Land, Politics and Society in Eighteenth-Century Tipperary

THOMAS P. POWER

D0002712

CLARENDON PRESS · OXFORD
1993

Oxford University Press, Walton Street, Oxford OX4 6DP

Oxford New York Toronto
Delhi Bombay Calcutta Madras Karachi
Kuala Lumpur Singapore Hong Kong Tokyo
Nairobi Dar es Salaam Cape Town
Melbourne Auckland Madrid
and associated companies in
Berlin Ibadan

Oxford is a trade mark of Oxford University Press

Published in the United States
by Oxford University Press Inc., New York

British Library Cataloguing in Publication Data
Data available

Library of Congress Cataloging in Publication Data
Power, T. P. (Thomas P.)
Land, politics, and society in eighteenth-century Tipperary /
Thomas P. Power.
Includes bibliographical references and index.
1. Tipperary (Ireland: County)—Politics and government.   2. Land
tenure—Ireland—Tipperary (County)—History—18th century.
3. Tipperary (Ireland: County)—Social conditions.   I. Title.
DA990.T5P69   1993   941.9'2—dc20   93–22481
ISBN 0–19–820316–0

1 3 5 7 9 10 8 6 4 2

Typeset by Cambrian Typesetters, Frimley, Surrey
Printed in Great Britain
on acid-free paper by
Biddles Ltd., Guildford and King's Lynn

To my parents,
Richard and Sheila Power,
in affection and gratitude

Acknowledgements

I am indebted to many institutions and individuals for assistance. I am grateful to the staff of the following institutions for making available material in their custody: in Dublin the National Library of Ireland; the National Archives; Trinity College Library; Genealogical Office; King's Inns Library; Dublin Corporation Library, Pearse Street; Registry of Deeds; Royal Irish Academy; Representative Church Body Library; Grand Lodge of Free-masons of Ireland; Church of Ireland College of Education; High School; and the Society of Friends Library. Outside Dublin in Ireland: Tipperary (SR) County Museum, Clonmel; Tipperary County Library, Thurles; St Patrick's College, Thurles; Arch-bishop's House, Thurles; Roscrea Heritage Centre; Limerick City Library; Mount Melleray Abbey, Co. Waterford; and the Public Record Office of Northern Ireland. In England, Cheshire Record Office; East Suffolk Record Office; Leicester City Archives; Kent Record Office; Hampshire Record Office; Lancashire Record Office; Sheffield City Library; Guildhall Library, London; Public Record Office; British Library; Historical Manuscripts Commis-sion; National Army Museum, London; Society of Friends Library, London; Petworth House; and the Bodleian Library, Oxford; and in Paris, the Bibliothèque Nationale.

For access to private collections I am particularly thankful to Mr Robert Armstrong, Mr Jim Condon, Revd Iain Knox, the late Mr Tim Looney, Mr Brian MacDermot, Mrs C. Murphy, Jim and Kate Nicholson, Miss Maura Ryan, Mr C. O. R. Phillips, and Revd David Woodworth. For their assistance in particular ways I am grateful to Dr Thomas Bartlett, Peter Connell, Dr David Dickson, Kevin Herlihy, Mrs Norma McDermott, Professor William Smyth, Julian Walton, and Dr Kevin Whelan. To Mrs Vickie MacLeod, of Audio-Visual Services, University of New Brunswick: I am grateful for her patience with my many demands on her knowledge of word processing. I wish to acknowledge the help I have received from the staff at Oxford University Press, particularly Tony Morris and Dorothy McCarthy, in guiding my

manuscript through the press. For helpful suggestions regarding the map I am grateful to John Callow. I thank my wife, Marlene, for her consideration and support in a number of ways.

This work has benefited significantly from the critical scrutiny of Professor L. M. Cullen, Dr Anthony Malcomson, and an anonymous reader. I have emphasized certain themes more than they might have wished, and any errors of fact or interpretation that remain are solely my responsibility.

The dedication acknowledges a personal debt to my parents for their encouragement and support over the years.

THOMAS P. POWER

Fredericton, New Brunswick
June 1992

Contents

List of Genealogies

List of Tables

Abbreviations

AH	*Analecta Hibernica*
Arch. Hib.	*Archivium Hibernicum*
BL	British Library
CA	*Cork Advertiser*
CDA	Cashel Diocesan Archives, Thurles
CEP	*Cork Evening Post*
CG	*Clonmel Gazette*
CH	*Clonmel Herald*
CO	Colonial Office
Coll. Hib.	*Collectanea Hibernica*
Comms. Jnl.(Ire.)	*Journal of the Irish House Of Commons*
CS	*The Civil Survey: Co.Tipperary*, ed. R. C. Simington (Dublin, 1931, 1934)
CSPI	*Calendar of State Papers Ireland*
DG	*Dublin Gazette*
EC	*Ennis Chronicle*
FDJ	*Faulkner's Dublin Journal*
FEC	Forfeited Estates Commission
FJ	*Freeman's Journal*
FLJ	*Finn's Leinster Journal*
GO	Genealogical Office
HC	*Hibernian Chronicle*
HMC	Historical Manuscripts Commission
HO	Home Office
IESH	*Irish Economic and Social History*
IHS	*Irish Historical Studies*
JCHAS	*Journal of the Cork Historical and Archaeological Society*
JWSEIAS	*Journal of the Waterford and South-East of Ireland Archaeological Society*
LC	*Limerick Chronicle*
LJ	*Leinster Journal*
Lords Jnl.(Ire.)	*Journal of the Irish House of Lords*
Mic.	Microfilm

NA	National Archives, Dublin (formerly Public Record Office and State Paper Office of Ireland)
NLI	National Library of Ireland
n.d.	not dated
n.p.	no place of publication
OP	Official Papers
PP	*British Parliamentary Papers*
PRIA	*Proceedings of the Royal Irish Academy*
PRO	Public Record Office, London
PRONI	Public Record Office of Northern Ireland
RCB	Representative Church Body Library
RD	Registry of Deeds
RIA	Royal Irish Academy
RO	Record Office
RP	Rebellion Papers
SCP	State of the Country Papers
SP	State Papers
SPI	State Papers Ireland
TCD	Trinity College Dublin
WC	*Waterford Chronicle*
WHM	*Walker's Hibernian Magazine*
WM	*Waterford Mirror*

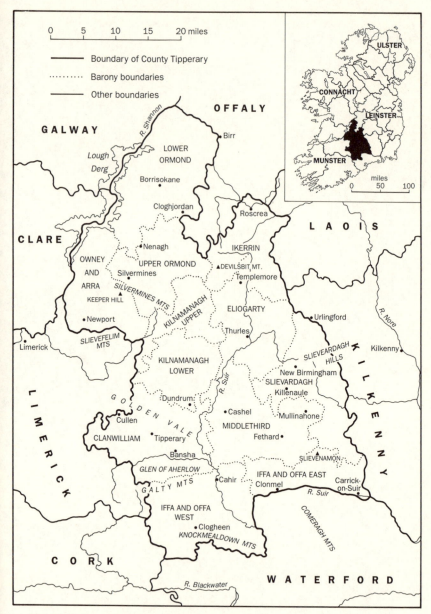

Map of Tipperary showing baronies and main towns.
Note: Kilmanagh Upper incorporates the former baronies of Ileagh and Kilnalongurty.

I

Introduction

Despite its size and the importance of its role in Irish history, Tipperary has until recently been neglected as a subject of historical enquiry. This alone would justify the undertaking of a work such as the present one. Tipperary's extent as Ireland's largest inland county, makes it an appropriate choice for an intensive regional study. Its extent and the relatively good survival rate of documentary source materials (although their potential might at first appear elusive), allows one to investigate political, economic, and social themes in an integrated way. Other studies have chosen the barony or county division (Marnane, Nolan), the estate (Maguire), the port hinterland (Dickson), or the natural geographical region (Elliott) as the unit of study. This study, however, is a composite one in that it attempts to provide a profile of the experience of one crucial Irish county in the critical and formative period of the eighteenth century. This regional dimension serves to indicate that select areas of the country in this period were not uniformly backward, subservient politically, or narrowly localized and uninfluential in their preoccupations as might initially be assumed.

In Irish terms Tipperary is a hybrid. The county occupies a central area in Ireland, placed as it is between the less well-endowed areas of the west, and the better lands of the east, though it incorporates characteristics of both. It occupies a frontier or contact zone between the provinces of Munster and Leinster, and between Munster and Connacht. The historic ecclesiastical divisions of the dioceses of Cashel and Emly, Killaloe, Lismore, and Ossory partition the county.

In physical geographical terms the county has a varied physiography and is characterized by six principal divisions. The dominant region is a lowland central plain based on carboniferous limestone encompassing an area roughly within a triangle formed by the points of Thurles, Clonmel, and Tipperary. This area is

drained by the River Suir and its tributaries and covers most of the baronies of Eliogarty, Middlethird, Clanwilliam, and Iffa and Offa East and West. Its western section, west of Cashel and running into east Limerick, forms the fertile grassland region of the Golden Vale. This core area is flanked by three ranges of upland or mountainous districts. On its north-western side is the hill complex formed by the Slieve Felim, Keeper Hill, Silvermines and Devil's Bit group. This region incorporates much of Kilnamanagh, Owney and Arra, and Upper Ormond. To its south-eastern side are the Slievardagh Hills and Slievnamon covering much of Iffa and Offa East and Slievardagh. On the south-west side the Galty mountains project into the county from adjoining Cork and Limerick. The northern tip of the county in Lower Ormond has features such as undulating lowland and bogland which are characteristic of the great central plain of the country. Finally, a distinct area of flat to undulating lowland containing basin peat is to be found in a broad arc from north-east of Cashel round to just east of Roscrea, giving eastern Ikerrin and Eliogarty bog and moorland characteristics.

The most extensive soil type covering the county is the grey-brown podzolics found on the flat to undulating lowlands and overlying the carboniferous limestone. These soils stretch from Clonmel in a broad sweep northward beyond Thurles and westward through Tipperary into Limerick. They are also extensive around Nenagh and Roscrea, and north-eastwards from Thurles stretching down the boundary with Kilkenny. Broadly speaking these soils cover Iffa and Offa West, Middlethird, Clanwilliam, Ikerrin, and large areas of Lower Ormond and Eliogarty.This soil type has a wide range of agricultural use being alternatively capable of supporting rich grassland, as in the Golden Vale or, in other districts, cereal and other crops. This dominant soil type has no serious limitations as regards its potential for agricultural exploitation. Its multi-purpose nature and wide usage were to be features in the agricultural changes of the eighteenth century.

This broad area of soil type is intersected and intruded upon by four areas of different soils. The first, in the south-east, is the acid brown earths associated with the Slievardagh Hills and the podzolic soils found in the mountain and hill terrain east of Slievnamon, and covering much of Iffa and Offa East and Slievardagh. The second extends west of Cahir forming an area of

peaty podzols and blanket peat centring on the Galty Mountains. The third comprises the complex range of hill and mountain formed by the Slieve Felim, Silvermines, Keeper Hill, and Devil's Bit group. This area has a mixture of soil types but is dominated by peaty podzols, brown earths, and gleys which are characteristic of mainly upland areas. They cover the major part of Upper Ormond, Ileagh, and Kilnamanagh. Finally, immediately north of Thurles stretching about half-way to Roscrea is an area of gley soils, while east of the town there is a parallel area which has basin peat as its principal soil. These four areas have limitations deriving from their soil type which make their range of agricultural uses more restricted than the main type area of grey-brown podzolics.[1]

Tipperary has a generally moderate and mild climate. Its inland situation and its physical geography means that the county seldom experiences a season too wet or a summer too dry. This mildness means that grass growth is good, and in favoured areas like the Golden Vale livestock can graze out all year.[2]

Historically the county espouses themes of continuity and change, unity and diversity. The region later to comprise the modern county was subjugated by the Normans in the late twelfth century and its lands parcelled out, the largest grant consisting of the entire northern half going to the founder of the Butler family. This northern area, though partly subdued, was not as heavily settled as the centre and south of the county where new forms of village and townlife began to develop. This basic division of settlement had long-term consequences. In the north a native Irish identity and lifestyle continued in an area only lightly settled by the newcomers. This accounted for the facility with which the Gaelic polity recovered its former position during the fourteenth century, leading to the removal of the chief Butler residence from Nenagh to Kilkenny in *c.*1400. The Gaelic recovery failed to overrun the heavily settled areas of Norman influence in the centre and south. Along this contact zone stretching from the south-west

---

[1] M. J. Gardiner and T. Radford, *Soil associations of Ireland and their land use potential* (Dublin, 1980); *Atlas of Ireland* (Dublin, 1979), 24–5, 28.

[2] P. K. Rohan, *The climate of north Munster* (Dublin, 1968), 4, 7, 10, 27, 30, 39, 41, 54; W. Patterson, *Observations on the climate of Ireland* (Dublin, 1804), 180; J. Rutty, *A chronological history of the weather and seasons and of the prevailing diseases in Dublin* (Dublin, 1770), pp. xxxvi–xxxvii, xl–xlvi.

to the north-east of the county a frontier, still evident in the seventeenth century, evolved.

Tipperary's fortunes were closely associated with its most prominent family, the Butlers. Their predominance was expressed in extensive landownership and in control of county politics and administration. From the original grant in the north the Butler interest expanded and despite losses to the native Irish in the fourteenth century (losses which were compensated by gains in the south) by the early fifteenth century their lands encompassed the basin of the Rivers Suir, Nore, and Barrow. The Butler lands, particularly those of the earl of Ormond, were further enlarged in the sixteenth century through royal favour and the acquisition of the lands of dissolved religious houses.

The concomitant to extensive landowning was local political predominance and control. From the creation of the earldom of Ormond and the elevation of the county to the status of a palatinate liberty in 1328, the most influential person in the county was the earl of Ormond. The palatinate jurisdiction conferred on him administrative and judicial powers of a virtual semi-regal nature. The institution maintained law and order at a distance from Dublin in an area where strife between Ormond and Desmond, and between rival branches of the Butlers, Cahir and Dunboyne particularly, was a recurring feature. By the early seventeenth century, however, the central government had re-asserted its control over the whole country and the existence of the palatinate came to be regarded as anomalous so that it was abolished in 1621. However, though the continuance of the jurisdiction depended on royal favour, while it operated it meant that the county could conduct its own affairs virtually immune from royal interference. The revival of the institution in 1662 was in administrative terms an incongruity, but in political terms it was a recognition of the part played by Ormond in the restoration of Charles II. By 1715, because Ormond was out of political favour, the process came full circle with the family agreeing to its removal (under 2 Geo. I, c. 8) because of the financial burden involved.

Nevertheless for over fifty years the administration of justice in the county was the responsibility of a department of Ormond's household. A system of courts was reconstructed after 1662.[3] All

[3] Copy of the letters patent in NLI, MS 11,044; *App. to the fifth report of the deputy keeper, Public Record Office of Ireland* (Dublin, 1873), 34–6.

sheriffs appointed in the period 1663–1715 were Ormond's appointees, as were the judges in the courts and minor officials.[4] The courts dealt with civil and criminal cases, with the exception of the four pleas of rape, treasure trove, burning houses, and forestalling which were reserved to the crown. The liberty claimed superior jurisdiction over specifically local courts.[5] Ormond, as lord of the liberty, claimed precedence in the granting of patents, and in the creation of manors within the county.[6]

The work of the courts was varied. On the criminal side between 1662 and 1690, for instance, the number of pleadings heard in the chancery court exceeded 800; while on the civil side the fee farm grants, granted on the Ormond estate from the late 1690s, were recorded in the chancery.[7] The courts also functioned in the enrolment of fines and recoveries relating to land, and of grants made under the act of settlement.[8] Ormond also sanctioned grants of fairs and markets, and created new manors such as Dundrum for Sir Robert Maude in 1711.[9] The existence of the palatinate was of material importance in the adjudication of cases of forfeiture for treason in the 1690s. This range of civil and criminal functions indicates that the palatinate exercised in Tipperary the role which the central courts and departments of state fulfilled at national level.

Given its concentrated level of litigation and business, the palatinate had a sizeable revenue. However, it proved to be an unprofitable institution, with expenditure matching or exceeding revenue. In 1672 the duchess of Ormond remarked that it now 'occasions a great charge unto my lord far above the profits of it', and by 1675 it was reported that the courts were in 'great arrears . . . and other arrears like further to incur and every day become more and more desperate'.[10] Out of revenue of £8,000 from the courts up to October 1671, only about £300 had come into the

[4] GO, MS 570, 71; NLI, MS 11,044, untitled document relating to the agency of the palatinate (n.d. [c. 1712]); *App. to the sixth report of the deputy keeper, Public Record Office of Ireland* (Dublin, 1874), 81, 82, 85, 86.

[5] NLI, MS 2340, 277; HMC, *Ormond* (1904), iii. 92.

[6] NLI, MS 11,044, document entitled 'The Duke of Ormonde's Title to Regalityes in Tipperary' [1684].

[7] NA, SP, Press A2/3/18 (index to Chancery pleadings in the palatinate 1662–90); *App. to the sixth report*, 46.

[8] *App. to the sixth report*, 80, 82, 84.   [9] Ibid. 83–4, 86, 87.

[10] NLI, MS 2503, 91; MS 11,044, indenture between G. Mathew and R. Lowe, 2 May 1675.

duke's hands by June 1673.[11] In addition, Ormond incurred further expenditure out of his own revenue to the amount of £2,240 which went towards repairing premises for the judges and covering their expenses and allowances, which left a net loss of over £1,940.[12] An attempt in 1675 to farm out the collection of fines was successful in the short term for in 1689 the profits of the courts were said to be 'very considerable'.[13] But the ensuing war eliminated this advantage, and it is apparent that by the late 1690s the duke's finances from the liberty were again in a critical state, a situation contributed to by the negligence on the part of some officials.[14] Despite some success in reducing debt on the Ormond estate as a whole after 1700, the unprofitability of the palatinate remained. By 1715 the institution was an administrative and economic burden on Ormond. Archbishop King remarked in 1715 that 'the Duke himself was weary of it, it being a considerable charge and a mere feather of no value in itself'.[15] Ormond's attainder in 1715 thus served to remove this costly and archaic survival, and in consequence the county was integrated into the regular framework of the Irish judicial and administrative system.

Ormond as the main landowner in the county furnished the area with continuity and stability. A common historical experience under Ormond and the other Butler branches since the Middle Ages gave cohesion to the county. With the exception of the Gaelic recovery there was virtual continuity of landownership in the county exemplified by the fact that by 1641, in contrast to neighbouring counties, extensive confiscation or resettlement had not taken place, and it had survived the Tudor breakup of the lordships. On the other hand, because it experienced change, Tipperary had a complex character. The county's continuity under Ormond was sufficient to absorb new elements, such that in the seventeenth century the so-called New English or recent settlers, Old English or descendants of the original Norman settlers, and Gaelic Irish were found within its confines. Also as a border county where the two provinces of Munster and Leinster meet, it

[11] NLI, MS 11,044, document entitled 'Stat[e] of ye Duke of Ormonde's advantage by his Liberty Courts, 2 June 1673'.   [12] Ibid.
[13] MS 11,044, indenture between G. Mathew and R. Lowe, 2 May 1675.
[14] Ibid., 'State of the case as to the fines and forfeitures of the County Pallatine of Tipperary' (n.d. [c.1700]); and untitled document relating to the agency of the palatinate (n.d. [c.1712]).
[15] King to Stanhope, 7 Oct. 1715 (PRO, SPI, 63/373/149).

combined influences from these historically different provinces. These considerations gave the county a complex historical character.

Tipperary has a key importance for an understanding of eighteenth-century themes, events, and attitudes. In elucidating this fact, this study seeks to test at local level some of the generalizations made concerning the Irish experience in that century. The century witnessed the integration of the local economy more intimately into the wider market economy (Chapter 2). Up to mid-century, pastoral farming was the prevailing agricultural pursuit, an activity which accorded with a low population in the countryside and an undercapitalization of agriculture. From the 1760s, however, stimulated by subsidies from central government, cereal cultivation expanded markedly and was reflected in the spread of flour mills and in the rise of a class of capitalized grain farmers. Almost contemporaneous with the expansion in cereal cultivation was the decline, protracted but definite, of the traditional textile industry especially in its main centre, Carrick-on-Suir, a process which entailed the transfer of Quaker entrepreneurial skills and capital from the declining textile to the emergent flour-milling industry. Sustained prosperity was also evident in the growth of fairs, the emergence of banking facilities, the expansion of towns, and changes in the merchant community.

Landed property was the basis of wealth, as well as being fundamental for political and social participation (Chapter 3). In the seventeenth century alterations in the pattern of landowner-ship were most radical in the northern part of the county; there was a high survival rate for the larger Old English proprietors, the lesser being displaced; and Ormond re-emerged as the main landowner following the Restoration. The pattern of landowner-ship in the county was largely unaffected by the Williamite land settlement. In the eighteenth century, a pattern of unmitigated stability among Protestant landowners and of decline among Catholic proprietors was not universal. In fact there were important structural and personnel changes in the county's landed class arising from the disposal of the Ormond, Everard, and Dunboyne estates in the early part of the century, and, later, from sales on the Mathew and Meade estates. The breakup of the first three estates stemmed from serious indebtedness, the solution to

which led to the rise of new families in the landed class; while in the case of the two latter, it led to the establishment of substantial Catholic head-tenants as owners in fee. The changing relationship between levels of income, expenditure, and debt created by the prosperity of the latter half of the century, allowed for a greater solvency among landed families as a whole, in contrast to the economically difficult conditions of the early part of the century. Prosperity served to widen the base of the landed class, a development which benefited Catholics particularly. Consideration of landed Catholics at the levels of owners in fee, head-tenants, and converts demonstrates that they formed an influential section of landed society.

Landlords were concerned to maximize the revenue-bearing capacity of their estates through the granting of leases to tenants (Chapter 4). In tenurial terms, the structures which emerged from the 1690s involved the granting of long leases at low or moderate rents for large acreages. This created the context out of which a considerable, entrenched middleman interest emerged. The loss of landlord control thus inaugurated was further increased by the Catholic relief act (1778) and the tenancy act (1780), both of which operated to reinforce the position of the large tenant in the 1780s and after. On the whole, landlords were unable to reverse the tenurial structure in their favour, a situation which was aggravated by subdivision. The prevailing tenurial structure did not allow the majority of landlords to pursue an improvement policy, the exceptions being those involved with projects of social and evangelical engineering, who promoted Protestant settlement on their estates.

The consequences of a rapid commercialization of agriculture were seen in acute phases of agrarian unrest after 1760 (Chapter 5). Unrest derived from the uneven effects of this commercialization as agriculture became more intensive and extensive in a society hitherto pastorally-based and lowly-populated, but now experiencing a shift to cereal cultivation and population growth. The rural unrest in the traditional grazing areas was a class one, while economic issues were more to the fore in southern parts of the county where grain had spread more rapidly. The narrow range of participation in unrest by rural social classes at times of economic growth, as in the 1760s, and the broader social composition of agrarian movements at times of general depression,

as in the 1770s and 1780s, is apparent. A particular category of unrest derived from the tenant market for land at the level of the large tenant and the smallholder, involving both categories in attempts to dictate conditions of tenure to the landlord. By the early years of the nineteenth century this challenge had become increasingly serious. The existence of a large and increasingly marginal element in rural society and of head-tenants whose position was being undermined, in association with the grievances of others like dairymen, gave unrest in the county a complex character in its pattern and persistence.

The decade of the 1760s and its aftermath had a significant impact on the politics and denominational relations of the county (Chapter 6). The Mathew family, whose senior members displayed a pattern of conversion to protestantism, was the initial focus of the sectarian conflict of the decade. That conflict derived from a unique set of circumstances in time and place, involving as it did a purge by Protestant extremists of propertied Catholics. However, the excesses of that decade provided the context out of which concessions to Catholics were made from the 1770s onward. The integration of Catholics into county administrative structures following the relief act of 1793 precluded them from active involvement in radicalism for the remainder of the 1790s (Chapter 7). This partly accounts for the absence of rebellion in the county in 1798, a situation also contributed to by the activities of the magistrates in disarming potential rebels, the role of the high sheriff in 1798, and the general absence of serious rural unrest in that decade.

2

Economic Development

1. The Seventeenth-Century Background

Tipperary formed part of the rich and extensive hinterland of the ports of south Munster. At the outset of the seventeenth century the economic character of the county was simple and under-developed: except in years of dearth an agricultural surplus of grain and livestock and their by-products was conveyed outward. The main export items for the ports of Cork, Limerick, Youghal, and Waterford in 1626 were hides, tallow, pipestaves, sheep, cattle, butter, frieze, and cereals, being the primary products produced in their respective hinterlands of which Tipperary formed a part.[1] With more stable and settled conditions prevailing in the first forty years of the century there was a gradual quickening of economic life in the county based primarily on a more intense exploitation of its livestock surpluses enhanced by external demand. Producers began to profit from the export of live cattle for which there was an increasing demand in England.[2] Evidence of losses in the early 1640s indicates how vital a role stockraising had assumed in the agricultural economy of the county.[3] However, the ravages of wartime in the 1640s caused considerable disruption of economic life, aggravated further by plague and famine in the early 1650s. Recovery subsequently, however, provided the basis for the high level of livestock exports in the early 1660s from which the recently arrived settlers profited much.[4]

---

[1] PRO, CO, 388/85/A 15, Ireland: exports, 1626.
[2] D. Woodward, 'A comparative study of the Irish and Scottish livestock trades in the seventeenth century', in L. M. Cullen and T. C. Smout, *Comparative aspects of Scottish and Irish economic and social history 1600–1900* (Edinburgh, 1977), 147–64.
[3] TCD, MS 821, fos. 12ᵛ, 15–15ᵛ, 84; HMC, *Egmont* (1905) i. pt. 1, 156.
[4] D. Woodward, 'The Anglo-Irish livestock trade of the seventeenth century', *IHS*, 18 (1973), 514.

The effect of the cattle acts (1663, 1667) was to virtually
eliminate live cattle and sheep exports for a century and to
reorient the nature of the livestock trade. Since lean cattle could
no longer be exported more of them were fattened and finished at
home, slaughtered and then sent as salted beef to service the
growing transatlantic demand in the West Indies by slave
populations and ships' crews. As opposed to other areas of
Ireland, Munster's favourable location allowed ready access to this
emergent Atlantic provisions trade. The strength of contacts with
this new market is exemplified by Sir William Stapleton, a native
of Tipperary, who was governor of the Leeward Islands, 1672–85,
and whose brothers were at different times deputy governors of
Montserrat.[5] As with the live cattle trade, the ports of Cork,
Youghal, and Waterford were well located to benefit from this
provisioning trade, becoming the main victualling centres for the
naval and mercantile fleets. Given its convenience and accessibility to these ports Tipperary continued its cattle production but,
after the mid-1660s in response to market conditions, becoming
more a fattening than a breeding county.[6] So as livestock exports
declined from the mid-1660s there was a concomitant rise in
processed products mainly beef, butter, hides, and tallow.
Dairying was noted as a specialist activity in the Carrick-on-Suir
area in the 1630s, but butter exports at this time were small.[7] In
the Restoration period commercial production expanded in
Munster, with Youghal becoming the chief export outlet. As part
of the hinterland of that port, south Tipperary sent butter
consignments. In 1688, for instance, one Clonmel merchant
consigned 144 casks of butter valued as £200 (on which he realised
a profit of £43), to Ostend and Rochelle via Youghal and
Waterford.[8]

The cattle acts and market trends combined led to an intensification of sheep husbandry. Before 1641 cattle and sheep were
probably equally important in the county. However, sheep were
increasing in importance. Even by 1635 most of the area between
Carrick-on-Suir and Waterford was already devoted to sheep and

[5] A. Burns, *History of the British West Indies* (London, 1965), 341, 349.
[6] NLI, MS 4908, fo. 50ᵛ; MS 4909, fos. 14, 60; TCD, MS 749/4/423.
[7] PRO, CO, 388/85/A15; C. L. Falkiner, *Illustrations of Irish history and
topography* (London, 1904), 403.
[8] W. P. Burke, *History of Clonmel* (Waterford, 1907), 102.

was said to have been 'converted' to that use.[9] Sheep numbers could be considerable. Ninety-two per cent of the sheep removed from Munster in the 1650s as part of the transplantation to Connacht came from Tipperary, and the number of sheep removed from the county was eight times that for the entire province of Leinster.[10] After the Restoration sheep became a capital resource much exploited by the new settlers. Indeed by the early eighteenth century the exploitation of wool in the county, along with areas in Connacht, was the most significant example of direct landlord participation in commercial farming in the country. Tipperary emerged as one of the chief sheep-rearing counties in the later seventeenth century with 40,000 sheep bred during one lambing season alone in 1694, for instance.[11] Intensified sheep-farming was accompanied by the rise of large flock-masters such as Richard Moore of Clonmel who in 1685 sold 128 bags of wool for £1,443 to William Vaughan, a Clonmel wool merchant, and Joseph Damer of Tipperary who in the 1660s was said to be exporting the fleeces of 10,000 sheep through Waterford.[12] They epitomize the participation by the new settlers in the commercial exploitation of the county's chief export resource.

The picture of a pastoral economy is reinforced by the foundation of fairs, which are also an index of the integration of the county into the larger economy. In the first half of the century there were thirty-two grants of new fairs, mainly in the first three decades.[13] However, only fourteen fairs are listed in the Civil Survey suggesting that in the intervening period the fairs had either failed to develop or had suffered dislocation, temporary or permanent, during the disruptions of the 1640s. Spatially there was a concentration of fairs in the southern half of the county. This would suggest that the movement of livestock outward from the county was through points there and that their location was influenced by the accessibility of Waterford, Youghal, Cork, and

---

[9] Falkiner, *Illustrations*, 402.

[10] W. H. Hardinge, 'On circumstances attending the outbreak of the civil war in Ireland on 23rd October, 1641', *Trans. of Royal Irish Academy*, 24 (1873), 415.

[11] PRO, SPI, 356/211 (NLI, Mic.P. 3273).

[12] Burke, *Clonmel*, 102; A. M. Fraser, 'Joseph Damer a banker of old Dublin', *Dublin Historical Record*, 3 (1941), 43; D. Dickson, *New Foundations: Ireland, 1660–1800* (Dublin, 1987), 104.

[13] For the full list of fairs see app. II in T. P. Power, 'Land, politics, and society in eighteenth-century Tipperary', Ph.D. thesis (University of Dublin, 1987).

Limerick. Many of the older fairs were revived after 1660, for in the last half of the century eleven new patents were granted, and in 1685 thirty-three fairs were being conducted at nineteen locations.[14] The cash and credit facilities generated by transactions at these fairs were of great benefit to the local economy. Indeed the desire of local patrons to benefit from the traffic passing through their areas often led to competition to establish fairs, as in the south-west of the county where much of the fatstock would have been purchased at local fairs by Limerick merchants.[15]

Grain cultivation in the early seventeenth century was more important than has been traditionally assumed. Losses of cereal crops are regularly mentioned in the 1641 depositions. By mid-century over 56 per cent of the surveyed area of the county was represented as arable, 21 per cent as pasture, and the remainder as mountain, bog, and wood.[16] The chief arable areas were in the baronies of Iffa and Offa, Middlethird, Clanwilliam, and Eliogarty where the county average was exceeded, and in Upper and Lower Ormond where one of the stated attractions of planting in the 1630s was that the area was very rich in grain.[17] On the whole these arable areas had the lowest proportion of unprofitable land and the highest land values. The pattern in the distribution of flour mills shows the majority in the southern area and extreme north, with few in the intervening region.[18]

Grain production was also important. In 1649 the grain applotment made on the county for the supply of Ormond's army was 2,333 barrels, with most of the quota being promptly delivered suggesting that harvests were good.[19] Many of the flour mills, however, suffered as a result of the wars of the 1640s while others declined because they were situated on or near frontier zones. Of the 128 mills recorded in the early 1650s, 92 were functioning while the remaining 36 were out of service.[20] The county is likely to have remained self-sufficient in grain with some small surplus for export. Tipperary contributed grain to the subsidy in kind in 1667, it was self-sufficient in grain supplies in the war period of 1690–1,

---

[14] Bourke's, *Almanack* (Dublin, 1685), *passim*.

[15] *CSPI, 1666–9*, 191; Oxford Bodleian Library, Carte MS 161, fos. 159–159ᵛ (NLI, Mic.P. 5452); Prendergast MS, ii. 391–6; NLI, MS 11,044 document entitled 'Copy of a war[ran]t for a writt of ad quod da[mnu]m', n.d.

[16] Computed from *CS*, i, ii.   [17] *CSPI, 1647–60*, 151.

[18] Computed from *CS*, i, ii.   [19] HMC, *Ormond* (1902), i. 140–2.

[20] Computed from *CS*, i, ii.

and the poll tax returns of 1696 show high values for the baronies of the south where arable farming remained important.[21] Certainly the southern part of the county was a grain region noted by outside observers in this regard, while the north was perceived as backward and underdeveloped.[22]

The expansion in the area under pasture was made possible in part by the clearance of woodland, timber from which was much in demand for both domestic and commercial purposes. This facilitated the extension of the settlement frontier already evident in enclosures and quicksets in newly won grazing areas where commercially exploitable woods were absent. Timber was a required material for the erection of new houses and there was already concern about the shortage of native timber needed for the construction of dwellings by the settlers.[23] Woodland was also widely exploited for timber, staves, and as a fuel in the iron industry. The acreage of woodland in the county in *c.*1654 was estimated at 18,750 acres (statute), being the second largest area in the country after Clare.[24] Surveyors of the county at this time distinguished the areas in which commercially exploitable timber existed, its extent, and its proximity to navigable rivers (e.g. Rivers Shannon and Suir) and ports (Limerick and Waterford).[25] The exploitation of woodland also served a semi-political purpose in that, since the woods gave shelter to so-called tories (outlaws), their clearance would have benefits for the security of the settlers.

The growth in the volume of wool exported gave merchants a profitable and stable return as prices were firm. A number of merchants from the county applied for licences to export wool mostly through Waterford and Youghal in 1678–9.[26] Of these the most notable was William Vaughan who in 1678 purchased land near Clonmel, rented further lands as sheepwalks, and stocked them with sheep. In addition to exporting wool on his own account, Vaughan performed a similar function for others. Based

[21] *CSPI, 1666–9*, 297; TCD, MS 749/2/180, 749/4/406; T. W. Moody, F. X. Martin, and F. J. Byrne (eds.), *A new history of Ireland*, iii. *Early modern Ireland, 1534–1691* (Oxford, 1976), 458, 475.

[22] L. Eachard, *An exact description of Ireland* (London, 1691), 96; W. Camden, *Brittania* (London, 1695), 983.

[23] T. Birch, *A collection of state papers of John Thurloe* (London, 1742), ii. 404.

[24] E. McCracken, *The Irish woods since Tudor times* (Newton Abbot, 1971), 162.

[25] *CS*, i. 123, 136–8, 140; ii. 23, 160, 185.

[26] HMC, *Ormond* (1906), iv. 665–76.

in Clonmel he purchased wool from the large flock-masters, had it packed in Clonmel, and then had it conveyed either down-river to Waterford or overland to Youghal from both of which it was sent to the ports of south-west England as supplementary raw material for the cloth manufactory there. His business in the wool export trade provided him with a substantial return.[27] The duke of Ormond was personally involved in the wool trade in this period also. As early as 1663 he received letters patent giving him authority to grant licences for the export of wool from Ireland.[28] In the autumn of 1673 8,000 stones of wool (worth £3,000 at the then current price of 7s. 6d. a stone), were brought into Carrick-on-Suir by his tenants as rent payments, but due to the wartime conditions Ormond experienced difficulty marketing the wool abroad.[29] In normal times the flow of raw wool from Ormond's estate in Tipperary through Waterford (which was largely a wool-exporting port in the seventeenth century, beef and butter being subsidiary export items) to English ports, merited no attention.

Already by mid-century the presence of twelve tucking or fulling mills for shrinking cloth attests that processes, however primitive, existed for the working up of raw wool.[30] These catered mainly for local needs, but with the growth in sheep numbers and in wool production in the 1660s, there was an opening for a more export-oriented manufacture. With labour costs low and with wool cheap (in 1677, 4s. per stone cheaper than in England[31]) entrepreneurs had a tempting outlet for investment. It was also encouraged by the relatively heavy charges on the export of wool.[32] In late 1674 Edward Nelthorpe, a London merchant, proposed to Ormond the setting up of a serge and cloth manufactory at Clonmel. A capital stock of over £20,000 was to be made available, families skilled in cloth-making were to come over from England, £500 was to be laid out on tools, and those involved were to make their own ships available to transport the finished goods overseas. For this large-scale project Clonmel was considered more convenient and accessible than other centres in Ireland to which the manufacturers

[27] Burke, *Clonmel*, 102; C. L. Vaughan-Arbuckle, 'A Tipperary farmer and Waterford tradesman of two centuries ago', *JWSEIAS*, 8 (1902), 80–9; NLI, D5235. [28] NLI, D4505, dated 13 Jan. 1662–3.
[29] NLI, MS 2357, 147; MS 2358, 33, 63–4, 118.
[30] *CS*, i. 41, 47, 64, 184, 220, 307, 322, 352, 388; ii. 8, 300, 321.
[31] NLI, D4816.
[32] O. Airy (ed.), *Essex papers* (London, 1890), i. 275.

had been invited.[33] About 500 families of French and Walloon
extraction at Canterbury were involved in the scheme.[34] The
venture was launched in late 1674. A schedule of 1676 shows that it
then had in stock 1,000 stones of wool, 5,400 pounds of other
wool, 550 pieces of serge, 8,000 pounds of yarn, 48 kerseys, 22
broad cloths, 10,000 pounds of dyeing stuffs, and 100 weavers'
looms.[35] In the 1670s also, Ormond established Dutch woollen
manufacturers at Carrick-on-Suir and the industry in the town was
to be one of the largest in Ireland in the eighteenth century.[36]

Prospects for the industry seemed good. In 1699, however, an
act (10 & 11 Will. III, c. 10) passed by the English parliament
prohibited the export of Irish woollens in order to safeguard the
English woollen industry which was then experiencing competition
from Irish goods. Despite the importance ascribed to the act in
subsequent historiography, its effects have been overstated.[37] The
goods largely affected by the act—old and new draperies—had
only assumed importance in the previous thirty years, their
manufacture was confined to towns like Clonmel and Carrick, and
the industry was far from being highly developed when the act
passed. Though some emigration of those employed in the
industry resulted, the number was not large. Rather the industry
successfully adapted to the new situation by concentrating on
production for the home market to fill the demand in the
eighteenth century for coarse and fine woollen cloth. Also wool
combing and spinning developed in the Suir valley as a significant
source of employment in the production of yarn for the English
market.

Economic activity was closely influenced by settlement changes.
The property changes of the seventeenth century introduced new
immigrants to the county. In the pre-1641 period New English
infiltration was limited, their absenteeism accounting for a lack of
promotion of colonization, though their head tenants did become
involved, as at Cullen and Silvermines.[38] These two centres

[33] NLI, MS 2360, 95, 99, 125.
[34] G. L. Lee, *The Huguenot settlements in Ireland* (London, 1936), 17.
[35] NLI, D4883.   [36] NLI, MS 2394, 163; MS 2404, 441.
[37] P. Kelly, 'The Irish woollen export prohibition act of 1699: Kearney revisited', *IESH*, 7(1980), 22–44; PRONI, Education Facsimiles, *Ireland after the
Glorious Revolution* (Belfast, 1976), 228.
[38] For Cullen: TCD, MS 821, fo. 276; S. Pender (ed.), *A census of Ireland c.1659*
(Dublin, 1939), 326; T. Laffan (ed.), *Tipperary's families* (Dublin, 1911), 60, 114;

represent exceptional concentrations of colonists before 1641, elsewhere the process was informal and dispersed. Clearly no large migration or formal plantation could proceed without the concurrence of the earl of Ormond, and such consent was not forthcoming. The main body of new settlers arrived in the decades after 1650 and, apart from the return of those who fled during the Williamite wars, no wave of fresh colonists came as a result of the Williamite land settlement.

The 1659 poll tax shows an approximate county ratio of English to Irish of 1 : 14. The four southern baronies of Iffa and Offa, Clanwilliam, Middlethird, and Slievardagh had a total return of 844 English inhabitants, whereas in the remaining baronies the total was 1,080, showing that the greater impetus for settlement came from the Cromwellians of military background. It was a 'military' barony, Lower Ormond, which had the greatest number of New English and also the highest total of New English persons of substance.[39] The hearth-money returns for the mid-1660s indicate that there were over 1,000 New English households representing 12.5 per cent of the total.[40] The pattern of New English settlement is one of wide dispersal, though there was a tendency for the newcomers to move towards the existing nuclei, outside of which they were generally sparse or isolated. Outside the towns, concentrations of New English were few. In the centre and south of the county, where they replaced the lesser Old English families as landowners, the newcomers displayed a tendency to settle on the older manorial and ecclesiastical centres, indicating that the arrival of the settlers into the Old English rural areas did not have a radical effect on existing settlement patterns.Their advent to the Gaelic areas of the north and west was more intrusive. In Lower Ormond more cohesive Protestant rural communities evolved to give it its distinctive character. The dependent tenantry or settler population arrived in this barony in

---

G. Story, *A true and impartial history of the last two years* (London, 1691), 135; Petworth House: Thomond papers, survey and maps of the Thomond estate, 1703 (NLI, Mic.P.4767). For Silvermines: *CSPI, 1633–47*, 5; *CSPI, 1647–60*, 150–2; *CSPI, 1660–2*, 153–4; TCD, MS 821, fos. 126, 145, 148, 163, 181, 187–8, 193–4, 197–9; T. C. Barnard, *Cromwellian Ireland* (Oxford, 1975), 39. Dineley's sketch of Silvermines is reproduced in *Jnl. of the Kilkenny Archaeological Society*, 5 (1864–6), 272.

[39] Pender, *Census*, 295–329.
[40] Based on Laffan, *Tipperary's families*.

sufficient numbers to provide the county's two instances of village promotion in the later seventeenth century, at Cloghjordan and Borrisokane. Of the northern baronies, Lower Ormond and parts of Upper Ormond were the most fertile and the most conducive to permanent settlement, while the other baronies were peripheral in terms of suitability for agricultural exploitation and presented a generally inhospitable environment for settlers. As a result in the eighteenth century some of the ancestors of the original grantees, notably Maude of Dundrum, experimented with introducing Protestant tenants on to their estates.

The county's towns were essentially medieval foundations. All the major centres owed their existence either to their favourable location on navigable rivers or to patronage by the Butlers, especially the earl of Ormond. In terms of size, population, and diversity of economic function, evidence from the hearth-money returns of the mid-1660s indicates that a wide gap existed between the four towns with the largest number of households, Clonmel, Cashel, Thurles, and Carrick, and the other centres. Only the former towns had expanded beyond their town walls and acquired large suburbs.

Clonmel was the county's largest town. A profile of occupations there in 1661, shows a predominance of the labourer (108) and servant (164) class, which together constituted over 57 per cent of all stated occupations, family relatives and unstated or unknown occupations excluded.[41] If the two last categories (330 and 50 respectively) are taken into account this indicates a large dependent population. The main activities were textiles, leather, alcohol, and the building trades, with some service and semi-agricultural pursuits. Clonmel's primacy was indicated in the extent of its trade and in its merchant community. Its trading links were influenced by its position in the hinterlands of Waterford and Youghal, from which two ports it was roughly equidistant. Clonmel merchants exported a range of primary materials especially hides, tallow, and woollen goods, and imported luxuries like wine and salt.

The Restoration period of prosperity saw a revival in the fortunes of the towns. First, the expansion in trade provided the context for town growth. The better situated centres grew at the expense of the less favourably located. There may have been an

---

[41] Compiled from Burke, *Clonmel*, 247–55.

increased concentration on Clonmel and, to a lesser extent, Carrick. Both centres are included among the seven market towns of Munster in 1691, and since the others were all ports this made them the most important inland towns in the province at that date.[42] The pattern in the movement of exportable products outward from the county was in a southerly direction through these two transit points to the southern ports. The attraction of textile industries to these centres in the 1670s further enhanced their importance. The upsurge in trade was also reflected in the formation of guilds in the towns as craftsmen and traders became more organized. At Cashel in 1673 the blacksmiths, carpenters, ironmongers, goldsmiths, masons, watchmakers, slaters, pewterers, braziers, glaziers, cutlers, and hammermen were grouped into one company, and in 1698 the merchant tailors and victuallers were incorporated.[43] Similarly at Clonmel the traders and craftsmen were organized into three guilds in 1681: brewers, cordwainers, and merchants.[44] The growth of trade, therefore, saw increased organization among the merchant community.

Secondly, towns experienced a significant influx of new immigrants. The tendency of the newcomers to settle in the existing nuclei is apparent. Clonmel, the largest town, had a considerable influx. In 1661 a poll tax return listed 870 individuals in the town about one quarter of whom were New English.[45] About one half of the households in the 1665 return for the town were New English. The arrival of new settlers in Carrick-on-Suir and Fethard was less pervasive. Significant Protestant communities were established at Cashel, Tipperary, Nenagh, and Roscrea. Thurles, Cahir, and Clogheen also experienced some inward movement, but this was on a less impressive scale. New English settlement had a sizeable urban dimension, but it was directed in the main at the older centres. No new urban focus emerged as a result of their arrival, comparable to the towns of the Ulster plantation. The advent of the newcomers simply served to supplement existing urban concentrations notably at Clonmel and Carrick.

Yet, at another level, their numbers were sufficient to occasion political, social, and cultural change which was to be of long-term

---

[42] L. Eachard, *Exact description*, 93.

[43] NLI, MS 5575, fos. 13, 21ᵛ, 40, and unfoliated section at end (in reverse): orders for blacksmiths 24 Mar. 1673, tailors 28 Mar. 1698, victuallers 29 Aug. 1698.

[44] Burke, *Clonmel*, 146.   [45] Ibid. 247–55.

effect. New Protestant oligarchies emerged though these were not at all times exclusive as in Clonmel where Catholic merchants appear as freemen, and conversely in the reorganization of the boroughs under James II Protestants were included in the newly constituted corporations.[46] Nevertheless a new ethos was emerging which was to become more sharply defined as time went on. There was a conscious policy of encouraging English manners and practices, as in 1673 when a newly organized guild in Cashel was required 'from time to time [to] goe in the English attire'.[47] The colonial ethos of the Protestant town oligarchies is epitomized by the marking of the anniversary of the 1641 rebellion, and their political preference exemplified in the celebration on the defeat of Monmouth in 1685.[48]

Thirdly, some towns experienced actual physical growth after 1660. The patronage of Ormond was an important factor in this process, particularly in Clonmel. His policy aimed to beautify 'this borough with such public and most useful structures as are not to be paralleled through this whole kingdom, and by a lasting fixation of several fairs within our walls and of the regality courts at our very doors'.[49] After the revival of the palatinate in 1662 Clonmel once again, after a lapse of forty years, became the centre of its officialdom and courts, and a new court house was constructed in *c*. 1675.[50] Further building activity is indicated by the erection of a new prison in 1677, by plans for the establishment of a free school in 1681, and by proposals in 1679 for 'erecting good houses without Kilsheelan Gate [on the east of the town], where the situation is pleasant, the water near, and one good slate house already built and converted into an inn'.[51] In the 1670s the corporation undertook the paving and repair of the streets and the demolition of fortifications as a hindrance to the passage of carriages, in 1681 the water supply was improved, and in 1699 ground was allotted for the building of a barrack.[52]

At the outset of the seventeenth century Tipperary was still

[46] Burke, *Clonmel*, 105–9.
[47] NLI, MS 5575, unfoliated section at end (in reverse).
[48] Ibid., fos. 56, 78.   [49] NLI, MS 2410, 413–14.
[50] E. Shee and S. J. Watson, *Clonmel: An architectural guide* (Dublin, 1975), 12; M. Craig, *The architecture of Ireland from the earliest times to 1800* (London, 1982), 202.
[51] NLI, MSS 2368, 15–16; 2391, 305; 2410, 413–14.
[52] NLI, MS 5575, fos. 7, 9^v, 19, 32^v, 35, 61^v, 62, 132^v, 133.

essentially medieval in character, and in its economic activity underdeveloped. By its close much change had occurred. The transition was not in the main a continuous process, for change accelerated only after 1641 in response to national political events, the consequences of which were a radically altered pattern of landownership in some parts and the introduction of new racial and religious elements into the county particularly to the existing towns. These developments were paralleled by economic change centring on more intensive sheep-farming and cattle-fattening which brought increased prosperity for some, displacement for others, and which served to bring the county into the mainstream of the market economy.

2. Pastoral Farming

In the eighteenth century there was a continued concentration on pastoral farming for four reasons. First, because economic conditions, particularly market demand and prices favoured pasturage.[53] Secondly, the leasing policy pursued by landlords was conducive to the emergence of large-scale grazing. Directly managed farming units devoted to pasture, with acreages of 3,000 to 6,000, and often 8,000 acres, characteristic of parts of the county in 1741, were still prevalent in the mid-1770s, and the pattern persisted into the nineteenth century.[54] These large grazing farms, most characteristic of the region stretching north-ward from Cahir to Cashel and westward to Tipperary and on a scale unrivalled elsewhere, were partly a consequence of tenancy arrangements and partly a function of the expansion in demesne sheep-farming in the late seventeenth century. In the most intense grazing area the most successful large-scale graziers were those on the Butler (Cahir), Mathew, Meade, Damer, Stanley and arch-bishop of Cashel estates. Some of the tenants on these estates held leases under a number of different landlords which explains the large size of grazing farms. Many of these head-tenants were

[53] L. M. Cullen, *An economic history of Ireland since 1660* (London, 1976), 48, 52–3.
[54] Publicola, *A letter from a country gentleman in the province of Munster to his grace the lord primate of all Ireland* (Dublin, 1741), 2; A. Young, *A tour in Ireland* (London, 1780; repr. Shannon, 1970), i. 390; *PP Stock*, 57, pt. ii. (1847–8), 12–13.

Catholic, with persons like McCarthy, Keating, Doherty, and Scully being the most extensive graziers in the region. Investment in livestock could be considerable with, for instance, McCarthy's stock in 1776 valued at £20,000, and Scully's stock for the 1781 season bought at a cost of £6,985.[55] After the relief acts of 1778 and 1782 and the tenancy act of 1780, Catholics took extra leases, stocked such grounds, and availed themselves of the favourable demand of the period 1783–1815. Thus these large Catholic tenants, far from indicating the detrimental effects of penal legislation, are witness to the fact that the striking accumulation of land by head-tenants could be preserved and even added to.

Thirdly, an important inducement to the maintenance of grazing was the fact that pasture lands were tithe-free. This exemption came into practice in 1735 (at a time when cattle and beef prices were beginning to show an upturn), and it received formal sanction in law in 1800. Finally, grazing allowed for large profits which were primarily responsible for making up head rents. Even with the existence of a guaranteed market for grain between 1758 and 1797 due to the subsidy system, the swing to cereals was mainly among small- or medium-sized farmers and not among the large graziers. Thus the agent for the Stanley estate remarked in October 1773 that 'we have some people under £2,000 a year rent and higher on those sort of lands and who have not so much trouble as a plow farmer of £300—all they do is buy in stock, graze or rear them, and sell out when the markets answer'.[56]

Thus the structure of agricultural activity in Tipperary was a two-tiered one. On the one hand, there was a system of extensive demesne farming by landowners and large head-tenants who engaged in pastoral farming. This adherence to grazing was reinforced by the economic environment, tenurial preferences, and tithe exemption. The direct management of farms was a barrier to agricultural innovation and was slow to respond to economic incentives, particularly the conversion of lands for cereals. This latter, on the other hand, became the activity associated with the farmer.

From the Restoration to the 1770s sheep-farming was the dominant activity in Tipperary both within agriculture as a whole

[55] Young, *Tour*, i. 390; NLI, MS 27,480 (stock book, 1775–82).
[56] A. McGuire to T. Dane, 25 Oct. 1773 (Derby papers (Preston), DDK, 1704, correspondence series 1747–77).

and within the grazing sector itself. Sheep declined in importance in the period 1780–1815 due to the emergence of arable farming as a profitable enterprise, but their significance in the local economy was renewed after 1815. Commercially sheep were valued for their wool and meat. Mutton was an important commodity in the home market and Tipperary was a supplier of mutton to Dublin in the spring.[57] Sheep were also dispatched to Cork butchers. The main commercial item from sheep was their wool which went to serve the domestic woollen industry in the county. The most intense sheep-grazing district was contained within the area comprising the country between Cullen–Thurles–Callan–Clonmel, with its western point extending into Limerick and its eastern into Kilkenny. From the 1770s, with the expansion of grain production around Clonmel, the southern tip of the sheep region receded, the shift being most noticeable between Clonmel and Cashel. The baronies of Upper and Lower Ormond were the most important sheep areas in the north where the sheep were maintained for breeding purposes mainly. The movement out of sheep-farming in its formerly established areas continued in the early nineteenth century, for the two Ormond baronies were by then the most important sheep areas with Iffa and Offa West, while the movement out of sheep is evident in the comparatively lower numbers in Iffa and Offa East, Clanwilliam, Middlethird, and Eliogarty where sheep-grazing had formerly been strongest.[58]

The sheep system was two-tiered: first, lambs were bred until they were three years old, fattened and sold in October, while the ewe lambs were fattened to replace the older ewes which were sold off; and secondly, part of the stock of fat three-year-olds were winter-fed for disposal on the Dublin market as mutton the succeeding spring.[59] This dual system ensured that the two elements which determined whether sheep-farming was to be profitable, i.e. an adequate lambing percentage and ewe replacement strategy, were present. Thus the arrangement of a flock of 2,500 sheep in Tipperary in the 1770s was such that there was an average lambing percentage of 20 per cent and an annual replacement level of 250 for old ewes, and so in proportion to larger flocks.[60] An integral component of the sheep system was the

[57] Young, *Tour*, i. 388–9.
[58] Ibid. 389, 395, 435; ii. 77–8; *PP Stock*, 57, pt. ii. 12–13.
[59] Young, *Tour*, i. 388–9.   [60] Ibid. 389.

sending of part of the flocks for the winter period to farms in east
Limerick rented by Tipperary graziers for the purpose. John
Keating of Garranlea held over 2,000 acres there in 1767, and
Richard Doherty of Kedragh had over 1,600 acres in 1769.[61] The
spring lambs were sent to the east Limerick farms in October and
maintained there until the ensuing May when they were returned
to the Tipperary home farms fattened.[62]

Important improvements in the breed of sheep took place in the
late eighteenth century. The native Irish sheep were of small
stature and their wool growth small, but their crossing with the
imported Leicester breed enhanced the quality of the stock
overall, improving its size and its wool type. The credit for the
introduction of new breeds in the county goes to Dexter of Cullen,
who was agent or steward on the Maude estate in the 1770s and
who also gave his name to a new breed of cattle.[63] Maude
encouraged the replacement of his sheep stock by the Leicester
strain, as did his relative Moore of Marlfield who by 1760 was
importing Leicester rams.[64] Once established the new breed came
into demand and the letting out of Leicester rams for breeding
purposes became a specialist activity in some areas especially
under Dexter's auspices in Clanwilliam, in the north-east of the
county around Urlingford, and in the Slievardagh Hills.[65] In the
north of the county, Thomas Johnston of Derry between 1765 and
1777 imported over 185 rams and 370 ewes from England at a cost
of £6,660, which he sold at various locations in order to
disseminate the new breed. It was claimed by Johnston that on the
basis that one ram produced 30 lambs in a season, his had
produced 27,300 in a six-year period 1765–71. He claimed that
sheep from his new strain were larger in size, gave a greater
quantity of wool and tallow, and obtained a higher price on the
Dublin market as mutton.[66] Individual sheep masters also undertook the direct importation of new breeds: John Hemphill of

[61] Young, *Tour*, i. 389; *FDJ*, 14–17 Feb. 1767; *CEP*, 11 Sept. 1769.

[62] Young, *Tour*, i. 382, 389, 452.

[63] Ibid. 390, 453; for Dexter: *FLJ*, 10–13 Sept. 1788; M. J. O'Shea, *The history of
native Irish cattle* (Dublin, 1954), 9.

[64] Young, *Tour*, i. 393, 396.

[65] W. Tighe, *Statistical observations relative to the county of Kilkenny* (Dublin,
1802), 321–4.

[66] *An account of Mr Thomas Johnston's improvement of the livestock of the
kingdom of Ireland* (Dublin, 1777), 9–11, 33.

Golden paid sixty guineas in 1779 for a ram of Robert Bakewell of Leicester; in 1791 Sir William Barker purchased two rams from Chaplin of Lincolnshire; and in 1792 Scully of Kilfeacle sent his son to purchase sheep from Bakewell.[67] By the early nineteenth century the Leicester breed were in general use though they were then supplemented by some further new strains notably the Merino and South Down breeds introduced by Lord Lismore in 1810 and 1813.[68]

Cattle and sheep were grazed together. This was a beneficial system resulting in higher lamb and cattle growth rates and higher output per farm, and the rise in cattle numbers reflected some degree of intensification in farming from earlier decades when sheep predominated even more markedly. Evidence from the farms of Keating of Garranlea, Doherty of Kedragh, Alleyn of Golden, and McCarthy of Springhouse in the 1760s and 1770s shows an average stocking ratio of sheep to cattle of 11 : 1.[69] Sheep flocks tended to be large. In the 1770s Alleyn maintained 2,000 sheep besides lambs on 1,200 acres; McCarthy kept 10,000 sheep (including 2,000 lambs) on 9,000 acres; and Keating had 16,300 sheep on 13,800 acres.[70] They were among the very large sheep graziers who were able to achieve a stocking level of five sheep per acre on the rich lands of Clanwilliam and Middlethird, whereas in north Tipperary this ratio fell to one sheep per acre.[71] Flocks were larger and the system more intense in the south.

In the grazier system the broad pattern of movement was from the small farmers of the west of Ireland who passed on their reared cattle to the store breeders of the south, the stock being subsequently fully fattened and finished by the large farmers of the east. In Tipperary the system in its most characteristic form involved the purchase of young bullocks at the major fair of Ballinasloe and the more local fairs of Banagher, Newport, and Toomavara from September to November. In this way north Tipperary and adjacent areas of Offaly developed as a feeding or store-supply region serving the local fairs, where the graziers

[67] *CG*, 26–30 Sept. 1782; *FLJ*, 1–5 Oct. 1791; NLI, MS 27580, entries for 13–15, 22–3, 26, 28–9 Sept., 2 Oct. 1792.

[68] *PP Public instruction*, 33 (1836), 295; T. Radcliff, *Reports on the fine wooled flocks of Lord Viscount Lismore* (Dublin, 1820).

[69] *FDJ*, 14–17 Feb. 1767; *CEP*, 11 Sept. 1769; Young, *Tour*, i. 389–90.

[70] Young, *Tour*, i. 389–91.   [71] Ibid. 389, 430, 435.

assembled to buy.[72] Such stock, maintained initially on coarse ground, were kept on hay until the following May when they were put out on grass for the summer and fattened up. Contracts with the butchers in the ports of Cork, Limerick, and Waterford were made in July and August, and the fattened stock came to market between September and December. A subsidiary practice to this main activity was to buy in six-month-old bull calves in September and October, feed them with grass and hay over the winter months, and sell them the following May and June. On those parts of the farm where such bull calves were not kept, sheep were substituted. A fourth system, linked with cattle grazing, was the practice of purchasing old cows in the March–June period, fattening them up and selling them.[73]

Improvements in cattle breeds enhanced the value and sale-ability of stock and, in consequence, profit margins. This did not take place to a marked degree until the 1760s. For ten years after 1765 Johnston of Derry introduced at great expense breeds from England and, by 1775, 500 to 600 of his new cattle were in circulation.[74] He claimed that they were superior in quality and size and produced better beef, hides, and tallow. Despite these new strains, the dominant breed of cattle continued to be the long-horned or lowland breed of the native Irish type.

The county was primarily a fatstock region, its products being directed towards the beef export trade. Before the passing of the cattle acts (1666–7) the emphasis in Ireland was on the raising of lean cattle for export to England for fattening. From the time the acts became operational up to 1758–9 when they were suspended, Irish cattle and beef were excluded from the English market. This loss, however, was compensated for by the development of the specialist needs of the colonial market, the victualling require-ments of armies and navies, and the continental demand. Cattle numbers all over Munster increased in the 1760s with Tipperary noted for bullocks, sheep, and dairy cows.[75] The perception locally was that the suspension of the cattle acts would not lead to any upsurge in live cattle exports. One visitor to the county in 1760

---

[72] C. Coote, *General view of the agriculture and manufactures of the King's County* (Dublin, 1801), 49–50, 94; Young, *Tour*, i. 430, 435, 443–4.

[73] Young, *Tour*, i. 451–2.

[74] *Comms. Jnl.(Ire.)*, ix. pt. i. 184; *An account of Mr Thomas Johnston's improvement*, 21.

[75] Anon., 'Mallow and its neighbourhood in 1775', *JCHAS*, 27 (1921), 9, 83.

enquired what effect the suspension of the act had had and he was told: 'none at all for that in the whole Kingdom, at least their part of it, there was scarce any [i.e.live cattle] exported'.[76] In fact the boom in colonial demand made the repeal of the cattle acts unimportant. It is clear that Tipperary graziers remained in the beef sector. Beef exports to England grew and quadrupled in the period 1770–1800 by which date it was the main export market, surpassing those of the Continent and the colonies which declined in importance after 1780.[77]

Cork, Waterford, and Limerick were the main ports for the disposal of cattle from Tipperary. All the leading Cork firms and contractors purchased bullocks there. Before the shift to arable in south Tipperary after 1770, beef cattle were still being supplied from that area to Cork firms.[78] There was a preference among graziers to dispose of their cattle at Cork because prices were more generally favourable there, payment was more prompt, and there was an assured demand with contracts for the army and navy. This dependence on the Cork market was emphasized at the time of the embargo on the export of provisions in the late 1770s. It prevented feeders in Tipperary disposing of their fat cattle and in turn made them unable to purchase new stock from the rearers because of accommodation problems, and also because the bar on trade denied them the funds to make such purchases. A credit crisis developed whereby the Cork dealers could not purchase new consignments from the Tipperary graziers until their existing beef stocks were disposed of, which was prevented by the embargo.[79] The crisis created by the embargo was temporary, as the beef trade usually benefited from wartime demand or anticipation of it. In 1790, for instance, speculation among the Cork merchants of an expected war with Spain caused them to buy up several hundred head of cattle in Tipperary and other counties for a ten-day period in May.[80]

Individual consignments of cattle were large, those of Scully to Cork in select years being 570 (1782), 810 (1792), and 509 (1802), and others also filled large orders on a regular basis.[81] Profits on

[76] BL Add. MS 29252, 48.

[77] L. M. Cullen, *Anglo-Irish trade 1660–1800* (Manchester, 1968), 18, 33, 69–71.

[78] W. Woulfe to J. and P. Comerford, Cork, 31 Mar. 1765; same to Rice, White, and Connor, Cork, 9 Apr. 1765 (NLI, MS 9629).

[79] NLI, MS 14157, 17. [80] *FLJ*, 26–9 May 1790.

[81] NLI, MS 27571, 28–9, 44, 52–3, 97–8, 136, 178–9, 255, 297.

the sale of stock could be considerable. This was because, though
the price of stock to the grazier displayed an upward trend after
1770, the sale prices obtained for beef were sufficient to give him
good and sustained profits. For the early period the profits gained
by a grazier from Kilnamanagh were continuous from the late
1730s except in two years. Between 1738 and 1767 the level of
profit grew almost fifteenfold from £27 to £400.[82] This demonstrates the return achievable by a small-scale grazier at a time of
growing demand. The profit margins of the larger grazier were
substantially higher. Thus Scully in November 1781 disposed of
stock at Cork at £7. 5s. each which he had purchased for £4. 5s.;
in 1785 stock bought for £4 each were sold for £7. 12s. 6d.; and in
1790 his profit per beast in Cork was £5. 14s., in 1792 £5. 10s.[83]
When translated into total sums these amounts gave a substantial
return even allowing for foddering and other costs. Thus in 1775
Scully calculated that his total revenue from beef sales would be
£3,700, and by 1798 it was expected to reach £12,000.[84] Thus
Scully achieved a threefold increase in revenue from beef sales
over a 23-year period. It is not apparent how typical he was.
Demand for beef between 1770 and 1815 was sufficiently consistent for most Tipperary suppliers to benefit, though in different
degrees depending on the scale and extent of their operations,
their location, their contacts in trade, and their business acumen.

Dairying was not an enterprise engaged in to any large extent by
landowners, gentry, or large grazier tenants. The nominal stocks
of cows maintained by McCarthy, Alleyn, and Maude were either
for their own use or for letting in small numbers to tenants, rather
than for their own active commercial exploitation. Large graziers
were not primarily involved in promoting dairying rather what
cows they kept were for convenience, calving, or fattening. That
dairying was not the primary agricultural enterprise is emphasized
by the function and character of the fairs in the county which was
to transfer surplus young stock from dairying and rearing regions
outside the county for fattening within it. Since the lowland
pastures were devoted exclusively to dry cattle and sheep, dairying
became a family enterprise conducted by dairymen and smallholders. Dairying fitted into the economic organization of the

---

[82] Computed from NLI, MS 498.
[83] NLI, MS 27571 *sub* [?] Nov. 1781, 5 Dec. 1785, 27 Nov. 1790.
[84] Ibid. 4 Aug. 1775, 7 June 1798.

small farm because of the moderately intensive production per acre involved, the regular income provided, and the availability of cheap family labour. Dairy farms were found in upland and mountainous areas and on bad land within grazing districts which, because of their light soil and poor growth, made them unsuitable for cattle fattening. For the smallholder, ground—usually of 1 or 1½ acres with a cabin and two cows—was let in the 1770s at rents varying from £3 and £4. 10s. in the Ormond baronies, to £6. 2s. between Golden and Clonmel, and to £8. 8s. 3d. in Clanwilliam, the most intense grazing area.[85] Cows kept by such smallholders provided milk for family needs and a valuable income in the form of butter (varying between areas, but about 1 cwt. per annum), and skimmed milk for areas adjacent to towns and, in their absence, a calf or calves (valued at 2s. 6d. to 3s. in the mid-1770s).[86] Possession by cottiers, landholding labourers, and smallholders of such an income-generating resource as cows, marked them off from the landless labourers, some of whom hired out their labour, and others who rented grassland for potatoes, but neither of whom could, because of lack of resources, secure land with cows.

Dairying was an important enterprise for smallholders near towns, particularly if such centres adjoined hill or upland areas. Tipperary town developed as a centre in a dairying region lying as it did between the Galty Mountains to the south and the Slieve Felim range to the north; so also did Cashel as it lay on the western extremity of the Slievardagh Hills; while Fethard and Mullinahone were significant subsidiary centres. The practice of landlords letting out cows to dairymen for an annual cash or butter rent, extensive in Cork, Kerry, and Waterford, may have developed to a moderate extent near such centres, and their scale of dairy operations was more considerable than that of the smallholders already described. Dairying advanced to a greater extent in the south-east of the county largely as an extension of the activity from south Kilkenny and Waterford from the 1750s. This was because of the town demand for milk and milk products in Carrick and Clonmel, and because of the demand from butter merchants in Waterford.[87] A dairyman lease from Carrick in 1755 involving the

---

[85] Young, *Tour*, i. 391, 429, 444, 455.   [86] Ibid. 453.

[87] Ibid. 400; W. S. Mason, *A statistical account or parochial survey of Ireland* (Dublin, 1814–19), ii. 119.

letting of 115 acres with 30 cows suggests that the initial expansion in dairying here was financed (in terms of land and cows) by town merchants who were also head-tenants to outlying lands.[88] Dairying remained resilient in this area with dairies of 200 milch cows being the average around Carrick in 1814, and a survey of Clonmel in 1813 reported that: 'A great part of the parish is pasture ground the farmers, especially those near the town, depending mostly on dairies for making their rents.'[89] By that date both towns had become important butter-exporting centres through Waterford.

A large export trade in butter existed through Cork, Limerick, and Waterford supplying the English and colonial markets. There had been a dependence on the French market in the late seventeenth century but this was subject to fluctuation and became restricted from the 1730s. Butter exports to Spain and Portugal remained important, however, largely for re-export to their colonies. In the 1780s an expanding demand for butter in the English market meant that this market came to dominate the Irish butter trade subsequently.[90] Information as to the volume of Tipperary's contribution to this trade is slight. In 1791–2 under half the amount of butter—7,337 casks out of a total of 17,955— supplied to a large firm of Waterford butter exporters came from merchants in four Tipperary towns. The 7,337 casks, valued at the considerable sum of £29,317, were consigned from Carrick, Clonmel, Cashel, and Tipperary.[91] These butter purchases were made from the farmers by merchants acting as intermediaries in their localities for the exporters in the port. The four centres represent the points around which dairying was most prevalent at this stage. Clonmel and Carrick grew to be major butter-exporting centres by the early nineteenth century, and 60,000 to 70,000 firkins were disposed of in Clonmel's market in the 1820s.[92] A large part of this trade consisted of butter redirected from

[88] NLI, Ormond deeds (unsorted), bundle 1756–7: memorandum from J. Butler, Kilcash to J. Power, Tiberaghny, Co. Kilkenny, dairyman, 22 Mar. 1755.
[89] Mount Melleray, Burke MS 72 (vi), fo. 2, 'A statistical account of the parish of St. Mary's in the town of Clonmel and the diocese of Lismore' [c.1813]; Mason, *Survey*, ii. 119.   [90] Cullen, *Economic history*, 21, 54–5, 59.
[91] Ledger of Courtenay and Ridgway, 1791–2, fos. 31–5, 39, 42, 191–2, 208, 215, 224 (NLI, Mic.P.4036); *Jnl. Royal Society of Antiquaries of Ireland*, 87 (1958), 172.
[92] Mason, *Survey*, ii. 123; *PP Butter (Ire.)*, 5 (1826), 56–7, 100–1, 146; Burke, *Clonmel*, 184–6.

Limerick where beamage rates were high, and from districts like Fermoy, thus avoiding Cork where there was a requirement that the butter be in firkins of Cork manufacture.[93] These factors explain the redirection of the butter via the markets at Clonmel and Carrick to Waterford where no stipulation requiring the firkins to be of local manufacture existed. A large proportion of the butter passing through both centres had its origins outside the county, so that the large volume of trade in butter is not an accurate index of local production levels.

Pig-rearing developed as an enterprise in dairying areas. Its main advantage as a source of income was that the return was likely to be more immediate since pigs accumulated body fat early in life and therefore matured earlier than cattle or sheep. Secondly, pig culture lent itself readily to being a small, easily managed enterprise absorbing surplus family labour. Thirdly, the feeding requirements of pigs were supplied from the by-products of the farm, especially whey, skimmed milk, and potatoes so that little extra cost was incurred for feeding stuffs. These advantages made pig-owning a viable cash pursuit for smallholders and small farmers. The result was that pig ownership became widely diffused throughout the county, especially in Iffa and Offa West, Clanwilliam, and Slievardagh which were strong dairying areas, and it was relatively unimportant in large grain producing districts notably Iffa and Offa East, centring on Clonmel.

The dairyman kept pigs in order to consume the waste products of the dairy. He generally sold the litter from his breeding sows to the cottiers and labourers who fattened them up for about six months when they were sold to bacon curers. The sale of a pig became an important source of income for the peasantry as it made a significant contribution to paying the annual rent. A typical cottier in west Tipperary in the mid-1770s derived his income from labour and the sale of commodities (a pig, poultry, a calf, and butter). Of the disposable items the sale of a pig, bought for 7s. and sold for 47s., brought in a profit of £2 equivalent to 12.8 per cent of total income. For a peasant at Gloster, Co. Offaly, the percentage was 7.5 per cent, at Johnstown it was 21 per cent, and at Derry 6 per cent.[94] Income from pigs thus made a substantial

---

[93] *PP Butter (Ire.)*, 56–7, 100–1, 146.
[94] Calculated from Young, *Tour*, i. 429, 436, 444–5, 455–6.

contribution to cottier rents just as cattle and sheep made up grazier rents.

Profitability from pigs was enhanced by improvements in breeds. The native Irish breed of pig was ungainly in size and aspect. The introduction of Berkshire and Hampshire strains had the effect of shortening the period of maturity, so that such breeds fattened more quickly. Johnston of Derry introduced the Hampshire breed and by the mid-1770s about 6,000 of the breed were diffused through the countryside.[95] Maude at Dundrum brought the Berkshire strain to his estate and fed them on clover, which was an innovation in the Irish context, given the established preference for farm by-products.[96] A relation of Maude's, Stephen Moore of Marlfield, also had the Berkshire breed and adopted a novel feeding system by feeding his pigs entirely on bran, a milling residue, which he had in plentiful supply from his large Marlfield flour mill.[97]

After the spread of dairying from mid-century pig-ownership became more common and an active trade in pigs evolved. In west Tipperary stretching into east Limerick pig numbers had greatly increased by the 1770s and an important twice-yearly pig fair in April and June developed in Cullen.[98] Pig-ownership also increased among cottiers in north Tipperary by the 1770s where the demand from Limerick port was an influential factor.[99] Similarly, in the extreme south-east corner of the county pig fattening developed as an adjunct to the spread of dairying and the demand for pig products in Waterford. Such demand was created by the need for salted pork in the British plantations. The pork trade through Waterford catered for the specialist needs of the Newfoundland market. Towards the end of the century a decline in pork exports was linked to the growth in demand for bacon in the English domestic market.[100] Waterford was supplied with pigs from south Tipperary and south Kilkenny. By the early nineteenth century Carrick and Clonmel had emerged as important dispatching points

---

[95] *An account of Mr Thomas Johnston's improvement*, 21.

[96] Young, *Tour*, i. 393.   [97] Ibid. 395, 396.

[98] Ibid. 453, 455; NLI, *Ordnance Survey name book*, vol. 122, Co. Tipperary, fo. 6.

[99] Young, *Tour*, i. 436, 444, 445; *PP Railway commissioners*, 35 (1835), 2.

[100] J. J. Mannion, 'Waterford merchants and the Irish–Newfoundland provisions trade, 1770–1820', in L. M. Cullen and P. Butel, *Négoce et industrie en France et en Irlande aux XVIIIe et XIXe siècles* (Paris, 1980), 28.

TABLE I. Pig meat and by-products processed at Carrick

	Nov. 1812–Nov. 1813	Nov. 1814–Nov. 1815
Bacon (flitches)	39,406	37,502
Lard (cwt)	1,482	1,394
Pork (tierces)	101	150
Pork (barrels)	163	150

Source: Mason, *Survey*, ii. 123 (export data); Burke, *Clonmel*, 186.

in the pig-export trade. An estimated 12,000 pigs were slaughtered in Clonmel in 1808, while the volume of pig meat and pig by-products processed at Carrick was substantial as Table I indicates.

Growth in the livestock trade integrated the local economy as the number of new fairs grew. The low density of fairs in the seventeenth century is indicative of the county's underdevelopment in that period. In 1685 the chief fair centres were at Cashel, Clonmel, Holy Cross, and Tipperary. The slow growth and poor demand of the early eighteenth century are seen in the meagre increase of only two new fairs between 1685 and 1723, and in the concessions which the proprietors of fairs had to offer, for instance the corporation of Cashel in 1721 ruled that its twice-yearly fair would be custom-free for three years.[101] Nevertheless, two new fairs at Dundrum and Clerihan illustrate a trend away from the south into the northern half of the county reflecting the growth in demand for cattle from there. This trend was reinforced in the 1720s and 1730s with the upsurge in demand for cattle. By 1732 eleven new foundations are on record and a further eight sites by 1743. The direction of new fairs by 1732 was northward with foundations at Borrisokane, Borrisoleigh, Nenagh, Toomavara, and Silvermines; and by 1743, though new fairs were widely spread, there was a certain concentration of new points west of Cashel like Galbally, Golden, and Kilfeacle, these adding to the already large number of fair locations in west Tipperary and east Limerick. The pace in the establishment of fairs continued between 1743 and 1760 with eleven new foundations. It is clear that fair centres were responding to the pattern of demand with

[101] *Dublin Courant*, 5 Aug. 1721.

modifications being undertaken as at Kilfinnane in east Limerick in 1750 when the fair green had to be enlarged to accommodate the growing number of cattle being brought for disposal there.[102] The most significant new fair founded at this time was that at Newport.

The most active periods in the establishment of new fairs were the 1720s, 1730s, and 1760s. Thereafter two trends are evident: the pace of foundation decelerated so that by 1815 new fairs were not being founded, and although the number of fairs held grew from 101 (1760), to 125 (1788), to 155 (1815), these were conducted at a static or declining number of centres.[103] Even the new centres established in the late eighteenth century, e.g. Templetuohy, display a northern orientation or were on landlord-sponsored sites in marginal areas within the existing catchment area, e.g. New Birmingham. The trend is further confirmed by the location of fairs held over a number of days. Thus Castle Otway had a two-day fair twice yearly in April and September, and Templemore held two three-day wool fairs in July. Cahir apart, these were the only centres where fairs were conducted over a number of consecutive days.

The business of the fairs shifted northward away from the southern centres. The shift to cereals in the south contributed to this. In 1784 it was said of the twice-yearly (May and November) fairs in Clonmel that they had been 'for some years past much neglected',[104] while in 1787 it was reported that the Cashel fairs in September and November were 'not being of late much attended'.[105] In both cases efforts were made by the corporations to revive the attendance of buyers and farmers. The revival of business in such centres had to await the sustained demand for livestock which became evident from the late 1780s. Already in 1786 the November fair in Clonmel experienced brisk demand and by 1790 the new fair at Callan in November witnessed a large number of cattle being disposed of to Cork buyers.[106]

Some of the Tipperary fairs were specialist in function. The

---

[102] *Munster Journal*, 9 Apr. 1750.
[103] For statistics on fairs, see Power, 'Tipperary', Table XXXII; for fairs in general see P. O'Flanagan, 'Markets and fairs in Ireland, 1600–1800: Index of economic development and regional growth', *Jnl. of Historical Geography*, 2 (1985), 364–78.
[104] *CG*, 15–19 Apr. 1784.   [105] Ibid. 6–9 Aug. 1787.
[106] *FLJ*, 11–15 Nov. 1786; 23–7 Oct., 3–6 Nov. 1790.

majority of fairs took place in the latter half of the year, especially in September and October which was the period when young cattle were bought for fattening by the county's graziers from small farmers. Specialist fairs evolved at Newport and Toomavara (stores), Golden (stores and fat cattle), and Clonmel and Templemore (wool). These fairs assumed a higher profile in the hierarchy of fairs unlike the remainder whose influence would have been local. Newport is the best documented of these specialist fairs. It developed as a meeting point for the transmission of stores from the west of Ireland particularly from Clare via Killaloe and O'Brien's Bridge, and from north Tipperary to the graziers of west Tipperary and Limerick for fattening, and also for the sale of fat cattle. The fair had a well-situated location as part of a landlord-promoted estate village in the early 1740s and it received further local support in 1762.[107] The proprietor of the ground, Richard Waller, offered a variety of incentives with the result that the fair prospered after 1760. In 1764 over 2,000 stores were sold there, yet even this number failed to satisfy the large demand from buyers; in 1765 over 10,000 stores were disposed of and yet again the demand went unsatisfied; and by 1768 the volume of business was so great that the fair had to be extended over two days.[108] The evolution of Newport fair shows the importance it had, especially after 1760, as an exchange point for livestock servicing the needs of the county's graziers.

3. Arable Farming

The emphasis in the county's agriculture at mid-century was largely pastoral, with the county's chief products being cattle, sheep, butter, rape-seed, and cereals. In the ensuing forty years, however, cereals were to advance significantly as a cash crop in an area extending north from Clonmel. The principal cereal crops were wheat, oats, and barley. By the mid-nineteenth century the main wheat-growing districts were in the area from Clogheen to Carrick, in the central region focusing on Cashel and Thurles, and in the north around Nenagh. Oats, because of its adaptability in

---

[107] *FDJ*, 9–12 Oct. 1762.
[108] Ibid. 27–30 Oct. 1764; 26–9 Oct. 1765; 15–19 Oct., 29 Oct.–2 Nov. 1768.

the crop rotation, was an important crop in all areas, especially in hill regions. Barley was less important in the south than wheat except in the south-west around Clogheen, and there were strong barley-growing areas in the centre of the county and north of Nenagh. Barley was grown to meet the needs of local distilleries and breweries, while wheat to an extent was almost entirely an export item.

The amount of pasture would have been correspondingly greater before the mid-eighteenth century. The southern orientation in arable cultivation is apparent from a comment made c. 1687 that 'The South p[ar]t is fertill, full of corn and hay', and from a further observation in 1732 that 'Tipperary County, excepting ye more northern parts of it, is reckoned ye finest in ye kingdom and indeed ye large vales here presented us with more barley, flax, and potatoes than we had seen anywhere in Ireland.'[109] The extent of cereal cultivation before mid-century in normal years satisfied local consumption needs and in good harvest years left a surplus for export. The balance between pastoral and arable shifted as a result of the introduction of subsidies on the inland carriage of grain and flour to Dublin from 1758. The serious food shortages experienced in the mid-1750s induced government to promote an expansion in the area under cereal crops beyond the traditional supply counties surrounding Dublin which had become exhausted through constant working. It was envisaged that counties such as Tipperary, where it was said that the land had become 'unwholesome for sheep from the length of time it has been under grazing', would be suitable for cereal growing.[110] An act of 1758 (31 Geo. II, c. 3) made provision for bounties on the conveyance of grain and flour to Dublin, and in the ensuing decades this acted as a stimulus to effect a transition to extensive cereal cultivation in the navigable river valleys of the county, precipitating a sharp rise in land values in such areas.

The initial local response to the subsidy system was meagre because of the traditional reluctance to set lands to grain farmers, who were normally undercapitalized and because the early 1760s saw an upsurge in livestock production. From the late 1760s, however, as the benefits of the system in terms of a guaranteed

---

[109] TCD, MS 4879/1; J. F. T. Loveday (ed.), *Diary of a tour in 1732* (Edinburgh, 1890), 43.   [110] *Lords Jnl. (Ire.)*, iii. 103.

market and price at the local mills became evident, cereals spread. In 1772 it was reported that 'The corn premiums has cutt up all the grass lands in the Golden Vales of Killcash and Limerick.'[111] The ready sale and guaranteed price available at the growing number of local mills served to capitalize the farmer and lessened the reluctance of landlords to encourage grain growers. One of the instructions issued by the county's freeholders to their MPs in November 1773 was to resist demands for the removal of the bounty, stemming from the government's policy of reducing expenditure.[112] This did not happen and by 1776 Tipperary was receiving 17 per cent or £10,320 of the total subsidies paid.[113] Spatially the catchment area where commercial cereal growing became most intense is defined by the distribution of flour mills, with evident concentrations around Clonmel and Fethard and along the River Suir. Something of the degree of intensification is shown by the fact that in 1788 one visitor was struck by the number of bags of wheat brought to Thurles for sale, and by 1818 that town was said to attract 1,000 cartloads of grain for sale on market day.[114]

The second phase in the growth of cereal production locally came after 1790. Despite the termination of the bounty system in 1797, grain producers found a new market in the war years (1793–1815) when Ireland became a granary for supplying Britain. Harvests locally were generally good in the 1790s, and harvest prices rose nationally by 50 per cent in the decade 1792–1802.[115] Prices in the ports influenced trends in their hinterlands and overall cereal prices rose more rapidly than prices for pastoral products, something which induced a further expansion in the area devoted to cereals. In 1791 one observer claimed that the county could grow twice as much grain as it did, and in 1813 farmers sowed near double the amount of ground with grain according to one grain merchant in Clogheen.[116]

Tipperary benefited substantially from the subsidy system which

---

[111] PRONI, D572/2/93.   [112] *FJ*, 30 Nov.–2 Dec. 1773.
[113] J. S. Donnelly, 'Irish agrarian rebellion: The Whiteboys of 1769–76', *PRIA*, 83 C (1983), 299.
[114] *The compleat Irish traveller* (London, 1788), ii. 7; P. Leahy, *Reference and rental to the map and survey now taken of the Thurles estate, 1818* (Dublin, 1819).
[115] NA, OP 525/162/114.
[116] *Comms. Jnl.(Ire.)*, xiv, ccxiv; Society of Friends Library, Dublin: Fennell papers, box iv, g, no. 11.

favoured counties at a distance from Dublin. The Quaker merchants, who came to dominate the grain trade locally, had a system of family links in the ports and canal towns which facilitated access to external markets via the river and canal system. On the surface the halting of the bounty payments could have had serious implications locally. Pressure for change arose from Dublin interests who felt that the city's export trade languished through the absence of an export bounty comparable to that which existed in other ports. A movement for the suspension of the bounties in favour of export subsidies through Dublin arose in the early 1790s, though local interests were actively petitioning against this as early as 1791.[117] In 1797 an act (37 Geo. III, c. 24) was passed whereby from September 1797 the inland bounties were to cease and be replaced by an export bounty on grain, flour, bread, and malt exported through Dublin, as operated in other Irish ports.

The local impact of the removal of the subsidies after 1797 was not adverse, its effect being softened by the vibrancy of the livestock sector, by the relative absence of barley and malting in the county, and by the reorientation of the trade towards exports through Waterford. Up to 1797 the internal market for grain was probably more significant than the export one. The volume of wheat exported declined over the period as a whole especially after the mid-1770s when it was increasingly diverted to the local flour-milling concerns which were then entering upon a phase of expansion. Similarly there was an overall fall in the amount of bere and barley as most of the crop came to be used in the malting concerns locally. Malt conveyed to Dublin from Tipperary displayed some increase in the period. Consignments of oats and meal to Dublin fluctuated reflecting the importance of these items in the diet of rural Ireland. Grain not utilized in the local flour mills was normally exported through Waterford and the export bounties there were availed of. The volume of Tipperary's contribution to this export trade is not readily deducible. However, individual consignments could be considerable. For instance, between September 1791 and May 1792 Thomas Taylor, a Clonmel grain merchant, sent 1,790 barrels of oats, 1,215 of wheat, and 200 of barley valued in all at £3,042 to a Waterford firm

---

[117] *Comms. Jnl. (Ire.)*, xiv. 342.

for export.[118] The result of the termination of the subsidy system in 1797 was to transform Clonmel, with Waterford close at hand, into a major centre of the grain trade.

4. Industry

Textile activity was the most widespread industrial pursuit in the county. The expansion in sheep grazing during the Restoration period provided the context for a growth in wool exports and for the promotion of woollen-manufacturing concerns at Carrick and Clonmel. This period of growth was followed by one of dislocation consequent on the disruption to economic life occasioned by the wars of 1688–91, as a survey of the Ormond estate, including the above two woollen towns, shows.[119] In 1692 most of Carrick was reset to Protestant tenants and plans were in hand to encourage a manufactory there which suggests the degree to which the earlier concern had been reduced by war.[120] The act of 1699, which prohibited the export of woollen goods from Ireland, induced manufacturers to concentrate on the home market. Carrick grew as a textile town to fulfil this demand. One revenue official observed in 1733 that it was 'very remarkable for the manufacture of rateens which is carried on in a very extensive manner'.[121] At Clonmel the making of serges, camblets, and yarn was firmly established and as the assize town it became the centre where contracts were made for wool, a function it was still fulfilling in 1773.[122] Ratteen or coarse woollen cloth was worn by a wide segment of Irish society and was distributed to many parts, particularly to the north-east of the country, to cater for the requirements of those in the linen-making areas.[123]

The woollen industry did not experience significant growth again until the 1740s, from which time there was a rise in worsted yarn which was combed and spun in the Suir valley. By mid-century Tipperary with Cork and Limerick were recognized as the

[118] Ledger of Courtenay and Ridgway, fo. 43.
[119] NLI, MS 2561, fos. 20–5, 34–7.   [120] BL, Add. MS 28877, fo. 282.
[121] NA, E. Thompson's report on the revenue, 1733 (2c, 36, 1), 27.
[122] G. T. Stokes (ed.), *Pococke's tour in Ireland in 1752* (Dublin and London, 1891), 125–6; *FLJ*, 7–11 Aug. 1773.
[123] C. Smith, *Antient and present state of the city and county of Waterford* (Dublin, 1746), 281; *Comms. Jnl.(Ire.)*, xix. pt. 2, p. dccccxcvii.

main counties where woollen manufacturing was conducted.[124] It
was during this period that a number of new locations in the
industry developed. It was reported of Clogheen in *c.*1750 that
O'Callaghan had 'encouraged artificers particularly manufacturers
of friezes and ratteens to settle here'.[125] In 1768 a Cork merchant
with local interests, Richard Pope, advertised his intention of
establishing a woollen manufactory at Tipperary town.[126] Thurles
in 1774 was noted as a thriving centre of the woollen industry, and
in 1779 John Bayly was seeking combers to settle at Farneybridge
near Thurles by offering accommodation, plots, and employment
for twenty combers capable of working-up 10,000 stones of
wool.[127] The industry also existed in Roscrea, Golden, Tipperary,
and Cahir.[128]

Coarse woollens or ratteens remained the mainstay of the
industry, particularly in Carrick, but in addition from the late
1760s there was an expansion into broadcloth making. This
development was initiated by the arrival in Carrick in 1769 of John
Moore, clothier, from Dublin whence he had been induced to
remove by the Dublin Society premiums. He experienced some
local opposition initially but later came to employ over 100
persons. Supported by premiums and a contract for the supply of
clothing to the army, Moore's enterprise achieved a good level of
output in the 1770s.[129] Other established manufacturers expanded
their operations to include the making of broadcloth. Despite this
diversification within the industry locally, the 1770s marked a high
point indicated by the levels of employment and the degree of
prosperity. These were aspects commented on by contemporaries,
one remarking in 1776 that 'the manufacture increases and is very
flourishing', and another in 1778 that ratteen making was
conducted 'in great abundance and give[s] a flourishing air to this
part of the country'.[130] From the early 1780s, however, the
industry began to decline because of difficulties associated with

---

[124] PRONI, T2368/1.   [125] RIA, MS 24. G. 9., 278.
[126] *LC*, 13 Oct. 1768.
[127] *FLJ*, 13–17 Aug. 1774; 13–17 Feb. 1779.
[128] Roscrea: RD, 33/467/20936, 33/303/20395, 35/133/21447, 123/190/84151;
FDJ, 26–9 Oct. 1765; *Comms. Jnl.(Ire.)*, xi. pt. 1, 145; Stokes, *Pococke*, 172;
Golden: Young, *Tour*, i. 335, 394; Cahir: NLI, MS 772 (4), 35.
[129] *Proc. of the Dublin Society*, 6 (1769–70), 251–2, 255, 259; 7 (1770–1), 7,
14–15, 106.
[130] Young, *Tour*, i. 402; P. Sandby, *The virtuosi's museum* (n.p., 1781), 38.

raw material, organizational problems, new technology, and imports.

Wool came to be in short supply. This trend was evident as early as 1760 when one visitor to the county commented that 'another reason they give for the dearness of wool is that there are not so many sheep bred in Ireland as formerly, the breeding and feeding of horn[e]d cattle being more profitable'.[131] There was a contraction in sheep grazing in the county in the last three decades of the century as pasture lands were increasingly devoted to cattle fattening, and as the spread of cereals took place. Indicative of the shift was the foundation of a six-day wool fair in July at Templemore, challenging Clonmel in the south as the centre where contracts were made.[132] Sheep numbers were falling: the number of sheep shorn by Scully of Kilfeacle declined from 2,800 in 1786 to 1,150 in 1808.[133] Consequent on a reduction in supply was a rise in the price of wool threefold from 5s. to 6s. per stone in 1776, to 19s. 6d. in 1806.[134] Reduced wool supply and higher prices meant an increase in production costs for the manufacturer. In 1786, for instance, the master combers of Clonmel had to lay off eighty journeymen combers because the rise in wool prices made it impossible for them to sell the finished product at a price which would give a profit, leaving thousands of pounds of unsold worsted on their hands.[135]

Shortage of raw wool and its high price led to the development of fraudulent practices in the industry. The main abuse arose out of the practice of stretching or pulling the piece of cloth. This stemmed from the position of the journeyman turned manufacturer who, having experienced insecurity of employment under a master manufacturer, set up on his own with some small capital. Due to the absence of a class of wool sorters he was obliged to purchase his supply of wool (generally of inferior quality) from the master manufacturer. Moreover, when working-up the yarn he lessened the amount of warp which his web should consist of and reduced the weft by laying it thin on the cloth. The result of this stretching process—undertaken to gain a rapid return on a small capital—was that goods of poor quality were brought to market

---

[131] BL, Add. MS 29,252, 48.   [132] *CG*, 25–9 Oct. 1794.
[133] NLI, MS 27,571, *sub* 21 June 1786, 1 Jan. 1806, 9 June 1808.
[134] Young, *Tour*, i. 388–9; NLI, MS 27,571, *sub* 1 Jan. 1806.
[135] *FLJ*, 12–16 Aug. 1786.

where they sold cheaply, thereby underselling those of the better manufacturer. Because these goods lacked firmness and decayed quickly when worn, the Dublin dealers eventually refused to buy them so that there was a loss of sales.[136] Attempts to eliminate abuses were made initially by the main clothiers in Carrick in 1774.[137] But their failure brought into greater focus the need for statutory provision. Only with a comprehensive act of 1800 (40 Geo. III, c. 36) was effective protection given to the legitimate manufacturer from his fraudulent opposite. By this stage, however, other factors had come into play to make the decline of the industry irreversible.

Difficulties in the industry were reflected in a fall in employment levels. The worsted branch was more labour-intensive than the woollen sector because of the greater number of processes involved in production. A census of Carrick in 1799 shows that textile manufacturing accounted for 20 per cent of total occupations out of a population of 10,907.[138] By 1814 the numbers employed in the industry in Carrick had experienced a sixfold decrease.[139] The period of prosperity in the industry between *c.*1740 and 1780 brought a degree of prosperity to a large number of people. The judgement of one observer in 1762 was that 'all the common people [of Carrick] live comfortably and are enriched [by the textile industry] to a very great degree',[140] while over twenty years later the belief was that the progenitors of the town's industry and their descendants had 'made great properties, improved the town and neighbourhood, and gave subsistence to great numbers of industrious poor'.[141] How this comfort was reflected in wage levels can be exemplified by the fact that in 1786 it was calculated that eighty combers in Clonmel could earn £8,000 in wages in one year working-up 25,000 stones of fleece wool, equivalent to £100 each per annum.[142] Any setbacks in the industry could, therefore, be damaging and widespread in terms of employment, income levels, and living standards.

The economic difficulties of the early 1770s caused a slump in

---

[136] The foregoing is based on T. Wallace, *An essay on the manufactures of Ireland* (Dublin, 1798), 155–6, 170–2, 181–2.   [137] *FLJ*, 5–8 Jan. 1774.

[138] L. A. Clarkson, 'The Carrick-on-Suir woollen industry', *IESH*, 16 (1989), 23–41, at 32 (based on an analysis of BL, Add. MS 11,722).

[139] Mason, *Survey*, ii. 120.

[140] J. Long, *The golden fleece* (Dublin. 1762), 13.

[141] *Comms. Jnl.(Ire.)*, xi. pt. 1, 108.   [142] *FLJ*, 12–16 Aug. 1786.

the domestic market for woollen goods and in 1773 the county's freeholders instructed their MPs to press for a removal of restrictions in the industry in order to make it more competitive.[143] The early 1780s was also a critical period as unemployment among the worsted weavers of Munster forced them to seek work in the manufacturing towns of the midlands (Mountrath, Mountmellick, Ballinakill, and Edenderry), but without success since these centres were also experiencing a recession.[144] The increasing level of unemployment in the industry and the consequent rise in poverty can be seen in Carrick at the end of the century. In 1799 there were 113 persons described as of 'no profession' and 91 as 'persons wholly dependent on charity' in the town; while in 1814 out of 1,424 families in the town and parish 1,217 were employed in trade and manufacture, 82 in agriculture, leaving 125 families with no designated occupation.[145] Assuming a uniform family size of 6 persons then a threefold increase in poverty in the 15-year period can be advanced.

The industry's urban location represented an organizational weakness because it added to employers' costs. In contrast to the linen industry in Ireland and the woollen industry in Britain, which were both rural in location, the urban character of much of the Irish industry meant higher wages and the prospect of industrial disputes. The income of £100 for a comber in Clonmel in 1786 was high by contemporary standards, and such wage levels were increasingly difficult for employers to sustain given the growing shortage of wool and its high price. The industry was also threatened by combinations among the journeymen weavers, the most serious of which was in 1764 in Carrick when 500 of them conducted a five-month strike chiefly over the issue of substitute labour and apprentices.[146]

Employment prospects were further diminished by the introduction of new technology in the 1790s. Traditional labour-intensive processes in the industry were slow and time consuming. More mechanical methods would assist in reducing employers' labour costs, a regular supply could be depended upon, and combinations in the industry would be defeated. Attempts by outsiders to

[143] *FJ*, 30 Nov.–2 Dec. 1773.
[144] *Comms. Jnl.(Ire.)*, xi. pt. 2, 449–50.
[145] BL, Add. MS 11,722, fos. 121^v–122, 125; Mason, *Survey*, ii. 109–110.
[146] *FDJ*, 17–21 Jan., 13–17 Mar., 29 May–2 June, 21–5 Aug. 1764.

introduce such techniques into a tradition-bound industry were
resisted in Carrick in the early 1790s. Thus a spring loom
introduced there in 1791, which would have allowed one man to do
the work hitherto performed by four, led to violent opposition.[147]
New techniques introduced by local partnerships, however,
appear to have been more successful.[148] The effect of the
introduction of new technology was to further erode employment
in an industry already suffering from inherent weaknesses.

Declining wool supply and its high price precluded any
expansion in Irish manufacturing to match the British industry
which, because of cheaper and better quality wool, was able to
produce goods more competitively. In the 1780s and 1790s imports
rose to compete successfully with home-produced goods on the
domestic market. In 1783 the worsted weavers of Roscrea
petitioned parliament for the imposition of protective duties to
mitigate their distress from rising imports.[149] The manufacturers of
Carrick also sought relief against imports, particularly coarse
woollens. They claimed that had they not in previous years
attempted to hold down their share of the market by lowering their
prices and by making inferior goods for the common country
people, then their industry would have become extinct.[150]
Although these complaints against imports were voiced at a time
of general crisis in the Irish economy, it is clear that the long-term
prospects for the industry were not auspicious. A permanent
decline took place in the woollen industry in the late eighteenth
century in the towns of Tipperary especially Carrick.

The woollen industry was the chief branch of textiles in terms of
employment, capital, and organization. The linen industry did not
develop to any prominent degree in the county, though there were
attempts to promote it. These attempts show experimentation on
the part of the local gentry in measures to advance linen-making at
a time when it was fashionable for their class to do so, or as
adjuncts to the promotion of Protestant settlement or charter
schools, factors which were unnecessary in Ulster, the heartland of
the industry. The earliest instance of such promotion comes from
the early 1730s at a time of soaring linen exports. In 1735 George

[147] *FLJ*, 14–18 May 1791.
[148] *JWSEIAS*, 15 (1912), 65.
[149] *Comms. Jnl.(Ire.)*, xi. pt. 1, 145.   [150] Ibid. 108.

Mathew granted 100 acres near Thurles adjoining the River Suir to a linen manufacturer on a three-lives lease and agreed to spend £200 in two years on buildings and equipment. This he failed to do and the linen manufacturer claimed that by 1740 he had accumulated debts of £800.[151] Other instances of gentry participation in linen schemes are recorded for Newport under the Jocelyn and Waller families when the charter school was established there in the 1740s; at Tipperary pupils from the Erasmus Smith School were bound apprentice to craftsmen in the town including one case in 1722 of apprenticeship to a linen weaver; at Shronell, west of Tipperary, a colony of northern weavers was introduced in the 1740s, and at Dundrum under Maude in 1771.[152] The industry is also mentioned after 1755 for other centres and gentry interest persisted into the nineteenth century, for in 1823 Lady Glengall introduced flax growing to the country people around Cahir where she also promoted a regular linen market.[153]

Despite premiums from the Linen Board, the growth of the linen industry locally was hindered because the amount of flax sown was insufficient and of poor quality. In 1823 a mere 640 acres of flax were sown in the county placing it twenty-fifth in order of magnitude, and the scarcity of flax seed continued to be a problem.[154] Also the industry was imposed from the top down: there was a concentration on the bleaching side of the industry, and at a lower level employment in linen was unreliable and unremunerative for rural dwellers compared with worsted spinning. These factors inhibited the 'take-off' of the industry compared with other areas of Ireland.

The cotton industry had a brief existence from the 1780s at Clonmel and Tipperary in response to bounties offered by the Dublin Society on the home sales of cotton. The Clonmel venture was promoted by a partnership of local (Grubb) and Dublin interests in 1788, and although the venture was initially successful, after 1800 it declined in line with the experience of the industry in

---

[151] RD, 86/428/61096; NA, 2A.12.38, pp. 66–9, 155; PRONI, D562/1112.
[152] Newport: *Report and observations of Robert Stephenson* (Dublin, 1764), 47; Tipperary: High School, Dublin, Erasmus Smith Schools committee book 1721–4 (abstracted in NLI, MS 16,931, 9); Shronell: *Compleat Irish traveller*, ii. 15; Dundrum: RD, 296/461/197728; *FLJ*, 9–13 Feb. 1771; Young, *Tour*, i. 392–4.
[153] PRONI, D207/28/365, 367, 369.
[154] Ibid. 369.

Munster at large.[155] The Tipperary concern was a partnership between two local merchants William Baker and Clement Sadlier, the latter possibly being an associate of the Cork firm of the same name which was the largest cotton manufactory in Munster at this time. The firm adopted the Manchester method of production and in 1788 it had a large number of workhouses for weavers, accommodation for sixteen apprentices, and an extensive bleach green.[156] By 1793, however, the partnership had been dissolved and the concern, including the stock of cloths, cottons, and drapery goods was assigned over for the payment of creditors.[157]

The bounty system provided the initial stimulus for the development of flour milling and this was later supplemented by the transfer of capital from the declining textile industry particularly among the Quaker community, with the transition taking place in the 1770s. Only in the post-1770 period does flour milling expand rapidly with the number of mills sending flour to Dublin growing from 8 in 1771–2 to 12 to 47 in 1791–2; with a commensurate increase in the volume of flour transported, from 14,203 cwt. in 1771–2 to 123,484 cwt. in 1791–2.[158] Despite the termination of the subsidy in 1797 flour milling had become sufficiently well established as to avoid any adverse effects. On the contrary, the industry was sustained by the years of external demand up to 1815 and beyond, new mills continued to be established, and nationally Clonmel emerged as a major centre of the industry.[159]

The mills were concentrated along the River Suir and its tributaries and also around Clonmel and Fethard. The riverine situation provided both the motive power for mills and the means of conveyance for the grain and flour down the Suir, initially to Dublin by canal via the Barrow navigation, and later to external markets through Waterford. The most intensive region of milling was in Clonmel and within a twenty mile radius of the town. The

---

[155] *Dublin Evening Post*, 28 Feb. 1788; *FLJ*, 12–16 July 1788; *CG*, 5–9 June 1788, 8–12 Feb. 1794; RD 503/155/322073; Paris, Bibliothèque Nationale, MS 20,099, fo. 99; D. Dickson, 'Aspects of the rise and decline of the Irish cotton industry' in Cullen and Smout, *Comparative aspects*, 109–111.

[156] C. T. Bowden, *A tour through Ireland* (Dublin, 1791), 158; R. Lucas, *A general directory of the kingdom of Ireland* (Dublin, 1788), 184.

[157] *CG*, 11–15 May 1793.

[158] Power, 'Tipperary', Tables XXXVI, XXXVII.

[159] L. M. Cullen, 'Flour milling in Ireland in the eighteenth century', *IESH*, 4 (1977), 24.

mills created an accessible and convenient market for grain at the farmer's doorstep. They were large multi-storey structures requiring substantial capital investment, and were significant also in terms of capacity and equipment. One of the largest mills in the country, Marlfield near Clonmel, had a storage capacity of 10,000 barrels of wheat; it processed 3,000 barrels at its opening but by 1776 this had risen to 20,000 barrels, equivalent to half the production of all mills in the county at that date.[160] A mill with its machinery required a large capital. Marlfield was erected in 1769 at a cost of £15,000.[161] Since this was the county's largest mill the cost of the other mills was much less, but altogether the forty-seven mills in 1791 represented a substantial investment.

The nature of the partnership structure in the milling business at a period of rapid growth, is shown by the case of Sir Cornwallis Maude of Dundrum, who in 1782 put up a capital of £5,000 and agreed to operate a partnership with Edward Collins of Clonmel in the Marlfield mill.[162] Investment in other milling concerns was also substantial. Maude's partner, Collins, leased the corporation mills in Clonmel in 1781 on which between £10,000 and £12,000 had been spent, while in 1805 a capital fund of £9,000 was involved in a joint milling venture by two other Clonmel merchants.[163] Much of the necessary funding for the expansion of flour milling came from the landed class, Moore and Maude being notable examples. Much of the essential working capital was provided by Dublin flour factors who provided the millers with advance cash with which to purchase quantities of grain from farmers. Thus in 1777 William Colville, a large Dublin flour factor, advanced £3,000 to Stephen Moore, the proprietor of Marlfield mill, a sum repaid on the basis of the amounts received for subsidy which in 1777–8 were over £6,200, the margin of difference being indicative of the scale of return obtainable.[164]

The largest and most influential group to emerge in the flour-milling sector locally, in terms of capital provision and extent of operation, were the Quakers, particularly in Clonmel. They had been traditionally associated with the textile industry, but with its

---

[160] Young, *Tour*, i. 395.   [161] Ibid.

[162] RD, Memorials of deeds of partnership 1/3/2, dated 18 Dec. 1782.

[163] RD, 627/343/432518, 619/472/425057; *PP Corporations (Ire.)*, 28 (1835), 486; *CG*, 30 Sept.–3 Oct. 1782.

[164] NA, M1418; *Comms. Jnl.(Ire.)*, x. pt. 1, p. li.

decline Quaker resources and skills were increasingly diverted
from the 1770s into milling. This movement was influenced by
their religious belief that failure in business was regarded as a
moral fault. The earliest Quaker mill was that at Anner conducted
by the Grubbs which was second only to Marlfield in output. After
1780 the Quaker presence became more evident: in 1791 they ran
ten large concerns, five in Clonmel itself, and five others in its
immediate vicinity. Their success in flour milling was sustained by
family connections in the ports, and sons were bound as
apprentices in the large mills.[165] The expansiveness of the industry
is clear from the fact that family members were established in their
own right in new concerns at locations such as Clogheen, away from
the main focus at Clonmel.[166]

Specifically urban industries were small-scale. As industries
deriving from grain, brewing, distilling, and malting, however,
merit attention. Brewing developed to some extent in a few of the
towns. A revenue report of 1733 shows that there were twenty-
four brewers in the Cashel walk of the Kilkenny revenue district,
and ten in the Roscrea walk.[167] In 1788 individuals for whom
brewing was the sole occupation are recorded for only three
centres: Carrick (1), Clonmel (1), and Tipperary (2); while those
who pursued it in association with other activities were present in
Cashel (1), Clonmel (2), and Thurles (2).[168] The small number of
these concerns, and the fact that half of them were carried on with
other occupations, indicates the non-specialist nature of brewing,
the small size of the operations, and the localized market.

The organization and scale of individual concerns is evident
from the Woulfe brewery at Carrick in the mid-1760s. In 1765
Matthew Woulfe established a brewery in the town with his son
Walter, in partnership with James Wyse, a Waterford merchant
with whom they dealt regularly. The essential supplies of bere
barley were obtained locally to some extent but mainly through
merchants in New Ross, Youghal, and Dungarvan. The hops were
imported through Woulfe's London contacts, M. Reilly and Dillon
and Cruise, and imported via Waterford or brought coastways

[165] Society of Friends Library, Dublin, Jacob correspondence, ST 70.
[166] RD, 500/31/311408, 506/231/329308, 606/585/417768.
[167] NA, Thompson's report, 1733 (2C 36 1), 85, 107.
[168] Lucas, *General directory*, from which all information is taken.

from Cork or Dublin.[169] There is no evidence of Quaker capital and enterprise in brewing, an association which was a key element in the growth of the industry in England at this time. Of the four concerns listed in 1788 none was Quaker. This non-involvement precluded the growth of large-scale brewing (comparable to inland Kilkenny) particularly in Carrick and Clonmel where Quaker resources were sunk in textiles and later in flour milling. Additionally during the 1790s the Irish brewing industry as a whole became concentrated in larger concerns in the port towns, and the smaller inland concerns like those in Tipperary contracted in consequence.

There were a number of small distilling outlets: in 1782, fifty-nine licensed stills at nineteen locations conducted by fifty-four individuals.[170] All the towns had at least one still in operation, but the main centres were Thurles (11 stills), Roscrea (9), and Carrick (5). The majority of these were small-scale concerns, their limited output being suggested by the fact that most were single operations, their individual capacity generally not exceeding 260 gallons. The exception was at Roscrea where the three stills conducted by Edward Birch had a capacity of 1,000 gallons.[171] Roscrea and Thurles were the chief centres of the industry, the former emerging after 1800 to predominance chiefly because of an expansion in Birch's concern.[172] By that stage Roscrea had benefited from the reduction of stills in other locations as a result of official policy. By 1791 the number of licensed stills in the county had fallen to twenty-two, and by 1835 to fourteen.[173] In 1791 excise duties on spirits rose and thereafter no stills of less than 500 gallons capacity were to be licensed. On the basis of the capacities of the Tipperary stills in 1782 this provision would have excluded the majority of them and favoured the larger concerns like that of Birch at Roscrea. The result was an increase in output by a lesser number of distilleries and a greater competition between them.

An essential process in brewing and distilling was malting. The

[169] NLI, MS 9629, *passim.*
[170] *Comms. Jnl.(Ire.)*, x. pt. 2, pp. dxxv–dxxvii, dxxix.
[171] Ibid., p. dxxix.
[172] RCB, MS O.9., 50; M. Byrne, 'The distilling industry in Offaly, 1780–1954', in H. Murtagh (ed.), *Irish midland studies* (Athlone, 1980), 213–28.
[173] *Comms. Jnl.(Ire.)*, x. pt. 2, pp. dxxv–dxxvii, dxxix; xv. pt. 1, p. cxli; *PP Railways (Ire.)*, 35 (1837–8) app.B, no. 13, 97.

number of malt houses recorded for Clonmel revenue district in
1785 was 191 which was the third largest after Maryborough (276)
and Wexford (243), the main centre.[174] Given the trend in the
brewing and distilling industries, malting as a related activity
experienced a similar trend of concentration. By 1835 the number
of maltsters in the Clonmel revenue area had fallen sharply to
fifteen, the number for the entire county being forty-eight, with
the main centres at Clonmel, Carrick, and Roscrea.[175]

A number of minor industrial pursuits developed out of the
main activities associated with the livestock trade. The 1788
trading list gives tanning and related leather trades as important
occupations in seven of the county's towns, chiefly in Carrick,
Clonmel, and Tipperary. Tanning existed in these centres from
early in the century at least, some even at that stage on a fairly
large scale.[176] A riverine location was a necessary requirement for
the industry as also was bark as a treatment agent. Bark appears to
have been available locally to some extent up to the mid-1760s
supplemented by imports from Wales, but these became depleted
and the tanners came to rely entirely on imports. In 1791–2, for
example, three main tanning concerns, one in Carrick, two in
Clonmel, imported between them through Waterford over 134
tons of bark valued at more than £1,300.[177] The basic raw material
was hides, and tanning developed inland where there was
slaughtering of animals, particularly in Clonmel and Carrick since
their situation on the Suir gave them a water supply and access to
external markets. Leather-working developed as a subsidiary
activity in the tanning centres, especially boot and shoemaking and
saddlery. As an off-shoot of the livestock business, chandling and
soap boiling developed to a degree in most of the larger centres.
As a service industry for the beef and pork trade (by providing
barrels), and for the butter trade (by providing firkins), coopering
existed mainly in Clonmel and Carrick, both of which developed
as points of exit for beef, pork, and butter exports. As an adjunct
to this, salt refining, essential for preserving meat exports, was
conducted near Clonmel.[178] These industries were essentially

---

[174] *Comms. Jnl.(Ire.)*, xi. pp. dccccvii–dccccviii.

[175] *PP Railways (Ire.)*, 97.

[176] RD, 18/240/8941.

[177] Ledger of Courtenay and Ridgway, fos. 19, 31, 165, 191, 224.

[178] Paris, Bibliothèque Nationale, MS 20,099, fo. 99ᵛ.

involved in working-up primary products and were unsophisticated in their structure.

Exploitation of the county's mineral resources also took place. The chief area of coal workings was in the Slievardagh Hills. The coal-bearing area situated on the plateau of these hills had been worked in the seventeenth century if not earlier.[179] Between 1730 and 1740 Langley discovered a new seam of coal at Coalbrook and Lisnamrock; Gahan at Coolquill also exploited coal; Going investigated a deposit at Earlshill; and Barker at Kilcooley and Vere Hunt at Glengoole did similarly.[180] The main focus of coal workings was at Killenaule under its landlord Newenham and his tenants the Lathams.[181] It is probably the best instance in the county of a landlord town developing around a mining activity, and Vere Hunt's promotion of the new town of New Birmingham was influenced by coal mining.[182]

The market locally for this coal was good if one can judge from a comment in 1814 that Cahir, Cashel, Thurles, Fethard, and Littleton were said to 'entirely depend on the collieries of Killenaule for fuel'.[183] The Slievardagh area also produced culm (coal dust) and limestone which were widely valued and widely distributed among farmers who used both in reclamation and manuring.[184] In 1757 the discovery of copper on the Stanley estate at Gortdrum led to an active involvement of local and outside interests in assessing the viability of working the mine commercially.[185] The workings at Silvermines were elaborate, of long

[179] *CS*, i. 102, 130.
[180] Langley: *Memoir on the coalfields of Ireland* (Dublin, 1921), i. 73; *CG*, 17–20 Sept. 1794; G. Holmes, *Sketches of some of the southern counties of Ireland collected during a tour in the autumn of 1797* (n.p., 1801), 15; NA, Lodge rolls, ix. 431; Gahan: *CG*, 16–20 May 1782; Going: *Memoir* (1921); Barker: TCD, Barker Ponsonby papers, P6/46; Hunt: *Trans. Dublin Society*, i. pt. 2 (1800), 114–15; W. Hunt to Sir Vere Hunt, 10, 24 Jan. 1788 (Limerick City Library, Vere Hunt correspondence).
[181] Killenaule: *CS*, i. 104; NA, Lodge rolls, ix. 377; RD, 70/341/4862; *CH*, 24 Nov. 1802, 8 Jan. 1803; *A description of the colleries of Killenaule now to be let, the estate of E. W. Newenham* (Dublin, 1814).
[182] Limerick City Library, Vere Hunt correspondence and diaries; *CH*, 28 Aug. 1802, 17 May 1815; *CG*, 11–15 Dec. 1802.
[183] *A description of colleries* (1814), 3.   [184] Ibid. 5.
[185] Lancashire RO, Derby papers (Preston), DDK, 1704 series, P. Hanly to Lord Strange, 20 Nov. 1757; S. Howard to same, 27 Aug. 1772; DDK, 1705 series, T. Patton to Derby, 18 May 1783; T. Smyth to same, 31 Dec. 1785; and undated proposal from R. Smyth, T. Stoney, R. Reddan, and M. Carroll.

standing, and of national significance. A revival in their working for lead was encouraged by Prittie in the 1720s and 1730s, but they seem to have remained inactive thereafter until 1802 when the Dunalley Mining Company was formed for exploiting the ore there, and there were other ore workings nearby and at a scatter of other locations.[186] Thus, though industry was small in terms of scale it was impressive in terms of its extent.

5. The Urban Dimension

The upsurge in economic activity in the course of the century is reflected in town growth. After a period of indifferent prospects in the early seventeenth century, the larger towns of Carrick and Clonmel grew in the Restoration period. Thereafter sustained growth may have halted until the second half of the eighteenth century, though the case of Tipperary town, where Smith, the landlord, granted numerous building leases in and from 1731, indicates activity.[187] Similarly overall physical growth can be implied from the rise in the valuation of town property, that for 'the minister's money' in Clonmel increasing from £476 in 1703 to £760 in 1796.[188] Such a rise is consistent with an extension in building activity over the century as a whole and with a growth in the county's population from an estimated 74,450 in 1706 to 99,500 in 1732, and from 169,000 in 1792 to 300,000 in 1813.[189] The larger towns experienced a complementary rise in their populations. A ranking of towns can be suggested with Clonmel the largest followed in order by Carrick, Cashel, Roscrea, Thurles, and Nenagh each about half as important as Clonmel in size and

[186] RD, 43/245/28057, 66/351/46690, 206/10/134647, 214/279/141170, 217/25/41307, 240/403/156116; NA, 1A.52.167, p. 5; PRONI, T2368/1; G. Holmes, *Sketches*, 39, 44; *LJ*, 1–5 May 1802; NLI, PC, 564 Trant, folder marked 'Miscellaneous Trant papers'.

[187] Cheshire RO, Smith-Barry papers, DCN, 1984/2/5, 1984/10/52; RD, 65/514/46710, 65/514/46711, 65/523/46758, 65/524/46759, 66/353/46709, 66/455/47497, 66/459/47536, 67/440/46714.

[188] T. P. Power, 'A minister's money account for Clonmel, 1703', *AH*, 34 (1987), 185–7. The figure for 1796 has been computed on the basis that the amount received that year was £38, which at the rate 1s. in the £, would give a total valuation of £760. Minister's money was the urban equivalent of tithe assessed at the rate of 1s. in the £ property valuation.

[189] Power, 'Tipperary', Tables LXIII, LXI.

population; and then the minor centres of Tipperary, Cahir, Clogheen and Templemore which were about one quarter of its size or less.

While most of the existing centres expanded, those with a strong industrial base and distributive functions grew more markedly than others. Clonmel and Carrick advanced relative to other towns because their riverine situation allowed them access to markets externally through Waterford and internally via the Barrow navigation system, and because of the presence of vibrant textile and later flour-milling sectors. Evidence from the window-tax returns of 1800 suggests that Clonmel was Ireland's third largest inland town, its population of 12,000 in 1806 making it an important regional centre.[190] With a population of 10,907 in 1799 Carrick was almost as important. Indeed it is an index of the volume of commerce in the region that two such large population centres could exist in close proximity. Yet in the long term Carrick lost out to Clonmel as a growth centre for three reasons. First, the decline in the textile industry in Carrick though long drawn-out was permanent and was not compensated by the grain trade and flour milling as in Clonmel. Secondly, the rise of pork and bacon as important exports through Carrick does not appear to have been sufficiently labour intensive to adequately compensate for the decline in textiles. Thirdly, the Clonmel merchant community, Quakers especially, began to engage in importing articles direct by by-passing Waterford, a practice for which Carrick, though closer to that port, was not suitable. While trade and urban functions were increasingly centralized in Clonmel, and Carrick to an extent, there was a corresponding decline in nearby centres formerly important like Fethard.

On a more modest scale the development of semi-urban functions can be seen in the estate villages which landlord sponsors hoped would ultimately develop into larger centres. Those most successful were based on an expansion of existing centres. The prime instances are Clogheen where O'Callaghan revived the functions of an older centre in the 1740s, and Templemore where Carden from 1766 developed an older manorial centre into a town with a long main street adjoining his demesne. This was supplemented by the granting of extra fairs in 1794 and the

---

[190] *Comms. Jnl.(Ire.)*, xix. p. dccclvii; RCB, MS, O.9., p. 70.

building of an infantry barracks in 1808 which stimulated the local economy and brought a large influx of Protestants.[191] The motivation in both cases was mixed: partly an exercise in social experimentation on the part of the landlords, partly a desire to enhance their own incomes, and partly security considerations by the promotion of Protestant settlement. A similar mixture of motives was evident in the case of the new centres. Newport was influenced in its foundation by the construction of the Nenagh–Limerick turnpike road from 1737, the establishment of a charter school in 1747, and by its growth as a fair centre in the 1760s. The development of Dundrum by Sir Thomas Maude from 1767 centred on the attraction of Protestant settlers, the advancement of the linen industry, and the promotion of novel farming practices. The stimulus to its foundation derived from the sectarian fervour of the early 1760s and from his commitment to improvement. When both factors ceased to operate—sectarian tension did not persist beyond the 1760s and Maude died in 1777—the progress of the new settlement waned. Maude's brother and successor, Sir Cornwallis Maude, contracted his farming and became involved in flour milling so that Dundrum's development, though not aborted, was slow.[192]

A similar pattern of fluctuating fortunes applies to New Birmingham on the western edge of the Slievardagh Hills. Deriving its inspiration from the English industrial city, New Birmingham was intended by its promoter, Vere Hunt, to be 'principally inhabited by English manufacturers',[193] and in August 1802 he received a patent for twelve yearly fairs (one per month), including a wool fair in July.[194] It was one of the few new centres to be given fairs at this time and they promised to be novel in that, exclusive of cattle, they were to have 'imported merchandise' for sale in addition to linen and woollen goods. Some dealers were attracted to the settlement early on and it did secure the functions of a post town, military station, spa, and chapel site. But despite this profusion of functions it is clear that by 1815 many of the buildings were unfinished and untenanted, and Hunt was still

[191] *FDJ*, 19–22 July 1766; *LJ*, 26–9 Oct. 1808; RD, 603/215/411650.
[192] *FLJ*, 13–16 Oct. 1784; S. Lewis, *Topographical dictionary of Ireland* (London, 1837), i. 117.
[193] NA, OP, 143/19.   [194] *CH*, 28 Aug. 1802.

trying to attract settlers, finance, shopkeepers, and tradesmen.[195] The long-term prospects for the development of this estate village were not good because the scheme was over-ambitious; the achievement of a multiplicity of functions based primarily on industrial enterprises proved unpromising, particularly in the post-1815 climate of economic decline; and with other towns in the region as well as a large number of fair centres, New Birmingham had little prospect of success.

Its fate is a reminder that the pattern of urbanization in the county must be assessed in the following terms: no new major urban focus emerged; economic activity was centred in the existing centres whose large number and distribution reflected an historical inheritance; Clonmel emerged as the major town because of its favoured location and because of its role in textiles and flour milling; new centres were few and often artificially induced; and the context and scale of the urban nexus can be more usefully gauged in terms of the diffusion of fairs.

The majority of the county's towns functioned primarily as market and trading centres for the collection of produce from their hinterlands and the exchange and distribution of goods from outside. The range of commodities constituting the inward trade of Clonmel in 1750 shows a concentration on grain and animal products.[196] This emphasizes the essential distributive function of the towns which is also apparent from a profile of the merchant and trading community in 1788. The towns were non-specialist in function: most of the merchants and craftspeople were engaged in more than one occupation, in some cases entirely unrelated trades.

Apart from their market and distributive functions, a few towns developed strong industrial bases. These focused on the working-up of agricultural produce into manufactured products, and in a number of centres specialist industries emerged as with textiles (Carrick, Clonmel, Clogheen, Thurles, Roscrea), distilling (Thurles, Roscrea), brewing (Carrick, Clonmel), and related industries. Towns like Cashel and Fethard did not develop manufacturing sectors but depended on their position as market-ing centres at key points in the road system, and such towns remained semi-agricultural in character. Many towns acquired the

---

[195] *CG*, 11–15 Dec. 1802; *CH*, 17 May 1815; Limerick City Library, Vere Hunt letterbook, ii. 4, 9, 14, 15, 23.   [196] Burke, *Clonmel*, 216–17.

functions of military centres, the best instance being Templemore. The presence of military barracks was significant not merely in a security sense, but also from the point of view of consumption as they required large amounts of victuals, particularly bread and biscuit, and also hay and forage for horses. In 1778 Carrick could cater for 3,000 infantry and 300 cavalry, Clonmel 6,000 and 2,000 respectively, figures which bear witness to the capacity of these centres to provide accommodation and food supply.[197] Additionally three centres were important because of their religious and ecclesiastical functions: Clonmel because it contained large numbers of Dissenters and because until the late eighteenth century it was the residence of the Catholic bishop of Waterford; Cashel because it was the capital of the Anglican ecclesiastical province of Munster and where at least two archbishops, Bolton and Agar, resided and contributed to the improvement of the town; and Thurles as it was the centre of the Catholic archdiocese of Cashel where the archbishop resided. A combination of functions appeared in Clonmel as it was the county's chief town and functioned as assize town, and military and ecclesiastical centre, with a strong industrial function supporting a large population.

Those towns closely involved in trade and industry experienced growth in their physical layout and in their suite of municipal buildings particularly in the period 1790–1814, when much of the modern streetscapes came into being. Indicative of this expansion is the displacement of the old town walls. As late as 1732 Clonmel and Carrick still had their town walls virtually intact, but these were breached as the towns grew as were those at Cashel by the end of the century.[198] On the other hand Fethard, which ceased to grow after the medieval period, retained its impressive array of walls to a much later date. So far as the layout of streets is concerned Clonmel, Roscrea, and Nenagh were regarded as being regularly built while Carrick and Cashel were irregular.[199]

---

[197] Kent RO, Pratt papers, U840/171/91, 145–6, 253–4 (TCD, Mic. 56); RIA, MS G.1.2., nos. 4, 12.

[198] Loveday, *Diary*, 36, 43–4; P. Deighan, *A complete treatise on the geography of Ireland on a new plan* (Dublin, [1810]), 228; H. Moll, *A set of twenty new and correct maps of Ireland with the great roads and principal cross roads* (London, 1728), description of Tipperary towns.

[199] Paris, Bibliothèque Nationale, MS 20,099 fo. 99ᵛ; Pococke, *Tour*, 125; G. Tyner, *The traveller's guide through Ireland* (Dublin, 1794), 63; R. C. Hoare,

Tipperary town's evolution from 1731 was based on its main street and the clearance of outlying cabins to accommodate new stone houses; Thurles developed along an axis of the bridge at one end and the Mathew residence at the other; and Cahir was influenced in its development by Lord Cahir's new residence (1785) at one end of the square and a new market-house at the other.[200] In the course of the century towns acquired many of the buildings regarded as necessary for their proper functioning as trading and manufacturing centres. Fethard had a market-house in 1712, a new one was building at Carrick in 1726, monies were allotted for the erection of one at Cashel in 1732, Tipperary had one by 1737, as had Thurles in 1743 erected by Mathew, and they were present at Clonmel and Nenagh before the end of the century at least.[201] Clonmel had acquired a new quay by 1788 and a new jail in the 1790s to add to the existing range of buildings which included a tholsel and court house; in 1748 a shambles with twenty-seven stalls for butchers was erected and by 1813 John Bagwell had built a new shambles rented from him by the town's forty-one butchers.[202] A distinctive and large new chapel was erected in Tipperary (1730), and Clonmel had a new meeting house by 1788, while coffee houses had made their appearance in Clonmel by 1774 at least and a new one opened in Tipperary in 1791.[203]

Towns were subject to a number of hazards the chief of which, fire, was particularly dangerous especially as many towns had large suburbs of cabins. In 1754 an accidental fire in Nenagh destroyed 112 houses besides outoffices and stables with the entire loss amounting to £5,000; in 1768 an outbreak of fire consumed most of Clogheen, destroying army stores and ruining many of the artisan families, an incident which accounts for the rebuilding of the town in the 1770s; and in 1798 a fire in Tipperary town made up to 500

Journal of a tour in Ireland AD 1806 (London and Dublin, 1807), 35; W. Wilson, *The post-chaise companion or traveller's directory through Ireland* (Dublin, 1786), 168, 213, 257, 331, 365; J. S. Dodd, *The traveller's director through Ireland* (Dublin, 1801), 72; Burke, *Clonmel*, 122–3.

[200] Loveday, *Diary*, 43; Wilson, *Post-chaise*, 213; NLI, MS 772 (4)/34; NA, Acc. 976/6/5.

[201] RD, 424/210/276008; Deighton, *Complete treatise*, 228; Wilson, *Post-chaise*, 365.

[202] RD, 308/19/203377; Tyner, *Guide*, 63.

[203] Loveday, *Diary*, 43; *FLJ*, 17–21 Dec. 1791; NLI, PC, 12,674 (i–iii), Bagwell, deed of 26 Nov. 1788.

persons homeless.[204] Such disasters often led to public subscriptions for relief of those in distress. However, what caused most
distress was a failure of the potato or reduced grain supplies
caused by an outflow to dearer markets elsewhere. During a
period of scarcity in 1729, particularly in the north of Ireland,
there were riots in Clonmel and Munster in an attempt to prevent
the conveyance of grain (of which there was a plentiful supply
available locally) outward to fill deficiencies elsewhere.[205] In April
1741 following a severe frost and famine, a mob of 1,000 at Carrick
prevented a consignment of oats being conveyed downriver; there
were food riots in Clonmel and Carrick in 1757 during general
dearth in the south; and in June 1782, with the prospect of a bad
harvest, the inhabitants of Clonmel had to be reassured that there
was sufficient wheat in the millers' stores to maintain them.[206] The
years 1799 and 1800 were difficult locally, producing near famine
conditions. In such times of scarcity the main merchants bought up
available grain supplies and sold them cheaply to the poor. Relief
had to be administered to over one quarter of the population of
Carrick as a result of the distress of 1799, and in 1800 a meal fund
amounting to £8,200 was set up in Clonmel to provide corn meal
and soup for poor relief.[207]

Experience of these disasters brought to the fore a new concern
with the underlying causes of poverty. The causes were identified
by a commentator on the situation pertaining in Carrick in 1799
when he wrote: 'The principal causes of poverty are sickness, old
age, want of employment, children becoming orphans, and very
principally idleness and intemperance.'[208] These causes contributed to making 6 per cent (or 660 persons) of the town's
population of 10,907 in 1799 dependent on aid or charity of some
kind, and it is clear that poverty was on the increase.[209] One of the
chief causes of poverty in the town was the decline of the textile

[204] NLI, MS 11,887, *sub* June 1754; *FJ*, 12–16 Apr. 1768; *FDJ*, 12 May 1798.
[205] H. Boulter, *Letters written by his excellency Hugh Boulter, DD, lord primate of all Ireland* (Dublin, 1770), i. 228, 230.
[206] *CG*, 6–10 June 1782; *Dublin Newsletter*, 2–6 June 1741; Burke, *Clonmel*, 126; *JWSEIAS*, 15 (1912), 67; PRONI, D354/851.
[207] Society of Friends Library, Dublin, SG.C.4; *JWSEIAS*, 15 (1912), 67.
[208] [W. M. Pitt], *A letter from Major Pitt of the Dorset regiment to the society for promoting the comforts of the poor established at Carrick-on-Suir in the County of Tipperary* (Dublin, 1800), 4.
[209] Ibid. 4–5; see also L. A. Clarkson, 'The demography of Carrick-on-Suir, 1799', *PRIA*, 87, C (1987), 13–36.

industry. In addition the seasonal migration to the Newfoundland fisheries which had been a feature of the south Tipperary area for half a century or more before 1800, was ceasing to be an option as a source of income for artisans and labourers.

Already, however, attempts were made to confront the problem through the foundation of almshouses, as Thomas Wadding of Cadiz did in Carrick in 1756, by charitable donations and bequests for the poor, and by public infirmaries like those founded in Cashel and Clonmel in 1767.[210] The imaginative and cost-effective proposals forwarded by William Morton Pitt for the relief of poverty in Carrick in 1799 were novel for the period. He observed that while charitable relief was praiseworthy it was insufficient to address the long-term problem of urban poverty. Instead of alms-giving he proposed that a society be established, of which the poor themselves would be members, with financial contributions coming mainly from honorary members. He advocated the establishment of an annuity society for widows with a small subscription, a loans system for manufacturers in temporary difficulties, and a savings scheme for the poor with regular and attractive interest payments. He also advocated a more systematic allocation of workers between different firms, cheaper fuel for the poor, and better hospital and educational facilities.[211]

Pitt highlighted the importance of educational facilities and these had developed to some extent. Clonmel had a free school endowed by the duke of Ormond in the seventeenth century and a charter school was added in the 1740s. Cashel had a separate new schoolhouse built in 1724; in 1789 John Bagwell endowed a new Sunday and daily school in Clonmel; and individual clergymen established schools in other centres, as at Carrick in 1792.[212] The prospectus for a Carrick establishment claimed to prepare candidates for the revenue, army, navy, and university through instruction in writing, arithmetic, and bookkeeping.[213] The appearance of such schools with this kind of programme shows the needs of the comfortable urban classes in terms of social and career advancement.

As part of the infrastructural development in the local economy

[210] NLI, MSS 133; 5578, p. 142; Burke, *Clonmel*, 291–3; *FDJ*, 29 Aug.–1 Sept., 12–15 Sept. 1767.   [211] Pitt, *A letter*, 4, 6–13.
[212] RD, 117/37/79588; NLI, MS 5576, *sub* 29 June 1724; *CEP*, 28 Dec. 789; *FLJ*, 26–30 Jan. 1792.   [213] *Waterford Herald*, 27 Dec. 1792.

improvements in the transport and communications network are an important index of greater integration into the wider market economy. The development of roads coincided with the upturn in economic activity in the 1730s. Roads developed in Tipperary by virtue of the needs of internal trade flowing towards Cork, Limerick, and Dublin. The need to have these ports linked more effectively with their hinterlands meant that Tipperary, encompassed within the triangular axis of these three ports, came to be well served by roads by the end of the century. The direction of traffic on these roads was such that the movement of grain tended towards either Clonmel or Limerick, butter moved towards Clonmel and Carrick, the movement of livestock was dictated by the location of fairs, and there was a lively cross-county trade in coal from Killenaule.

The River Suir, which was tidal to Carrick and navigable for boats to Clonmel, was the main artery of trade. An index of the growth of trade along it were demands for improvements in the facility in order to make the flow of traffic more efficient. In 1755 local gentry and merchants with their Waterford counterparts sought a parliamentary grant to remove impediments in the river to allow an increase in the carrying capacity of boats; also the construction of a towpath for horses to draw the boats, thereby eliminating one third of the heavy expense of employing men in such work, and reducing markedly the time involved; and with a reduction in operating costs, freight charges would fall.[214] A grant of £1,500 was made, but it was another decade before the works were satisfactorily completed.[215] The advance in grain production in ensuing decades brought the need for further improvements in the river system.

Much of the building boom in towns after 1790 was financed by the credit facilities made available by banks. The export and import trade was facilitated by the system of credit which had been evolving over a long period. By the eighteenth century a system of payment based on bills had developed between merchants inland, their colleagues in the ports, and Dublin and London discounting houses, as the practice of a Carrick merchant in the 1760s illustrates.[216] Actual discounting and banking facilities at inland locations evolved more slowly. In time, however, Clonmel

---

[214] *Comms. Jnl.(Ire.)*, v. 237; Burke, *Clonmel*, 128–9.
[215] Burke, *Clonmel*, 128–9.   [216] NLI, MS 9629, *passim*.

emerged as the main inland town where banking business of any volume was conducted.

Banking had some early precursors in the county before 1700, which developed out of surplus accounts in the hands of rent receivers transmitting payments to absentee landlords.[217] The most notable exponents of this practice were William Vaughan, Phineas Riall, and Joseph Damer. Only with the Bagwell establishment does a concern of any significance emerge. John Bagwell, merchant, acted as a country correspondent in Clonmel for the Dublin banking house of La Touche and Kane in the 1720s.[218] Out of this association Bagwell developed a banking business of his own based in Clonmel which was still being conducted by a third generation in 1760. By this stage the Rialls had become established in banking and by 1788 they were the town's only bankers, Bagwell having by then entered the flour-milling business. The Riall concern was considered to be secure as it survived the crises of the early 1770s and 1793, and by the end of the century the Rialls were reputedly worth £70,000.[219]

The growth of trade and the long period of high prices after 1793 encouraged an expansion in banking. Four new concerns at three locations were established: Watson at Clonmel (1800), Scully at Tipperary (1802), Carshore at Carrick (1806), and Sause at Carrick (1807).[220] On the basis of the amounts paid in stamp duty between 1800 and 1804, Clonmel was the main inland banking centre and, taken in conjunction with the banks in Carrick, this is further evidence of a concentration of wholesale trade in both centres, Clonmel particularly.[221] In 1808 the note circulation of the Clonmel banks was said to be £200,000.[222] Note circulation and issue was only the final stage in the evolution of these banks for at an earlier stage their main function was the discounting of bills and, to some extent, receiving sums of money for safe-keeping. With the exception of Scully's bank all those which emerged in

---

[217] L. M. Cullen, 'Landlords, bankers, and merchants: The early Irish banking world, 1700–1820', in A. E. Murphy (ed.), *Economists and the Irish economy from the eighteenth century to the present day* (Dublin, 1984), 31–2.
[218] Burke, *Clonmel*, 175; NLI, MS 2785, ledger of La Touche and Kane, 1719–26.   [219] Burke, *Clonmel*, 188.
[220] *Report from the committee on the circulating paper, the specie, and the current coin of Ireland* (1804) repr. as *PP*, 5 (407) (1826), 147–53; E. O'Kelly, *The old private banks and bankers of Munster* (Cork, 1959), 23–4; NLI, MS 27,571, 315.
[221] *PP*, 5 (407) (1826), 147–50.   [222] Burke, *Clonmel*, 189 n.

Tipperary were mercantile in origin and exhibit a distinct element of kinship links in their evolution. The progression of those involved in banking out of trade into land was uneven. Bagwell used the surplus accounts on hand and the profits of trade to purchase the Dunboyne and other lands in the late 1720s and early 1730s, and the Rialls did the same in the 1770s. Yet both families retained their links with trade: Bagwell in flour milling, Riall in banking. Catholics, like Sause, on the other hand, tended to progress out of trade entirely using the profits obtained therein to establish themselves in landed society. Scully is exceptional in being of landed status and becoming involved in banking.

The merchant community reflects the changing character of economic development closely. A 1788 directory, although incomplete (Roscrea and Fethard are excluded, and for those centres included the lists are deficient), allows one to profile the personnel of the merchant community for seven towns.[223] For the different sectors of manufacturing, distribution, building, personal and professional services, certain groups dominated certain pursuits. In manufacturing Catholics dominated the textile sector in Carrick with fourteen of the seventeen clothiers (who controlled the industry) being Catholic. In Clonmel Protestants dominated textile activity with only one Catholic out of seven clothiers named. The textile industry in Tipperary town, in its cotton and woollen branches, was in the hands of the Sadliers at this time.

In the alcohol industries, Catholics dominated distilling in Thurles (which, with Roscrea, was the main centre), and they were also to the fore in Carrick and Cashel, while Protestants were its sole conductors in Borrisoleigh, Nenagh, and Tipperary, and in Clonmel representation was about even. Brewing as a sole pursuit in Carrick, Clonmel, and Tipperary was the monopoly of Catholics. Flour milling was a widely disseminated activity but in its main centre, Clonmel, it was the preserve of Quakers. Allowing for the fact that Carrick was not as good a location for milling as Clonmel was, there appears to be an implicit reluctance on the part of Catholic clothiers in the former to make the transition to flour milling with this gap being filled by Quakers.[224] Yet in a

---

[223] R. Lucas, *General directory*. What follows, unless otherwise indicated, is based on this source.
[224] J. Hall, *Tour through Ireland* (London, 1813), i. 135.

related area, the baking and confectionery trades, Catholics dominated, especially in Clonmel.

In the various sectors of the leather industry Catholics were to the fore in tanning in Carrick, Nenagh, and Thurles with representation about even in Clonmel and Tipperary; boot and shoemaking was the preserve of Protestants in Clonmel and of Catholics in Nenagh, and mixed elsewhere; and saddlery and leather-cutting was dominated by Protestants. Tallow chandling, soap, and candle-making were mainly in the hands of Protestants particularly in Clonmel, but in Thurles Catholics had a monopoly. Coopering was largely the preserve of Catholics. The heavy metal industries like ironmongering, smithing, and pewtering tended to be evenly distributed. Activities such as coach-making, gun-making, glass, china, and glazing were not dominated by any one group.

The retail distribution of goods was the most pervasive activity of traders. Where the occupation is given as grocer, either separately or in combination with other trades, Catholics were prominent especially in Thurles, Cashel, Tipperary and Carrick, with Protestants also involved in Clonmel. In the area of alcohol distribution, incorporating vintners, porter-room owners, and spirit dealers, no one group dominated. The textile drapery trade in linen and woollen goods was monopolized by Catholics especially in Carrick, Cashel, and Tipperary, while in Clonmel Protestants were involved. In the area of personal service, in occupations such as that of apothecary for instance, representation tended to be mixed. In the different professions attorneys were present in all centres and, with conversion as a requirement for entry to the legal profession, surnames like O'Kearney (Thurles) and Dwyer (Tipperary) show the Catholic presence, though most attorneys tended to be Protestant, notably in Clonmel and Cashel where the ecclesiastical court functioned.[225] For the professions of doctor and surgeon (from which Catholics were not excluded under law), representation was mixed.

Overall, accepting the fact that the primary function of the merchant community in the towns in Tipperary was distributive

---

[225] For legal conversions see T. P. Power, 'Conversions among the legal profession in Ireland in the eighteenth century', in D. Hogan and W. N. Osborough (eds.), *Brehons, serjeants, and attorneys: Studies in the history of the Irish legal profession* (Dublin, 1990), 153–74.

rather than specialist, Protestants were to the fore in the manufacturing areas of flour milling, chandling, and textiles (Clonmel), and in the distributive sector in textiles (Clonmel) and in grocery. Catholics dominated manufacturing in Carrick, distilling in Thurles, brewing, tanning, and chandling (Thurles). As general grocers and textile drapers Catholics were prominent in all centres outstripping Protestants except in Clonmel. Representation was mixed in the heavy industries like metals, the alcohol distribution trade, and in the professions. In this way the Protestant merchant community was predominant in Clonmel, the Catholic in Carrick and Thurles, and elsewhere no clear hegemony emerged.

Subsequent changes in the merchant body can be most readily assessed as far as Clonmel is concerned in 1820.[226] Although Clonmel cannot be taken as representative, as the largest town with a greater diversity of functions than others, it should indicate general trends. The overall pattern was of a decline of 19 per cent in the numbers engaged in manufacturing, and of an increase of 5 per cent in those engaged in personal service, coupled with the sharpest increase (15 per cent) in the area of distribution. The successful transition made by the Quakers out of textiles into milling ensured their continued pre-eminence in the merchant community. They monopolized the occupations of flour miller and grain merchant, and were to the fore in banking, boat transport, and the bacon trade. In contrast Catholic merchants and traders retained a connection with the secondary pursuits of retail grocery, baking, linen and woollen drapery, and taverning, and were not well represented in the primary manufacturing sectors.

The religious factor in trade was reinforced by external trading links. The correspondents of Catholic merchants in Tipperary in the outports tended to be their co-religionists. Walter Woulfe of Carrick dealt mainly with Wyse in Waterford, Comerford in Cork, and Connor in Dublin.[227] By such links Catholic merchants in Tipperary became tied into a network of Irish mercantile interests overseas. In Woulfe's case this reflected his main trade which was

---

[226] The following is based on Lucas, *General directory*, and Pigot, *The commercial directory of Ireland* (Manchester, 1820), tabulated in Power, 'Tipperary', Tables XLV, XLVII.

[227] NLI, MS 9629, index *sub* J. Wyse, J. & P. Comerford, J. Connor, W. Coppinger, and L. Sall.

in wines and spirits, obtained through expatriate Irish merchants
in Bordeaux. Such external trading links were used to launch
younger members of some Catholic landed families into trade. In
1766 Woulfe promised to provide George Ryan of Cadiz (his
nephew and son of Daniel Ryan of Inch) with an order for £500
worth of goods in order to launch him into trade in the West
Indies.[228] Protestants also had extensive trading contacts. The
Quakers in particular depended on a network of kinship links
among their co-religionists in the textile and grain trades. In the
1760s and 1770s evidence shows the contacts between the Gurneys
of Norwich and their fellow Quakers in the south-east for the
supply of yarn from south Tipperary (via the Clonmel group, the
Grubbs especially) through Waterford.[229] The grain trade also
benefited from these kinship links.

[228] W. Woulfe to G. Ryan, 19 Oct. [1766] (NLI, MS 9629).
[229] Society of Friends Library, Dublin, 'Diary of J. Grubb of his travels in
England, 1766' (Grubb SGB, 2/1); Society of Friends Library, London, Gurney
correspondence, 1769–84, especially letters of 3 Oct. 1770, 6 Aug., 12, 26 Nov.
1772.

3

Landed Society

1. The Seventeenth-Century Background

In 1641 about 60 per cent of the land in the county was owned by Catholics, a body comprising over 300 Old English and over 900 native Irish proprietors.[1] The Old English landowning class was dominated by a group of nine main families, of whom the Butlers were the most influential. The Old English were concentrated in the east, south, and centre in the mainly fertile areas of singly owned property units, high land values, and an established tradition of urban settlement and commercial activity.[2]

The large number of native Irish proprietors was due to the high level of shared ownership. In areas where the native Irish lands were concentrated, i.e. in the west and north, joint or multiple ownership was characteristic. With the exception of the lowlands of Upper Ormond much of the area held by the Old Irish was marginal with generally low land values, poor soil quality, and subsistence agriculture.[3] Protestant New English settlement in the pre-1641 period was limited, with only 21 such owners recorded for 1641, the majority absentees.[4] The promotion of English Protestant tenants was not confined to incoming New English

---

[1] J. G. Simms, *The Williamite confiscation in Ireland 1690–1703* (London, 1956), 196; the number of proprietors from *CS*, i, ii.

[2] W. J. Smyth, 'Land values, landownership and population patterns in Co. Tipperary for 1641–1660 and 1841–1850: Some comparisons', in L. M. Cullen and F. Furet (eds.), *Ireland and France 17th–20th centuries: Towards a comparative study of rural history* (Paris, 1980), 59–68; idem, 'Property, patronage and population: Reconstructing the human geography of mid-seventeenth century Tipperary', in W. Nolan (ed.), *Tipperary: History and society* (Dublin, 1985), 109–14.

[3] Smyth, 'Land values', 68–74; id., 'Property'. 116–18.

[4] *CS* i, ii *passim*; NLI, D3786; H. F. Kearney, 'The court of wards and liveries in Ireland, 1622–1641', *PRIA* 57 C (1955), 29–68.

landowners. For instance, it was said of Sir Richard Everard, an Old English Catholic landowner, that 'before the Rebellion [he] planted moste of his estate with English tenants', and the evidence suggests that they were eighty-eight in number.[5] However, the larger blocks of Protestant land were located on the periphery of the Old English area, so that their intrusion did not radically alter the structure of landownership.

Ormond, though born a Catholic, was raised in the Anglican faith and became the Protestant head of an Old English family whose leading members were mainly Catholic. With his Catholic relatives he shared a staunch support for the royalist cause, and with the New English a common religious sympathy. Both loyalties were to influence Ormond's dealings with the two groups in Tipperary. Ironically it was the Protestant Ormond branch which was responsible for introducing in the pre-1641 period two families of Catholic New English background. Sir George Hamilton, who held Nenagh and Roscrea on lease from his mother-in-law the countess of Ormond, was responsible for promoting New English settlement at Silvermines.[6] In 1620 George Mathew, possibly a younger son of a long-established gentry family of Glamorgan, Wales, married into the Ormond family (see Figure 1(a)). His arrival was part of the movement from south Wales and the Severn basin to Munster,[7] and it indicates that New English infiltration, however limited in scale, was not solely Protestant in its composition.

The effect of the Cromwellian land settlement was to permanently alter the structure of landowning in the county. With over 77 per cent of its area affected, Tipperary had the highest percentage of land confiscated of any county in Ireland, much of which was Butler property.[8] The county was reserved for division between the adventurers and the army. The 204 adventurers, owed £60,000 out of the county, were to be compensated by grants of land in Clanwilliam, Eliogarty, Iffa and Offa, Ikerrin, Ileagh, and Middlethird, the main Old English region. Of the 204 grants, 48

---

[5] King's Inns Library, Prendergast MS, iii. 145 (account of the rebellion in Tipperary written for Ormond, 1680).
[6] See Ch. 2, n. 38.
[7] N. Canny, 'Migration and opportunity: Britain, Ireland, and the New World', *IESH*, 12 (1985), 7–32, at 29.
[8] Hardinge, 'On the circumstances', 418; Moody, Martin, and Byrne, *New history of Ireland*, iii, 358; Smyth, 'Property', 111.

were in excess of 1,000 acres each, and were given mainly to individuals who were to maintain their interest, and to corporations and philanthropists like Erasmus Smith. The majority of adventurer grants, however, were under 1,000 acres with 129 of them under 500 acres made to small investors, mainly London merchants and tradesmen, who were subsequently to dispose of their claims.[9] The other group was the army whose officers and privates drew grants in Upper Ormond, Lower Ormond, Owney and Arra, Kilnamanagh, Kilnalongurty, and Slievardagh and Compsy which, with the exception of the last, were Old Irish areas. Since their grants were very often minute and uneconomic, many of the privates sold their lands to their officers like Lieutenant John Otway who purchased from soldiers debentures for lands in Upper Ormond in the 1650s and 1660s, with the price usually less than half the amount owed in pay or in debentures.[10] In this way large estates owned by officers (Abbott, Finch, Prittie, and Sadlier) became a feature of landowning in the three baronies of the north-west.

The successful establishment of the new owners on their estates depended on the effective removal of the forfeiting proprietors to Connacht and Clare. Over 200 Catholic landowners from Tipperary were assigned holdings west of the Shannon.[11] Though there were some dispensations, 8,635 persons were transplanted in the first six months of 1654, a figure which was nearly half the entire total recorded as removing from Munster and which exceeds that for all of Leinster.[12]

A new situation presented itself with the restoration of Charles II. The act of settlement (1662) provided for the restoration of 'innocents' and a large number of named Catholics, while the Cromwellians in possession were to be compensated by grants elsewhere. Decrees were issued by a court of claims but these

[9] Computations based on statistics compiled from the schedules in J. P. Prendergast, *The Cromwellian settlement of Ireland* (London, 1922), 389–400.

[10] Leicester Archives Department, Braye of Stanford papers 23 D57/718, 724–5, 728–34, 736–7, 739, 740–1, 745–6, 748 (abstracted in Nat. Reg. of Archives list 9254).

[11] Estimated from R. C. Simington, *The transplantation to Connacht 1654–1656* (Dublin, 1970).

[12] Hardinge, 'On the circumstances', 416; for the articles of surrender: *CSPI 1647–60* (1903), 375 (Mathew); NLI, D7403 (Fethard); Hardinge, 'On the circumstances', 418; Prendergast MS: Collections, i. 634–5, ii. 541; Prendergast, *Cromwellian settlement*, 181; RIA, MS 4.A.42 (2h).

proved unenforceable because the Cromwellians were reluctant to move and there simply was not enough land available to satisfy all needs. The act of explanation (1665) sought to rectify this deficiency by proposing that Cromwellians give up one-third of their lands and out of the resultant accumulation Catholics were to be reprised. Attempts to reconcile the opposing claims continued throughout Charles II's reign.

Some New English in Tipperary refused to accept the Restoration. Alarmed at the large number of Catholic officers returning to claim their former estates, some Cromwellian officers and adventurers met in Cashel in August 1660 to formulate a petition to be circulated in the county aimed at the 'preservation and advancement of the Protestant English interest'.[13] Attempts to obtain general consent to the petition foundered, however, when the large group of newcomers around Nenagh (more secure in number than their more isolated counterparts in the countryside around Cashel) declined to lend their support. On the contrary their spokesman declared his willingness to keep the county quiet.[14] Elsewhere, however, grantees were outspoken in their reluctance to accept the restored royalist political order and the new landowners vowed to resist attempts by the former owners to re-establish themselves.[15] In the two decades after 1660 there are a number of cases of former owners forcibly re-entering their lands and ejecting the newcomers, and also of the latter resisting.[16]

The character of the Restoration land settlement locally was directly influenced by Ormond. Enjoying enormous prestige after 1660 for his role in effecting the king's recovery of power, Ormond was created a duke in 1661 and was lord-lieutenant for 1662–9 and 1677–85. Because of his office, his outlook, and his family connections he was uniquely positioned to influence decision-making. As lord-lieutenant he influenced applications for restoration, for a list of over 200 persons from Tipperary was submitted to him in 1664 and on his recommendation they were to be restored.[17] In Tipperary his policy was to confirm the New English in possession and then, in descending order of priority, the

[13] Prendergast MS: Collections, iv. 24.   [14] Ibid. 26–8.

[15] NLI, MS 4908 (Clonmel assize book 1663–75), fos. 4, 7ᵛ.

[16] Ibid., fos. 20ᵛ–21, 55, 94, 104ᵛ–105ᵛ.

[17] Prendergast MS: Collections, iv. 521 *et seq.*, printed in *Irish Genealogist*, 4 (1972), 429–34.

interests of his own family, his relatives, and close connections among the leading Old English families. The Old Irish fared worst out of the Restoration settlement and met with no favouritism from Ormond, at least where the ownership of land is concerned. Some New English, who may have suffered as a result of Ormond's role, did not allow the matter to go unnoticed.[18] However, such cases were exceptional and the New English in general seem to have been satisfied with Ormond's performance.[19]

The books of Survey and Distribution show how uneven the Restoration land settlement was in its effects.[20] As a class the Old English had mixed fortunes with those who were large proprietors in 1641—the Butlers of Cahir, Dunboyne, and Ikerrin with the Everard, Purcell, Mandeville, and Morris families—retaining most or nearly all of their lands.[21] Lesser families like Tobin, St. John, Mockler, Archer, Stapleton, and Burke were displaced as proprietors. The Old Irish areas experienced a virtual transformation in proprietorship, though in certain cases some, like John Egan who in 1669 received a lease from Ormond of 700 acres at Uskane, continued as head-tenants on their former holdings.[22] The case of Charles Carroll, who became attorney-general of Maryland in 1688, and whose kin were to rise to landed and political prominence in that colony, illustrates how a displaced family could recover and extend their fortunes in the New World.[23]

New English grantees who had some or all of their lands confirmed after the Restoration, established themselves in areas where the Old Irish and lesser Old English had formerly been. Those of the officer class seem generally to have been resident, those of the adventurer class less so. A number of large estates belonging to absentees like Erasmus Smith were created. Such absentee estates served to introduce to the county tenants or agents who, in the eighteenth century, were to become landowners in their own right. The best instance is Joseph Damer who purchased land from departing Cromwellians and who was also agent for Erasmus Smith. The Restoration land settlement

---

[18] NLI, MS 4908, fo. 14ᵛ.   [19] Prendergast MS, vii. 596–7.
[20] RIA, MSS H.3.2., H.4.2.
[21] Prendergast MS, ii. 642, 689–91, vii. 817–18.
[22] NLI, MS 2350, 161–4.
[23] R. Hoffman, ' "Marylando-Hibernus": Charles Carroll the Settler, 1660–1720', *William and Mary Quarterly*, 45 (1988), 207–36.

involved a reduction of about half in the proportion of land owned by Catholics. Ormond not merely recovered his large estate but also supplemented it. The Old Irish and lesser Old English families were displaced and the larger of the Old English owners, particularly the Butlers, maintained their interest. A large number of New English established themselves on their estates and in the towns where Protestant oligarchies emerged. In the north and west of the county, where New English immigrants formed durable and cohesive rural communities, there could be some sense of security, but outside the towns in the centre, south, and east, where a significant amount of land remained in Old English hands, the New English could only feel the Restoration land settlement to be incomplete.

The accession of James II instilled in Catholics hopes of recovering the political prominence they held prior to 1641. After 1685 Catholics were installed in those local civic offices which were subject to royal appointment.[24] Commissions in the army were granted to a number of prominent Catholics, notably Nicholas Purcell who was also made a privy councillor and was a member of parliament for the county in the 1689 parliament.[25] King James revoked the charters governing Cashel, Clonmel, and Fethard, and issued new charters in 1687 and 1689. All those holding office in the newly constituted towns were obliged to take an oath declaring that James was the lawful king, a stipulation which gave Catholics a majority position in the corporations.[26] But Ormond consistently chose from the ranks of the New English class for the office of high sheriff and continued to do so during the 1680s.[27] Protestants were actively discouraged from taking the office of justice of the peace. Thus Sir Robert Cole, a large landowner in Upper Ormond, in 1685 was ordered 'to suspend acting or intermed[d]ling in the office of Justice of [the] Peace within the said county tyll further ord[e]rs'.[28]

Catholics not restored after 1660 sought a reversal of the

[24] W. King, *The state of the protestants of Ireland under the late King James's government* (London, 1691), 326, 329, 335–6.

[25] J. D'Alton, *Illustrations historical and genealogical of King James's Irish army list* (1689) (Dublin, 1855), i. 272–8, and for other commissions, 78–9, 104–5, 133–6, 206–7, 215, 239–41, ii. 402.

[26] W. Harris, *The history of the life and reign of William Henry* (Dublin, 1749), pp. vii, xv.   [27] GO, MS 570; RIA, Upton papers, no. 28, fo. 6.

[28] NLI, MS 11,044, document entitled 'Sr Robt Cole'.

settlement in their favour. Ormond, who was identified as having frustrated this objective, became an object of hostility, informing a correspondent in 1685 that it was the current view that 'but for me [Ormond] they should long since have obtained an act of indemnity and restitution of all their estates'.[29] Ormond was no less suspiciously regarded by Protestants who generally viewed his Catholic connections as too strong to make him trustworthy. In these circumstances Ormond's moderating policy, evident in the 1660s and 1670s, operated to make his position untenable in the 1680s.

For Protestants in Tipperary the accession of King James deepened existing fears of a political turnabout. Tension increased when a rumour spread in the north of the county in June 1685 that a repeat of the 1641 massacre was intended. The rumour made eighty Protestants take refuge in Borrisokane but the massacre never materialized. However, those who gathered in the town were indicted for arming themselves and for unlawful assembly, but out of the sixty who attended for trial only ten were found guilty and imprisoned.[30] Other meetings were held in which about fifty of the New English landowners are reported to have participated. As a result of all these proceedings about 100 persons described as 'of the richest men of the county' were returned on charges of treason, sedition, and unlawful assembly at the autumn assizes of 1686, but were acquitted.[31] These events in 1685–6 are important in the long term in that they contributed to the perceptions and fears of Protestants locally, and doubtless were part of the folk memory which fuelled the animosities of the 1760s. In 1688 the only option for Protestants was to leave Tipperary, and at least forty landowners fled to England, while Protestant tenants on Ormond's estate fled to the north and elsewhere.[32]

The comprehensive nature of the Williamite victory, though qualified by the continued presence of tories and rapparees, was

[29] NLI, MS 2445, 354.
[30] King, *State of the Protestants*, 90; T. Crosby, *The history of the English Baptists from the reformation to the beginning of the reign of King George I* (London, 1740), iii. 43; NLI, MS 2445, 185.
[31] BL, C21 fo. 12 (14), proclamation dated 24 July 1685; NLI, MSS 2443, 309–10, 377–81; 2445, 7–12, 181–5, 205–6, 435; 2446, 109–18, 163–8, 289, 375–6, 383–91; 2447, 167–8, 203–7; 2451, 33–7.
[32] TCD, MS 847, fos. 1–16, *passim*; Harris, *History*, p. lv; Prendergast MS, ii. 549.

not—in contrast, for instance, to neighbouring Kilkenny[33]—
reflected in any policy of confiscation or in any radical alteration in
the structure of landownership. Ormond, as lord of the palatinate,
was entitled to all lands forfeited for treason in the county, a right
which he asserted over the commissioners of forfeited estates.[34]
This action possibly accounts for the fact that officials of the
palatinate court were slow to make returns of outlawed Jacobites,
and those who remained unconvicted by 1699 escaped outlawry
altogether. A number of Tipperary Jacobites were, however,
outlawed in Dublin notably Sir John Everard, but such cases were
few.[35] Only four individuals with a total profitable acreage of
11,633 acres forfeited land and were not restored, the largest was
Everard (6,500 acres) and his forfeiture was not permanent.[36]

Over 100 Catholic landowners submitted claims for a total of
just under 7,000 acres and were restored under the articles of
Limerick or Galway. They included important figures like Purcell
of Loughmoe, Ryan of Inch, and Lord Dunboyne, with some Old
Irish.[37] In addition three persons were restored by special royal
grant: Sir John Morris, Sir Laurence Esmond, and Lord Cahir
with their combined acreages totalling 13,367 acres. Lord Cahir
was confirmed in over 10,000 acres.[38] Ormond's Catholic relatives,
Butler of Kilcash and Mathew of Thomastown, though they did
not come under the articles of Limerick or Galway, retained their
interests. With the exception of Everard, and his experience was
temporary, Catholics supporting the Jacobite cause in Tipperary
did not fare adversely as a result of the Williamite land settlement.
Two additional elements of the settlement were the land grants
made by King William, and the disposal of the forfeited estates.
The king had made a number of grants of land in Ireland to
individuals for services rendered during the reduction of the

[33] M. Brennan, 'The changing composition of Kilkenny landowners, 1641–
1700', in W. Nolan and K. Whelan (eds.), *Kilkenny: History and society* (Dublin,
1990), 161, 174–5.
[34] BL, Add. MS 28,939, fo. 77; NLI, MS 11,044, documents entitled 'Case D.
Ormonde Liberty Courts & Sr. Jon. Meads opinion', n. d.; 'The humble Peticon of
James Duke of Ormond ' (n.d. [c.1690]).
[35] TCD, MS 744, book i: outlawries, fos. 14, 14^v, 16–17, 47^v (printed in *AH*, 22
(1960), 32–65).   [36] Ibid. 91^v–92, 99^v.   [37] Ibid. 103^v–150^v.
[38] Ibid. 91^v–92, 99^v. Cahir was outlawed by the palatinate court, but this was
reversed by special act of parliament, I Anne, c. 38, and a restriction on Catholic
inheritance was not apparently enforced in his case (Annesley MS 22, fos. 130–8
(NLI, Mic.P.264), and Simms, *Williamite confiscation*, 130).

country and to court favourites. These grants included lands in
Tipperary but their precise extent is uncertain.[39] One special grant
was made to Thomas Prendergast as a reward for revealing a plot
to kill the king in 1696, and as a result he recovered lands lost by
his ancestors at the Restoration.[40] This particular grant was
confirmed by the trustees for forfeited estates, but they revoked
other grants made by the king and these, with the forfeited lands,
were to be sold.

Under the act of resumption (1700), 116 claims were submitted
for forfeited lands in Tipperary and over half of these were
allowed.[41] The nature of these claims varied widely but most
related to interests in leases for 31 years granted in the 1670s and
1680s. Two tenants under Lord Cahir, James Nagle of Garnvella
and Robert Keating of Knockagh, had their interest in leases
confirmed and they continued under Lord Cahir in the eighteenth
century. The remainder of the forfeited estate amounting to about
12,000 acres was put up for public auction, and between April and
June 1703, twenty-three individuals paid over £25,000 for land
purchases.[42] What remained unsold was made over to the Hollow
Sword Blades Company, a joint stock company directed mainly by
London merchants. A schedule of the lands held by the company
in Ireland in 1709 does not include Tipperary, implying that it had
disposed of its lands there by that date.[43] Most of the forfeited
property sold was purchased by local interests, mainly New
English. The largest single purchaser, however, was Sir Thomas
Prendergast who paid about £6,300 for over 1,800 acres much of
which he already held as a leaseholder. Indeed purchase of their
interests by existing tenants is recorded in five cases.[44]

The property changes resulting from the Williamite land
settlement were not as catastrophic in their effects as those of the
1660s. Those with an existing interest consolidated their position
by benefiting from the break-up of King James's estate. There was
no radical removal of existing proprietors, nor on the other hand
was there any perceptible influx of new settlers. Catholic proprie-

[39] TCD, MS 744, book vi, nos. 2, 5, 44, 64, 69, 74.
[40] NLI, MS 19,904, 64–8.   [41] NA, M2547–8.
[42] NA, M2578, 101–31.
[43] *A list of the estates in Ireland of the Hollow Sword Blades with acres in each*
(Dublin, 1709). For sales of the company's land in the county: RD, 11/304/4593,
12/116/4594, 15/478/8280; NA, Lodge rolls, x. 187–205.
[44] NA, M2578.

tors were not adversely affected by the settlement which, by its relative moderation, allowed a number of large owners, notably Lord Cahir, to continue into the next century. This contrasts with the situation obtaining in Wexford at this date, and the disposal of the estate of the Catholic earl of Clancarty in Co. Cork at this time contrasts with the survival of Lord Cahir.[45]

2. Property

The landed class was composed of families who derived their standing and income from landed estates. Estate and income are the basic determinants which distinguish the different groups composing landed society. A categorization of the incomes of 130 named individuals in Tipperary in 1775 shows that landed society on an income basis was narrow at the top and broadened out as one descended in the level of incomes. Only two persons, the earl of Clanwilliam (£14,000) and Lord Cahir (£10,000), had incomes of £10,000 or over, and both were absentees. Beneath them in the hierarchy was a group of twenty-five persons whose incomes ranged from £2,000 to £10,000, the majority of them in the £2,000 to £3,000 range. This group as a whole comprised the leading landowners of the county. Beneath them were those on smaller incomes of under £2,000, in all 104 persons who comprised the lesser landowners and smaller gentry. At the base of landed society were the freeholders who in 1776 numbered less than 1,000 individuals.[46]

From this categorization one can postulate a four-tier structure for the landed class. At the apex was a small group of very large landowners, usually titled; below them a more numerous group of large landowners; beneath them a larger body of lesser land-owners; and finally at the bottom a wide base of freeholders. If the latter are excluded from consideration, the 1775 list indicates that over 160 individuals of consequence composed the landed class. The contention can be advanced that in the early part of the

[45] D. Gahan, 'The estate system of county Wexford, 1641–1876', in K. Whelan and W. Nolan (eds.), *Wexford: History and society* (Dublin, 1987), 213–14; D. J. Dickson, 'An economic history of the Cork region in the eighteenth century', Ph.D. thesis (University of Dublin, 1977), 67–70.
[46] *AH*, 12 (1943), 137–47; RIA, MS 12.D.36.

century the landed class consisted of about 100 families, that this increased to 150 by the 1770s, and by the end of the century it stood at about the 200 mark. On this basis there was a doubling in the size of the landed class in the course of the century.

Changes in the size of the landed class are related to changes in property ownership. A dramatic transfer of property through confiscation, the consequence of radical political change, took place in the seventeenth century. The eighteenth-century experience was less dramatic being characterized by the circumstances of individual families and by changes in the distribution of wealth in society. Changes in landownership took place first through marriage and inheritance, which was the normal method whereby existing landed families extended their estates; and secondly, through sale and purchase which was motivated by the desire to consolidate estates, to transfer wealth, or to repay debts, and which was the chief means whereby newcomers obtained an estate. The land market in Tipperary in the first half of the century was dominated by the disposal of three large properties: Ormond, Everard, and Dunboyne.

The estate of James Butler (d. 1688), first duke of Ormond and his grandson, also James (d. 1746) second duke, experienced heavy indebtedness. In May 1688 total debts stood at a colossal £98,500. Yearly interest payments on this debt were £6,000 which with other charges (£10,500), brought total annual outgoings to £16,500. Gross income for one year to May 1688 was £22,600 leaving a net income of £6,100, so that in 1688 the main debt exceeded gross income fourfold.[47]

Excessive charges accumulated because the social and political status of the first and second dukes required them to provide for themselves and their families to a degree commensurate with their social position. This led to heavy borrowing and the imposition of charges on the estate. Heavy personal borrowing indulged in by the two dukes made the reduction of the estate necessary. In 1688 such debts were £86,500, excluding portions (£12,000). When over £81,000 of this amount was paid off through fines in 1701, most (£59,000) went towards personal debts and the balance (£32,000) was applied to repayment of the second duke's personal debts incurred in England.[48]

[47] BL, Add. MS 28,939, fos. 237–241ᵛ.
[48] NLI, MS 23,787, fos. 69–74ᵛ.

The level of debt could not be sustained because income was inadequate. The main source of income for Ormond was rents but in 1688 net rents were a meagre £6,100, which was clearly insufficient. Low rental income had as its source serious mismanagement of the first duke's estate in the period 1660–88.[49] This situation was further aggravated by the devastation wrought by the Williamite wars which extensively impoverished the Ormond estate. Also, as we have seen, the palatinate jurisdiction was proving unremunerative as its revenue was not sufficient to cover the cost of running it. The level of debt on the estate was thus of serious proportions with little prospect of it being ameliorated by revenue from the estate, rather its very solvency was threatened. In this situation Ormond's creditors made increasing demands that the annual payments on the principal debts be honoured more punctually. The need to meet current interest payments and, more critically, to tackle the substantial accumulated principal occasioned the adoption of radical and novel measures.

The genesis of a scheme for relieving the debt originated in April 1692.[50] Its main elements were embodied in a private act of parliament in 1695 which placed the estate in the hands of trustees empowering them to sell it off, and giving the second duke authority to raise fines on the granting of leases and to impose various family charges.[51] An amending act of 1696 arose because Ormond was unwilling to contemplate any outright sales of land by the trustees.[52] Accordingly he and his brother, Charles, earl of Arran, were empowered to grant leases for lives or years on which two-thirds of the rent levels prevailing in 1687 should be payable. Income from the fines levied on the granting of these new leases was to be applied in the first instance to defraying the debts of the first duke and then those of the second duke.

Under £115,900 was received from the fines, of which amount about £45,000 was raised in Tipperary mainly from town property in Clonmel and Carrick, and from lands elsewhere in the county; while further sums were raised from the estate elsewhere in Ireland, notably in counties Kilkenny, Wicklow, and Mayo.[53] A

[49] BL, Add. MS 28,877, fos. 232–232ᵛ, 265–6, 384–5; Add. MS 28,939, fo. 341.
[50] BL, Add. MS 28,877, fos. 280–1.
[51] *Comms. Jnl. (Ire.)*, ii. pt. 1, 123, 127, 396, 401.
[52] *An act for the more speedy payment of the creditors of James late duke of Ormond and of the present duke of Ormond* (Dublin, 1701), 1–2.
[53] NLI, MS 23,787, esp. fos. 67ᵛ–68.

further act of 1701 authorized Ormond first to sell the fines on the renewals of leases, and secondly to create fee farms of existing leases, for which conversion the tenants were to pay.[54] In this way a further £6,386 was received in 1701–4, and the operation of the act was extended.[55] As a result of these measures the level of debt on the estate was reduced to £41,634 by March 1711.[56] In the ensuing decade, however, debt crept steadily upward again and by 1720 exceeded £100,000.[57]

Debt reduction was disrupted by political events. As a result of his role in the Jacobite rising of 1715 the second duke was attainted for high treason, his annual pension of £5,000 withdrawn, a £10,000 reward offered for his capture, and his estate, alone of estates in Ireland at the time, forfeited to the crown. In a unique decision, however, the final settlement of the estate allowed the earl of Arran by special act of parliament (7 Geo. I, c. 22) to purchase back the residue forfeited estate in 1721 for £50,000.[58]

The effects of these proceedings internally on the Ormond estate and more broadly on the structure of landowning in the county were significant. In the period 1697–1701 the granting of leases for lives renewable on payment of a lump sum or fine and the fining down of rents to the levels of 1687, was followed in the period after 1701 by the conversion of these and other leases into fee farm grants. This process had the effect of giving tenants on the Ormond estate, who had hitherto held their lands on leases for years, a virtually absolute perpetuity interest. It is clear that the opportunity to transform an interest for years into one in perpetuity was widely availed of by the tenants. In the period up to mid-1700 there were 167 purchasers spread over the county with a large participation from Clonmel and Carrick, paying a total of £45,000. The areas where Ormond property was most concentrated, i.e. Eliogarty, Iffa and Offa, Middlethird, and Clanwilliam, witnessed the largest sums paid in fines. A survey of 1715 shows

---

[54] *An act for the more speedy payment*, 6, *et seq.*
[55] *Comms. Jnl. (Ire.)*, ii. pt. 1, 396, 401.
[56] NLI, D5492.
[57] *A state of the value of the forfeited estate of James, late duke of Ormonde* (n.p. [*c.*1720]).
[58] NA, M6862: *An act for enabling Charles earl of Arran to purchase the forfeited estate of James Butler late duke of Ormond* (n.p. [1721]), 408–9.

that the fee farm was the most common form of tenure on the estate by that date.[59]

This transformation in proprietorship was availed of by two classes of tenant: those who were tenants of Ormond's alone, and those who were tenants of his but who also owned land in their own right. The majority of the participants were not grantees or the descendants of grantees under the acts of settlement and explanation. A number of families who were however, used the opportunity to extend or consolidate their lands, notably Moore (Chancellorstown), Sadlier, Coote, Langley, Baker, Cleere, Dawson, Dancer, Harrison, and Mathew. They were out-numbered by those who were not grantees under the acts of the 1660s and who used the Ormond sales to establish themselves as large landed proprietors for the first time. Most significant in this category were Lowe, Carleton, Carden, Latham, Toler, Roe, Bayly, and Armstrong. These families were to establish new estate foci, Carden and Toler in addition were to receive a baronetcy and peerage respectively, and all were to function as grand jurors at different times.

A good instance of the process in operation is the case of the Armstrongs of Farneybridge. Captain William Armstrong held Farneybridge (803 acres) as a tenant to Ormond under a 21-year lease from 1670 at a rent of £120. In 1697 John Armstrong, his son, on payment of a £451 fine, received a new lease for three lives renewable forever at a rent of £80. In 1702 this perpetuity lease, on payment of a further fine of £335, was extended to be a fee farm at the same rent of £80. This remained the position until 1724 when William Armstrong bought out the fee farm rent of £80 for a lump sum of £1,933.[60] Thus in the course of three generations the Armstrongs rose from tenants to landowners. A similar pro-gression can be documented for Roe of Roesborough and Bayly of Ballynaclough, and these cases were typical of the process.[61]

Of the second category of tenant the most impressive instance of a family altering their status was that of the Meades. The initial

---

[59] PRO, Forfeited Estates Commission (hereafter FEC), I, O.99, An account of the estate of James late duke of Ormond in the kingdom of Ireland [Lady Day and May, 1715]; *App. to the sixth report of the deputy keeper, Public Record Office*, 46.

[60] NA, D23,404, D23,378, M5259 (2); NLI, D5281.

[61] Roe: NLI, D5256-7; NA, D20, 786-20, 788a,b; Bayly: Nenagh, Bayly papers, deeds of 13 Aug., 30 Nov. 1697, 26 May 1699, 23 May 1720, 18 Sept. 1732; NA, Lodge rolls, ix. 390.

association of the family with Tipperary derived from office (John Meade was a chief judge in the palatinate court), and marriage links (the same John married a daughter of Lord Ikerrin, Ormond's cousin). In 1697 Meade paid two fines amounting to £2,300 for perpetuity leases of nearly 4,000 acres centred on Golden. These were converted into fee farm grants in 1702 and 1703, and finally bought out in 1724. This large addition of lands contributed to the rise of the Meades as a county family for, though they were absentee (their main estate being at Ballintober, Co. Cork), their marriage and personal ties with Tipperary were close, instanced by the fact that the family chose the title of earl of Clanwilliam when elevated to that dignity in 1766.[62]

In general those benefiting within the county from the downturn in Ormond's financial position were New English of the post-1640 period. In addition there was a significant participation from individuals from outside the county mainly from Kilkenny with some Dublin interests and a scatter of others, including Joseph Ivie a Waterford merchant who acquired extensive lands at Holy Cross and Borrisoleigh.[63] Although sizeable fines were paid by outsiders, in total these were less than the amount contributed by interests within the county.

Outright purchases constituted the more important contribution of the outside interests to the breakup of the Ormond estate. Ormond was reluctant initially to entertain the prospect of outright disposals but overawed perhaps by the size of the debt, encouraged by the return gained from the fines levied after 1697, and induced by the prospect of ready cash from purchasers, he made provision for limited and selected sales after 1703. The 1715 survey records thirteen individuals to whom parcels of land were sold outright, the largest being Sir Alexander Cairnes, an Irish banker in London, who paid £18,600 in 1710.[64] The next most important were two Dubliners. In 1703 Nehemiah Donnellan, a baron of the exchequer, paid £5,274 for 3,188 acres in north Tipperary, including Nenagh, to all of which he was already head-

---

[62] J. Lodge, *The Peerage of Ireland* (rev. M. Archdall) (Dublin, 1789), iii. 295–8; NLI, D5246, D5273 (also summarized in NA, Lodge rolls, ix. 113, 116, 395); PRO, FEC, I, O.99 denominations 596, 610, and 629; RD, 44/40/27427.

[63] NLI, D5269; NA, Lodge rolls, x. 43–5.

[64] PRO, FEC, I, O.99, *passim*, and for Cairnes, denominations 585, 588, 599, 607, 618, 631, 638, 643–7, 672.

tenant.[65] By 1733 the Holmes family were head-tenants on the Nenagh property and were responsible for developing the town in succeeding decades.[66]

A similar development is evident in relation to Roscrea, which was part of an outright sale of 2,867 acres for £3,399 to Robert Curtis, also in 1703.[67] In 1722 the Curtis interest in the town was sold to John Damer of Tipperary for £22,000, a sum nearly seven times the amount of the original purchase price.[68] John Damer was established in the county by his elder brother Joseph (d. 1720), the founder of the family, who had been steadily gaining in wealth and influence since the seventeenth century. Thus the Damers acquired a semi-urban base in Roscrea where the family soon after constructed an impressive mansion-house unique for its size at this time in provincial Ireland.

Thus a situation of acute indebtedness led to the adoption of an innovative leasing policy and the selective selling-off of the estate, a process initiated in 1697 and culminating in the 1720s. This process had a twofold effect on the composition of the landed class. First, it diminished the Ormond stake in landed estate and in the status and leadership of the landed class which this conferred. There was a clear break with the past as one of the great lordships to survive from the medieval period lost its economic unity due to insolvency. This process on the Ormond estate paralleled that on the Boyle, Thomond, and Antrim estates elsewhere in Ireland in the same period, and like them it witnessed local resident gentry gaining from the financial straits of large landowners.[69]

Decline in landed influence combined with the demise of the family politically, was characterized by the long thirty-year exile of the second duke after 1715, spent in a futile adherence to the Jacobite cause; the abolition of his private jurisdiction, the palatinate, in 1715; and the permanent loss of the family's highest attainment, a dukedom. After the second duke's death in 1746 the residue estate was inherited by his brother, the earl of Arran, following whose death in 1758 it devolved on his cousin John Butler of Kilcash. Following his death without issue in 1766 ownership of the Tipperary estate was transferred to the Garryricken, Co. Kilkenny branch of the Butlers, who had converted, at

[65] NLI, D5416.
[66] RD, 74/501/52279.
[67] NA, Lodge rolls, ix. 387.
[68] RD, 36/127/21789.
[69] Dickson, *New Foundations*, 104; id., 'Cork', 73–85.

least nominally, to Anglicanism. It was this branch which assumed the Ormond title after its official revival in 1791. Further estate shedding in 1815 meant that by the mid-nineteenth century the Ormond estate was only the fourth largest (15,765 acres) in the county, a reversal of the position of a century and a half earlier when Ormond was its leading landowner.[70] The eighteenth-century reversal of fortunes was compounded by the consolidation of the family's centre of influence to Kilkenny, and at another level by the difficulties of other Butler branches: the absenteeism of Lord Cahir, and the disposal of Lord Dunboyne's lands in Tipperary in 1729.

The second effect was on the landed society of the county. Out of the Ormond estate a large body of new owners was created made up of former tenants and supplemented by outside pur-chasers. Although the disposal of the estate created some new absentee owners, most new proprietors were resident. Politically Ormond's removal from the hierarchy of the landed class meant that local society became less cohesive, leaving the way open for competing interests to vie for political leadership of the county.

Another estate which traced its origins to the medieval period and which also underwent difficulties in the early eighteenth century was that of the Old English family of Everard. Here again the twin factors of indebtedness and a close association with the Jacobite cause were present. The Everard estate was confiscated on the outlawry of Sir John Everard in 1691.[71] By a private act of parliament in 1702, however, the attainder of Sir John was reversed in consideration of £2,000, the estate being conveyed to trustees. A further proviso in the act required that Sir John's heir, Redmond, be reared a Protestant, and if he had not formally converted at the age of 18 years, then he and his heirs would be barred from inheriting the estate.[72]

Born in 1690 Sir Redmond must have conformed on or before 1708 in order to ensure his succession. This can only have been nominal, however, for although a convert, Everard was elected to

---

[70] In 1815 3,439 acres producing a rental of £5,000 were advertised for sale (NLI, Ormond papers, bundle for 1809–29, document for the sale of the fee simple estates of Walter, earl of Ormond in Co. Tipperary to be sold, 1 June 1815).

[71] NA, Lodge rolls, ix. 40–1.

[72] NLI, PC, 46 (i), Barton papers, document entitled 'Abstract of title to the estate late belonging to Sir Redmond Everard', 1.

the 1713 parliament by the Catholic interest in Fethard, and after 1714 he was actively involved in France with the advancement of the Stuart cause.[73] In 1716 he appointed an agent to manage his Irish estate and soon after became closely associated with the duke of Ormond.[74]

In 1721 total debts stood at £22,161 but an opportune marriage in the same year brought him a dowry of £10,000 which, with the sale of that part of the estate situated in the barony of Iffa and Offa for £11,500, combined to cancel this debt at one stroke.[75] The reduction of a separate debt of £7,000 was provided for in an act of parliament in 1727 which appointed trustees to sell off parts of the estate in the barony of Middlethird, while an additional debt of £7,904 was to be satisfied out of the remaining unsold lands.[76] In this way the encumbrances on the estate were successfully eliminated during the course of the 1720s.

While this development was decisively advantageous in one respect, in another it meant that the size of the estate and its revenue-bearing capacity were sharply reduced. What remained of the estate yielded less than £1,000 annually in the 1730s.[77] Rent remittances were made by the agent to Everard in France where he claimed that he and Lady Everard were engaged in 'extravagant living', while one of his creditors claimed that by 'some mismanagement attending his estate in Ireland he [Everard] was so ill supplied with money that he lived entirely upon credit for five or six years'.[78] The result was that debt began to emerge again in the 1730s.

As it happened fate intervened, for Sir Redmond and Lady Everard died childless in 1742. The estate devolved on his near cousin, James Long, a Catholic who converted for the purpose of inheriting.[79] In 1750 total debts due out of the remainder of the estate amounted to £27,137, which were to be satisfied by sale.[80] This was soon achieved when Thomas Barton, a successful

[73] *Historical studies*, 4 (1963), 91 n. 5; *Studies*, 32 (1943), 108.
[74] Clonmel Museum, O'Callaghan papers 1985/180, schedule of deeds relating to the Everard estate 1674–1721 (no. 6); HMC, *Stuart*, 5 (1912), 54.
[75] NLI, PC, 46 (i), 'Abstract', 1–2, marriage articles of Sir R. Everard and Mary Drake, 30 May 1721.
[76] TCD, Private acts of parliament, i: *An act for vesting certain manors, lands, and hereditaments the estate of Sir Redmond Everard, bart. in trustees* (n.p. [1727]).
[77] NLI, PC, 46 (i), case in Chancery of *R. Dawson v. James Long Everard and others* (1750), 8, 18, 20.
[78] Ibid. 2, 17.   [79] Ibid. 3–4.   [80] Ibid. 28–37.

Bordeaux wine merchant, paid £30,500 for the estate in 1751.[81] This represented a considerable financial outlay, indeed Barton was later to claim that it 'exhausted the greatest part of [my] stock in trade and other personal fortune'.[82]

Everard's difficulties provided the occasion for the introduction of two important new families into the landed class of the county, one having a background in the law, the other in trade. Cornelius O'Callaghan was a small Co. Cork landowner and successful Dublin lawyer who, apart from facilitating Everard with mortgages, had much in common with him politically. O'Callaghan like Everard was a convert and as such sat in the 1713 parliament with Everard as representatives for Fethard.[83] It is reasonable to surmise that O'Callaghan's return was a political favour rendered to him by Everard in part repayment of debts. In 1721 O'Callaghan paid £11,500 for the Everard property located in Iffa and Offa and centring on Clogheen.[84] This purchase was to form the basis of the family's subsequent rise in the landed class. The family obtained the title of Lords Lismore in 1785, it forged important political marriages with the Ponsonby and Ormond families, and by the mid-nineteenth century they were the county's largest landowners.

The purchase of the Fethard estate was motivated by Thomas Barton's concern to provide for or compensate his son William on his marriage and for other reasons. By virtue of the purchase the Bartons made a successful transition from trade into land, and acquired a political interest in Fethard borough, but unlike O'Callaghan they did not obtain a peerage. The Barton and O'Callaghan estates are the two main new interests which arose out of the breakup of the Everard property. A separate development was that under the 1727 act certain of the Everard lands in Middlethird were sold off for £7,379 to six individuals with some town property in Clonmel.[85] This sale served to establish a group of minor gentry: Power at Barrettstown, Power at Gurteen, Jacob at Coolmore.

The Catholic family of Butler, Lords Dunboyne, became

---

[81] NLI, PC, 46 (i), Articles of agreement between James Long Everard, Robert Marshall, and Thomas Barton, 8 Mar. 1750–1.

[82] King's Inns Library, House of Lords appeals 4a: *Barton* v. *Barton* (1765), appellant's case, 2.

[83] *Historical studies* 4 (1963), 91, n. 5.   [84] RD, 33/487/20997.

[85] NLI, PC, 46 (i), 'Abstract', 1; RD, 60/52/39865, 64/33/42487, 66/418/47202.

indebted in the 1720s and as a result were forced to dispose of considerable lands in the county. The family exhibits a history of heavy borrowing on mortgage from the 1680s at least.[86] Additionally between 1711 and 1732 Pierce and Edmond Butler (eighth Lord Dunboyne, d. 1732), accumulated judgment debts of £9,000.[87] To alleviate these, Dunboyne in 1729 sold about 900 acres of the ancestral lands in Middlethird barony to John Bagwell, a Clonmel merchant, for under £6,000.[88] Bagwell, apart from his direct mercantile interests, was a Munster correspondent for the Dublin banking firm of La Touche and Kane. These functions of merchant and agent may have provided him with the necessary funds for investment in land. At any rate this purchase marked the entry of the family into the landed class. The Dunboyne purchase was supplemented by the acquisition of 1,500 acres centring on Kilmore near Clonmel, the estate of John Slattery a Catholic lawyer and agent to Lord Cahir, and by three other properties totalling 413 acres.[89] In this way by the early 1730s Bagwell had acquired a substantial rural estate of 2,730 acres and entered into landed society at the expense of largely Catholic debtors.

The subsequent history of the Bagwell property is of interest in illustrating the shifting fortunes of a landed family, and its tendency, like Barton, to retain links with trade. The Kilmore property was used to establish an elder son on his marriage in 1736 and this remained the rural base of one branch of the family.[90] The Dunboyne acquisition, however, only remained in Bagwell possession for about fifty years until 1778 when due to debt it was purchased by the Riall family of Clonmel, who like Bagwell in an earlier generation also had a background as bankers and merchants.[91] This marks the advent of one of the town's leading

---

[86] NLI, reports on private collections no. 48, p. 798; PC, 260–1, Riall papers, deeds of 14 May 1681, 3 Sept. 1684, 8, 21 Oct., 1 Dec. 1698; RD, 17/269/8785.

[87] NLI, PC, 260–1, 'A list of judgments against Pierse (sic) & Edmund, Lord Dunboyne', in folder marked 'Lord Dunboyne'.

[88] 'Tipperary deeds, 1720–49', deeds of 19 Sept. 1729.

[89] Ibid. 27 May 1736.

[90] Ibid.

[91] NLI, PC, 260–1, Riall papers, 'Certificates of judgments against J. Bagwell of Kilmore'; 'Certificates of judgments being satisfied against J. Bagwell of Kilmore' in folder marked 'John Bagwell'; and 'Tipperary deeds 1750–69', deed of 15 Jan. 1778. Between 1756 and 1776 John Bagwell of Kilmore incurred judgment debts of

Quaker merchants into landed society. The younger branch of the Bagwell family remained in trade and banking in Clonmel and in 1780 purchased the Marlfield property and flour mill of the indebted Stephen Moore, and proceeded to become the major political interest in Clonmel after 1800 when the borough was bought from Lord Mount Cashell.

The most important changes in the personnel of the landed class emanated from the experience on the Ormond, Everard, and Dunboyne properties. These changes were profound in their consequences for the composition of the landed class in the county in the first half of the century, leading on the one hand to the decline of three long-established families, and on the other to the introduction of new elements.

Changes in the composition and personnel of the landed class in the second half of the century were less dramatic than in the preceding period. There were a number of cases of the outright disposal of lands to satisfy debts but these involved small landowners; their purpose was to consolidate larger estates held elsewhere in Ireland, and they did not have a widespread effect on the land market or on landowning structures. Changes in the period 1750–1815 must be assessed from a different perspective than those of the early part of the century. The earlier period was distinguished by an adverse economic environment characterized by static, low, or declining rents making borrowing common. The later part of the century, however, witnessed more favourable conditions with agricultural prosperity producing rising rentals. Rising overall incomes and the better management of estates created the context in which landed families were able to borrow without damaging the solvency of the estate. To borrow on mortgage from fellow landlords, merchants, and others became a more widely accepted practice. Yet despite its greater incidence it did not lead to the breakup of estates and there were fewer cases among landed families of chronic indebtedness or insolvency. Some leading families like Mathew and Meade indulged their expectations and schemes of expenditure to the full, leading in

£32,640, about £12,650 of which was satisfied leaving £19,990 outstanding. This was partly satisfied by the sale of the former Dunboyne property to Riall in 1778 for £11,800.

both cases to the necessity to dispose of property. They were the exceptions however.

With insolvency due to indebtedness being less likely it is clear that change within the landed class in this period did not stem largely from this cause. On the contrary it derived from the effects of the wider dissemination of wealth in society at large. Agricultural prosperity served to create a larger number of solvent tenants and farmers. Indicative of their number and wealth is the number and value of freeholds in each of the categories 40s., £20, and £50 registered in the county between 1807 and 1815. In the first classification (40s.) Tipperary had the largest number (13,900) registered in Munster and compared well with northern counties like Down. It is in the higher valuations of £20 and £50, however, that Tipperary outstrips other counties. In the former category there were over 1,600 registered and in the latter 2,270. The total value of the freeholds registered, assuming a uniform rate in each category, was in excess of £173,300.[92] This shows that Tipperary was very wealthy and that it possessed a higher proportion of farmers holding more highly valued lands than elsewhere. From this one can imply that a more silent transition was occurring in rural society: generated by agricultural prosperity there was a movement upward into and beyond the farmer/tenant class. All sectors rose but farmers rose markedly relative to others. This happened without a displacement at the apex of landed society: rather the landed class became enlarged at its base.

This model provides the conceptual framework within which the changing relationship between income, expenditure, and debt can be considered. The income of the landed class depended on prevailing land values and the level of rents obtainable. An examination of certain estates before c.1750 indicates that the picture is not a uniform one and where increases in rent are evident their scale varied. Lands were cheap in the first half of the eighteenth century. If average land values for the county in the mid-seventeenth century can be put at under 1s. 6d. per acre then by the end of the century this had increased three times to 4s. 6d.[93] Land values grew only slowly thereafter. Because of differences in

---

[92] *Clonmel Herald*, 20 Mar. 1816.
[93] Land values calculated from information in the Civil Survey by dividing the total value per barony by total acres. Values for 1696 from *Comms. Jnl. (Ire.)*, ii. pt. 2, p. xxxviii.

TABLE 2. Rents and incomes on select estates

Date	Estate	Amount (£)	Date	Estate	Amount (£)	Date	Estate	Amount (£)
1697	Barker	226	1767	Mathew	6,000	1780	Mathew	12,600
1699	Butler[a]	3,485	1767	Butler[a]	2,500	1780	Stanley	3,000
1718	Mathew[b]	8,000	1770	Butler[a]	6,000	1786	Ryan[d]	1,596
1721	Smith[c]	230	1770	Stanley	2,592	1791	Stanley	4,430
1724	Ryan[d]	205	1772	Mathew	10,000	1794	Smith[c]	1,386
1735	Ryan[d]	430	1774	Stanley	2,734	1797	Stanley	4,544
1736	Barker	616	1775	O'Callaghan	6,000	1800	Smith[c]	1,386
1743	O'Callaghan	477	1775	Barker	5,000	1807	Ryan[d]	1,941
1744	Mathew[e]	2,600	1775	Butler[a]	10,000	1808/9	O'Callaghan	15,000
1750	Smith[c]	510	1778	Ryan[d]	1,368	1808/9	Mathew	28,000
1756	Stanley[f]	1,872	1779	O'Callaghan	6,000	1808/9	Barker	10,000
1759	Mathew	8,000				1808/9	Butler[a]	36,000
						1811	Ryan[d]	2,132
						1818	Ryan[d]	19,700
						1822/3	O'Callaghan	17,120

[a] Refers to the Butler (Cahir) estate. For 1808/9 the amount is one expectant upon reletting.

[b] Refers to the Thomastown estate only.

[c] All figures for the Smith estate are derived from rental sources.

[d] The amounts for 1778, 1786, 1807, 1811, and 1818 are gross amounts; the net amounts are respectively £194, £751, £917, £1,146, and £674.

[e] The amount for 1744 refers to the Thurles estate only, and is adjusted to one year from the half-year amount.

[f] Adjusted to one year from half-year amount.

Sources: Barker: TCD, Barker Ponsonby Papers P11/14, 15, P1/1/12, P1/4/22; *AH* 12 (1943), 140; Wakefield, *Account*, i (1812), 276. Butler (Cahir): TCD MS 744, fos. 91ᵛ–92; *A list of the absentees of Ireland* (1767); PRONI D 151/9/109; *AH* 12 (1943), 143; Wakefield, *Account*, i. (1812), 276. Mathew: Sheridan, *Life of Swift* (1785), 359; rent roll for half year, Nov. 1744 (Tipperary County Library, Thurles); Fitzpatrick, *Union* (1867), 157; *A list of the absentees of Ireland* (1767); NLI, Byrne papers, 'Memo'; *An act for vesting in trustees* [1780], 29; Wakefield, *Account*, i (1812), 276. Smith: NLI MS 16,929, p. 133; E. Smith papers, leases of 1750 (High School, Dublin); PRONI DIO 4/8/9/17, 21. Ryan: Ryan papers (Thurles), rent roll, c.1724; rent roll Nov. 1735; ledger of accounts and rents, 1780–1811; green pocket book marked 'D. Ryan, 1805'; rental, May 1807; rental 1811; 'Memo of debts due by D. Ryan, Apr. 1818'. O'Callaghan: O'Callaghan papers (Cahir), rent account book, 1736–54; rent roll, 1780; Lismore's account with E. Taylor, Aug. 1822–Apr. 1823; *AH* 12 (1943), 138; Wakefield, *Account*, i. (1812), 276. Stanley: Derby papers (Preston), DDK 1702/3, 15, 22, DDK 1701/13, 22, 26.

land quality in various parts of the county and on individual estates, a consistent average for acreable rent by mid-century is difficult to determine accurately. However, a general average of not more than 10s., and in the majority of cases much less than that amount, would not be inconsistent with the available evidence.[94] On this basis land values hardly more than doubled in the half century after 1700 which contrasts with the threefold increase in the half-century before that date. Evidence from four estates—Barker (Kilcooley), Erasmus Smith (Tipperary), Ryan (Inch), and TCD (Templemore, Tipperary, Thurles)—indicate an average increase in rents up to c.1750 of the order of 180 per cent (Table 2). However, elsewhere rents in this period were declining. Thus on the 5,000-acre Bayly estate, located largely north of Nenagh but also near Cashel, while rents rose from £1,400 in 1707 to £1,600 in 1717, by 1730 this level had fallen to £1,080 representing a decline of 32 per cent. The conclusion is that before mid-century one can not generalize too readily: evidence indicating rising rentals can be complemented by contrary data showing a fall.

Land values doubled to 20s. by the mid-1770s.[95] Lands in the more fertile areas like Clanwilliam (22s. 9d.) and Middlethird (25s.) exceeded this average, while areas with significant portions of bad lands like Owney and Arra (12s.) and Ikerrin (18s.) were below it. In Cork rents averaged only 5s., in Limerick 10s. 6d., and in Waterford 7s. and 10s.[96] Thus even the worst of Tipperary lands were more highly valued at this time than some other Munster counties. Acreable rents in Tipperary fell by 4s. or 5s. between 1771 and 1776, reflecting the economic downturn of these years, a fall which would suggest that the average in 1770 can more accurately be put at 25s., representing a rise of two and a half times in the 20-year period 1750–70.[97] Landlords themselves attested to a doubling of rents in the county in the 20-year period up to the mid-1770s.[98]

Land values remained depressed from the early 1770s into the 1780s and a steady upward trend resumed only after 1790.[99] The

[94] Power, 'Tipperary', 45–6.
[95] Young, *Tour*, i. 391, 394, 432, 451; NLI, MS 14,157, 17.
[96] Young, *Tour*, i. 400, 401, 451.
[97] Ibid. 391, 426.   [98] Ibid. 432, 442.
[99] W. W. Seward, *The Hibernian gazetteer* (Dublin, 1789), lx.

main cause of this was the local effect of the American war and its aftermath whereby a slump in the prices of meat, butter, and grain reduced the value of agricultural holdings.[100] The diary comments of a large grazier, James Scully, for the years 1775–90 record the effects of poor prices and low demand for beef (1775, 1777, 1782), bad weather leading to the scarcity of hay and loss of livestock (1776), the failure of provision merchants in Cork (1778), poor demand at fairs (1784), and credit restrictions and bank failures in Cork (1779, 1784).[101] In a county where so much of the profits of farming depended on cattle and sheep grazing, stock mortality meant disaster with tenants becoming insolvent and unable to meet rent commitments. Describing the general distress in 1784 the agent on the Stanley estate referred to the fact that tenants on the Tipperary lands were 'near ruined by the death of cattle'.[102] In consequence there was emigration, ruin, farms were abandoned or surrendered though some landlords like Lord Cahir cancelled arrears, accepted surrenders, and abated former rents, thereby helping tenants over a difficult period.[103] After 1790 the sustained demand for agricultural produce meant that land values resumed their upward movement. Acreable land values rose from an average of 20*s*. in 1790, 30*s*. in 1800, 40*s*. by 1810, and under 50*s*. by 1815. In 1790 Scully noted in his diary: 'a great prospect of a good season next year for butter, beef, sheep, and wool', and in 1791: 'land seems high in demand now owing to two good seasons'.[104]

Following the depression of the early 1770s the upward surge in rents resumed (Table 2). On the Mathew estate worth £12,600 in 1780 income was then expected to rise to £20,000 (58 per cent increase) on the fall of leases, and by 1809 was producing £28,000 (40 per cent increase). Income on the Barker estate rose by 100 per cent between 1775 (£5,000) and 1809 (£10,000), while the O'Callaghan estate witnessed a rise in income from £6,000 (1775) to £15,000 (1808/9) or 150 per cent to £12,840 in rents by 1822/3. The level of income on the Cahir estate grew from £10,000 (1775)

---

[100] L. M. Cullen (ed.), *The formation of the Irish economy* (Cork, 1969), 15, 117; NLI, MS 14,157, 17.

[101] NLI, MS 27,571, under the respective years.

[102] McGuire to Derby, 27 May 1784 (Derby papers (Preston), DDK, 1705 series). [103] *WM*, 11 May 1811.

[104] NLI, MS 27,571, entries for 24 Apr. 1790, 17 Mar. 1791.

to an expectant £36,000 in 1809 (160 per cent increase). The 15,000-acre Maude estate in Kilnamanagh experienced a rise of £4,000 (50 per cent) in income between 1789 and 1808/9. Substantial growth in rental income on the Prittie, Toler, and Bayly estates is also evident. Rent increases were not universal however, reflecting the leasing situation on particular estates. On the Ryan (Inch) and Erasmus Smith estates, for instance, lands reset in the mid-1770s were not out of lease by 1800, thereby impeding their owners from increasing rent levels in line with the rise in land values. Nevertheless the overriding trend is of an emphatic growth in rental income in the later eighteenth century.

The broad pattern of rent movement in Tipperary is of a slow increase in the first half of the century, a sharp increase in the 1750s and 1760s, a static phase in the 1770s and 1780s, followed by rising rents in the 25-year period after 1790. Although the amounts differ, this pattern of rents broadly concurs with other areas of the country like Ulster and with the findings of Large nationally for 1790–1815.[105] However, in Tipperary the most impressive rise is evident in the middle decades of the century with the increase in the period 1790–1815 being more modest in comparison. This was the case despite the fact that land values grew more sharply in the latter period than they did in the former. The implication from this is that rising land values were not being substantially reflected in enhanced landlord incomes at least on the sample of estates cited here, suggesting that a large proportion of the wealth of the period passed into the hands of those beneath the landowner. This further substantiates the contention that a widening of the landed class at its base occurred in the latter part of the century.

Agricultural rents were the main source of landed incomes. A few landlords such as Smith-Barry, the archbishop of Cashel, Mathew, Damer, and Lord Cahir benefited from urban rents at Tipperary, Cashel, Thurles, Roscrea, and Cahir respectively. Other landlords like Prittie at Silvermines, Stanley at Gortdrum, Langley at Coalbrook, and Vere Hunt at Glengoole at one time or another had lead-, copper-, or coal-mining operations but they entailed considerable financial risk, were not always successful,

---

[105] P. Roebuck, 'Rent movement, proprietorial incomes and agricultural development, 1730–1830', in P. Roebuck (ed.), *Plantation to partition* (Belfast, 1981), 90; D. Large, 'The wealth of the greater Irish landowners, 1750–1815', *IHS*, 15 (1966), 29.

and did not generate substantial revenues for their owners. More successfully, as the main sponsors of the larger flour-milling enterprises established from 1770, landlords benefited to a greater or lesser degree from this extra-agricultural source of income. Office holding was an additional source of income for a few landlords like John Hely-Hutchinson who in his own right had a combined income from offices of all kinds of £4,900 in 1775; John Toler had a salary of £500 as a judge in 1784, advanced to being solicitor-general and later an earl; and John Scott, who married into the landed class, had an official income in 1787 of £15,000 and in 1799 of £20,000, and he advanced to being attorney-general and earl of Clonmell.[106] They are the exception in having such supplementary sources of income as most landlords depended primarily on their estates as the chief source of support.

Impressive though the overall increase in income levels is it has to be offset against the level of expenditure incurred by landlords. There were three main areas which absorbed incomes: personal charges, family, and estate expenses of which the two last were the most important. Because of the dominance of the strict settlement in the financial regulation of estates, family charges constituted a large drain on landed incomes. Family pride and social considerations reinforced the need to provide adequately for daughters and younger sons once the practice of primogeniture catered for the eldest son. Before c. 1750 the amount in portions paid to daughters on marriage was less than £1,000 for smaller families like Fogarty, Kearney, Purcell, and Tobin; £1,000 or £1,500 for middle-ranking families like Kennedy, Bunbury, Holmes, Green, and Mathew (Thurles); while leading families like Prittie, Mathew (Thurles and Thomastown), O'Callaghan, Maude, Barker, Bagwell, Minchin, and Butler (Cahir) could expect to give or receive portions ranging from £2,000 to £6,000.[107]

[106] W. Hunt, *The Irish parliament in 1775* (Dublin, 1907), 26–7; *PRIA*, 71 C (1971), 204; *DNB*, xvii. 981–3; W. J. Fitzpatrick, *Ireland before the union* (Dublin, 1867), 14.

[107] Marriage articles with main partners: A. Mandeville and K. Tobin, 5 Oct. 1681 (NA, Acc.1079/1/2/1); J. Kennedy and C. Latin, 1735 (NLI, Reports on private collections no. 11, p. 287); R. Purcell and B. Comerford, 1684 (TCD, Barker Ponsonby papers, P4/2a); C. Fogarty and M. Kearney, 28 Feb. 1696 (GO, MS 171, pp. 197–9); J. Mandeville and C. Green, 1 Apr. 1725 (NLI, Minchin papers, Mic. P.5701); J. Mandeville and E. Kennedy, 20 Feb. 1720–1 (NA, Acc. 1079/1/2/2); Mathew: settlement of 11 Mar. 1713 (NA, M5302, 4); J. Bayly and B. Holmes, June 1750 (Bayly papers); R. O'Callaghan and M. Bunbury, 16 May 1746

In the 1760s portions of leading families, e.g. Prittie, Minchin, were in the range £2,000–£3,000, one or two were £6,000 (Mathew, Lane), but few were in excess of that.[108] Leading families could expect substantial dowries as in 1765 when Francis Mathew, heir to the vast Thomastown property, received £10,000 with Ellis Smyth of Co. Wicklow; £5,000 was paid with Anne Roche, daughter of a leading Limerick merchant, on her marriage with George Ryan of Inch in 1783; and a similar sum applied on the marriage of Lord Dunalley and Maria Trant of Dovea in 1805.[109] Leading head-tenants came to be in a position to provide substantial dowries for their charges. Thus James Scully, who received a dowry of £500 on his marriage to Catherine Lyons of Croom in 1760, was able to portion his own daughter to the amount of £2,000 when she married in 1791.[110] Leading families would appear, therefore, to have been able to afford average portions of £2,000–£3,000 in the 1760s and £5,000 by *c.*1800.

Annuities or jointures paid to wives if they survived their husbands were normally calculated on the basis of 10 per cent of the portion depending on whether or not the marriage had issue. This can be documented for a number of marriage settlements over the century.[111] Widows from marriages entered into in the

(RD, 132/467/90048); H. Prittie and E. Harrison, 27 July 1720, citing deed of 2 Feb. 1702 (NLI, Dunalley papers); G. Mathew and I. Brownlow, 6, 7 Aug. 1745 (*An act for vesting in trustees certain lands the estate of Francis Mathew* (n.p. [1780]), 10); C. O'Callaghan and E. Ford, 13, 14 Aug. 1733 (RD, 85/136/59465); W. Barker and M. Quin, 16 June 1733 (TCD, Barker Ponsonby papers, P1/4/24); J. Bagwell and A. Calwell, 27 May 1736 (NLI, Riall papers); P. Minchin and H. Bunbury, 4 May 1749 (NLI, Minchin papers, Mic. P.5701); J. Butler and C. Moore, 17 Dec. 1739 (RD, 98/243/68283); Sir R. Maude and E. Cornwallis, *ante* 1723 (RD, 39/499/26695).

[108] Marriage articles with main partners: P. Holmes and E. Prittie, 3, 4 Feb. 1765 (*A bill for vesting certain lands in the King's county part of the estate of Peter Holmes* (n.p., 1784), 4–5); D. Toler and R. Minchin, 28, 29 Nov. 1760 (RD, 209/67/137591); W. P. Vaughan and M. Synge, 21, 22 May 1764 (NA, M4917, 5); W. Barker and C. Lane, 23 Jan. 1760 (TCD, Barker Ponsonby papers, P1/9/7–8); A. Roe and C. Mathew, 7 Apr. 1767 (NLI, Byrne papers); J. Butler and M. Keating, 26 Sept. 1760 (RD, 211/63/137570).

[109] *An act for vesting in trustees*, 20; NA, M5306, 8–10; RD, 547/539/361730.

[110] RD, 222/21/145209, 433/410/283766.

[111] G. Ryan and A. Roche, 1783 (NA, M5306, 8–10); P. Holmes and E. Prittie, 1765 (RD, 244/296/157786); W. P. Vaughan and M. Synge, 1764 (NA, M4917, 5); R. Read and E. Hall, 1722 (NA, Lodge rolls, x. 124–5); J. Brooks and A. Hunt, 1758 (ibid. x. 314–15); E. Butler and M. Walsh, 1766 (RD, 239/362/158622); R. Butler and C. Roe, 1755 (NA, D17,539); C. Hart and F. White, 1765 (Roscrea Heritage Centre, A37/0/82).

1760s could expect jointures of £300 or under, those of forty years later ones of about £500. These figures reflect the arrangements for leading families, those of less wealth and status could expect more modest settlements in proportion.

Providing for younger sons and daughters put a considerable charge on estates depending on the numbers to be provided for and this had to be borne by a succeeding generation, sometimes the original provision taking little account of its ability to bear it. A sample drawn from the available evidence indicates a range in individual amounts of £2,000–£4,000 for smaller families and £5,000–£11,000 for larger.[112] In the period after *c.* 1750 for smaller families the amount increased to £4,000–£8,000, and for larger like Meade, Mathew, and O'Callaghan up to £20,000.[113] Daughters' portions apart, much of the provision for younger children was intended to facilitate education and advancement to a professional career in the law, the church, or the army, and the fulfilment of these obligations could constitute important charges. In the normal course of events portions, jointures, and provision for younger sons could be met by a prudent management of affairs. They came to be viewed as oppressive however, when other areas of expenditure became excessive or when unexpected circumstances intervened.

The purchase of additional land for economic, political, family, or social reasons could involve a considerable outlay of funds. It has been seen in relation to proceedings on the Ormond, Everard, and Dunboyne estates that land purchase tended to be characteristic of rising families or those entering the landed class. Thus the O'Callaghans had a voracious appetite for land acquisition once they became established. Lord Lismore in his will of 1787 stipulated that his younger son lay out £9,999 in the purchase of lands, and in 1803 his heir bought an estate in County Laois for £43,620.[114] Land acquisition could be less ambitious however, in

[112] Will of T. Butler, Kilcash, 7 Oct. 1730 (NLI, Ormond papers, bundle 1729–30); will of J. Bayly, Debsborough, 23 Jan. 1776 (Bayly papers); Prittie: deed of 12 Oct. 1726 (NLI Dunalley papers); Roe: deed of 18 Oct. 1745 (NA, M5427 (9)); Minchin: deed of 4 May 1749 (NLI, Minchin papers, Mic. P.5701); Vaughan: deed of 2, 3 Oct. 1738 (NA, M4917, 4).
[113] P. Holmes and E. Prittie, settlement of 1765 (n. 111 above); Mathew: *An act for vesting in trustees*, 30–1; Meade: *An act for the sale of the estates of Rt. Hon. John, earl of Clanwilliam* (n.p. [1795]), 3; O'Callaghan: will of C. O'Callaghan, Lord Lismore, 4 Feb. 1787 (Clonmel Museum, Acc.1985/80).
[114] Clonmel Museum, Acc.1985/80; RD, 553/57/365286.

some cases having as its purpose the consolidation of an existing interest. Thus in 1768 Peter Holmes bought out his interest in the town and lands of Nenagh for £12,400, of which sum £7,000 was borrowed. By 1784 when £9,000 of this mortgage (including interest) was outstanding he disposed of his small (377 acres) Offaly estate to pay it off, in order to concentrate instead on his more substantial (1,200 acres) Tipperary estate.[115] The result was a more rational estate unit.

Management costs for the administration of estates affected only a minority of landlords. Professional estate agents began to be appointed more widely in Tipperary only from the 1780s. This development was not before its time, for duplicity in the running of estates was not absent in previous decades. On the Mathew estate in the 1760s receivers were appointed by chancery and it was said that by their 'mismanagement the rents of the said estates to a very considerable amount had been squandered'.[116] The appointment of professional staff could, therefore, be a welcome development. The cost of such agencies nationally has been estimated at 5 per cent of the gross rental (6–7 per cent on larger estates) and the total cost of running the estate at 10 per cent.[117] Given the late appearance of professional services on estates in Tipperary this particular cost was less important as a drain on estate finances before 1780.

Tipperary landlords spent little of their incomes on estate improvements; there is little evidence of a regular reinvestment in estates, and what improvements took place were carried out by tenants. There were exceptions however, notably O'Callaghan at Shanbally, Carden at Templemore, Osborne at Newtown Anner, Maude at Dundrum, and Barker at Kilcooley. They sponsored large-scale remodellings of the landscape, drainage schemes, estate villages, new tenants, and resettlement. Such endeavours could entail substantial capital investment the scale of which is indicated by the fact that in 1775 the principal debt owed by Sir Thomas Maude stood at £27,000 at a time when his improvement schemes were most intense.[118]

While landlord assistance to tenants was generally minimal,

[115] *A bill for vesting certain lands. . . part of the estate of Peter Holmes.*
[116] *An act for vesting in trustees*, 26.
[117] W. Maguire, *The Downshire estates in Ireland 1801–1845* (Oxford, 1972), 69, 76–7.   [118] RD, 312/57/207330; Young, *Tour*, i. 392–4.

their expenditure on demesne embellishment and house building was greater. Both Clarendon in the 1670s and Swift *c.*1718 refer to the extensive improvements to the Mathew seat at Thomastown.[119] These were achieved by prudent management and, as noted by one observer, 'strict economy'.[120] George Mathew (d. 1738) of Thomastown reportedly lived frugally on the Continent in the 1710s for seven years on £600 yearly in order to devote his £8,000 rental to the laying out of a 1,500 acre demesne and fitting out the house with forty guest rooms.[121] His successors were less circumspect in their expenditure on the estate. When Francis Mathew died in 1806 the rental was much depleted and the estate indebted due to his sponsoring a private bill to bring a water supply to Thomastown Castle.[122] As we shall see the causes of Mathew's indebtedness were more complex, but this statement does indicate the common perception that landlords as a class were spendthrift by inclination and that much of their expenditure on improvements was unnecessary, self-indulgent, even wasteful.

Associated with demesne embellishment was house building. Nolan has shown that in 1777 there were 184 gentlemen's seats in the county with particular concentrations in Iffa and Offa, Middlethird, Clanwilliam, and the Ormond baronies.[123] Many of these mansions were erected in the 1750s and 1760s when incomes rose sharply. Some of the wealthier landowners like Damer at Roscrea, Mathew at Thomastown, O'Callaghan at Shanbally, Sadlier at Sopwell Hall, Pennefather at Marlow, Moore at Barne, and the archbishop of Cashel already had large and impressive mansion-houses from an earlier period. New residences were constructed in the mid-eighteenth century by Carden at Templemore, Otway at Templederry, Toler at Beechwood, and Pennefather at Ballyowen.[124] So that the picture evident in 1777 is largely the product of the previous twenty or twenty-five years of prosperity. After stagnating in the 1770s, when prosperity resumed thereafter incomes rose again. If one accepts a landed class of around 160 in the 1770s and one of 200 in 1800, then

[119] T. Sheridan, *The life of the Rev. Dr. Jonathan Swift* (Dublin, 1785), 359–66; *Correspondence of Henry Hyde, earl of Clarendon*, ed. S. W. Singer (London, 1828), ii. 6; St. Patrick's College, Thurles, Skehan notebooks, Thurles parish, ii. 90.
[120] Sheridan, *Swift*, 362.   [121] Ibid. 359.
[122] Skehan notebooks, ii. 90.   [123] Nolan, *Tipperary*, 293–4.
[124] Burke's, *Guide to Irish country houses* (London, 1976) under the individual houses concerned.

something of the order of forty new mansions may have been erected in that period.

House building involved a large-scale capital outlay on the part of landlords, but never to such an extent as to result in a crippling financial burden. Even though the Damers started to erect a substantial mansion-house (Damers' Court) on their estate at Shronell in the 1750s and 1760s, the costs of the uncompleted project did not influence its ability to survive as a landed family.[125] There is no pattern of reckless overspending on new mansion-houses, except to a degree in the case of the Mathews who, as British landowners and MPs in the imperial parliament, acquired greater models of grandeur to aspire to. What house building took place among the Tipperary gentry was of a scale not to be an excessive drain on incomes.

Two main families had problems of financial management the resolution of which had important results in terms of the personnel comprising the landed class. The case of the county's leading family, the Mathews of Thomastown, illustrates the dire consequences which could ensue from debt accumulation and marriage settlements. Under the will of George Mathew (d. 1760), the Thomastown and Thurles estates, then valued at £8,000 annually, came to Thomas Mathew of Annfield for life with remainder to his son Francis.[126] Particular provisions in the will allowed the inheritor to charge the estate with a jointure of £600 and portions totalling £6,000; to make leases of three lives and 41 years; and to pay legacies amounting to £9,000. In due course Thomas Mathew inherited the Thurles estate (as tenant in tail by a settlement of 1713), and the Thomastown estate (as tenant for life under George Mathew's will of 1759). At that stage the estate was said to be 'incumbered to a very great amount', due to the debts of a previous generation and because of charges provided for in the will of 1759.[127]

Two settlements of 1765 added to the financial burden on the estate. One made previous to the marriage of Francis Mathew to Ellis Smyth, in consideration of her portion of £10,000, charged a

[125] D. Marnane, *Land and violence: A history of West Tipperary from 1660* (Tipperary, 1985), 25; A. P. W. Malcomson, *The pursuit of the heiress: Aristocratic marriage in Ireland 1750–1820* (Belfast, 1982), 3–4, 39, 41.
[126] All details from *An act for vesting in trustees, passim.*
[127] Ibid. 19.

jointure of £1,000 and £8,000 as provision for younger children on the Thurles and Thomastown estates. By a second settlement Thomas Mathew made over to trustees the mansion-house and lands of Thurles as a maintenance for his son Francis following his marriage. In accordance with the will of 1759, Francis Mathew agreed to charge the lands with £600 part jointure and £6,000 for portions. In addition both agreed to apply for an act of parliament to allow Francis to charge the lands with a further annuity of £400 and £2,000 for portions, so that the entire arrangement would conform with the sums agreed on in his own marriage settlement.[128] This settlement had disastrous consequences because by it Thomas Mathew was deemed to have curtailed his powers as tenant in tail of the Thurles estate under the 1713 settlement. As a result he was precluded from raising any money on the estate by way of sale or mortgage to satisfy debts. Creditors sought the satisfaction of their claims, the court of chancery appointed receivers, and by their mismanagement the rents were depleted.

In accordance with the settlement of 1765 an act of parliament was duly applied for in 1772 seeking to have provision made for the enlarged jointure and portions, and for the payment of debts.[129] By 1780, when the act was finally obtained, debts on the estate stood at £70,000 made up of a principal of £40,504, interest payments of £19,824, and legal costs of £9,672. The principal creditors were Michael Aylmer and Justin McCarthy. By this date the estate was producing a rental of £12,600 but this was likely, in consequence of leases falling in, to rise to £20,000 annually. Nevertheless the arrears of principal, mounting interest payments, and the cost of law suits were deemed to be a great drain on the estate following its inheritance by Francis Mathew after his father's death in 1777. These difficulties were compounded because Francis Mathew had to make provision for his own offspring, three sons and two daughters, to the amount of £20,000 and because his wife's jointure was enlarged to £1,500. The 1780 act placed the Mathew estate in the hands of trustees.[130]

In the ensuing years the trustees proceeded to dispose of lands and by 1810 most of the debts were discharged. However by that date a separate debt amounting to £60,000 had arisen, largely from judgment debts and from personal borrowing indulged in by

[128] RD, 240/521/156651. [129] *Comms. Jnl. (Ire.)*, viii. pt. 1, 481–2.
[130] *An act for vesting in trustees*, 26–8.

Francis Mathew, first earl of Llandaff, and his two sons Francis James, second earl and Montague Mathew.[131] They borrowed from neighbours like Thomas Lanigan (£5,400), from head-tenants notably James Scully (£12,000), and from the Dublin financier David La Touche (£2,400 in 1792).[132] These sums constituted additional claims on the estate and their satisfaction resulted in a number of outright sales. In the period 1809–14 sales on the Thomastown estate raised £148,950 of which £97,750 was applied to debts.[133] The principal purchasers were Nicholas Maher (£26,000), Thomas Scott, second earl of Clonmell (£34,000), William Plunkett (£22,750), Daniel Kinahan (£23,000), Thomas Ryan (£8,000), Laurence Waldron (£25,000), and James Scully (£33,200).[134] Maher and Scully were existing tenants on the estate who bought out their interest and became landowners in their own right. Scott excepted, all the major purchasers were Catholics showing that a substantial proportion of the wealth generated in the late eighteenth century was in their hands. Scully, one of the county's leading Catholics, was very wealthy and had established his own bank in Tipperary in 1802.[135]

A neighbouring family which experienced indebtedness and sale at this time also was Meade, earls of Clanwilliam. In 1765 on the marriage of Sir John Meade to Theodosia Magill, heiress to a Co. Down estate, the settlement made provision for her jointure of £3,500 (£2,500 of which was chargeable on the Tipperary estate), and a sum for younger children of £30,000 (£20,000 on the Tipperary estate).[136] Thus about two-thirds of the charge was placed on the Tipperary estate. Three factors made this charge untenable subsequently. First, the large progeny resulting from the marriage; secondly, the heavy personal debts incurred by Sir John Meade; and thirdly, income from the estate was insufficient to satisfy the debts.

The marriage issue of five sons and five daughters made the provisions of the 1765 settlement seem inadequate, indeed disastrous. More seriously by 1787 debts had, through lavish

---

[131] D. Scully to J. Scully, 16 Aug. 1814 (NLI, MS 27,488 (iv); MS 27,494 (i)).
[132] Lanigan: NA, M5331; Scully: MS 11,422, bonds of 1 Oct. 1802, 13 Aug. 1814; La Touche: NA, M5302, 25.   [133] NLI, MS 27,494 (i).
[134] Ibid.; RD, 682/121/469267, 694/333/476621.
[135] NLI, MSS 27,488 (iii, iv), 27,494 (i), 27,571, 451–2.
[136] *An act for the sale of the estates of the Rt. Hon. John, earl of Clanwilliam.* What follows is based on this source, unless indicated otherwise.

spending by the earl of Clanwilliam (as he became in 1766), reached £53,807 (exclusive of interest) plus a mortgage of £8,000 on the Tipperary estate and £10,328 in bills and notes, making in all £72,135. Although the debt from bills and notes was settled in annuities of £5,525 to the creditors out of the estate, clearly the earl's income of £14,000 in 1775 was inadequate to satisfy the total debt and to cater for the family charges. In consequence, in 1787 it was agreed that part of the earl's estate in Cork and Kilkenny (remaindered on the eldest son under the 1765 settlement), be sold or mortgaged to pay off the debts. The Tipperary estate was to remain charged with the £20,000 and £2,500.[137] The marriages soon after of two daughters, Ann and Catherine Meade, to Lord Powerscourt and John Whaley respectively, required the payment of portions of £4,000 raised on the Cork and Kilkenny estates, leaving Richard the eldest son without a sufficient maintenance. To rectify this in 1788 Richard was granted a maintenance of £1,700 charged on the Tipperary and Down estates.[138]

By 1791, debts including the Tipperary mortgage stood at £31,327 and in that year the earl consented to forgo his life interest in the estate in return for £1,000 annually with a similar amount for his wife out of the Down estate. However, debt continued to grow to £46,251 in 1795, and the choice lay between satisfying this and paying the portions of younger children. It was agreed that the former option should take precedence, the sums to be raised by sale of the Tipperary estate. As a prelude to this it was necessary to resettle the estate by a transfer of the jointure and portions on to the Down estate and for this purpose an act of parliament was applied for and obtained in 1795. Already a trustee was appointed in 1793 for the disposal of the Tipperary lands of 4,870 acres centring on Golden with head rents of £3,341.[139] This trusteeship facilitated the disposal of the estate, while the act of parliament provided for the transfer of encumbrances.

Although the sales were initiated in 1793 they were not finalized until after 1805. Of the fifteen head-tenants on the estate the most substantial were the McCarthys who held the 1,000-acre Spring-house lands at a head rent of £1,000 and which gave a profit rent of £500 in 1793, £1,000 in 1805.[140] The McCarthys purchased the fee

[137] RD, 388/173/25741.   [138] RD, 395/535/262709.
[139] RD, 457/341/300308; *CG*, 27–31 July 1793; cf. Malcomson, *Pursuit*, 22, 24.
[140] *CG*, 27–31 July 1793; NA, M2197.

simple for £18,000.[141] Another large Catholic head-tenant on the estate was James Scully who held 291 acres in all with a head rent of £172, profit rent of over £300.[142] Scully laid out at least £19,380 in purchases on the Clanwilliam estate in 1806 and 1808, effectively buying out his own interest and that of others.[143] The Meade estate in Tipperary, created essentially out of the Ormond estate, passed by virtue of debt accumulation and the contingencies of family settlement into the ownership of some leading Catholic head-tenants like McCarthy and Scully, thereby duplicating the contemporaneous trend on the adjoining Mathew estate. In contrast to these transfers in the south, landownership in the northern part of the county continued to be stable. On the whole the main changes in landownership in the late eighteenth century were concentrated in the south of the county, principally in the baronies of Clanwilliam and Middlethird revolving around the Mathew and Meade sales.

The majority of landed families were able to manage their debts without incurring insolvency. For instance, between 1755 and 1775 Sir Thomas Maude accumulated debts of £27,000 which passed to his brother Cornwallis Maude, Viscount Hawarden (d. 1803), after 1777.[144] A successful marriage by Thomas Ralph, second Viscount (d. 1807) to the daughter of the archbishop of Cashel (later earl of Normanton) may have served to reduce debt, for the Hawarden estate survived intact to be one of the largest in the county in the nineteenth century.[145] In the 1770s also the level of debt on the Butler (Cahir) estate stood at £51,000 exclusive of 5 per cent interest, which had mounted since 1750 through heavy borrowing from London merchants.[146] This degree of debt probably precipitated a general releasing of the estate between 1779 and 1788 which brought in immediate and badly needed cash. Debt continued to be a feature of the estate subsequently, though a fortuitous marriage in 1834 brought in £200,000 which was applied to debts which then stood at between £250,000 and £300,000.[147] In the Maude and Cahir cases opportune marriages

[141] RD, 481/8/300269.   [142] NA, M2197.
[143] NLI, MS 27,571, 340, 368; J. Scully to D. Scully, 4 Feb. [18]09, S. Alleyn to [D.] Scully [1809] (NLI, MS 27,485 (34)).
[144] RD, 176/117/118008, 176/537/119855, 186/450/125405, 276/297/177346, 282/217/182849, 312/57/207330.   [145] Marnane, *Land and violence*, 173.
[146] RD, 138/580/96084, 178/161/118229, 190/569/128268, 312/524/210716.
[147] Malcomson, *Pursuit*, 9, 21.

played a prominent role in reducing debt thereby avoiding loss of landed estate. At a lesser level good financial management appears to have been the general norm. For instance, John Bayly of Ballynaclough near Nenagh incurred judgment debts of £41,000 between 1745 and 1788, but satisfied £30,000 of that amount in the same period leaving only £11,000 outstanding by the 1790s.[148] A similar pattern of successful financial management can be documented in the case of the Ryans of Inch.[149]

So far income, expenditure, and debt have been considered together with the circumstances and influences determining changes in the pattern of landownership. A number of additional questions must now be addressed so far as marriage alliances are concerned, since they constitute the second method whereby changes in the landed class occurred. First, to what extent was marriage a main cause making for the enlargement of estates? Secondly, what is the pattern of inheritance achieved through less conventional methods?

It was through marriages to heiresses that estates were extended. The outstanding example of this at the outset of the century is the marriage in 1702 of Henry Prittie of Kilboy to Elizabeth daughter and heiress to James Harrison of Cloghjordan (see Fig. 2). This alliance added to the sizeable Prittie estate of 3,600 acres a further 900 acres centring on Cloghjordan which had the advantage of being in the same region as the home estate. The joining of the estates brought the Prittie family important political benefits, since by the extension of its landed interest it gained in freeholder strength in an area where rural Protestants were more numerous than elsewhere in the county. In this way the displacement of one landed family consolidated the interest of another and enhanced its political prospects, which for the Pritties were largely built on a family interest. In the next two generations each of the heirs to the Prittie estate married heiresses: Deborah Bayly in 1736 and Catherine Sadlier in 1766, thereby further consolidating the family's interest, landed and political.

At the other end of the county a marriage in mid-century to an heiress also had important consequences for landed society and

[148] Bayly papers, list of judgment debts against J. Bayly in the Exchequer 1745–88, endorsed by Lord Earlsfort, 10 Mar. 788.
[149] Power, 'Tipperary', 60–1.

politics. In 1751 John Hely, an ambitious barrister of modest origins from Co. Cork, married Christian Nickson, niece and heiress of Richard Hutchinson of Knocklofty near Clonmel.[150] The marriage was costly for Hely in that he agreed to pay off Hutchinson's debts of £11,000, received no portion and only a reversionary interest in the estate of over 3,000 acres.[151] However, in return for adopting the name Hutchinson the estate was to devolve on him and his heirs and he had power to charge it with £2,000 for younger children. In the process Hely obtained a rural estate and a foothold in the landed class. In this case the presence of an heiress served to introduce a new person into county society who was later to advance the prestige of the family, for it achieved an earldom (1800), was primarily responsible for carrying the act of union in Tipperary, and was also distinguished for its support of Catholic relief.

Instances of inheritance through co-heiresses are few, but the outstanding case is that of the estate of Hugh Smith, son of the original grantee Erasmus Smith. This was an estate distinct from that of the Erasmus Smith Schools, though situated in the same district. With no male heirs the estate devolved on his two daughters, Dorothy and Lucy, who married respectively Hon. John Barry, youngest son of the fourth earl of Barrymore, and James Stanley, Lord Strange, their son inheriting the title earl of Derby.[152] Both families were substantial landowners in Cheshire and Lancashire already and both adopted the patronymic Smith. In 1755 a division of the Tipperary estate was agreed on with Smith-Barry obtaining 4,908 acres and Stanley 6,108 acres in Clanwilliam and Middlethird.[153] In this way the large estate of an absentee was partitioned and absorbed into the larger estates of the earls of Barrymore and Derby by virtue of the failure of male heirs and descent through co-heiresses. This increase in absenteeism was not necessarily detrimental for in the Derby case at least, an improvement in the management of the Tipperary estate ensued.

There were less conventional methods by which progress into and within the county's landed class was attained. The underhand

[150] TCD, Donoughmore, B1/13; GO, MS 573, 16.
[151] Ibid.; Malcomson, *Pursuit*, 30–1.
[152] Derby papers (Preston), DDK, 1703/6.
[153] Cheshire RO (Chester), Smith-Barry papers, DCN, 1984/25/9.

methods adopted by John Scott, solicitor (1774) and later attorney-general (1777), involved an opportunist marriage to the daughter of Thomas Mathew and the appropriation of certain leasehold interests.[154] As a younger son of Thomas Scott of Mohubber (an estate of 1,400 acres), John Scott advanced in the legal profession, being called to the Irish bar in 1765.[155] Initially on friendly terms with Thomas Mathew, Scott intruded himself as a trustee for lands which Mathew had settled on his mistress and in 1771 obtained its possession.[156] Secondly, Scott in 1768 married Catherine Marianne Roe, widow of Philip Roe (d. 1767) and daughter of Thomas Mathew, and eventually laid claim to monies in right of his wife following her death in 1771.[157] By these methods Scott established himself by 1778 in a new mansion-house at Dovehill between Carrick and Clonmel; in 1784 he was created baron Earlsfort and in 1789 viscount Clonmell; and his income rose from £15,000 in 1787 to £20,000 in 1799.[158]

These details reveal how advancement could be gained through legal skill, astuteness, opportune marriage, and calculation (a personal trait espoused in Scott's private diary),[159] leading to landed estate, the peerage, and social eminence. It shows that the landed class of the county was fluid allowing a younger son with talent and ambition to achieve advancement. Scott is perhaps the best exponent of those whom a correspondent of James Hutchinson of Timoney referred to in 1759 as 'people who fish for estates'.[160] The appropriation of the traditionally inalienable See estate of the archbishop of Cashel by Charles Agar, archbishop (1779–1802) to form part of his private estate as earl of Normanton, must also be viewed as a manifestation of this tendency.[161]

Two outstanding cases exist to indicate that abduction could

[154] NLI, Byrne papers, documents entitled 'Memorandum of the Mathews', and 'The case of Edward Byrne esq. and Mary Ann Byrne his wife'; Fitzpatrick, *Union*, 156–83.

[155] F. E. Ball, *The judges in Ireland 1221–1921* (1926), ii. 222.

[156] Fitzpatrick, *Union*, 166.

[157] Ibid. 164; NLI, Byrne papers, 'Memorandum' and 'Case'.

[158] G. Taylor and A. Skinner, *Maps of the roads of Ireland surveyed 1777* (Dublin and London, 1778; repr. Shannon, 1969), 120; *DNB*, xvii. 981–3; Fitzpatrick, *Union*, 14.

[159] J. Scott, *Private diary of John Scott, Lord Earlsfort* (n.p., n.d.)

[160] J. Pilkington to J. Hutchinson, 13 Nov. 1759 (NLI, MS 8924/4).

[161] A. P. W. Malcomson, *John Foster: The politics of the Anglo-Irish ascendancy* (Oxford, 1978), 284 n.

serve as a means of social advancement. The successful abduction by a large middleman, Henry Grady, of Susanna Grove on his second attempt at Tipperary in 1756 brought him significant benefits in the form of leasehold interests in town property in Tipperary and title to lands in Clanwilliam which he used to pay off debts on his Limerick property.[162] By 1775 his income was £7,000, the fourth largest of those landlords listed for that year.[163] Benefits of a greater magnitude accrued to Samuel Phillips as a result of abducting his young cousin Mary Max, an heiress, in 1777. Already well-endowed by her father, she became more so on the death of her brothers in 1775 and 1777 when she became entitled to a large property midway between Cashel and Thurles estimated to be worth £30,000–£40,000.[164] In August 1777 Phillips abducted her and in the course of time he came to acquire a large property in her right. A survey of 1798 shows this property at Gaile to contain 880 acres.[165] So important an addition did this represent that in the next generation the Phillipses moved from their Co. Kilkenny base to make Gaile their main residence.

3. Catholic Proprietorship

Catholic proprietors experienced particular problems in the eighteenth century deriving from political and social exclusion sanctioned by penal legislation. Yet it is evident that by virtue of a series of devices and fortuitous circumstances—single male heirs, legal protection through assignment of estates, preferential leasing arrangements, and conversion—Catholics survived in sufficient numbers to constitute an important segment of the landed class at the close of the century. Indicative of this is the number of Catholics of status who subscribed to the oath of allegiance in 1775 being 133 in all, made up of 23 esquires, 64 gentlemen, and 46

---

[162] NA, proclamation of 30 Mar. 1753; J. Brady, *Catholics and Catholicism in the eighteenth-century press* (Maynooth, 1965), 83, 85; Marnane, *Land and violence*, 26–7; J. A. Froude, *The English in Ireland in the eighteenth century* (London, 1872–3), i. 419–21; *DG*, 8–12, 15–19, 26–9 June, 9–13 Nov. 1756; RD, 219/358/144037, 307/15/202752, 310/93/205644, 321/366/216825.

[163] *AH*, 12 (1943), 143.

[164] Phillips papers: 'Will of John Max, Killough, Co. Tipperary, 13 Aug. 1769'; 'Case for the opinion of the Attorney-General, John Scott, 28 Dec. 1777'.

[165] NLI, MS 8797 (7).

farmers; between 1778–91 Catholic landed oath subscribers numbered 220 comprising 1 peer, 12 esquires, 17 gentlemen, and 190 farmers; and between 1793–6 it was 364 divided between 12 esquires, 40 gentlemen, and 312 farmers.[166] These figures show that Catholics formed a significant group within the county's landed class, and their participation is further enlarged if landed converts, who totalled 94 in 1751–90 (59 gentlemen, 21 esquires, 11 farmers, 3 peers/peeresses), are included.[167] In 1807 it was estimated that, of the 6,500 freeholders in the county, 5,500 or 84 per cent were Catholics showing that beneath the level of gentleman the base of the Catholic landed class was wide.[168] The experience of landed Catholics can be treated under three headings: owners in fee, converts, and head-tenants.

A substantial Catholic interest, including Lord Cahir and Everard, survived from the Williamite wars. Yet the number of such families who remained Catholic right through the century was few. Though Everard became a nominal Protestant and the Dunboyne Butlers were reduced as a result of the 1729 sale and later converted, the Butlers of Cahir remained Catholic without being obliged to convert, forfeit their estate, or subdivide their estate as required by the penal laws. Neither does the family appear to have fallen victim to hostile discovery proceedings.

Theobald Butler, fifth Lord Cahir, had issue a single male heir who inherited before 1703 (see Fig. 3). The provisions in the penal laws on inheritance did not therefore affect him. The problems of the family did not become acute until after his death in 1744, when by law the estate (of 10,000 acres) should have been divided among his five surviving sons. Apparently to avoid that eventuality the estate was then vested in trustees and subsequently mortgaged at various times in the 1750s, with the proviso that it was not to revert to the owner until the borrowed money was repaid.[169] These mortgages were still outstanding in the 1770s when the stipulation regarding repayment was renewed.[170] Thus

---

[166] NA, Catholic qualification rolls, 1778–91, 1793–7; *Comms. Jnl. (Ire.)*, xv. pt. 1, p. clxxxv; *Fifty-ninth report of the deputy keeper, Public Record Office* (Dublin, 1956).

[167] NA, Calendar of convert rolls, i. 1703–89, ii. 1789–1838; Lodge MS, 'Alphabetical list of converts'; BL, Egerton MS 77; Brady, *Press*.

[168] *Southern Reporter* (Cork), 6 June 1807.

[169] RD, 138/570/96083, 138/581/96084, 180/69/119543, 190/569/128268; *WM*, 11 May 1811. [170] RD, 312/515/210715–6, 365/61/243128, 363/88/243129.

the devices of trusteeship and the vesting of the legal estate in the mortgagee were used to ensure continuity of ownership. Additionally the outbreak of war with France and a renewed interest by the Irish parliament in framing anti-Catholic laws in 1756, stimulated the family into anticipating possible legal proceedings over the inheritance and their participation in the French service, by entering into collusive discovery arrangements.[171]

James Butler became *de facto* seventh Lord Cahir, and was an absentee. In the mid-1770s he returned briefly to reside in Tipperary. By the time he died in 1788 the penal restrictions on Catholic inheritance were repealed by the act of 1778, but ironically despite their repeal the estate passed into Protestant hands in 1788. James died without issue, his brothers were either dead or unmarried, and his sisters were ineligible. Since the two brothers then living were in the church, the estate devolved on the son of a relation, Richard Butler of Fethard, who was or became a Protestant, tenth Lord Cahir and later first earl of Glengall.[172] Thus, having survived the vicissitudes of inheritance for half a century from 1744, the estate came to a Protestant by choice rather than compulsion.

The experience of more modest Catholic landowners in fee can be outlined with reference to the Ryans of Inch. Following the death of his father Daniel in 1692, John Ryan inherited lands in Inch parish which had been purchased and assembled since 1668.[173] These were added to by further purchases in 1703 making the entire estate into a formidable block of 3,000 acres.[174] Having succeeded before 1700 John Ryan was unaffected by the penal legislation on succession, and on his death in 1723 he left a single male heir, Daniel. Though the latter's death in 1767 received notice in the press, and though he left three sons (John, George, and Denis—the two last being in foreign parts), no partition of the estate occurred nor is there any evidence of discovery proceedings.[175] At this point the outcome becomes similar to that of the

---

[171] RD, 185/98/122373, 187/480/126091.

[172] Mount Melleray: Burke MS, will of James, Lord Cahir, 31 Aug. 1784, with codicils (copy). For a different account of the succession of Richard, tenth Lord, see D. Herbert, *Retrospections 1770–1806* (London, 1929), ii. 308–9.

[173] Ryan papers, 'Sketch of title to the estate of Inch, May 1821'; M. Callanan, *Records of four Tipperary septs* (Dublin, 1938), 105; will of Daniel Ryan, 22 Apr. 1692 (NLI, Mic.P.5489).   [174] Callanan, *Records*, 105.

[175] *FLJ*, 24–8 Oct 1767; will of D. Ryan, 22 Aug. 1757 (NLI, Mic.P.5489).

Cahir Butlers in that John Ryan died without issue in 1778 passing on the inheritance to his brothers. Possible acrimony would have ensued had a bill under the discovery clause filed by Denis (a younger brother who returned from military service in Austria for the purpose) for a moiety of the estate been proceeded with. However, a compromise was reached whereby George Ryan, who returned from South America to inherit, agreed to pay Denis an annuity of £100 for life in return for the withdrawal of the bill.[176] Thus a pattern of succession before 1700, inheritance by a single male heir in 1723, and an agreed succession in the 1770s characterized the fortunes of the Ryans. The fortuitous circumstances which favoured the survival of the Butlers of Cahir and the Ryans, both representatives of different strata of Catholic landownership, were first, inheritance before enactment of the penal laws in the first decade of the century; secondly, succession in the next generation by a single male heir; and thirdly, continuity of ownership up to *c.*1780 by stratagem (Cahir) and good fortune (Ryan), after which the legal bars on succession were removed.

Both families had overseas connections in the military and commercial spheres, indicating that this was an important component in Catholic lifestyle. The movement of Catholic sons into officerships on the Continent established itself as a distinct movement from the late seventeenth century, and Tipperary was prominent in this. The genealogies of Tipperary Catholic families show that many younger sons went into continental military service. Thomas Butler, second son of Thomas, eighth Lord Cahir, was sent at 16 years in 1737 to France to be an officer in the French army; in a year he was made a second lieutenant in Dillon's regiment of foot and was later promoted to the rank of captain in Lally's foot, and he fought at the battle of Fontenoy.[177] The Daltons of Grenanstown near Nenagh had a distinguished military service in the Austrian and German armies. Peter Dalton received the title of count from the German emperor. While they were absent from Ireland their landed interests appear to have been attended to by the Pritties of Kilboy. In 1796 Dalton could write to Prittie of that 'mutual friendship that has so long existed between

[176] NA, M5306, 6–7; W. Woulfe to G. Ryan, 28 Dec. 1779 (Ryan papers).
[177] PRO, SPI, 63/412/15–15ᵛ.

our families'.[178] In the commercial area there were strong overseas links between Catholic landed families and their overseas relations, a nexus which centred on the port of Waterford through its commercial contacts with France and Spain. The McCarthys, for instance, were one of the largest mercantile interests in Bordeaux, and the Ryans of Inch in Spain. These overseas military and commercial activities provided career outlets for younger sons of Catholics of gentry status, thereby facilitating inheritance by a single heir to the home estate.

The fact that one can document only two cases of Catholic owners in fee in such detail signifies perhaps their exceptionality. More representative of the fate of Catholics in fee was the resort to conversion as a device for keeping estates in their ownership. The estimated total number of converts for the county in the period 1705–1810 is less than 600, with the number for the early part of the century (1705–50) low at 188, 337 for the period 1751–78, and only 48 for the years 1779–1810 following the relaxation of the penal laws. While in the majority of cases the social or occupational status of those converting is not specified, in cases where it is specified the number of persons of landed status converting between 1705 and 1750 was 72, consisting of 53 gentlemen, 11 esquires, and 8 farmers. There was a sharp rise in the number of converts after mid-century, and the number of landed converts in 1751–90 was 94. So that between 1705 and 1790 the number of landed converts was in excess of 160 individuals, though a small minority of these were persons who converted twice, particularly in the 1760s.[179]

The position and experience of the Mathew family is crucial. How the estate descended in the period up to 1760 can be demarcated by four key dates: 1713, 1736, 1738, 1760. The Thurles branch, in contrast to that at Annfield, was fortunate in having a succession of three single male heirs following the death of Theobald Mathew of Thurles in 1699 (Fig. 1(b)). There is in

---

[178] Dalton to Prittie, 6 Jan. 1796 (NLI, Dunalley papers PC, 870, correspondence file 1790–1811).

[179] Based on evidence in NA, calendar of convert rolls, i. 1703–89, ii. 1789–1838; Lodge MS, alphabetical list of converts; BL, Egerton MS 77; E. O'Byrne, *The convert rolls* (Dublin, 1981) from which references to individual converts throughout are taken. See also T. P. Power, 'Converts', in T. P. Power and K. Whelan (eds.), *Endurance and emergence: Catholics in Ireland in the eighteenth century* (Dublin, 1990), 101–27.

consequence no pattern of conversion in this branch. The succession was provided for by a settlement of 1713 whereby, in the event of the failure of heirs male in the Thurles line, the estate was to go to the Annfield and Thomastown branches success-ively.[180] In 1738 the Thurles and Thomastown estates were joined because of the failure of direct heirs to the latter, and thereafter continued as the inheritance of one person until 1760. The heir to this enlarged estate was George Mathew of Thurles who converted in 1740 in order to succeed to the Thurles and no doubt to the Thomastown property which he later inherited.[181] An earlier conversion in 1702 by the heir to the Thomastown estate ensured his inheritance and that procedure at gavelkind (or an equal division of the property) among two brothers was avoided.

The Annfield branch displays a different experience (Fig. 1(c)). On the death of Thomas Mathew in 1714 the Annfield fee simple estate should by law have been divided between his three sons. But the eldest son, Theobald, inherited with a residue of the personal estate going to two younger sons.[182] There is no evidence that Theobald converted to mitigate any possible threat of disinheritance or discovery. On the marriage of his eldest son, Thomas Mathew, in 1736 a settlement was entered into whereby Theobald agreed on his death to leave Thomas £20,000 should the estate not descend to him solely, and bonds to this amount were executed at the same time to secure its future payment, but Thomas did not join in these bonds.[183]

On Theobald's death in 1745 the estate descended to Thomas Mathew and neither of his three brothers initiated proceedings to convert the estate into gavelkind.[184] All the members of the Annfield branch were still Catholic at this stage. Thomas Mathew, however, converted in 1755. This event was opportune for on the failure of heirs male of George Mathew of Thurles and Thomas-town on his death in 1760, and by a clause in his will of 1759, and in accordance with the settlement of 1713, Thomas Mathew became the sole heir to the whole estate which for the first time was

---

[180] RD, 37/454/23458.

[181] NLI, Reports on private collections no. 109, p. 1096.

[182] Will of Thomas Mathew, Annfield, 13 Nov. 1714 (NLI, Mic. P.4546).

[183] NLI, Byrne papers, 'Memorandum on the Mathews', *sub* the recited deeds, 5 July 1736; Reports on private collections, no. 109, p. 1100.

[184] NLI, Byrne papers, 'The case of Edward Byrne and Mary Byrne his wife'.

consolidated under the ownership of a single individual.[185] This was an event of major significance in the evolution of landed interests in the county. It showed that conversion rather than being a stage in the decline of families could, in combination with the devices of trusteeship and failure of heirs, act to consolidate a Catholic interest.

After the Mathews probably the most significant conversion before 1760 was that of John Butler of Kilcash in 1739. Thomas Butler of Kilcash, a colonel in the Jacobite army and a leading Catholic, died in 1738 when the estate came to his son John as single male heir.[186] Given this situation it is initially surprising to find that he converted in 1739.[187] It becomes comprehensible because in addition to inheriting the Kilcash estate John Butler was also heir apparent to the earl of Arran on whom, as already noted, devolved the residue Ormond estate and title. This point was stressed in the public notices of his conversion.[188] The rights of remainder to the Arran/Ormond estate had already been applied for by the Kilcash branch and confirmed.[189] Arran died in 1758 following which John Butler experienced an addition to his estate and became *de jure* fifteenth earl of Ormond, though he never assumed the title. Despite this new prominence problems emerged in the 1760s. John Butler was in his dotage and insane and left no heir on his death in 1766.[190] Instead he was succeeded by his first cousin Walter Butler of Garryricken, Co. Kilkenny whose only son, John, converted in 1764, inherited, married into the Wandesford family, and in 1791 had the Ormond title restored and formally recognized.[191] So while problems of succession could be overcome in the short term by conversion, ultimate descent in the Kilcash branch in the direct line became frustrated due to more human factors. In the process there was a loss of one of the leading Catholic families and also the passage of ownership to a Butler branch outside the county. Conversion can also be detailed for

---

[185] NA, Betham's genealogical abstracts of prerogative wills, 47, pp. 39–40.

[186] NLI, Ormond papers, bundle 1729–30, will of Thomas Butler, 7 Oct 1730 (and codicil, 7 Nov. 1730).

[187] Ibid., bundle 1743–7, certified copy of the conformity (dated 23 Dec. 1747) of John Butler, 26 July 1739.   [188] Brady, *Press*, 60.

[189] *The case of Thomas Butler of Kilcash esq., John Butler of Garryricken esq., and James Butler of Kilveleagher esq.* [c. 1720] (TCD, 25 bb 22, no. 21).

[190] RD, 239/88/156267.

[191] Lord Dunboyne, *Butler family history* (3rd. edn., n.p., 1972), 17.

other major families like Morris (motivated out of apparent conviction), Mandeville (representing one element in the confused affairs of that family throughout the century), Butler (Dunboyne) (culminating in the decision of John Butler, Catholic bishop of Cork, to convert in 1787 thereby ensuring the continuance of the title), and Fogarty.

These case-histories of the part played by conversion in the descent of estates exemplify the adoption of specific strategies to ensure continuity in the ownership and descent of ancestral estates. Conversion, at this level, was a carefully decided strategy, and not one lightly undertaken. Its undertaking did not necessarily imply that the individuals concerned identified with the ethos of protestantism particularly as it expressed itself on political issues. Conversion, as a requirement devised by the Anglican state at the outset of the century to curb Catholic inheritance, was successfully adapted to the needs of individual Catholic families and had unforeseen results for the composition and outlook of the landed class.

A numerous group of Catholic gentry existed at the level of head-tenant. The majority of those of esquire and gentleman rank who subscribed to the oath of allegiance in 1775 were in this category.[192] Taking that year as a bench-mark the spatial spread shows a concentration of large Catholic tenants in the south of the county in a line stretching from south of Cahir to north of Cashel; and a second grouping is found in a broad stretch of countryside stretching northward from a line linking Carrick and Clonmel. Over much of this region large Catholic head-tenants were the dominant social and proprietorial group. McCarthy of Springhouse and Keating of Garranlea held multi-thousand acre holdings which brought them to the notice of Young.[193] Catholics like Keating of Knockagh and Nagle of Garnvella dominated the head-tenantry on the vast Butler (Cahir) estate, and the bulk of the remainder were also Catholic. Others of prominence in the region were Doherty, Butler (Keylong), Meagher, Kearney, Scully, Lalor, Long, and Prendergast. They were former landowners such as Keating, Kearney, and Meagher whose ancestors had been expropriated in the seventeenth century but who had maintained

---

[192] *Fifty ninth report*, 52–63.   [193] Young, *Tour*, i. 388–91.

their position by securing advantageous leases. Or they were new families like McCarthy, Nagle, and Scully who had come into the region in the late seventeenth and early eighteenth centuries and who established themselves as large head-tenants. Some like McCarthy and Scully were to progress to being landowners in fee, but even before this they had a standing in the landed class.

In contrast substantial Catholic head-tenants were few in the northern part of the county. A return of Catholic tenants in the half-barony of Ikerrin in 1750 shows only eight proprietorial units of over 100 acres in size.[194] Even they were minute compared to the multi-townland units held by their counterparts in the south. There were no Catholics with holdings in excess of 100 acres in the barony of Kilnamanagh in 1765 and only four with acreages between 50 and 100 acres.[195] Catholics, however, were numerous at the strong farmer level (i.e. with holdings between 10 and 50 acres), with 93 (or about one-quarter of the total) in the Ikerrin and 89 (or half) in the Kilnamanagh returns. This was also true of other areas as the large and increasing number of farmers who subscribed to the oaths shows: 46 in 1775, 190 in 1778–91, and 312 in 1793–6. This group was upwardly mobile due to the agricultural prosperity of the late eighteenth century.

4. Marriage Patterns

There are three distinct features in the marriage pattern of the landed class of the county in the eighteenth century: one, the cohesive system of marriage alliances established by the Pritties of Kilboy; two, the integrated pattern of Catholic marriages; and three, the isolation of the Mathews in the landed class.

In the course of the century the Pritties established direct marriage links with nine leading families: Sadlier, Harrison, Bunbury, Holmes, Otway, Head, Bayly, Meade, and Clutterbuck (see Fig. 2). Through them the Pritties became linked to about thirty other major and minor families in the north. These alliances formed the basis of a unified gentry and cohesive landed class in the northern part of the county. They served to elevate the Prittie

[194] NLI, MS 8913.   [195] NLI, MS 19,822, 273–85.

family to a leadership position based on family ties and, by extension, command of freeholders which were most numerous in the north before 1793. The marriage with the Meades, future earls of Clanwilliam, in 1736 was an important factor in extending this power base outside the north as it brought a further accretion of freeholder support from a large estate in the south, a dimension consolidated by links with the Armstrong, Bradshaw, Chadwick, and Smithwick families via the Sadlier marriage.

Traditionally the Pritties stood for the established order in church and state, a fact reflected in its marriage pattern. However the marriage in 1802 of Henry Prittie and Maria Trant, a family supportive of Catholic relief, was contemporaneous with a shift in the political stance of the family. The marriage of Francis A. Prittie to Elizabeth Ponsonby consolidated this for the Ponsonbys were already married into the O'Callaghans, Lords Lismore who also favoured relief. Given the position of prominence already established by the Pritties as political leaders of the northern gentry, this transition was a highly significant one for the landed class in the county as a whole.

Outside the north the pattern of marriages is more diffuse, characterized by the existence of a number of subgroupings. The Quakers, the Fennells for instance, exhibit a pattern of alliances with co-religionists from outside the county, and only after 1760 with a new generation and the profits of flour milling were Quakers propelled more evidently into the landed class.[196] The Presbyterians, headed by the Jacobs, were a closely knit group displaying a marriage pattern among a narrow range of families, notably Ashe, Sankey, and Latham.[197] Mercantile advancement into the landed class was progressive in the case of the Bartons who display a pattern of intermarriage with the Massys, but less so in the case of the Bagwells who clung to their origins in trade for two generations at least, shown by marriages to Bristol (1736) and Cork (1749) mercantile families.[198]

The pattern of marriage among major Catholic families was one of integration. All such major families were related. The Butler

---

[196] NLI, MS 10,947.
[197] A. H. Jacob and J. H. Glascott, *An historical and genealogical narrative of the families of Jacob* (n.p., 1825), 108–12.
[198] B. F. Barton, *Some account of the family of Barton* (Dublin, 1902), 60–76; GO, MS 139, 70–3.

(Cahir) family were married to members of the Everard, Mathew, and Morris families (see Fig. 3); Butler (Dunboyne) to Everard, Keating, and Butler (Kilmoyler); and Butler (Kilcash) to Mandeville, Mathew, and Tobin. A blurring of social distinctions is evident where Catholic landowners forged marriage ties with members of large middleman families. Thus the Mandevilles had alliances with the McCarthy and Nagle families, as had the Ryans of Inch with the former; while the Lalors were related to Doherty, Meagher, Phelan, and Scully all of whom were substantial middlemen. In terms of marriages to leading Catholic families outside the county the Butlers of Kilcash were to the fore with marriages to the Burkes, earls of Clanricarde, Kavanaghs of Borris, and Brownes of Kenmare. Indicative of the social position attained by the McCarthys is that they forged extra-county ties with important Catholic families: Tuite, Wyse, Shee, and Farrell. Catholics were married into some of the leading Catholic merchant families in the southern ports. The Scullys, for instance, had marriage connections with Wyse of Waterford, Arthur and Sexton of Limerick, and Sause of Carrick; the Ryans of Inch married into the Roches of Limerick and Woulfes of Carrick; and the Nagles were connected with the Longs of Waterford. These connections tied the Tipperary Catholic families into a far-flung network of mercantile links with Catholics overseas, especially through Waterford.[199]

A further index of the standing and status of Catholics was their ability to obtain official confirmation of their genealogies and grants of arms. Some junior families received such grants from the exiled Jacobite court in the early part of the century, and there were some privately sponsored attestations of gentry status as with O'Neill of Ballyneale in 1724.[200] More significant were those grants made by the Ulster King of Arms. Such grants are on record for Egan of Uskane (1715), Walsh of Tenerife late of Tipperary (1732), O'Kearney of Ballyduagh (1750, 1772), Purcell of Loughmoe (1757), McCarthy of Springhouse (1772), Ryan of Cadiz from Kilkeill, Co. Tipperary (1773), Fanning of Ballingarry

---

[199] For this genealogical information see Power, 'Tipperary', Genealogies III–VIII, X–XI.

[200] HMC, *Stuart* (1902), i. 146, 160, and 179, 214 for others; and certification of nobility of Timothy O'Neale, 10 July 1724 (NLI, Mic.P.5404); K. Whelan in *The Irish Review*, 7 (1989), 139–43.

(1775), and O'Dwyer of Spain formerly of Kilnamanagh (1776).[201] In 1785 the Daltons of Grenanstown were permitted to have their arms and title of count, obtained in the German service, for use in Ireland despite the reservation that they were Catholic.[202] In this way, despite their official exclusion from the normal paths to ennoblement and gentility, prominent Catholics did receive confirmation of their genealogies and grants of arms.

There were few significant cross-marriages between Catholic or convert families, and Protestants. In this respect it is striking how isolated the Mathew family was in the landed class despite a pattern of conversion among its leading members. Advantageous marriages to widows and heiresses played an important part in the advancement of the family in the course of the seventeenth century. Initially a marriage with the widow of viscount Thurles formed the basis on which the senior branch of the Mathews became established on the Thurles estate (see Fig. 1(a)). The standing of the family was further enhanced in the next generation by the marriage of George Mathew, a younger son and a half-brother to the first duke of Ormond, to the widow of Lord Cahir, and he was to establish a second branch of the family at Thomastown in 1671. However, the family's range of marriage partners was not confined to those of their own religion, rather it diversified into matches with representatives of the new interest (Foulke, Eaton, and Hume). Indeed marriages with the last two families brought substantial benefits to the Mathews. George Mathew of Thomastown's second marriage to Lady Ann Hume (widow of Sir Thomas Hume, a relation of Ormond's who was assigned the large estate of a departing Cromwellian grantee) brought him an estate worth £10,000 in 1680, the title to which he converted to his own use and that of his heirs, and used the money to make further land purchases.[203]

These were the most illustrious, beneficial, and in two cases controversial marriages entered into by the Mathews before c.1710. They brought advancement in terms of social standing, wealth, and land. Family connections also brought promotion to

---

[201] GO, MSS 103, p. 18; 160, pp. 158–60; 161, pp. 81–4; 162, pp. 48–9, 104–5; 165, pp. 173–9, 212–14, 269–72, 289–94.
[202] Rutland to Sydney, 29 Sept. 1785 (PRO, SPI 100/171/159–159ᵛ).
[203] Prendergast MS, vii. 583, 737–8.

positions of trust and office, and also favourable leasing arrangements.[204] After *c.*1710 the pattern of Mathew marriages continues
to exhibit social ambition. In the male line, the Thurles branch
made matches with the Catholic Butlers of Kilcash and the
Protestant Brownlows of Lurgan, Co. Armagh; the Annfield
branch married into the prestigious Shelley family, the local
Morris family, and the heiress of a wealthy Indian nabob named
Mathew (no relation); and the Thomastown line forged links with
the Butlers of Ballyragget and with the widow of the last earl of
Tyrone. The female side featured alliances with the local Catholic
Butlers of Kilveleagher and Ryans of Inch, Sir James Cotter and
the Nagles in Co. Cork, and the O'Haras of Annaghmore, Co.
Sligo.[205] Thus in its period of formation the Mathews exhibited a
mixed and controversial marriage pattern, in three directions:
first, links with the older Catholic families of Butler (Cahir),
Morris, and Butler (Kilcash); secondly, alliances with the New
English families of Hume, Foulke, Eaton; and thirdly, inter-
county marriages with prominent Catholic (Cotter, Butler (Ballyragget)) or convert (O'Hara) families, and others (Brownlow).

This pattern was more flexible in the seventeenth century than it
became in the eighteenth when, due to a more restricted religious
environment, the choice of marriage partners became more
confined. It is clear that the Mathews did not utilize their
conversion to forge marriage links with the leading Protestant
families of the county. Given that the Mathews were leading
landowners (especially after 1760 when the estate was unified
under one owner), the landed class outside the north, where the
Prittie diaspora dominated, was less unified by marriages. The
family was, therefore, isolated in the landed class not integrating
with its Protestant element through marriages, and therefore not
able to benefit socially and politically to the degree Prittie could.

[204] *CSPI 1647–60*, 375, 538–9, 802; Prendergast MS, ii. 879–95; *Correspondence
of Henry Hyde*, i. 468; NLI, D4813, D4838, D5027, D5061, D5070, D5071; NLI,
MS 2504, fo. 6; PRO, FEC, I, O.99, nos. 598, 602, 648, 662; NLI, Reports on
private collections, no. 109, pp. 1097, 1099; RD, 43/55/27352.
[205] T. Bartlett, 'The O'Haras of Annaghmore *c.*1600–*c.*1800: Survival and
revival', IESH 9 (1982), 34–52.

4

Land Tenure

With the onset of the Williamite wars the common experience of landowners was one of devastation, dislocation of economic life, and disruption to tenurial arrangements. In their wake land values slumped, rents were depressed, and reliable solvent tenants were in short supply. It was reported in January 1692 that 'by reason of ye late warr ye price of lands in generall throughout this Kingdom is much lessened at p[re]sent, but more especially in this county [Tipperary], being so near Lymerick ye seat of warr dureinge ye two campanes, so that it is impossible for the ten[a]nts whose leases are not yet expired to pay the old reserved rent.'[1] In addition to established armies, tories and rapparees caused much disruption in the county preventing many existing tenants from retaining possession of their lands, and discouraging prospective tenants from offering more than one-third or one-quarter of the former value of lands.[2] It was the nature of the response by landowners in Tipperary to the critical situation of the early 1690s which was to influence the kind of land-tenure system which was to prevail in the eighteenth century.

1. Tenurial Pattern, 1690–1750

The new leasing arrangements devised on the Ormond estate in the 1690s were formulated against a background of tenant impoverishment and landlord indebtedness. A large arrear of rents had arisen as a result of the wartime devastation, a situation compounded by a general scarcity of money. The total arrear for two years in early 1690 on the Tipperary estate was in excess of £9,780 out of a total for the entire estate in Ireland of under £17,300 recorded as unpaid in 1693.[3] These arrears arose from the fact that the few tenants,

---

[1] NLI, MS 5575, fo. 98ᵛ.   [2] BL, Add. MS 28,877, fo. 16ᵛ.
[3] Computed from NLI, MS 2561.

who remained on their lands during the course of hostilities after 1688, found on the cessation of war that they were impoverished. Other tenants who fled the county never returned and those who did found their lands lying waste. In 1691 it was reported of Ormond's estate that 'all my lord's lands but in the county of Tipperary are in [a] good condition'.[4] However, the characteristic feature of the estate in the immediate post-war period was that most tenants had abandoned their holdings, were unaccounted for, or were dead leaving a large arrear of rent and little assets or stock from which distress could be had. Given this situation, Ormond's lands were repossessed and retained in his hands until reset in 1692 either to relatives of former tenants, temporarily to under-tenants or, in the majority of cases, to others by the commission headed by Lord Longford.

The second factor contributing to a reformulation of policy on the Ormond estate in the 1690s was the indebtedness of the landlord. In May 1688 the debts of the first duke amounted to over £98,500 on which there were annual interest payments of £6,000.[5] So far as the estate is concerned, this indebtedness arose from the practice of the commissioners who managed the duke's affairs in the 1660s of granting leases to themselves and their relations from whom they were lax in demanding rent payments. The result was that a large arrear began to accumulate forcing the duke to borrow heavily. The death of the first duke in 1688, the succession of the second duke, and the intervention of the Williamite wars were events which signified a break in continuity in dealing with estate and overall debt. Only with the appointment of the commission under Longford in 1691 was the serious management of the estate renewed.

The commission had two objectives: to regulate the position of the existing tenants, and to procure new tenants for lands which had gone out of lease or become untenanted during the war. The existing tenants comprised those who had remained on their lands and those who returned having fled in 1688, and as a group they were clearly incapacitated and required the indulgence of the commission. The untenanted lands were more extensive than the tenanted and there was an urgent need to have them reset. A dual approach to the setting of lands was adopted. Outside the two

---

[4] BL, Add. MS 28,939, fo. 162.   [5] Ibid., fo. 67.

northwestern baronies of Lower and Upper Ormond, leases for 31 years or three lives at the old rent, with a recommendation for abatement for 4 or 5 years, were to be granted. In these two baronies, however, short yearly tenancies at the old rent were to be given which, it was calculated, would only be an interim arrangement which, once the tenants proved themselves able to meet rent payments, could later be revised to the benefit of the landlord.

The major part of the untenanted lands in Tipperary was reset by the commission in Kilkenny in March 1692. In general the rents agreed on with the new tenants, who were described as 'very substantial English and Protestant',[6] reached the old 1687 level and in some cases exceeded it. The offer of terms of 31 years or three lives, combined with abatements for a few years, attracted tenants to accept rents at at least the 1687 level.[7] In the difficult circumstances of the early 1690s the granting of long leases at the 1687 level of rent, cushioned by a system of short-term abatements, seemed the best possible arrangement from the landlord's viewpoint.

However satisfactory the arrangements made elsewhere, the special circumstances of the Ormond lands in the baronies of Upper and Lower Ormond made the outcome of dealings with tenants there less clear cut. These baronies had formed a frontier zone during the Williamite wars and in consequence had been particularly ravaged, and in the aftermath of war were waste and possessed few inhabitants. Two of the most valuable blocks of land to be set in the region were those centred on Roscrea and Nenagh. The former tenant to Roscrea failed to get his tenancy renewed despite pressing a claim of tenant right. Instead the farm was set for a term of three years at the old rent to John Carden, an outsider from Carlow, who was preferred because he was considered reliable, he could stock the land, and he undertook to settle forty Protestant sub-tenants on the farm.[8] A similar arrangement was arrived at with Carden's brother with respect to the lordship of Nenagh.[9] Of the remainder of Ormond lands in this region some farms were set for only one year. For Lackagh the only proposals came from 'Irish papists' whose offers were rejected by the commission, though the Egans were continued as

[6] BL, Add. MS 28,877, fo. 265. [7] Ibid., fos. 269–269[v].
[8] BL, Add. MS 28,878, fos. 21–2. [9] Ibid.

tenants on their former ancestral lands at Uskane.[10] On the whole, in the context of lands in the Ormond baronies, policy had to be guided by the consideration that tenanted lands at moderate rents were preferable to untenanted ones yielding no revenue.

In the event however, the 1687 levels of rent agreed on in March 1692 proved excessive and over-ambitious. As much can be implied from the contemporary scarcity of money, and because in July and November 1692 the commission was forced to concede additional abatements. The promotion of tenant petitions in favour of such concessions owed much to the vigour of local officials in Tipperary notably Valentine Smith, Sir John Meade, and Sir Thomas Butler.[11] The successful advancement of abatement claims could only result in declining or at best static income. In this situation the need to satisfy the demands of Ormond's creditors, who had been fairly tolerant in the immediate post-war period, but who by late 1692 were threatening re-entry on lands assigned to them as security, became more critical.[12] The solution to the dual problems of static or declining revenue from rents and the pressing demands of creditors was found in the adoption of an innovative system of fining, which brought in immediate sums of money in large amounts and also had the simultaneous effect of transforming the standing of participating head-tenants on the estate.

To appreciate the scheme's significance, the pre-1690 leasing history of the estate may be stated briefly.[13] Before 1641 most leases were for 21 years and were granted mainly in the period 1628–34. During the 1640s fines were taken on the granting of long leases usually for 99 years, while in the 1650s (when the estate was out of the ownership of the family), few leases were given and those that were were for short terms. In the period 1658–90 a significant resetting was undertaken with leases for lives being granted on an extensive scale for the first time. For this period 53 leases for three lives, 34 for 21 years, 12 for 31 years, and 6 for other yearly terms, were granted on Ormond's Tipperary estate.

---

[10] BL, Add. MSS 28,877, fos. 286–286ᵛ; 28,878, fos. 384–5.

[11] BL, Add. MS 28,877, fos. 276, 286, 390, 392.

[12] Ibid., fo. 385.

[13] Information on the pre-1690 leasing pattern is derived from T. B. Butler's catalogue of the Ormond papers (NLI, Special list 165), covering NLI, D3579–5573.

In total this represents about an even number of leases for lives and leases for years.

The scheme as advocated by Richard Warburton, a member of the commission, envisaged the upgrading of this two-tier tenurial structure by the granting of a perpetual term in the form of leases for lives renewable forever to the existing tenants holding for leases for lives, and the advancement of the tenants for years to tenures for lives, both groups paying fines in the process. Warburton's recommendations were embodied in a private act of parliament (1696) which empowered Ormond and the earl of Arran to grant leases for lives or a term of years (not to exceed 41) on payment of a fine and at two-thirds the rent of 1687, renewable on payment of one year's rent as a fine on the fall of each life.[14] Accordingly between 1697 and 1700 a number of substantial fines were received for lives renewable leases from individuals within the county like Sir John Meade (£3,325), John Carden (£1,671), and Nicholas Southcoot (£1,100). Others from outside the county like Joseph Ivie, Waterford (£1,525), Robert Curtis, Dublin (£1,933), and Sir Thomas Butler, Dublin (£1,025) also participated and are likely to have become aware, through legal and official circles in Dublin, of the investment potential the lands had.[15]

The scheme proved so effective that a further private act (1701) was obtained in order to satisfy the remaining debts more speedily. In tenurial terms the most important provision of this act was that it brought the process initiated in 1697 a stage further. Thus if tenants holding on renewable leases desired to hold their lands free from the future cost of renewal, they could now do so. They could now buy out prospective, future renewal fines for a lump sum (generally calculated at four times the existing rent), and have their tenures transformed into fee farms at a nominal rent. The existing tenants opted to pay the fines and accept fee farm grants.[16] Between 1703 and 1714, 106 notifications recording such grants were enrolled in the chancery of the palatinate and in chancery in Dublin.The sixty grants enrolled in the former accounted for a total of 13,377 acres, dispersed over seven baronies.[17] A survey of the estate in 1715 shows that a distinct

[14] *An act for the more speedy payment of the creditors*, 1–4.
[15] NLI, D5246, 5248, 5255, 5261–3, 5269, 5273–5, 5279, 5281, 5317, and 5321.
[16] Individual fee farm grants are recorded in NA, Lodge MS rolls, ix. *passim*.
[17] *Appendix to the sixth report*, 46.

alteration in the leasing structure had occurred. If lands sold
outright and lands settled on Arran are excluded, the remaining
220 leasing units consist of 131 fee farms, 21 leases for lives, 55
leases for lives renewable forever, 5 31-year leases, 3 from year to
year, 3 special grants, and one each for 200 and 900 years.[18] Thus
the most common and characteristic form of tenure on the
Ormond estate in Tipperary by 1715 was that of the fee farm,
followed by the other kinds of perpetuity lease, with the number of
leases for years being of minimal significance. A number of further
fee farm grants were made after 1715 which, with those pre-dating
1715, were liable to the fixed annual rent which a number of
individuals like Bunbury, Armstrong, Meade, and Mathew bought
out in the 1720s.[19]

The strategy, as provided for in the 1696 act, of inserting a
renewal clause in new leases had a simultaneous dual effect: it
raised ready finance for Ormond from fines, and it gave the tenant
a long-term interest. The leases for lives renewable forever
granted between 1697 and 1700 were in effect perpetuities
conferring on their possessors a degree of security unavailable to
other classes of leaseholders. The fee farms given after 1701
developed the process further by the establishment of a fixed
annual payment of a fee farm rent: tenants who paid the additional
fines and obtained the fee farm grants were freed from the
obligation to pay any future renewal fines. In this developed form
fee farm tenure approximated more closely than the lives
renewable forever lease to the fee simple estate. In fact it was in
legal terms equivalent to a fee simple estate but incurring a
nominal, fixed rent.

The exact chronology of diffusion in Ireland of the lease for lives
renewable and the fee farm is difficult to ascertain precisely. The
granting of such tenures is associated with the Ulster plantation of
the early seventeenth century. Their employment on the Ormond
estate in the 1690s suggests sparsity of solvent tenants and
underdevelopment in the county in the wake of the Williamite
wars, a view given further substance by the stated aim of the 1696
and 1701 acts to promote English Protestant settlement. Indeed

---

[18] PRO, FEC, I/O.99.
[19] For those after 1715: NA, Lodge rolls, x. 52, 74–5, 89–93, 98, 106, 109, 112,
117, 130; for purchase of fee farm rents: RD, 41/494/27041, 41/495/27044, 42/462/
27042, 43/55/27352, 44/40/27427; NA, M.5259 (2).

the judgement of one contemporary observer was that the lands had in fact passed into the hands of 'English improvers', and this was also the perception of a later generation.[20] The advancement of English tenants was in response partly to a shortage of solvent tenants and partly as a device to strengthen Ormond's claim to forfeitures in the county.[21] These considerations were, however, subsidiary to the primary purpose which was the alleviation of his acute indebtedness. The broader effect, though, was to give the new form of lease a wider currency on the estate. This bears out the view of later writers that the Ormond family can be credited with the more general dissemination of the perpetuity lease, at least in the southern part of Ireland.[22]

It is clear that a significant transition in tenurial arrangements took place from 1697. Families such as Armstrong, Bayly, Carden, Carleton, Bunbury, Latham, Lowe, Southcoot, and Toler became established as landowners in their own right, such families not being recorded as grantees under the acts of settlement and explanation in Tipperary at least. Families who were grantees elsewhere in the county under these acts but who took tenancies on the Ormond estate and participated in the new leasing scheme by paying fines, also advanced their interests. The most important of such families were Alcock, Baker, Coote, Dawson, Langley, Moore, and Sadlier. Some of these families acquired town bases in Carrick and Clonmel complementing their lands in adjoining baronies.[23] The landlord's financial straits and the procedures adopted to alleviate them thus facilitated the emergence from tenant status of a significant group of families on the Ormond estate whose subsequent role as county families was important, and also enhanced the position of existing landowners who supplemented their estates with Ormond lands. The creation of new estates and the expansion of existing ones was the general pattern in relation to the Ormond estate in Kilkenny also.[24]

The dispersal of the Ormond estate over several baronies serves to illustrate general conditions in the county in the 1690s.

[20] NLI, MS 11,044, document entitled 'A state of the Palatinate'; J. Finlay, *A treatise on the law of renewals in respect to leases for lives renewable forever in Ireland* (Dublin, 1829), 3, 6.   [21] BL, Add. MS 28,877, fo. 283ᵛ.
[22] Finlay, *Treatise*, 3, 6.   [23] PRO, FEC, I/O.99 *passim*.
[24] W. Nolan, *Fassadinin: Land, settlement, and society in south-east Ireland, 1600–1850* (Dublin, 1979), 86–7.

However, other landowners were not as successful in attracting tenants as Ormond was and those who succeeded did so only by conceding lower rents. In consequence much land remained untenanted for long periods after 1690. After his tour through the county in April 1692 Warburton commented that 'the country thereabouts belonging to other proprietors does generally lie wast[e] for want of tenants and what they have set are at much lower rates'.[25] In addition he ascribed the success of the commission in concluding with tenants for the Ormond lands to a recognition of Ormond's status and of his zeal for the Protestant and Williamite causes, factors which were articulated by the commissioners in their negotiations to gain tenants. A view also promoted by them was that Ormond, above other landowners, was prepared to take into account the difficult contemporary situation and accommodate prospective tenants accordingly.

Nevertheless the context was similar for all landowners: tenant impoverishment or untenanted lands, depressed land values, and a shortage of solvent tenants. There was as a result a heavy turnover of tenancies after 1690 which presented landlords with three options. First, where the larger of the existing tenants could vouch for their solvency they were retained as with the Keatings on the Butler (Cahir) estate. Secondly, landowners were tempted to offer themselves as head-tenants for other lands because of their cheapness and the advantageous terms, with the prospect of a profit rent in the long term. Examples of this are Baker and Damer taking leases on the T.C.D. estate. Thirdly, the general shortage of suitable tenants within the county and the low price of land, served to attract outsiders who took up leases on a number of estates. The arrival of Carden and Bunbury from Carlow to take leases on the Ormond estate is an instance of this, as is the participation of Curtis and Donnellan from Dublin, and Ivie from Waterford, while the advent of Nagle and McCarthy from Cork to the Butler (Cahir) and Mathew (Thomastown) estates respectively in the 1690s further exemplifies this pattern. In order to attract or hold tenants landlords had perforce to be moderate, flexible, and concessionary in the terms they offered.

Lands were cheap at the outset of the century and the rise in land values subsequently was spread out over a long period. The

[25] BL, Add. MS 28,877, fo. 280.

taking of lands appeared an attractive prospect to those with capital, but to attract such persons into lease commitments landlords needed to grant long terms. On the Butler (Cahir) estate out of a total of 141 leases and tenures recorded as being granted on the estate between 1720 and 1750, a majority (97) were for 31 years or under.[26] This reflects the landlord's compliance with the penal restrictions confining Catholic landowners to the granting of such terms. This compliance was not absolute as the existence of seven leases for lives to tenants like Bagwell, Fennell, Keating, and Nagle (the two latter being Catholic), testifies. A similar general compliance is also evident on the Butler (Kilcash) estate in the 1720s and 1730s with the recorded leases being for 31 years or less, though here again two leases for lives were given by this Catholic landowner in 1723 and 1726.[27] The 31-year lease was also predominant on the neighbouring Catholic Mandeville estate, though 21-year leases were not unknown in this district.[28] On the O'Callaghan estate at Shanbally between 1739 and 1750 leases of 31 years and three lives renewable were granted.[29] The pattern on the Mathew (Thomastown) estate to 1740 was the granting of 31-year or three lives leases to a small group of large tenants. The phrase employed in a lease to one of them in 1705 to the effect of including 'all other usual covenants in said George Mathew's other leases for lives renewable',[30] suggests that this duration of lease was commonly given on the estate at this stage. The lettings on the Smith estate in and near Tipperary and Cashel (estimated to contain 13,648 acres) between 1729 and 1745 comprised 41 three lives leases, 10 31-year leases (to Catholic farmers) for rural farms, and longer terms (41, 61, 99 years) for town property in Tipperary.[31]

Further north in Kilnamanagh evidence for 1723 indicates that the Maude estate had nineteen tenants but their lease terms are

[26] Butler (Cahir): RD, 138/57/96083.
[27] Butler (Kilcash): Kilcash estate deeds for the period in NLI, Ormond papers (unsorted), and RD, 37/495/23625, 51/372/34040.
[28] Mandeville: RD, Mandeville estate deeds.
[29] O'Callaghan: RD, 97/158/67748, 127/429/87334, 126/350/87649, 128/31/85860, 141/547/99372, 138/189/92705, 199/246/132102; Clonmel Museum, Acc.1985/67–8, 76, 84, 91.
[30] Mathew: Roscrea Heritage Centre, Mathew deeds (unsorted), G. Mathew and M. Bunbury, 28 Sept. 1705 (copy).
[31] Smith: Derby papers (Preston), DDK, 1701/4, rent roll 1749.

not specified, though an advertisement for untenanted lands on
the estate in that year had a stated preference for 21 or 31 years
which may suggest the norm, though leases for three lives were not
unknown for favoured individuals.[32] In Clanwilliam the Meade
estate preferred 31-year terms for Catholics like McCarthy, and
lives leases for Protestants like Alleyn and Smithwick.[33] On the
Damer estate, which maintained a large Protestant head-tenantry,
three lives leases were the norm before mid-century.[34] In
Slievardagh leases on the Pennefather estate show a pattern of 31
years for Catholics and three lives for Protestants.[35] In the 1720s
advertisements for lands in Lower Ormond, Owney and Arra, and
Eliogarty display a preference for the 21-year lease term, though
longer terms were not unknown.[36] On private estates over the
county, therefore, the tendency was to grant long leases with
denominational considerations being an influential factor. This
parallels the situation in neighbouring Cork where by the 1720s
and 1730s the standard lease was either for 31 years or three lives
(Protestants only).[37]

On institutional estates the situation was theoretically different.
The most extensive of these was that of the Anglican church
divided into lands held by the bishops and other clergy composing
the cathedral chapters of Cashel and Emly, Killaloe, and Lismore,
and the vicars of parishes holding glebe land.[38] In the leasing of
their estates the bishops were restricted to the granting of leases
for a maximum of 21 years. This stipulation was intended to
safeguard future incomes of successive occupants of a see, but it
was circumvented by the granting of renewals on payment of fines
before the full term had expired. This was more likely to be
resorted to if it became apparent that the bishop's occupancy of
the see seemed likely to be brief. For the See of Cashel the average
period of tenure for the ten archbishops between 1661 and 1779
was just under 12 years, for Killaloe 8 years, and for Waterford

[32] RD, 39/499/26695, 63/520/44718; *Dublin Courant*, 31 Dec. 1723.
[33] RD, 26/11/14483, 73/504/52178, 79/282/55837.
[34] RD, Damer estate deeds.   [35] RD, Pennefather estate deeds.
[36] *Dublin Courant*, 22 Feb. 1719–20, 30 Oct. 1720, 2–5 May 1747; *DG*, 14 Sept.
1726, *Pue's Occurrences*, 22 Mar. 1726; NLI, Parker deeds (uncatalogued), deed of
14 Nov. 1732; NA, M3957, BR/CAV/17/21; Roscrea Heritage Centre, Maxwell
papers A/1/1/5.   [37] Dickson, 'Cork', 158–9.
[38] *Dublin Courant*, 22 July 1721; *CS*, ii. 358–412; Hampshire RO, Winchester,
Agar papers, 'A rent roll of the Archbishop of Cashel's estate 1779'.

and Lismore 20 years. The relatively high turnover of bishops at Cashel suggests that they may have regularly taken fines and granted renewals. The sixfold increase in the gross income of the See lands from £664 in 1640 to £4,000 in 1779 implies that the practice became well established.[39] The system appears to have attained final definition and wider application under archbishop Theophilus Bolton (1730–44). A similar restriction applied on the Erasmus Smith Schools estate which was rigidly adhered to in contrast to the Cashel See estate.[40] In contrast to the latter, a system of graded rent increases was implemented, giving a structured rise in rents within the strictures of the 21-year rule. Much the same situation prevailed on the estate of Trinity College.[41] Thus evidence from a number of estates for the first half of the century suggests that lease terms were usually of long duration, usually 31 years or three lives for the larger denominations, and although a 21-year lease term was obligatory on institutional estates, civil and ecclesiastical, this stipulation could be circumvented by various devices.

A situation where there was a sparsity of solvent tenants, where lands were cheap, and where landowners gave long leases was complemented by the fact that units of tenure were large, consisting of townland or multi-townland units. A pamphleteer, writing from Cashel in May 1741, referred to county Tipperary as a place where 'vast tracts of land are held by single persons, where not only farmers but gentlemen keep from three to six or seven, nay, eight thousand acres in their own hands'.[42] Evidence from the Butler (Cahir) estate for 1750, shows a large number of holdings of 10 acres or under comprised of town plots in or near Cahir usually held on 31-year leases or at will. The holdings between 11 and 100 acres (two-thirds of which were under 50 acres) belonged to the middle and strong farmer class on the estate consisting of fifteen individuals including three partnership arrangements. The tenantry, however, were dominated by fifteen persons who held

[39] *CS*, ii. 358–412; Agar papers, 'A rent roll'.

[40] *The charter of King Charles the second empowering Erasmus Smith esquire to found grammar schools in Ireland* (Dublin, 1897), 14, 16–17, 24–5; High School, Erasmus Smith papers, Tipperary deeds.

[41] TCD, MUN, P/22/139, P/23/485, 706, 838, 1525; MUN, D174/322, 511, 526–7; MUN, V/78/4/4–5; V/80/1/62–5, 153–9, 160–6, 338–41, 354–7, 562–5, 609–12; V/81/1/507–9; MUN, ME/4/53–6.

[42] Publicola, *A letter from a country gentleman*, 2.

denominations in excess of 100 acres. Principal among these were the Nagles who held 1,744 acres spread over six townlands, and the Keatings (five members of which family are named in 1750) whose interest comprised 1,100 acres. The estate in 1750 is, therefore, characterized in structure at the bottom by a large number of town plots of 10 acres or under, a middling group averaging 50 acres in holding size, and at the top a group of large head-tenants who between them controlled over 7,000 acres on the estate and whose individual holdings ranged in size from 101 to 1,744 acres, averaging at 540 acres.[43] The neighbouring O'Callaghan estate exhibits a similar structure at this time for it was dominated by a group of eight or nine resident middlemen holding multi-townland units.[44] On the Mathew (Thomastown) estate the average size of lettings between 1703 and 1740 was about 480 acres, but ranged as high as 1,000 acres in the case of a lease to McCarthy in 1703.[45]

However, as can be implied from the remark of the 1741 pamphleteer, it was not merely that certain individuals were large tenants on single estates alone in the region, rather the fact that they took perpetuity or long leases on a number of adjacent estates which made them into multi-thousand acre tenants. Thus in addition to being tenants on the Butler (Cahir) estate, the Keatings appear also as large tenants on the Butler (Kilcash), Ormond, Everard, and Bayly estates.[46] Similarly the McCarthys, having gained an initial three lives lease for 1,000 acres on the Mathew estate in 1703, progressed in 1719 to obtaining a further 1,600 acres on the nearby Meade estate.[47] By the 1770s the McCarthy holdings extended to 9,000 acres.[48] The McCarthys and Keatings are the prime examples of the engrossing tenants in this region in the early eighteenth century. The pattern was general however. The presence of the Bunburys initially on the Ormond

[43] RD, 138/570/96083.
[44] W. J. Smyth, 'Estate records and the making of an Irish landscape demesne', *Irish Geography*, 9 (1976), 39.
[45] Mathew (Thomastown) leases in RD, and Roscrea Heritage Centre.
[46] RD, 12/151/4671; lease to J. Keating, 29 Oct. 1755 (NLI, Ormond papers, bundle 1756–7); Everard: NLI, PC, 46, (i) Barton papers, case of *R. Dawson* v. *J. Long Everard and others*, 15 Sept. 1750, 8–10, 18; PRO, FEC, I/O.99; Bayly papers, J. Bayly lease to J. Keating, 9 Dec. 1754.
[47] Roscrea Heritage Centre, Mathew deeds, G. Mathew and D. McCarthy, 14 June 1703; RD, 26/11/14483. [48] Young, *Tour*, i. 390.

estate, and later on the Mathew (Thomastown), Maude, Smith, and T.C.D. estates; the Bradshaws on the Mathew (Thomastown) and Damer estates; Smithwick on Damer and Meade; Alleyn on Mathew and Meade; and Lockwood on the Smith and Cashel See estates, testifies to this general pattern of a concentration of holdings in the hands of a few individuals in this region.[49] This trend evolved in two stages in the early decades of the century. The first stage was when they became tenants to lands on a single estate as with McCarthy (1703), Nagle (1695), and Bunbury (1697). Landlords gave low or graded rents, long leases, and large holdings to encourage such tenants. As time went on and as the solvency of such tenants became apparent, a second stage followed. They were entrusted with additional lands in the 1710s and 1720s either on the same estate as with Nagle and Keating or, having established their credibility with other landlords, on neighbouring estates as with Bunbury and McCarthy.

Elsewhere the pattern of holding size was somewhat different. In 1723 the nineteen tenancies on the Maude estate (which was not fully tenanted at this date) were composed of single townlands held by ten individuals and five partnerships, and multi-townlands held by two individuals and two partnerships.[50] A survey of the holdings held by Catholic tenants in the barony of Kilnamanagh in 1765, most of which consisted of the Maude estate, shows no holdings in excess of 100 acres held by Catholics. The bulk of the 181 holdings were in the range 5–10 acres (68) and 10–20 acres (70), with only 22 in the range 20–100 acres, 17 between 1 and 5 acres, and none less than 1 acre.[51] There were no multi-townland Catholic tenants in this barony at this date comparable to those in Clanwilliam, Middlethird, and Iffa and Offa. This pattern may be a reflection of the evangelical preferences of Maude who favoured Protestants with larger holdings. A different emphasis is evident for Catholic tenants in the barony of Ikerrin in 1750. There were eight persons who had holdings in excess of 100 acres: Kennedy (400), Lalor (340), Meagher (300), Lalor (200), Kennedy (500), Carroll (240), Meagher (150), and Carroll (150). Though these were large in themselves and contrasted sharply with the pattern in

---

[49] RD, 20/61/9733, 31/118/18369, 58/364/39804, 64/21/42437, 73/504/52178, 74/156/50496, 79/282/55837, 113/277/78253, 127/390/87204; NA, D16,339; Agar papers, rental, 1779.   [50] RD, 39/499/26695.
[51] NLI, MS 19,822, 273–85.

Kilnamanagh, again they did not approach the pattern evident further south. At the other extreme Ikerrin shows that at the base of proprietorship almost half (187) of total holdings (415) were of 1 acre or less.[52] Neither of the two baronies can compare with the pattern of large Catholic tenants evident in the southern half of the county.

The situation in which landowners found themselves in the years after 1690 required novel solutions because they were in a weak negotiating position where tenants were concerned. The long leases, large holdings, and moderate rents granted to tenants had the advantage of giving landlords a stable income however moderate. Such concessionary terms, conceded at a time when economic prospects seemed inauspicious, were to have unforeseen consequences. The difficulties of the post-1690 period and the way in which landowners adapted to them in the long-term entailed a loss of control on their part and an undermining of their position in local society, particularly if they were absentee. Something of this derogation of authority was mentioned by Warburton as a possible objection to his scheme of granting perpetuities on the Ormond estate in 1692. In answer to the objection that the plan might 'lessen ye dependancy a tenant should have of his landlord', he advanced the view that 'gratitude will oblidge ten[an]ts ye more to hon[ou]r and esteeme their landlord when they and posterity are to remaine under them [and] the Duke is above ye slight of any ten[an]t, and his hon[ou]r and eminency as well as meritt will ever gaine reverence unto (and dependancy on) his person and favour'.[53] This contention was valid so far as the lives leases are concerned and so long as the landowner remained in a position of eminence. Warburton could not have foreseen the consequences of the extension of his scheme into the granting of fee farms, nor the political demise of the Ormond family. The result of both was a lessening of social bonds between landlord and tenant.

Large head-tenants became entrenched and established a vested interest as well as social prominence in rural society. It was in the region where their most notable exemplars—Alleyn, Doherty, Keating, and McCarthy—became deeply rooted that they are taken notice of by Young in the 1770s. Attempts by the landlord or his agent to remove such interests were rare, difficult, and where

---

[52] NLI, MS 8913.   [53] BL, Add. MS 28,877, fo. 280ᵛ.

eventually successful, costly. A similar situation prevailed on seven estates in Carlow, north Wexford, and south Wicklow where half the tenantry were middlemen holding 120 acres or more.[54] Their position of dominance was in part created for management considerations. For in addition to being large head-tenants, some acted as agents for their landlord. Nagle acted in this capacity for Lord Cahir, and McCarthy for Mathew, and he also attended to the Ryan of Inch estate in the years 1737–56.[55] Such responsibility added to their influence and prestige locally. It gave them access to surplus funds which they loaned to local interests, and this function developed to such a degree in McCarthy's case that it gave him an influence over Protestant borrowers which he used to mitigate the application of the penal laws, an issue which became a source of resentment in the 1760s. Entrenched though such interests were, by their residence they nevertheless provided a social presence and cohesion in local society in the absence of such landowners as Butler (Cahir), Meade, Moore (Lords Mount Cashell), and Damer. Indeed it seems that the rise to prominence of middlemen occurred because of economic considerations, and that factors of religion and the absenteeism or residence of the landowner were subsidiary, at least initially.

2. Tenurial Pattern 1750–1815

In the half century after 1690 there is a positive correlation between long leases, low or moderate rents, and relatively sizeable leasing units. This pattern was consistent with an underdeveloped agricultural economy which emphasized grazing in an under-populated countryside. Related to this was the emergence of entrenched interests across the county. After mid-century this stable pattern altered markedly because an expansion in agri-cultural production, coupled with a growing diversification into cereals, created a more widely disseminated prosperity which

[54] D. Gahan, 'Religion and land tenure in eighteenth-century Ireland: Tenancy in the south-east', in R. V. Comerford, M. Cullen, J. R. Hill, and C. Lennon (eds.), *Religion, conflict and coexistence in Ireland: Essays presented to Monsignor P. J. Corish* (Dublin, 1990), 105–7.

[55] House of Lords appeals, 2 (TCD, 202 r 32), *Cahir* v. *Nagle,* 28 Feb. 1717; RD, 138/570/96083; Ryan papers: D. Ryan's account with Justin McCarthy, Feb. 1737–Apr. 1756.

served to increase land values, and multiplied the number of potentially solvent tenants. Competition for access to land became more intense. Agricultural prosperity and population growth reacting upon each other served on the one hand to create a more stratified society locally thereby modifying the earlier pattern, and on the other found expression in a series of agrarian movements in which certain interest groups sought to protect themselves against the unequal effects of prosperity. Thus the determinants by which leasing policy was formulated shifted markedly after mid-century.

Land values rose sharply in the middle decades during which significant amounts of property came on the market for reletting especially in the south and west of the county. A pattern of resetting is evident on the Mandeville, Bagwell, and Butler (Cahir) estates in the south, and on the Damer, Mathew, and Maude estates in the west for the 1760s.[56] Lesser, though still important, segments of property were relet in the Ormond baronies particularly Lower Ormond. Tenants who took lands at high rents in the 1760s found it difficult to meet their rent commitments in the depressed years after 1770. Landlords, enjoying enhanced incomes as a result of the 1760s, found it hard to obtain tenants after 1770 at these rent levels for lands then coming up for resetting.

For the 1770s as a whole no overall pattern of reletting can be observed comparable in scale to a decade earlier. Nevertheless on twelve estates between 1770 and 1776 a total of 7,900 acres were advertised all contained within the area joined by Kilcooley, Cashel, Cahir, and Carrick. The major estates being relet included Bagwell (Kilmore) near Fethard, Barker at Kilcooley, Cooke at Kiltinan, Lowe near Killenaule, Minchin at Ballingarry, Perry near Clonmel, Power (Barrettstown), Power (Gurteen), Taylor at Noan, Walshe between Clonmel and Fethard, Watson near Cashel and Killenaule, and Butler (Cahir).[57] Such large segments of land coming on the market within a defined area and within such a short period were bound to affect existing tenancy arrangements. In addition the fact that such public solicitation of bids from

---

[56] Based on advertisements in the *Munster Journal, CEP, FDJ,* and *FLJ.*

[57] *FLJ,* 21–4 Mar., 7–11, 14–18 Apr., 2–6 June, 8–11 Aug., 13–17 Oct., 24–8 Nov., 8–12 Dec. 1770, 26–30 Jan., 30 Jan.–2 Feb., 23–7 Feb. 1771, 4–8 Jan., 4–7 Nov. 1772, 7–10 Apr. 1773, 1–5 Oct. 1774, 11–14 Jan., 23–6 Aug. 1775, 7–10 Aug. 1776; *WC,* 12–15 Nov. 1771, 20–4 Sept. 1776.

prospective tenants was sought in this way represented a departure from the customary practice of renewing the term and tenure of the sitting tenant. That these were not lands being let for the first time can be implied from the inclusion in the public notices declaring the landlord's intention of auctioning them, of the terms 'no preference given', 'proposals in writing only', and 'now in the possession of'. The result was the introduction of new tenant farmers, some from Waterford, over the heads of the existing tenants. They, with their landlords, became the objects of intimidation with the aim of forcing them to quit their farms and return them to their former tenants.[58]

Some landlords were motivated to replace their existing tenants because they were unable in the economically difficult period of the early 1770s, to meet the high rent commitments entered into in the inflationary period of the early 1760s. A visitor to the county in October 1772 wrote of the farmers being 'to[o] hardly tied up in all their leases'.[59] Farmers who, stimulated by the premiums on the carriage of cereals to Dublin, had invested in the conversion of their pasture ground in the late 1760s found that they were unable to meet their rent obligations in the early 1770s because of the economic downturn. Landlords, anxious to have regular rent payments, were forced to distrain the goods of such defaulting tenants as on the Stanley (1773) and Cooper (1775) lands.[60] Much of the unrest associated with the rescuing of stock distrained for rent arrears arose out of this context. Ejectment of head-tenants was proceeded with where distress could not be obtained.[61] With almost 8,000 acres being publicly advertised for reletting the turnover of tenants was substantial. Those still in possession or those displaced reacted in the form of violence against the newcomers, whether dairymen-occupiers or those of greater substance who took the lands over the heads of the sitting tenants and who were likely absentee. In response to the action of the landlords (whom the 1772 visitor labelled as 'as wild and savage as

[58] *FLJ*, 25–9 Jan. 1772, 24–8 Apr., 19–22 May, 11–15 Sept. 1773, 3–6 May, 25–9 Nov., 2–6 Dec. 1775, 17–20 Feb. 1779; *FJ*, 20–3 Mar. 1773, 16–19 Mar. 1776; *WHM*, July 1775, 4336; *LJ*, 3–6 Apr. 1805.

[59] E. Smith to Sir G. [Macartney], 13 Oct. 1772 (PRONI, D572/2/93).

[60] A. McGuire to Derby, 18 Aug. 1772, 7 Jan., 5 Mar. 1773 (Derby papers (Preston), DDK, correspondence series 1747–77); TCD, MS 9865, *sub* June, 1 Sept. 1775.

[61] *FLJ*, 16–19 Aug. 1775.

tis possible to be conceived') of introducing outsiders in order to guarantee rents at a time of economic difficulty, the formulation of strategies to regulate the transfer of property among displaced tenants began to emerge as a result of the experience of the early 1770s. Already by 1777 tenants on the lands of William Minchin at Fole near Ballingarry were reportedly obliged to take an oath which stipulated that they were 'not to propose for or take any part of each other's land at the expiration of their leases'.[62] This notion of regulating property transfer by trying to ensure that the sitting tenant had a prior claim on renewal of a lease before the landlord could entertain other bidders, developed further in the 1780s.

In the 1780s, as in the early 1770s, considerable segments of land were publicly advertised for letting. On fifteen of the larger estates 20,676 acres were so advertised in the period 1780–8, representing two and a half times the amount of land coming on the market compared to a decade previously.[63] This acreage covered the following estates: Barker, Damer, Derby, Lloyd, Langley, Lowe, Lockwood, McCarthy, Massy, Otway, Palliser, Perry, Prittie, Roe, and Willington. Other evidence indicates that in addition the following estates were actually reset in the 1780s: Butler (Cahir), Butler (Ormond), O'Callaghan in the south; Damer, Erasmus Smith, Stanley, Cashel See, Meade in the west; and Ryan (Inch), Carden, Langley, Bayly, and Prittie in the north. Landlords were in a weak bargaining position, though this was balanced somewhat after 1784 because of the demand by tenants for land due to high grain prices. A number of landlords offered facilities for fining down the rents on new lettings: on the Massy estate fines were one-third of the rent.[64] How much this could amount to in individual cases is exemplified by the case of one Cashel attorney who in 1784 was prepared to make £2,000 available as a fine for a three lives lease.[65]

Tenants who took lands at low or moderate rents on long leases

[62] *WHM*, Mar. 1777, 215.

[63] *CG*, 1–4 Oct., 5–8 Nov., 10–13 Dec. 1781, 3–7, 14–17 Jan., 2–6 May, 21–5 Nov. 1782, 20–3 Jan., 5–9, 13–17, 20–24 Feb., 10–13, 13–17, 17–20 Mar., 4–8, 18–22 Dec. 1783, 5–9 Feb., 11–15 Mar., 29 Mar.–1 Apr., 1–5, 15–19 Apr., 12–15 July, 6–9 Dec. 1784, 17–20 Jan., 31 Jan.–3 Feb., 14–17 Mar., 12–16 May 1785, 13–16 Feb., 22–6 June, 7–10 Aug. 1786, 29 Jan.–1 Feb., 29 Oct.–1 Nov. 1787, 3–7 Apr. 1788; *CEP*, 22 Jan. 1781.

[64] *CG*, 10–14 Oct. 1783, 10–13 Apr. 1786; *CEP*, 22 Jan. 1781.

[65] *CG*, 27–30 Dec. 1784.

in the 1780s were to benefit substantially from the sustained demand and favourable prices for agricultural produce during the period 1790–1815. A Scully family history compiled in 1806 recorded of this time that 'Lands were then generally low and solvent punctual tenants difficult to be had, the American War and the succeeding event of a peace having much depressed the markets, consequently the rents of lands about 1788 began to rise again and thenceforward have so advanced that those leases antecedently taken are of high and increasing value.'[66] Landlords had little opportunity to benefit more substantially from this situation by adjusting rent levels in line with the rise in agricultural prices. Few if any of the major estates were reset in the 1790s or the first decade of the nineteenth century, and no pattern of general reletting is evident, the exception being the Otway (1801), Rous (part) (1791, 1806), and Erasmus Smith (1810) estates. Thus the 1780s is a vital decade, comparable to the 1690s, when much land came up for reletting, at low or moderate rents based on slumped land values, and on long leases. However, unlike the indifferent economic prospects which ensued in the half century after 1690, the 1780s were followed by twenty-five years of accelerated economic growth from which tenants more than landowners reaped the benefit.

Leases generally continued, as in the past, to be of long duration (see Tables 3 and 4). Though in the newspaper advertisements in many cases the term on offer was unspecified or was given merely as years or lives—stipulations which suggest that a degree of negotiation was involved—in practice 31-year or three lives leases were granted. Indeed this could be general estate policy. In 1764 when Thomas Mathew granted John McCarthy a power of attorney, he empowered him to make leases of any part of his estate then out of lease for terms of three lives or 31 years.[67] The 31-year term was regarded as normal in the improvement leases granted on the Barker estate in the early 1770s.[68] It was also preferred on the Rous estate, with one prospective tenant remarking in 1806 that 'y[ou]r L[ord]ship has an aversion to grant any other lease'.[69] The three lives lease was the preferred term in a

---

[66] NLI, MS 27,491, 16–17. [67] RD, 239/554/163536.
[68] *FLJ*, 1–5 Oct. 1774; TCD, Barker Ponsonby papers, P6/49.
[69] T. Carpenter to Rous, 28 Mar. 1806 (East Suffolk RO, Rous papers, HA, 11/D8/4).

TABLE 3. Profile of leases on select estates

Lease term	Smith 1749	Butler (Cahir) 1750	Cashel See 1779	O'Callaghan 1780	Damer 1787	Roden 1803	Ryan 1807
in years							
999					1		
400					1		
300					1		
99	1				1		1
61.5					1		
61	9						
60			1				
49.5					1		
41	1						
40			2				
31	10	82		31	6	2	5
30.5		1					
30				1			
28		2					
25				1			
21		12	36	19			
20.75				1			
20.5				2			
20				3	1		
19.5				1			
14							2

	Smith	Butler	Agar	O'Callaghan	Damer	Roden	Ryan
8				1			2
3				1			
2				1			
1				1			
in lives							
4			1				
3, renewable forever	1				12	17	
3, renewable			2		1	1	
3	41			19	36	16	3
3 and 2 renewals			4	2	1	1	
3 or 31 years					2	2	5
2 and 21 years					1	1	
3 and 99 years					1		
2					1		
1 or 31 years				1	1		
1			1	3			
'Lives & renewals'				4			
Year to year	1						
Fee farm	1				2		
At will			20	14	1		
Out of lease				9			
Not specified			16	10	19	19	

Sources: Smith: Lancashire RO; Derby papers DDK 1701/4; rent roll, 1749. Butler (Cahir): RD 138/570/96083. Cashel See: Hampshire RO; Agar papers; rental 1779. O'Callaghan: O'Callaghan papers (Cahir); rent roll, 1780. Damer: Tipperary County Library; Damer papers; rent roll, 1787. Roden: An act for the sale of part of the estates of the Rt. Hon. Robert, earl of Roden [1803]. Ryan: Ryan papers (Thurles); rental 1807.

memorandum outlining leasing policy on the Stanley estate in 1774 when it was about to be relet.[70] Where a choice of three lives or 31 years appeared in advertisements, it seems to have been normal that the former term was actually given sometimes with the choice of renewal being optional. Even tenants who took a 31-year term could have the lease renewed yearly, as with Latham's Killenaule lands in 1778.[71] Most of the extensive Butler (Cahir) estate was relet between 1779 and 1788 on long 61-year leases whereby the existing middlemen (Ross and Nagle for instance) had their interests renewed.[72] This reletting followed the Catholic relief act of 1778 which revoked the earlier restriction on leases to Catholics. Thus in a period of falling or static land values in the 1770s and 1780s the long lease continued to be favoured by most landlords.

This pattern is confirmed by a profile of the leasing structure on a number of estates (Table 3). On the O'Callaghan estate in 1780, the 31-year and three lives leases predominated, though the number of 21-year terms was also important. On the Damer estate in Clanwilliam, Kilnamanagh, and Ileagh a survey of leases current in 1787 indicates the three lives lease to be almost universal. Like the situation on the Butler (Cahir) estate, these long leases ensured the perpetuation of the large interests whose leases were renewed in 1768–9. The Roden estate (7,346 acres), scattered over five baronies (mainly in Upper and Lower Ormond but also in Eliogarty, Owney and Arra, and Middlethird), displayed a similar preference for the three lives lease as indicated by a profile of 1803. Long-lease terms also characterized the Ryan (Inch) estate in 1807.[73]

Attempts to introduce shorter-lease terms were limited in scale. The 21-year head leases evident on the O'Callaghan estate in 1780 are an expression of the landlord's desire to give shorter leases to under-tenants or occupiers as part of the process of replacing the

[70] Derby papers (Preston), DDK, 1712/4.

[71] *FLJ*, 17–21 Oct. 1778.

[72] NA, Acc. 976/6/5: memorandum on the Cahir estate by the earl of Glengall, (n.d. [1845]), D17,557; *PP Occupation of land (Ire.)*, 20 (1845) 240, 888–90; RD, 320/605/220359, 325/285/220358, 340/371/229869, 349/45/232812.

[73] O'Callaghan papers, rent roll 1780; Damer papers, rent roll 1787–98; Ryan papers, rental May 1807; *An act for the sale of part of the estates of the Rt. Hon. Robert, earl of Roden* (n.p. [1803]), schedules 1–3; Ryan papers, rental May 1807.

TABLE 4. Age of leases on select estates

Period	Cashel See 1779	O'Callaghan 1780	Damer 1787	Roden 1803	Ryan 1807
1700–09			1		
1710–19					
1720–9		2		1	
1730–9	2	1	2	4	
1740–9	9	10	2	3	
1750–9	16	16	1	7	
1760–9	13	14	27	1	
1770–9		35	16	5	
1780–9			19	14	9
1790–9				2	6
1800–09				2	4
No date	2	22	17	1	

Sources: As for respective estates listed in Table 3.

large middlemen taken on in the 1740s when capitalized tenants were needed but whose role subsequently was viewed as anachronistic.[74] The 21-year term was, of course, obligatory on institutional estates: church lands, Erasmus Smith, and T.C.D. Some landlords sought to adopt the 21-year lease as the norm on their estates. Thus Anthony Parker of Castlelough specified in his will of 1766 that his wife, as main beneficiary, was not to make any leases for longer than 21 years.[75] In consequence when 635 acres of the estate were set in 1774 the 21-year term was preferred, and in 1784, of the leases then current on the estate, seven were for 21 years, four for 31 years, two for three lives, and one had expired.[76] References to the 21-year lease being the preferred term are rare in newspaper advertisements and its currency did not become more widespread as time went on. There is evidence of both trends: a continuing preference for long leases to existing large tenants, and limited attempts to introduce shorter terms on a

[74] Smyth, 'Estate records', 37, 41.
[75] NLI, Parker deeds (uncatalogued), will of 23 Sept. 1766.
[76] NLI, MS 11,416, 'An account of the tenants of Anthony Parker 1784' and MS advertisement dated 5 Feb. 1774.

select number of estates. By the early nineteenth century new leases in the county were generally 21 years and one life, instead of 31 years and three lives.[77] Attempts to alter tenancy structures led to a conflict of interests between landlords and chief tenants.

The overall pattern was one of long leases. In this context the removal of the restriction on leases taken by Catholics by the 1778 relief act has been judged to have been of little significance in tenurial terms.[78] However, since the decade following its passing coincided with a time when large amounts of property came up for letting and when land values were depressed, then its importance locally must be re-evaluated. It is clear that many Catholics availed themselves of the relaxation to accept longer lease terms in the 1780s particularly. The best instance of this is the Scullys. The 1778 act emerges as a keystone in the evolution of that family's extensive interests. As a result of the act the Scullys took long leases of new farms and, by paying fines, received longer leases for their existing interests mainly in the 1780s.[79] In this way Scully took out three lives leases on the Damer estate in 1782 and 1786, and on the Mathew estate in 1789.[80] The result of these transactions was that the Scully leasehold interest doubled from 2,000 acres in 1776 to upwards of 4,000 acres in 1792, to over 6,000 acres in 1803.[81] Of Scully's 4,000 acres in 1792 he stocked about 1,500 acres and sublet the remainder (62 per cent) for profit.[82]

A similar practice is evident among the large tenants renewed on the Butler (Cahir) estate after 1779.[83] This had disastrous consequences so far as the under-tenants were concerned, but it also influenced the landlord's position. As a consequence of the long leases granted in the 1780s, he was unable to benefit greatly from the rise in agricultural prices after 1790. Middlemen like Scully and others prospered enormously from substantial profit rents because their head rents were moderate. In 1803, for instance, for the 6,000 acres held by Scully there was a gross rent of £7,670 and a profit rent of £6,700; and in 1793 the McCarthys,

[77] E. G. Wakefield, *An Account of Ireland, statistical and political* (London, 1812), i. 276–7.   [78] Cullen, *Economic history*, 79.
[79] NLI, MSS 27,491, 16; 27,479, 100.
[80] NLI, MS 27,571, *sub* 28 Aug. 1782, 13 Jan. 1789; County Library, Thurles, Damer estate rental 1787–98, at 1787; A. M. Sullivan, *New Ireland* (London, 1878), 364.
[81] NLI, MS 27,480 (unfoliated), 'The rent I pay May 1776'; MS 27,490; MS 27,491, 17.   [82] NLI, MS 27,491, 17.   [83] NA, Acc. 976/6/5.

holding their Springhouse lands under a 61-year lease from May 1781, paid a head rent of £1,000 and had a profit rent of £500 which had increased to £1,000 by 1806.[84] These profit rents appeared all the more substantial because head rents were modest and continued to be so. The 1778 act is important in the local context for a select group of Catholics who took perpetuity or long leases in the 1780s, who benefited materially from the moderate rent levels then established which continued subsequently, and from the profit rents from subletting. On the one hand this situation tended to erode the landowner's influence over the head-tenants on his estate, and on the other as it occurred at a time of emergent consciousness among Catholics, it had important political implications.

The position of the perpetuity tenant was further enhanced by the passage in 1780 of the tenancy act. This legislation was occasioned by a decision on appeal in the British House of Lords in 1779, whereby the failure of a tenant to make known the fact that a life in his lease had expired and to pay the renewal fine in due time, was adjudged to give the landlord the right of repossession.[85] The effect of this decision in Ireland, where perpetuity tenure was uniquely extensive, would have been to undermine the position of many of the lesser landlords whose title derived from this form of tenure, and upon which many family settlements and mortgages were dependant. It has been noted how, due to the shortage of tenants in the early part of the century, many landowners became tenants to lands. This situation continued to subsist later on, for instance Anthony Parker of Castlelough as well as owning an estate in fee of 1,438 acres, also held under six landlords in Tipperary (to whom he paid £351 annually in rents), and seven in Limerick (£563 in rents).[86] The legislation of 1780 was advanced to protect such tenants and to mitigate the effects of the 1779 judgment.

The act (19 & 20 Geo. III, c. 30) enacted that failure to pay a renewal fine, where not fraudulently intended, was not to lead to the defeat of a tenant's interest, so that the flexibility of the

---

[84] NLI, MS 27,490; RD, 494/690/339615; *CG*, 27–31 July 1793; NA, M2197.

[85] M. R. O'Connell, *Irish politics and social conflict in the age of the American revolution* (Philadelphia, 1965), 266–81.

[86] NLI, MS 11,416, 'A list of the several landlords of Anthony Parker esqr.' (n.d. [*ante* 1777]).

arrangement between when a life expired and a renewal fine paid was enshrined in law. Within landed society and in parliament the controversy over the issue was between those holding in fee who wished to avail themselves of the 1779 judgment to repossess property which could have been out of their effective control for generations, and those with perpetuity interests who wished existing arrangements to stand. The balance of opinion came out in favour of the latter stance. Locally the issue was supported by the earl of Clanwilliam, John Toler, Peter Holmes, Richard and John Hely-Hutchinson, Francis Mathew, and William and Richard Pennefather, while its most vigorous opponent was the archbishop of Cashel. Appointed to the See in the year before the act passed, Charles Agar was concerned to oppose the measure because of his experience of perpetuity tenants on the See estate, in particular the largest one Dr John Palliser who delayed payment of his renewal fine (annual value £1,000) for long periods.[87] On his estate in the same region Lord Milton (Damer) was obliged in October 1783 to issue a notice to his lives renewable lessees warning them that if they did not immediately pay fines on the death of lives in their leases, then his law agent would proceed against them.[88] The subsequent appointment of the Coopers as professional agents to manage the Damer and other estates (including the Cashel See) locally, may be viewed as a strategy to circumvent or restrict the flexibility given to the perpetuity tenant under the 1780 act. Significantly by 1787 the number of lives renewable leases on the Damer estate was less pronounced.[89] Nevertheless attempts to repossess estates where head tenants had failed to renew their interests contributed to a number of celebrated cases of forcible possession in the 1780s.

The position of sitting tenants was bound to be affected. The 1780s witnessed the head-tenant of substance involved in rural agitation for the first time. Where they were unsuccessful in being renewed in their tenancies, new tenants became the objects of resentment. Often this resulted in their ejectment and the forcible reoccupation of the lands by the former tenants. Forcible or illegal possession was a prominent feature of unrest in the 1780s. In 1784

[87] *HC*, 21–4, 24–8 Aug. 1780; S. Cooper to the archbishop of Cashel, 20 Feb. 1783, 16 Apr. 1786, 18 Jan. 1789, and his replies of 23 Feb. 1783, 22 Jan. 1789 (Agar papers, box 5).

[88] *CG*, 6–9 Oct. 1783. [89] Damer rent roll, 1787–98.

its common incidence was represented by the high sheriff to government with the request that additional military aid would be required to suppress the practice.[90] In 1784 the archbishop of Cashel informed government of the fact that 'many forcible possessions are kept at this moment [in Tipperary]'; government proclamations against the practice were issued subsequently.[91] Clearly the large amount of land advertised caused apprehensions among sitting tenants about their positions, and they responded to this threat by maintaining illegal custody of their holdings.

The two most serious cases involved the forcible occupancy of Ballinulta near Cullen on the Damer estate, and of Ballynamona near Golden owned by Richard Kiely. In the former case the trouble arose out of attempts by the head-tenant, English, to safeguard his position against efforts by the landlord to deal directly with the occupying tenant. By at least October 1784, and for a year thereafter, English and his followers established and maintained illegal custody of Ballinulta and defied successive attempts at their removal.[92] The event caused a sensation at the time. It elicited a government proclamation in 1785 and land-owners were anxious that those concerned be quickly subdued or else, as the archbishop of Cashel remarked in an alarmist tone, 'all the gentlemen of the county will be dispossessed'.[93] In another equally serious case in October 1784 a party entered the lands of Ballynamona, then held by Michael Mulcahy, farmer, for several years under lease from Kiely, who was an absentee in Co. Waterford. They took forcible possession of the lands, expelled Mulcahy, fortified themselves in a strong castle on the lands, and defied initial attempts by the military to remove them.[94] These cases and others show that as the position of head-tenants was threatened by the large amount of land being publicly auctioned in

[90] [W. Pitt] to Orde, 23 Oct. 1784 (NLI, MS 1007. 94–5).

[91] Agar to [Bolton?], 8 Nov. 1784 (NLI, MS 16,350/59–60); NA, Privy Council Office, index to the proclamation books 1618–1875, *sub* 1785, 1789, and 1A. 52, 159, p. 268.

[92] *CG*, 20–4 May 1784, 3–7 Apr. 1785; *FLJ*, 23–7 Oct., 3–6, 24–7 Nov. 1784, 7–11 May, 16–19 Nov. 1785, 21–5 Jan., 15–18 Feb., 3–6 May 1786; NLI, MSS 27,571, 119, 16350/53, 59–60; Damer estate rental 1787–98; and for the legal background W. Ridgeway, *Reports of cases on appeals and writs of error in the high court of parliament* (Dublin, 1795), ii. 192–203.

[93] NLI, MS 16,350/59–60.

[94] *CG*, 21–4 Nov. 1784; *FLJ*, 16–20 1784; J. D. White, *Anthologia Tipperariensis* (Cashel, 1892), 54; HMC, *Rutland*, iii. 259–60.

the 1780s, their response was forcible possession or repossession in order to protect their interests. In large measure the unrest of the 1780s, in so far as head-landlord and head-tenant are concerned, can be interpreted as an attempt by the former (e.g. Damer, and the archbishop of Cashel), to challenge the position of the latter through an attempt to frustrate the operation of the 1780 tenancy act by the repossession of lands for which tenants neglected to promptly renew lives in their leases. The cases of forcible possession represented confrontation undertaken in response to the actions of a few landlords, but on the whole the majority of landlords renewed their existing tenantry at this time with generally long leases, as on the Butler (Cahir) estate.

Tenants on a number of estates were slow to fulfil their lease obligations in relation to meeting rent payments in the 1780s. The situation appears to have been most serious on the extensive Damer estate near Tipperary. In October 1783 the tenants holding renewable leases on the estate were publicly cautioned that as one or more of the lives in the majority of their leases were dead and that renewals had not been made, legal proceedings would ensue unless the situation was rectified immediately.[95] This cajolement of the tenants may not have had the desired effect as much of the Damer lands were subsequently advertised for letting. Rent was a matter of contention, not surprisingly perhaps, as so much land was up for leasing in a decade in which conditions were exceptionally difficult both because of bad harvests in 1782 and 1783 and a post-war slump. In fact the event which sparked off the so-called Rightboy disturbances in the county was the murder of the absentee landlord Lyons Cane in October 1785, when he came to collect rent from one of his tenants, William Doherty, whose son shot Cane.[96] Tenants defaulting in rent payments faced the prospect of distraint by the landlord. While distress was obtained in a number of cases, it is evident that it was also rescued or recovered by tenants. A further indication that rents were difficult to obtain in the early 1780s is shown by the appointment of agents or rent receivers for a number of estates including those of Damer and Perry where unrest was to the fore. The extensive occurrence of the practice of forcible possession by tenants represented an

---

[95] *CG*, 6–9 Oct. 1783.
[96] Hamilton to Sydney, 5 Nov. 1785 (PRO, HO, 100/17/171). For the Rightboys see Ch. 5.

advance in the formulation of notions of tenant right compared to a decade previously.

The tardiness with which renewal fines were paid and the inability of landlords to enforce their punctual payment was given legal support by the act of 1780. Ostensibly promoted by those in parliament who had their own interests to protect, the measure by default came to give protection to the extensive perpetuity sector in the countryside. In Tipperary this sector was entrenched on a number of estates and after 1778, when Catholics were permitted to take longer leases, a trend marked in the 1780s, the 1780 act was beneficial in protecting their position. On the other hand, the act must be regarded as a defeat for landowners (at least those less resolute than Lord Milton) who were anxious to regain control of tenancies. The 1780s represented a critical phase in the evolution of landlord and tenant attitudes. At one level the early 1780s had as its background stagnant land values, rent arrears, and a large amount of property coming up for reletting; and at another level the relief act of 1778, whereby Catholics extended their interest by taking both longer leases for existing holdings and new leases for other lands, and the tenancy act of 1780 which confirmed the position of the perpetuity tenant. The attempt to confront the large tenant was unsuccessful. In consequence, as the 1780s, unlike the 1690s, were followed by economic prosperity, tenants more than landlords benefited from high prices and moderate rents in the period up to 1815. The bargaining position of the landlord was weakened because few of the large estates fell out of lease in the 1790s, a fact which strengthened the position of the tenant.

There were attempts after 1800 to break long leases so that landlords might benefit more fully from the prosperity of the period through granting shorter leases at higher rents. Lord Cahir was unsuccessful in his attempt and large middlemen remained on the estate until the 1840s when the 61-year leases granted in the 1780s fell in.[97] It was calculated that had he succeeded in such an attempt in 1811 the consequence of resetting the lands would have been an increase in his rent roll of £3,000 per annum.[98] But a test case, on which the position of fifty other tenants on the estate depended, brought in that year went against him.[99] In another case

---

[97] *PP Occupation of land (Ire.)*, 21, iii. (1845), 888–9.
[98] *WM*, 11 May 1811.   [99] Ibid.

the trustees of the Ormond estate brought a legal action in 1805 with the intention of impeaching all the three lives and 31-year leases granted on the former Kilcash estate between 1766 and 1796, on the ground that the previous owner, John Butler of Kilcash (d. 1766), had laid down in his will that only 21-year leases were to be given.[100] The action was unsuccessful because the will (dated 1764) was shown to be of dubious legal standing, and the position of the lessees on the estate was upheld. These attempts illustrate the inability of landlords to reverse the tenurial situation on their estates in their favour.

3. Denominational Character of Tenantry

As part of the Williamite settlement it was a decided preference of landowners to advance Protestant tenants where possible. However, this objective was not always achievable, Edward Cooke admitting in 1737 that 'I and every other gentleman wou[l]d have good substantial Protestant tenants if we cou[l]d get them, but as they are not to be had we must take the best we can get, or have our land wast[e] w[hi]ch is next to having no estate.'[101] It is the policy of adaptability and economic realism implicit in this remark which illustrates the compromises which landowners had to accept in the early eighteenth century in order to make their estates viable. It was from the response of individual landowners across the county that a characteristic type of tenant distribution established itself.

Moving westward from Carrick-on-Suir it is evident that Catholic head-tenants (Butler, White, Esmond, Neal) dominated the Butler (Kilcash) estate with at least one Protestant, Shaw.[102] The neighbouring Mandeville estate was mostly sublet to members of the family on 31-year leases, but for the rest the surnames Davin, Power, Walsh, Hickey, Quinlan, and Coroban suggest a strong Catholic presence.[103] On part of the Bagwell estate at

---

[100] *WM*, 1 Aug. 1810.

[101] E. Cooke to Sir W. Fownes, 17 Mar. 1737 (Cooke papers NLI, Mic.P.1560).

[102] RD, 37/495/23625, 57/419/39121, 92/372/64993; NLI, Ormond papers bundle 1726–7 (T. Butler and H. White, 16 Mar. 1726), 1729–30 (T. Butler and W. Esmond, 8 Jan. 1730).

[103] RD, 44/326/29573, 45/357/29574, 47/126/29789, 72/1/49413, 111/337/76868, 145/384/98900, 148/134/98890, 148/481/102451.

Lisronagh, north of Clonmel, in 1757 half of the 646 acres were in lease to John Keating, and the other half divided between Carleton, Birmingham, Fahy, Burke, and Doohy.[104] On the other lands acquired by Bagwell in this region Protestant tenants like Edwards (1732) and Bacon (1740) were encouraged with improvement leases, though some leases still subsisted at the time (1729) Bagwell purchased these lands and they were then in the tenancy of Catholics on 31-year leases.[105] On the 3,000 acre Hely-Hutchinson estate at Knocklofty in 1771 only four surnames (Bagnell, Miles, Cuffe, Serjeant) can be identified that would suggest Protestant tenants, for the estate was dominated by branches of the Prendergasts and Lonergans, former proprietors in the region.[106] The vast Butler (Cahir) estate adjoining was dominated by large Catholic head-tenants: Keating, Nagle, Shee, Fitzgibbon, Butler, Ross, and Griffith, with Bagwell and Fennell being the only Protestants of identifiable significance in 1750.[107] The Nagles had acquired a considerable interest on the estate since the 1690s, while the Keatings represented Catholic ex-proprietors maintaining their social position as substantial head-tenants.

To its south-west the Butler (Cahir) estate was flanked by the O'Callaghan estate where an improving landlord in the 1740s introduced a group of Protestant head-tenants coupled with artisans and craftsmen settled in the revived village of Clogheen.[108] The O'Callaghan estate is noteworthy for the conversion of the landlord to the Established Church and his promotion of Protestant tenants in the 1740s. In September and October 1747 twenty-two individuals including eight couples converted on the estate. This number included six farmers, the rest being tradesmen or merchants in Clogheen.[109] Of these farmers the surnames of Curtin, Fennessy, Murphy, and Walsh imply Catholic status, while those of Bradshaw and Burnet would

---

[104] NLI, 21.F.46 (15).

[105] NLI, PC 260–1, Riall: Tipperary deeds 1720–49: J. Bagwell and J. Edwards, 5 May 1732; marriage settlement J. Bagwell jun. and A. Calwell, 27 May 1736; Clonmel, Bagwell Estate Office, J. Bagwell and T. Bacon, 21 Mar. 1740.

[106] NLI, MS 2735.

[107] RD, 138/570/96083; House of Lords appeals, 2 (TCD, 202 r 32) *Cahir v. Nagle*, 28 Feb. 1717.

[108] RD, 97/158/67748, 127/429/87334, 128/31/85860, 141/547/99372, 199/246/132102; O'Callaghan papers: rent account book 1736–54, 19–22.

[109] NA, Lodge MS, convert rolls.

suggest non-Catholic background. Bradshaw was a tenant on the estate from at least 1741 and the pressure on both to convert may have stemmed from the fact that their wives were Catholic, a status increasingly incompatible with the new evangelical preferences of the landlord. This demonstrates that the pressure to convert emanated from the landlord and not from a desire among Catholics to gain more advantageous leases than they would legally be entitled to. The estate was dominated by newly introduced Protestants, with an attendant group of convert farmers, under the direction of a landlord intent on pragmatic changes in the tenancy structure.

Moving northward into the baronies of Clanwilliam and Middlethird, Protestant tenants were more numerous and possessed larger holdings. Between Cashel and the border with Limerick were a number of estates on which Protestant tenants were dominant. The extensive Damer estate, for instance, was characterized by the granting of head-leases between 1708 and 1750 to thirteen Protestant tenants.[110] Evidence for 1742 indicates that Damer almost exclusively favoured these large Protestant tenants for the better lands. For the less attractive lands in Kilnamanagh and Ileagh to the north he took on Catholics, notably the Burkes and Fogartys, though the presence of Cooke, Middleton, and Richardson reinforces the overall preference for Protestants.[111] In 1748 a rent roll of the neighbouring Smith estate shows that Protestants dominated the head-tenantry. Catholics were notably absent on this estate, those like Phelan being advanced to favourable leases only because of conversion.[112] In the same region the estate of the Erasmus Smith Schools displayed a similar preference for Protestants, as did the estate of Trinity College reflecting the espoused Protestant ethos of those bodies.[113]

An interesting mixture is apparent on the estate of the

[110] RD, 14/175/6007, 27/36/15056, 31/118/18369, 34/375/21976, 37/230/22512, 43/434–5/2881–2, 45/174/28843, 45/271/29198, 55/217/36643, 115/163/80036, 62/399/43381, 74/105/50199, 74/156/50496, 104/144/72334, 127/390/87204, 126/559/88949.

[111] RD, 106/46/74723.

[112] Derby papers (Preston), DDK, 1701/2 rent roll for one year ending 25 Mar./1 May 1748; Smith-Barry DCN, 1984/10/52: three leases between H. Smith and Barnaby Phelan dated 27 May 1740, 16 June 1744, and 1 May 1745, for 555 acres in all. He converted in 1736.

[113] High School, E. Smith papers, Tipperary deeds of 18 Sept. 1710, 22 Feb. 1715, 2 July 1720, 1 July 1729, 4 May 1749; TCD, MUN/ME/2/1/12; MUN V 80/1/153–66, 507–9.

archbishop of Cashel. Although half the acreage was taken by the Pallisers (7,325 acres), significantly the next three tenants in order of magnitude of acres, i.e. Hickey (1,280), English (1,031), and Heffernan (1,000), were Catholics reflecting the facility which the 21-year lease for bishops' land allowed them.[114] In this instance the stricture of the penal law that leases to Catholics not exceed 31 years operated to their advantage. Catholics were to the fore on the Meade estate with McCarthy holding over 1,000 of the 3,300 acres with a small group of Protestants, Smithwick and Alleyn being the largest, holding lesser amounts.[115] The same individuals, Alleyn and McCarthy, occur as large tenants on the neighbouring Mathew (Thomastown) estate where, though McCarthy appears as the largest single tenant, numerically Protestants are in a majority, though other Catholics like Egan (836 acres) and Walsh (658 acres) were important also.[116] Further north on the Mathew (Thurles) estate a rental of 1744 shows that the largest payments (over £20) were made by Keating and Shee. By 1819 the numerical strength of Protestants on the Thurles part of the Mathew estate was diminished with Armstrong remaining the largest, but the others being replaced principally by the Meaghers.[117]

Flanking the region to the west was the barony of Kilnamanagh dominated by the Maude estate. The nineteen tenancies on the estate in 1723 consisted of single townlands held by ten individuals and five partnerships, and more than one townland held by two individuals and two partnerships.[118] Protestants were present in both categories. This varied pattern of tenancy exhibits the landlord's inability to obtain sufficient numbers of British tenants to take multi-townland units, the single or shared unit being largely predominant. This is partly explicable on the basis of the inhospitable agricultural environment of the barony compared to Clanwilliam further south where, because of the fertility of the soil and presence of an assured return, tenants could be entrusted with

---

[114] Agar papers, rent roll 1779.

[115] RD, 26/11/14483, 79/282/55837, 73/504/52178.

[116] RD, 10/361/3834, 22/60/11386, 24/128/13280, 46/64/27669, 58/364/39804, 64/21/42437, 69/37/42088, 80/532/56815, 113/277/78253, 139/79/93072.

[117] Tipperary County Library, Thurles, 'A rent roll of the lordship of Thurles due to George Mathew Esqr. for the half year ending Michls. and Nobr. 1744' (xerox); Leahy, *Thurles estate.*

[118] RD, 39/49/26695; *Dublin Courant,* 31 Dec. 1723.

large acreages not only on one estate but on a number. The deficiencies of the tenurial arrangement were to be addressed by Sir Thomas Maude in the next generation through an active policy of promoting Protestant settlement and adapting the landscape for its success. This process was less in response to the need to redress any imbalance of Catholic tenants on the estate than to bring untenanted lands into lease. In 1723 Catholics held nine of the tenancies and were either former proprietors like Dwyer holding single townlands, or were involved in partnerships of single townlands. Significantly the return of 1765 gives no Catholic holding over 100 acres.[119]

Further north on the Ryan of Inch estate in 1724 there were twenty-two tenancies, the majority held by Catholics with two Protestants.[120] By 1807 no Protestants are self-evident from the surnames of the nineteen head tenants on the estate.[121] In Ikerrin the return of 1750 shows that there were eight units of over 100 acres held by Catholics, and though these were inferior in size to those held by Catholics in Clanwilliam, Middlethird, and Iffa and Offa, they were superior to those in Kilnamanagh.[122] Protestant tenants appear on the Carden estate at Templemore and Barnane before mid-century.[123]

The three northern baronies of Upper Ormond, Lower Ormond, and Owney and Arra had a greater proportion of Protestant tenants than elsewhere as a result of the seventeenth-century land settlement. On the 3,000 acre Cole-Bowen estate in 1760 only two of the eighteen tenancy units were held by non-Anglicans, and Protestants continued to predominate here.[124] Similarly on the Bayly of Ballynaclough estate near Nenagh where in 1707 its tenants included Rose, Brogden, Watson, and Cole.[125] A survey of Castle Otway in Upper Ormond in 1725 gives four tenants on 840 acres: Lee, Wright, Tool, and May. A schedule of tenancies on eleven denominations (covering 4,580 acres) on the Otway estate in 1803 indicates that twelve of the thirty tenancies belonged

[119] NLI, MS 19,822, 273–85.
[120] Ryan papers, rent account book, 1724–31.
[121] Ryan papers, rental of the Inch estate, May 1807.
[122] NLI, MS 8913.
[123] RD, 172/359/11695, 179/70/118843, 150/409/102654, 175/61/116185.
[124] NLI, MS 2043; Tipperary County Library, Thurles, Cole-Bowen rentals 1788, 1805.
[125] Bayly papers, rent roll 1707.

to Protestants. The largest single tenant was John Brenan (2,400 acres), the next in magnitude were Revd Richard Lloyd (721), Henry Hunt (447), and James Otway (317).[126] Although some leases for Owney and Arra are in evidence, much of the land here may not have been set until the 1740s.[127] In 1784 of the fourteen head-tenancies on the Parker estate only two can be said to be Protestant: Shouldice and Switzer (40 acres), and John Basketville (33 acres), and their holdings were modest in size.[128] Because of its unattractive aspect Owney and Arra may have experienced the same difficulties in attracting tenants until the 1740s, as was partly the case in Kilnamanagh. This factor may also have operated with reference to Slievardagh not merely because of its difficult terrain but also because it was a region particularly disturbed by tories and rapparees, thus making its recovery slower and hindering the attraction of tenants there.

The head-tenantry on a select number of estates across the county was largely Protestant. In the three most northern baronies (at least those under lease before the 1740s), they were numerous, and were also found in Clanwilliam, on the Mathew, Maude, and O'Callaghan estates, and around Clonmel. However, it is the interjection of a group of large Catholic tenants into this pattern, on the southern estates at least, that was most significant so far as tenant denominational distribution is concerned. They can be said to form a linking interest in a frontier zone stretching from Carrick to Cahir to Cashel and onward to Thurles, being entrenched on the Butler (Kilcash), Mandeville, Butler (Cahir), and partly on the Mathew estates. A more hybrid pattern is apparent on the Meade and Mathew estates, in the case of the latter this mixed tenantry paralleling the accommodation arrived at by the family itself with the Protestant establishment. This overall pattern parallels that on seven estates in Carlow, north Wexford, and south Wicklow where the chief tenantry was mainly Protestant and the Catholics accounting for about one-third; and on the Wandesford estate in Kilkenny in 1746, where the two largest tenants were Catholic.[129]

[126] NLI, 21.F.129 (4); NA, M3391.
[127] RD, 31/360/19450; NLI, MS 13,794 (5), 21.F.113 (24); Roscrea Heritage Centre, Maxwell papers A/1/1/5; *Dublin Courant*, 2–5 May 1747.
[128] NLI, MS 11,416 (unsorted): 'An account of the tenants of Anthony Parker esq. in the counties of Tipperary, Cork, and Limerick 1784'.
[129] Gahan, 'Religion', 108–10; Nolan, *Fassadinin*, 98–9.

4. Estate Management

To what extent did the circumstances already discussed influence
the degree to which landlords were able to administer their estates
effectively? This can be considered in relation to five areas of
estate administration: holdings, rent, agents, courts, and improvement.

The size of holdings leased in the early eighteenth century was
large. While maintaining a preference for the individual solvent
tenant after mid-century, landlords were prepared to take on a
number of tenants for a single leasing unit. In advertisements the
terms 'in whole or divisions' and 'entire or in parcels' occur
suggesting that landlords were prepared to split up leasing units.
While making a public declaration of such a choice, in practice
some landlords preferred to take on the individual tenant and give
him the entire farm. The landlord in such cases was satisfied to
obtain a guaranteed rent, and it normally implied that the tenant
was absentee. On the other hand, resident improving landlords
embarked on a policy of dividing up their estates into smaller more
viable farming units as old leases fell in. Thus Sir Thomas Maude
of Dundrum in 1767 sought 'Protestant manufacturers' for over
270 acres which he proposed to let in lots of 5–10 acres on three
lives leases.[130] Tardy rent payments by large tenants in the early
1770s led some landlords to favour more compact farming units.
On the Stanley estate an integral part of the new leasing policy
enunciated in 1774 was direct letting to the tenants in small
parcels, the agent recommending that 'you will find farms of 200
acres or thereabouts most suitable', and as old leases fell in
subsequently there was a policy of dividing up the farms and
letting direct to the occupier.[131] Barker at Kilcooley was also
involved in a similar process in the 1770s.[132]

More characteristic was the subletting into smaller units by large
middlemen or those who became middlemen by so doing. On the
Butler (Cahir) estate, following its resetting on long 61-year leases
in the 1780s, the lessees proceeded to sublet extensively, dividing

---

[130] *FDJ*, 10–14 Feb. 1767.
[131] A. McGuire to T. Dane, 25 Oct. 1773 (Derby papers (Preston), DDK/1704,
correspondence series 1747–77); McGuire to Derby, 20 Dec. 1788 (DDK, 1705
series); DDK, 1712/4.   [132] Barker: TCD, Barker Ponsonby papers, P6/46.

the estate into an array of small sub-tenancies from which they reaped large profit rents between 1790 and 1815.[133] In the judgement of a later owner the Cahir estate was 'subdivided and loaded with paupers', and the leases were 'shamefully abused, the lands were sub-let and ruined, and the farmers pauperized by the lessees'.[134] It can be argued that the result achieved by an improving landowner, like Maude, setting farms in small units to tenants directly, was no different than that of the middleman. The difference relates to a question of control: Maude, with direct control over the size of leasing units, was able to implement an improvement policy and to enjoy the full benefit of rising rents from occupying tenants; whereas, more commonly, landlords like Lord Cahir had lost control over the regulation of holdings below the level of head-tenant. In consequence it was impossible to implement any extensive reforms or undertake direct letting to the occupying tenant on the Cahir estate until the 1840s. This experience was general: by 1815 it was remarked that 'The land in Tipperary generally is not let directly by the landlord to the cottier, but most certainly through the intervention of the middlemen.'[135] This was typical of the situation in Munster generally. Thus for the majority of landowners, except when leases expired, there was a general inability to control the actual size of holdings on their estates. While in theory they could regulate them through lease covenants, these commonly were unenforceable. As a result while the size of holdings remained nominally large for chief tenants, in practice smaller-sized units became the norm.

In large part the proliferation of small holdings reflected the composition of peasant society and its inherent problems. There was a basic threefold division in peasant society. First, there were smallholders or cottiers who in Tipperary occupied less than 10 acres usually, held from a middleman, with a cabin on a year-to-year basis; those holding in excess of 5 acres paid a cash rent, those with less paid in labour. But generally, cottiers paid rent in cash. Secondly, there were landholding labourers holding a cabin and garden from farmers which they paid for in labour and who depended on the cultivation of potatoes for subsistence, in combination with what work became available. By 1816 a social

---

[133] *PP*, 21, pt. iii. (1845), 888–91.   [134] NA, Acc. 976/6/5.
[135] [A.] Gregory (ed.), *Mr. Gregory's letter box 1813–30* (London, 1898), 102.

differentiation had emerged among this class in Tipperary based on the amount paid for the plot and the amount paid in wages.[136] In addition such labourers received the grass for a cow from their farmer employers paid for in labour at the same rate as the cabin and garden. Labourers with a cabin, potato ground or conacre, and milk from their employers (which was normal), were considered to possess one-third or one-half of the wage equivalent.

Thirdly, there were landless labourers, a numerous group who were unmarried farm servants who lived with their employers, receiving food and wages in return for their labour. To this group belonged labourers in the county not bound by the year and the migrant workers from south-west Ireland whose labour was particularly in demand at harvest time and when potatoes were dug. At such times wage rates paid to this group were three times higher (2*s.*–2*s.* 6*d.*) than those (8*d.*–10*d.*) paid to bound labourers with land.[137] This class was entirely reliant on employment compared to the two preceding groups. The viability of each of these three groups depended on a combination of constants remaining in place: food being cheap and plentifully available, and conacre rents being reasonable and commensurate with wage levels. It was when these constants shifted that conflict arose within and between these groups themselves, and between them and their employers.

The term 'conacre' referred both to the contract made between the farmer and the labourer or cottier, and to the portion of potato ground so contracted for. The contract, usually made verbally, granted the right of occupancy for a specific period and did not create a legal relationship of landlord and tenant. There were two characteristic forms which the system could take. First, a farmer ploughed and manured a plot of ground and then let it for a season (normally an eleven-month period expiring on 1 November) at a high rent to a labourer who took one or more crops of potatoes from it. Alternatively, potatoes might be set in ground given rent-free to a labourer who undertook to supply the manure, and who paid for it by his own or his family's labour.[138] The choice between

[136] [A.] Gregory (ed.), 98–9; see also M. Beames, 'Cottiers and conacre in pre-famine Ireland', *Jnl. of Peasant Studies*, 2 (1976), 352–4.

[137] Ibid. 99; cf. Young, *Tour*, ii. 37, 39–40.

[138] J. P. Kennedy, *Digest of evidence taken before her majesty's commissions of inquiry* (Dublin, 1847–8), i. 519–22; *PP*, 33 (1836) app. F, 409.

the two kinds of system ultimately depended on the status and resources of the parties concerned: a labourer lacking in resources would be unable to supply seed and manure and therefore had to offer labour services in order to make up the rent; while more capitalized cottiers and labourers were in a position to pay the high conacre rent as well as supply seed and manure.

The conacre system was exploitive because it involved risk and insecurity. The fact that the contract was for an eleven-month period made the arrangement inherently insecure, and the contract entailed the prospect that if the season was good then a good crop was forthcoming, but if it was bad and the crop failed then the labourer was ruined. Secondly, since the contract did not have the status of the lease, the position of the labourer was precarious as he had no legal standing if the terms of the contract were disputed. Thirdly, rents for conacre tended to be high because, as it was essential as a basis for food supply, competition pushed up its price; because the presence or absence of manure tended to be an additional determinant of price; and because there was a reluctance on the part of graziers to break up prime pasture ground for conacre. Therefore, it might not be worth the high price paid for it. Despite its high price, access to conacre was essential for the peasantry to ensure food supply and so the high rent was vouched for without any necessary guarantee of ability to pay, but with the hope that any deficiency might be made up by labour services.

Landlords did include clauses in leases against subletting to under-tenants and prohibiting the alienation or selling of an interest without prior written consent, with infringement incurring penalties in the form of extra rent payments.[139] The degree to which this operated in practice varied. For instance, it can be shown that even in the case of an improving landlord like Barker his approach to alienation developed from one of deterrent in the 1770s, to incentive in the 1780s, to accommodation in the 1790s.[140] Most landlords, however, did not intervene in the subletting

---

[139] Such penalties can be documented for the Erasmus Smith Schools, Bagwell, Minchin, Riall, Otway, and Butler (Carrick) estates: High School, E. Smith papers, Tipperary deeds dated 17 June 1789, 16 May 1791, 17, 19 Mar. 1792, 5 July 1794, 27 Feb. 1810, 11 Mar. 1814; NLI, Riall papers, deeds of 10 May 1759, 11 Jan. 1770, 9 Aug. 1798; Minchin deeds (Mic.P.5701), deed of 23 June 1766; Braye papers, 23 D57/18, 19, 22, 33 (abstracted in NRA, list no. 9254); *LJ*, 24–8 Dec. 1811.   [140] TCD, Barker Ponsonby papers, P6/46, 49, 54, 59, P7/74.

activities of their head-tenants. This partly reflected the entrenched position established by the latter over a wide area of the county after 1690, and it partly demonstrates the lack of resolution by landowners to confront a major social group. Such a process became redundant at any rate after 1790 since many of the large head-tenants like McCarthy and Scully bought out their interests becoming landowners in their own right.

Clauses against subletting were contained in the leases granted on the Butler (Cahir) estate in the 1780s, but due to the boom in agricultural prices in 1790–1815 particularly for grain, these tenants sublet to a large degree thereby obtaining large profit rents, a process the landlord was unable to stem. Those tenants of Lord Cahir's, such as the Fennells of Rehill who exceptionally had not engaged in rampant subletting, were using the threat, as Cahir himself reported, 'to cut up this noble place into cottier tenancies if I did not give them a renewal of the lease [of Rehill], which I refused to do'.[141] This experience relates to the post-1815 period when a slump in cereal prices undermined the solvency of middlemen, allowing landlords the collective incentive to proceed against them more resolutely. Also, before 1815 landlords who had a high political profile were not themselves entirely blameless. For, after the act of 1793 readmitted Catholics with the required freehold value to the franchise, an impressive number of 40s. freeholders were created through the granting of life tenancies across the county, and those who were politically active in the 1790s and 1800s gave leases to smallholders to enhance their political prospects.[142] Thus where size of occupiers' holdings is concerned landowners could exercise little direct influence, a situation condoned by political self-indulgence on their part. The long-term consequence was that, in reaction to the situation, landowners became reluctant to grant leases at all, but preferred to allow tenancies at will, as on the Butler (Cahir) estate where subletting and subdivision were acute.[143] It may well serve as the exemplar for other, similarly circumstanced estates.

The main concern of landlords was a solvent tenant. Proposals were normally made in writing. While the process of auctioning lands through public advertisements operated to produce the

[141] NA, Acc. 976/6/5.   [142] Kennedy, *Digest*, i. 417.
[143] NA, Acc. 967/6/5; *PP*, 21, pt. iii. (1845), 239–41, 888–91; Kennedy, *Digest*, i. 418.

highest bidder, the other method of rent fixing was by fining, i.e. paying a lump sum for entry to the farm and having subsequent rent payments adjusted downward. In some cases the fining down of part of the rent or a small fine was specified, in others the choice of whether a fine was taken or not was often a matter of agreement rather than obligation with the option being left with the tenant.[144] In general the landlord's immediate need of cash determined whether a fine was taken. The amount of a fine could range from an arbitrarily chosen sum to a proportion of the annual rent. On the Massy estate in 1782 a tenant was given a choice of fining down one-third part of the rent, and on lands let by Walter Woulfe near Carrick, also in 1782, £20 or more per year could be fined down at 5 per cent.[145] These inducements and adjustments to the rent level were incentives to the tenant to commit himself to a lease.

Upon entry the tenant was expected to be punctual with rent payments. Times of payment were twice yearly, either 25 March and 29 September for leases in mixed farming areas, or 1 May and 1 November on pastoral farms. Rents were almost universally paid in cash or bills, though on some estates, e.g. O'Callaghan, Otway, and Hely-Hutchinson, some individual tenants paid in kind at least in part.[146] Leases usually stated a period of 21 days before distraint for non-payment took place, and 41 days (as on the Erasmus Smith estate) before possession was resumed. The custom of having a running or hanging gale, whereby the tenant was not expected to pay one-half year's rent until the second was due, became prevalent.[147] On estates where a more strict management was emerging there were attempts to reverse this practice. Thus the new leasing policy on the Stanley estate in 1774 specified that 'The first half year's rent to be paid before the second is due.'[148] This was exceptional however.

This running arrear, kept within limits in normal years, could extend itself in periods of economic difficulty. As a result of the distress of the early 1740s an arrear of £2,500 accumulated on the Butler (Kilcash) estate by 1747, £700 of which had to be written

[144] *FDJ*, 14–17 Feb., 17–21 Mar. 1767; *FLJ*, 12–16 Feb. 1780; *CG*, 4–8 Dec. 1783, 10–13 Apr. 1786, 5–8 June 1793, 30 Oct.–3 Nov., 3–6 Nov. 1802.
[145] *CG*, 10–14 Oct., 18–21 Nov. 1782.
[146] Clonmel Museum, Acc. 1985/81; Braye papers, 57/D/975–6; TCD, Donoughmore, Z/14, fo. 1.　　　　　　　　　　　　[147] Kennedy, *Digest*, ii. 757.
[148] Derby papers (Preston), DDK, 1712/14.

off.[149] At such times a degree of indulgence was required of a
landlord or his agent in order to tide tenants over hard times, as on
the Stanley estate in the early 1770s or the Barker estate in
1810.[150] When arrears mounted, resort was had to distraining the
tenant's stock either to make up part of the rent through public
auction, or to hold them as security until the tenant paid up. At
this point, as we have seen, relationships could become strained:
unless the landlord agreed to cancel the arrear and allow the
tenant to continue, then on his refusal to surrender a situation of
forcible possession arose. Alternatively if the arrear was cancelled
this set a precedent which other tenants might seek to take
advantage of, or if the old tenant was successfully removed
through ejectment proceedings, the new tenant was commonly the
object of threats from the displaced tenant. Ejectment was a last
resort because it was cumbersome and costly, rather the threat of
ejectment was more commonly employed. Payment of rent and
rent arrears required delicate management on the part of the
landlord. Yet in normal times there was great flexibility, and even
in periods of distress difficulties were not insurmountable. In the
1780s when arrears rose on some estates, tenants were allowed to
settle accounts and re-establish their tenancy. Thus in 1782, when
tenants were sought for 1,250 acres near Thurles, bids were
welcomed 'provided the [sitting] tenants should not redeem, being
lately evicted for non-payment of rent',[151] and other instances of
flexibility are on record.

   With difficulties being experienced in the 1780s in the collection
of rents this decade witnessed a closer management of estates,
reflected in a more widespread appointment of agents. At the
outset of the century the role of the agent was confined to the
narrow one of making leases and collecting rents, generally on the
larger, absentee estates. Both were the dominant considerations in
the work of the Longford commission on the Ormond estate in the
early 1690s. What made the commission unique as an agency at the
time was the way in which its members, notably Warburton and

[149] Ignatius [?] to J. Butler, 9 [?] 1747 (Kavanagh papers, NLI, Mic.P.7155).
[150] Derby papers (Preston), DDK, 1712/4; McGuire to [Derby], 7 Jan. 1773
(DDK, 1704 series); P. Walsh to Lady H. Ponsonby, 11 Aug. 1810 (Barker
Ponsonby papers, P2/3/8).
[151] *CG*, 24–8 Jan. 1782; and for other instances of flexibility: Derby papers
(Preston), DDK, 1701/13, 1702/19; TCD, Donoughmore, Z/14, rent receipt book
1784–6; High School, case of *M. Carroll* v. *J. Thrustout* (19 Mar. 1792).

Longford, formulated ideas on estate management and improvement novel for the period. More characteristic were agents like Damer on the Erasmus Smith Schools, Nagle on the Butler (Cahir), Purcell on the Everard, and Meade on the Smith estates, whose functions were more narrowly defined.[152] The greater amount of property coming regularly on the market after mid-century at the least brought an intensification in these functions. The downturn in the 1770s and 1780s caused a rise in arrears of rent, making landlords employ more resolute agents to enforce their collection. The large amount of land relet in the 1780s heralded the appearance of more professional agents notably the Coopers. Already by this stage the agent whose main function was to implement the landlord's estate improvement initiatives had made his appearance. One of the earliest was Daniel Lenihan on the O'Callaghan estate in the early 1740s.[153] The number of improving landlords, however, was few, consequently the agent with a role primarily as rent receiver continued to be the norm.

Salaried agents like the Coopers appeared late. At an earlier period agents were more commonly found among the landlord's relatives, large head-tenants on the estate, or from the ranks of attorneys or merchants in the larger towns. Two of the main requirements of the agent, trust and security, were most conveniently found among those related to the landlord. Thus the McCarthys attended to the estate affairs of their in-laws the Ryans of Inch between 1737 and 1756.[154] Head-tenants who had proved their solvency and who held large acres might also possess the credentials of reliability. In the early part of the century Nagle on the Butler (Cahir) and McCarthy on the Mathew estates acted as rent receivers, a function still fulfilled by the McCarthys in the 1760s.[155]

Valued for their specialist knowledge, the existence of attorneys as agents was most likely where the owner was a permanent absentee. Before its division in 1755 the Smith estate, situated in four counties (Louth, Limerick, Meath, and Tipperary) was managed by Edward Meade of Drogheda.[156] After the 1755

[152] Clonmel Museum, Acc. 1985/80, see also 1985/68; TCD, MS 3577/2.
[153] Clonmel Museum, Acc. 1985/76.
[154] Ryan papers, D. Ryan's account with J. McCarthy, 1737–56.
[155] TCD, House of Lords appeals 2, *Cahir* v. *Nagle* (1717); RD, 239/554/163536.
[156] NA, D16,339.

division the agency for that part of the estate which passed to Lord
Strange (Stanley), came to the Dublin attorney family of McGuire
who retained it until the 1820s.[157] The Stanley estate espoused
good management with rents paid regularly, tenants' arrears
tolerated through bad times, and sub-agents employed to provide
a local presence, all indicating that the estates of absentees were
not necessarily badly conducted. Indeed attorneys might be
preferred as new agents in cases where landlords had suffered at
the hands of unscrupulous agents. The Mathews of Thomastown
had a run of bad agents in the late 1760s and 1770s in the persons
of Ignatius Browne and Denis O'Brien, who contributed to the
alienation of estate revenues at this time, and who were replaced
by a Dublin attorney in 1781.[158] Similarly the agent who
fraudulently granted the long leases on the Butler (Cahir) estate in
the 1780s was replaced following the landowner's death in 1788,
again by a Dublin attorney.[159]

Merchants, who from situation could conveniently remit rents,
appear as agents occasionally. Thus Martin Murphy, a Waterford
merchant, was Lord Cahir's agent in the 1760s.[160] Two Carrick
merchants, Valentine Smith and James Sause, were agents to the
Arran and Scott estates respectively in the 1780s.[161] Among the
spate of new agents appointed in the 1780s were the Clonmel
merchant-banker Phineas Riall and Edward Collins who was given
the management of the Barton estate.[162] This illustrates the
different range of persons who functioned as agents. Their
interchangeability is shown in the case of the Butler (Cahir) estate
which experienced all three types in the course of the century:
from Nagle the head-tenant in the early eighteenth century, to
Murphy the merchant in the 1760s, to Scott the attorney in 1789.

The decade of the 1780s, with its rent arrears and relettings,
provided the context out of which a more professional agent
emerged. The prime example of this is the Cooper family. The
family originally settled at Killenure near Cashel in the 1740s as
part of the household of archbishop Price and later rose to

---

[157] Derby papers (Preston), DDK, 1702/3, 6, 10, 22; 1701/26.
[158] *FDJ*, 5–8 Dec. 1767; *FLJ*, 5–8 Sept. 1781; *CG*, 24–7 Dec. 1781; *An act for vesting in trustees*, 26.
[159] *CG*, 23–7 Oct. 1788.   [160] *FDJ*, 6–10 Jan. 1767.
[161] *CG*, 10–13 Dec. 1781; *WC*, 5–8 Sept. 1785.
[162] *CG*, 29 Feb.–1 Mar. 1784, 17–21 May 1787.

prominence in the Treasury Office in Dublin.[163] In the 1780s they used their position to pick up agencies on the Damer, Lloyd, Cashel See, Erasmus Smith, and Maude estates.[164] That their appointment sprung from the accumulation of arrears and debts is clear from a public notification as to their new agency on the See estate in May 1782.[165] In addition to those already mentioned, new agents were appointed in the 1780s to the Newenham estate; others were appointed in that decade also to the Cole-Bowen estate near Toomavara and the Massy estate near Golden.[166] Sub-agents or stewards became more plentifully evident in the 1770s and 1780s, their work being taken up with buying and selling cattle, tillage management, laying out grounds, keeping labourers' accounts, and running a large house.[167] The professionalization of the office of agent was a general feature in the management of estates in Munster in the late eighteenth century.[168]

Just as the appointment of more professional agents in the 1780s can be viewed as a reassertion of the landlord's power, so also can the revival of manor courts in that decade. These institutions were largely medieval in origin though some came into existence in the seventeenth century. About 1650 there were thirty-seven locations which had manorial jurisdiction, but by the 1830s this number had fallen to six.[169] Functionally the manor court was divided into a court leet and a court baron. In the former, which was convened twice yearly by the manor's seneschal who was appointed by the landowner, matters like land boundaries, roads, regulation of markets, weights and measures were dealt with. The court baron, also summoned by the seneschal, adjudicated in cases concerning the recovery of cash debts (£5 or under), promissory notes (£10 or under), and trespass. The court proceedings for the manor of

[163] L. Price (ed.), *An eighteenth-century antiquary: Austin Cooper 1759–1830* (Dublin, 1942), 3–5; Thurles, County Library, draft pedigree of the Cooper family (xerox); R. A. Cooper, 'Genealogical notes on the Cooper family in Ireland, 1660–1960', *Irish Genealogist* 3 (1964), 351–5.

[164] *CG*, 1–4 Apr., 30 May–3 June 1782, 29 Nov.–3 Dec. 1787, 16–19 Mar. 1789, 16–19 Mar. 1803. [165] *CG*, 30 May–3 June 1782.

[166] *CG*, 17–20 Dec. 1781, 11–15 Mar. 1784, 30 May–2 June 1785.

[167] *FLJ*, 15–18 Jan. 1772, 13–17 Apr. 1776; *CG*, 2–6 May 1782, 4–8 Sept., 2–6 Oct., 24–7 Nov. 1783, 3–7 July 1788; NLI, Mic.P.5489 (will of J. Ryan, Inch, 1 May 1773 mentions his steward Oliver Grace). [168] Dickson, 'Cork', 235.

[169] *CS*, i, ii; *PP Manor courts (Ire.)*, 15 (1837), 455–6; 17 (1837–8), 137, 141; court baron: W. H. Crawford, B. Trainor (eds.), *Aspects of Irish social history, 1750–1800* (Belfast, 1975), 131.

Coolkill near Thurles in *c.* 1790 shows it to have been mainly taken up with disputes between tenants, adjudicating small debts, and awarding costs.[170] The business of the courts could be considerable because of their accessibility and inexpensiveness, particularly if the jurisdiction of the court was extensive, as with Lord Lismore's, for instance, which extended over thirty-eight townlands.[171] The business of the manor courts grew subsequent to an act of 1785 (25 Geo. III, c. 44) which confirmed and enlarged their powers in civil cases. Following its passage a number of manor courts were revived. In the same year as the act passed, George Ryan of Inch appointed a seneschal to the manor of Coolkill; in 1792 following the revival of the Ormond title the manor courts of Carrick were reinstituted; Lord Cahir appointed a seneschal for his three manors in 1802, as did Lord Llandaff for his manor of Thurles in 1817.[172] The revival of these courts reflected the desire of certain landlords to reassert control over their estates, which in Lord Cahir's case had been sharply diminished in the 1780s.

The chief deficiency on estates where the above situation persisted was that progress towards improvement was impeded. While the aspiration towards improvement existed in the early eighteenth century, formulated on the twin pillars of a preference for Protestant tenants and solvency, this was compromised due to an insufficiency of the former and a toleration of the large head-tenant who did no more than pay a regular rent. From mid-century, however, landlords increasingly encouraged the solvent, improving tenant who would undertake a range of building and landscape schemes in return for generous lease terms. The landlord might be in a position to offer the land with the benefit of improvements already executed. Land was expected to be suitable for agriculture and in Tipperary land had a wide suitability and use range. Where fertility levels were inadequate, manuring programmes might be undertaken, and other advantages which could be offered the tenant were running water, shelter, orchards, and deer parks. A good dwelling-house for the farmer was a distinct advantage, particularly if it was slated and if it had a stable or barn adjoining it. The extent to which fields were enclosed and orchards

[170] Ryan papers, court book for the manor of Coolkill, *c.* 1790.
[171] *PP*, 15 (1837), 236, 455–6; 17 (1837–8), 140.
[172] Appointment of P. Fogarty by G. Ryan, 3 Sept. 1785 (NLI, Mic.P.5489); *CG*, 20–4 Nov. 1802; *FLJ*, 21–5 Apr. 1792; NA, M5330.

and deer parks walled were also important pre-conditions. Locational factors were also important, notably the fact that lands being leased were convenient to fair centres, market towns, and turnpikes.

The landlord was not the main agent in the execution of improvement schemes, rather his function lay in providing a range of incentives in the form of access to additional resources on the lands, and attractive lease terms. Landlords increasingly allowed tenants access to limestone, marl, and culm deposits as a form of encouragement. Accessibility to coal pits for culm to burn limestone in kilns was advantageous, and in this respect lands adjacent to the collieries in the Slievardagh Hills were particularly favoured.[173] This helped to reduce the cost of improvement in this region where the terrain was difficult environmentally. In general where the provision of lime is specified, the lands concerned were capable of being better improved. Other resources offered by the landlord to a new tenant might be crops or stock remaining from the old tenant. Where land had lain waste in the transition between tenancies—between May and November for instance— the benefit of this would normally be given to the new tenant. The choice of purchasing the stock on the lands on attractive terms might be given to the incoming tenant, while timber might also be offered.[174]

Commonage formed an incentive to the tenant. Valued for its convenience as rough pasture ground for cattle and sheep, commons were traditionally accessible for the benefit of all tenants in adjoining lands, and the numerous cases in which it was included in advertisements indicates that it was a valuable resource with which the landlord could attract the tenant.[175] The enclosure of commons took place in response to a sharp growth in demand for pastoral products in the late 1750s. To meet this demand landlords repossessed commons in order to stock them themselves or to let them to those who would, thereby overriding traditional

[173] *FDJ*, 13–17 Aug. 1771; *FLJ*, 2–6 Mar. 1771, 28 Feb.–2 Mar. 1776, 31 Jan.–4 Feb., 1–4 Mar. 1797; *LJ*, 28 Dec. 1805–1 Jan. 1806; *CG*, 13–16 Feb. 1786.
[174] *CG*, 4–8 Oct. 1781, 2–6 Oct., 18–22 Dec. 1783, 1–5 June, 13–16 Nov. 1786, 28 Apr.–1 May 1788, 23–7 Mar. 1793; *LJ*, 2–6 July 1808; *FLJ*, 22–6 Dec. 1770, 18–21 Nov. 1778; *FDJ*, 12–15 Mar. 1763; *CEP*, 6 Apr. 1769.
[175] For examples: NLI, D11,314; Church of Ireland College of Education, Purser Griffith papers, deed of 4 Mar. 1791; *FDJ*, 5–8 Jan., 14–18 Feb. 1764; *LC*, 27 Nov. 1769; *WC*, 8–12 Mar. 1771; *CG*, 15–19 May 1783, 20–3 Feb. 1793.

grazing rights in order to increase profits. Common lands were of two kinds. The first category was that adjoining the towns of Cashel, Clonmel, Fethard, Nenagh, and Thurles. By mid-century some of this common land was coming into the possession of private individuals. At Fethard, for instance, the extensive commons near the town, which were by report 'time out of mind grais[e]d in com[m]on by the people bounding and mearing the same and the inhabitants of Fethard',[176] were appropriated from the early 1740s. The corporation of the town allocated about forty acres of the commons for a proposed charter school in 1742, and the remainder was leased to Thomas Hackett one of the burgesses. He proceeded to enclose much of this land thereby excluding the customary access, for he was a victim of Whiteboy levelling activity in 1762.[177]

The second category of common land was more widely distributed, but was particularly evident on mountain slopes like the Galtees, Knockmealdowns, and Comeraghs. Due to the mid-seventeenth-century land settlement, large tracts of unreclaimed land were left in common between neighbouring estates. Their proprietors conceded grazing rights on these commons to their tenants but retained ultimate ownership including the right to enclose. That enclosure was proceeding by mid-century is indicated by the comment made regarding the lands of Kilcash in the 1750s when it was said that they had been 'enclosed and taken into John Butler's [the landowner] own hands'.[178] When enclosure such as this took place resistance by those affected would appear to have been unjustified as the original arrangement was informal and the landlord was within his rights. In other cases, however, there was a genuine cause of complaint. This was because some landlords set lands at a high rent to smallholders and in order to ease the burden allowed them tracts of common as part compensation. In response to favourable external demand for livestock and a rise in land values after mid-century, landlords like Barker and Perry in the 1760s, were induced to enclose these commons thereby providing

---

[176] NLI, PC, 46 (ii) Barton, folder marked 'Fethard Corporation', document containing an account by the inhabitants relative to the commons of Fethard, [c.1750].
[177] NLI, PC, 46 (i), 'Necessary questions and inquirys with respect to the Commons of Fethard, 25 Sept. 1757'; *FDJ*, 3–6 July 1762.
[178] NLI, MS 11,051, valuation of tithes in Kilcash parish in folder marked 'Lands in Co. Tipperary'.

an expanded area for grazing by new tenants or by stewards installed by landlords themselves.[179] This constituted an overriding of the privileges previously accorded to the sitting tenants. Their reaction was to register their discontent by attacks on the new or prospective occupiers of the commons and their property.

The reorganization of tenures consequent on the enclosure of commons led to the displacement of some villages. On part of the Butler estate at Kilcash, for example, only four tenants (who were the more substantial if one is to judge by the amounts they paid in tithe) remained out of the original twenty-three when John Butler, the landowner, enclosed the lands and took them into his own hands.[180] Contemporaries were struck by the depopulation which they saw as coinciding with the rural unrest of the early 1760s. At the least this unrest occasioned a certain mobility among the poor.[181] All of this was expressive of an erosion of traditional rights of access to commonage, which had been used as an incentive by landlords to induce tenants into lease commitments.

The second inducement landlords offered was a range of attractive lease terms. A moderately long lease was judged desirable if the tenant was to undertake long-term improvements. Very long or perpetuity leases, however, were self-defeating as was proven on the Butler (Cahir) estate. In preference the 31-year lease was regarded as sufficiently long, and for tenants who engaged to build a longer term or renewal of their leases might be promised.[182] In conjunction with a moderately long lease some in-built adjustment to the level of rent whether in the form of an abatement or a graded increase, could be made to aid the tenant in the initial period of the lease when, usually, the most expensive of the improvements were required to be executed.[183] Exceptionally, individual landlords might also forgo a renewal fine on the fall of a

---

[179] *FLJ*, 29 Sept.–2 Oct. 1764, 28 Sept.–1 Oct. 1768, 2–6 June 1770.

[180] NLI, MS 11,051, valuation of tithes.

[181] *Wilson's Dublin Magazine*, Apr. 1763, 197; J. Bush, *Hibernia curiosa* (London, 1769), 30.

[182] *FLJ*, 21–5 Mar. 1772, 1–5 Oct. 1774; *FDJ*, 17–20 Jan. 1761; *CG*, 26–9 Nov. 1781, 13–17 Nov. 1788, 9–12 Feb. 1789, 15–19 Jan. 1803; TCD, Barker Ponsonby papers, P6/49.

[183] Barker Ponsonby papers, P6/59; NLI, Riall PC, 260–1, Tipperary deeds, 1750–69 (G. Evans, 24 Oct. 1760), 1790–9 (deeds of 9 Aug., 30 Oct. 1798); High School, Tipperary deeds (R. Maunsell, 4 May 1749, and others of 27 Feb. 1810, 11 Mar., 18 Apr. 1814); *CH*, 27 Oct. 1804.

168 *Land tenure*

life during the early stages of an improvement lease.[184] In addition to the tenant's solvency, that he should reside was contingent for improvement schemes to proceed, and a preference for resident tenants is openly stated for lettings over a wide area.[185]

The requirement that prospective tenants be Protestant was of special significance. It had existed as a stated preference in the 1690s and to a degree it was achieved in the settlement of the Ormond estate. The policy was readvocated from time to time particularly in the aftermath of disaster. One farmer near Cashel in May 1741, after the heavy frost and snow, advocated the settlement of colonies of linen-workers from Ulster to replace the labourer and cottier population which was decimated through loss of the potato crop.[186] Such a proposal was novel being advanced in response to particularly harsh circumstances. In normal times landlords had to compromise their ideal of having a full comple-ment of Protestant tenants on their estates. Its re-emergence in practice was foreshadowed by the settlement schemes promoted by O'Callaghan around Clogheen in the early 1740s, with one tenant, Bagnell, for instance, in a lease of Shanrahan in 1741, being obliged to 'make, encourage, and continue two Protestant freeholders'.[187] The main stimulus to its revival as a preference came as a result of the events of the 1760s. Sir Thomas Maude and Sir William Barker, who were closely involved in the events of that decade, were subsequently associated with schemes to promote Protestant settlement on their estates. As early as February 1767 Maude was seeking Protestant manufacturers for settlement on his estate at Ballintemple, and in the 1770s he promoted the linen industry.[188] Barker's promotion of German Palatine settlers from Co. Limerick at Kilcooley derived from three sources: he had an estate in Co. Limerick; his mother was a Quin of Adare, a family which also sponsored Palatines; and difficulties were experienced

---

[184] NLI, Riall, PC, 260–1, Tipperary deeds 1750–69, lease to G. Evans, 24 Oct. 1760, has an endorsement that a new life was added on 18 May 1763 without fine.
[185] On solvency: *FDJ*, 31 July–4 Aug. 1764, 28 Oct.–1 Nov. 1766; *FLJ*, 9–13 June 1770, 6–9 Mar. 1793; *CG*, 1–4 Oct., 10–13 Dec. 1781, 10–13 Mar. 1783, 31 Jan.–3 Feb. 1785, 31 Dec. 1794–3 Jan. 1795. On residence: *FLJ*, 1–5 Oct. 1774, 7–10 Aug. 1776; 31 July–1 Aug. 1779; *CG*, 1–4 Oct. 1781, 20–3 Jan. 1783, 29 Mar.–1 Apr. 1784, 19–22 Mar. 1794, 20–7 Oct. 1804; *LJ*, 24–8 Dec. 1811; *CH*, 10 Nov. 1802; TCD, Barker Ponsonby papers, P6/49, 54.
[186] Publicola, *A letter from a country gentleman*, 2, 7.
[187] Clonmel Museum, Acc. 1985/47.
[188] *FDJ*, 10–14 Feb. 1767; RD, 296/461/197728.

by the original colony in Limerick after 1760 when a sixfold
increase in their acreable rents in new leases forced them to seek
new outlets.[189] Barker offered the settlers lands at a low rent in
1773 and by 1776 many families had settled in a colony in the
Slievardagh Hills later known as Palatine Street.[190] Other cases of
an active promotion of Protestants are on record: the Limerick
connection may also have influenced the settlement by Anthony
Parker of Castlelough of Palatines on his estate; on the Osborne
lands near Carrick; under Prittie at Silvermines; and the schemes
of Sir John Carden at Templemore.[191]

There were four areas in which improvement was undertaken:
building, planting, enclosure, and land use. The requirement of
residence necessitated a scheme of building, and the building
clauses in improvement leases were to be found in their most
precocious form in the estate village. The earliest, at Clogheen in
the 1740s, shows houses being erected of a standard and uniform
type intended to accommodate artisans and manufacturers. One
head-tenant on the estate in 1740 was required 'to throw down as
much of ye house where Squib [the previous tenant] lives as shall
appear not to be built with lime and sand, and rebuild and raise ye
same so as there shall be two lofts well floor[e]d, the walls and
chimneys to be of lime and sand and ye stair case without side ye
house, the whole to be new roofed, slated, and completely finished
within two years with a stable for 6 horses'.[192] Such a structure
reflected the status of this particular tenant, Daniel Lenihan, who
was O'Callaghan's new agent. The farmhouses of larger tenants on
other estates were equally ambitious and formidable.[193] The time
period within which the building had to be completed varied
between one and four years, and the cost ranged from £10 to £200.[194]

---

[189] D. L. Savory, 'The Huguenot-Palatine settlements in the Counties of
Limerick, Kerry, and Tipperary', *Proc. Huguenot Society of London*, 18 (1949–52),
215–17.

[190] H. Jones, *The Palatine families of Ireland* (Calif., 1965), fos. 41, 48, 55, 56,
58, 61.

[191] NLI, MS 11,416, 'A list of the landlords of Anthony Parker esq' (n.d.[*ante*
1777]), 'An account of the tenants of A. Parker 1784'; *FLJ*, 16–20 July 1768; *CG*,
3–7 Apr. 1788.

[192] Clonmel Museum, Acc. 1985/76, and for other cases, ibid. 67, 91, 138, 147.

[193] NLI, Riall, Tipperary deeds 1750–69, dated 24 Oct. 1760, 13 May 1769.

[194] NLI, MS 11,422, deed of 12 Feb. 1796; NA, D23,388; Clonmel Museum,
Acc. 1985/67, 76, 91, 138, 147; NLI, Riall, PC, 260–1, Tipperary deeds 1750–69,
deeds of 24 Oct. 1760, 13 May 1769.

The planting of an orchard sought to provide a long-term resource from which the tenant could benefit. Apple growing was widely spread over the county (except in the Keeper Hills, Slievardagh, and Eliogarty) by the mid-seventeenth century with eighty orchards on record, and in the south of the county (south of a line from Bansha to Fethard and Callan) cider-making grew as a side industry in the eighteenth century.[195] When mature an orchard could be very productive for the tenant, so that its planting was deemed a highly desirable form of improvement. The number of acres planted with cider fruit trees varied from one to four acres, and the period within which planting was to be completed was four to five years. Normally the orchard had to be fenced in with a stone wall or double quickset ditch, and any apple trees that died had to be replaced.[196] Timber was also a valuable resource but until mid-century tenants had little incentive to engage in planting trees, since they were traditionally reserved by the landlord in leases. However, an act of 1765 (5 Geo. III, c. 7) made provision whereby the tenant became entitled to all trees planted or their value on the expiry of the lease.

The enclosure of fields was the most widespread manifestation of improvement on the landscape. It had advanced to an extent, particularly in the south, by the mid-seventeenth century. The process continued piecemeal thereafter. It received a boost with the rising demand for pastoral products (emphasizing the need for closer management of stocking levels), and was promoted by the enclosure of common land to accommodate extra stock. Involving as it did a considerable deployment of time, labour, and resources, enclosure could prove as costly as building. A tenant on the Bagwell estate near Cashel in 1759 undertook to lay out £100 on ditching and improvements within seven years.[197] Enclosure advanced from the 1760s: lands were enclosed, subdivided with walls and quicksets in districts near Clonmel, Fethard, Killenaule, Cashel, Tipperary, Ballina (near the Shannon), and Roscrea

---

[195] I. Leister, 'Orchards in County Tipperary', *Irish Geography*, 4 (1962), 292–301.
[196] Clonmel Museum, Acc. 1985/76,138; NLI, Ormond bundle 1752–4 (3 Apr. 1752), bundle of 'Miscellaneous old deeds' (3 May 1757); Riall deeds, 10 May 1759, 24 Oct. 1760, 13 Mar. 1767; *CEP*, 10 Jan. 1760.
[197] Riall, Tipperary deeds, 1750–69, 10 May 1759.

during that decade.[198] Enclosure was also a feature of demesne agriculture, and it could also be associated with the development of roads.

Landlords were concerned to preserve the fertility of the soil, fearing that it might be exhausted by overcropping in the last few years of a tenant's lease. Such concern, expressed in lease covenants, sought to restrict the amount of land devoted to tillage and to stipulate a course of manuring. The restriction on tillage might apply to the entire property as on the Butler (Kilcash) estate in the 1750s and the Erasmus Smith Schools estate.[199] But as time went on the restriction became more specific with the preferred ratio of tilled to untilled land emerging as 1 : 10.[200] If, however, land was ploughed or tilled then a course of manuring was required. In the O'Callaghan leases of the 1740s this was required after every third crop, and by the 1760s after every second crop.[201] The burning of land was occasionally indulged in as a cheap way of providing manure in the form of ashes, but increasingly this became shunned as detrimental. Many acts were passed prohibiting the practice but only with that of 1765 (5 Geo. III, c. 10), which tightened up the judicial process and the system of penalties, may it have declined. References in leases obliging tenants to reclaim lands are few, those relating to the Palatines on the Barker estate and on the Erasmus Smith estate are exceptional. Drainage schemes involved a heavy capital outlay, and at any rate the proportion of unprofitable land in the county was low.

In-built into these improvement leases were penalties to enjoin the carrying out of their provisions. Commonly these were compounded into an overall sum at so much extra per acre rent as on the Butler (Kilcash) and Bagwell estates in the 1750s and 1760s.[202] Where improvements were more detailed separate penalties might be specified. The penalty for ploughing-up land

---

[198] *CEP*, 22 Sept. 1763; *FLJ*, 12–15 Oct. 1768, 15–18 Feb. 1769, 2–6 June 1770, 2–5 Jan. 1771; *FDJ*, 5–8 Oct. 1765, 18–22 Mar., 26–9 Apr. 1766; *LC*, 29 Mar. 1770.

[199] NLI, Ormond bundle 1756–7 (24 July 1756), 'Miscellaneous old deeds' (3 May 1757); High School, Tipperary deeds, particularly 4 May 1749.

[200] NLI, Ormond bundle 1770–4 (24 Oct. 1770), cf. bundle 1780–2 (16 Oct. 1782); Bagwell, PC, 12,674 (i–iii) (2 Feb. 1808); Riall, Tipperary deeds (9 Aug. 1798).

[201] Clonmel Museum, Acc. 1985/68, 76, 81, 83, 205.

[202] NLI, Ormond, bundle 1756–7 (24 July 1756), 'Miscellaneous old deeds' (3 May 1757); Riall deeds, 1750–69 (10 May 1759, 24 Oct. 1760).

without licence reached a norm of £5 per acre rent by the early nineteenth century.[203] Penalties for non-performance of enclosure works appear to have been particularly heavy, and similarly with reclamation and the abuse of turbary rights.[204]

Improving landlords might also provide direct incentives in the form of capital investment or aid, or more usually an allowance or remission in the rent, or an adjustment in the term of the lease. Direct capital input by the landlord was exceptional and was indulged in only by the most committed of improvers. Thus in 1747 O'Callaghan paid a tenant £10 towards the erection of a dwelling; in 1769 Barker spent £300 on ditching and draining a mountain farm of 300 acres; in 1769 also Bagwell agreed to compensate a tenant for two-thirds of the cost of improvements estimated at £100; and in 1807 Henry Otway agreed to repay a tenant £250 for the repair of Lissenhall mansion-house over the succeeding seven-year period.[205] It was more common to offer a rent allowance on the completion of certain works, which could amount to half.[206] Where works were partly undertaken by the landlord on the tenant's land, some compensation might be paid as on the Barker estate.[207] Alternatively a certain proportion of land might be given rent-free on the completion of designated works or an extension in the lease term might be offered.[208] However, such cases were as exceptional as the evidence for direct capital investment by landlords, a pattern which parallels the situation elsewhere, for example the Wandesford estate.[209]

The degree to which an improvement policy was implemented depended on the prevailing leasing structure on individual estates and on the commitment of individual landlords. The tenurial

---

[203] High School, Tipperary deeds (4 May 1749, 12 May 1750, 19 May 1770, 17 June 1789, 27 Feb. 1810, 11 Mar. 1814); NLI, Ormond bundle 1752–4 (3 July 1752), bundle 1770–4 (13 Apr., 21 May 1770); Bagwell, PC, 12,674 (i–iii) (2 Feb. 1808); NA, BR/CAV/17/21.

[204] NLI, Ormond bundle 1800–9 (24 Oct. 1776); Braye, 23 D.57/997; TCD, Barker Ponsonby papers P6/46.

[205] Clonmel Museum, Acc. 1985/67; NLI, Riall deeds (13 May 1769); Braye, 23 D57/1022; *FLJ*, 2–6 June 1770.

[206] NLI, Riall deeds (9 May, 4 Oct. and 30 Oct. 1798); High School, deeds 27 Feb. 1810, 11 Mar. 1814; RD, 403/348/267736; *CG*, 14–17 Mar. 1785; [J. Lidwell], *Lidwill's life* (Dublin, 1804), 39.

[207] Barker Ponsonby papers, P6/46a, 49, 54.

[208] NLI, MS 11,422 (12 Feb. 1796); High School, deeds, 19 May 1770; RD, 372/513/250109, 428/313/280258, 532/4/347908.

[209] Nolan, *Fassadinin*, 110–11.

situation on the majority of estates was inimical to improvement. The experience on the Butler (Cahir) estate was typical. Leases given to tenants on that estate in the 1780s contained clauses against subletting and, in most cases, for the building of good farmhouses.[210] But in following decades subletting became rampant, scarcely any houses of value were built, the land was exhausted through overworking, and by the 1840s there was little evidence of any improvement. The landowner at that stage commented despairingly: 'The lands have been sub-divided and loaded with paupers, not a house stands on them worth a farthing, the land is given up in a miserable state, not a single covenant in the leases is fulfilled'.[211] This experience illustrates the fact that the over-large tenant holding on a long lease was not the best choice when it came to improvement. This constrained the capacity of the landlord to act, and only when leases expired could an improvement policy be implemented. Even when this occurred and conditions were favourable, the motivating factor was the commitment of the landlord himself. Improving landlords were in a minority. Less than twenty persons from the county were elected to membership of the Dublin Society, for instance, between 1766 and 1782, and a farming society founded in 1802 had an initial membership of only forty-four.[212] The number of improvement schemes receiving premiums from the Dublin Society is impressive and suggests that most success was achieved at the level of the small farmer or cottier, as opposed to the large tenant.[213] Overall, however, whatever the aspiration towards improvement and however widely shared, its implementation was restricted in the case of the majority of landowners due to the leasing structure inherited from earlier in the century.

[210] *PP* 21, pt. iii (1845), 888. [211] NA, Acc. 976/6/5.
[212] *Proc. Dublin Society*, 2 (1765–6), 300, 317, 325; 3 (1766–7), 496; 4 (1767–8), 38, 42, 95; 6 (1769–70), 88; 8 (1771–2), 340; 9 (1772–3), 156, 191; 18 (1781–2), 79, 97; *CG*, 30 Oct.–3 Nov., 22–5 Dec. 1802, 2–6 Apr., 14–18 May 1803; *LJ*, 3–6 Nov., 11–14 May 1803.
[213] *Trans. of the Dublin Society*, 5 (1806), 132–4.

5
Rural Unrest

Agrarian unrest has loomed large in the history of county Tipperary not merely because of its persistence over time but also because of the violence of its expression. This unrest was a complex phenomenon neither uniform in its range of grievances, in its methods and organization, nor in the social groups or regions affected. At its most basic it derived from the unequal effects of economic change. Before mid-century the county was devoted to sheep and cattle grazing. After mid-century, however, while grazing continued to be important in certain areas, increasingly from 1770 there was a swing to cereal cultivation by farmers in areas adjacent to the River Suir, around Clonmel in particular. This shift to a more labour-intensive agricultural enterprise occurred at a time when population was growing. A combination of rapid commercialization and very large leasing units, largely pastoral, meant that tenurial problems were acute.

While Tipperary was a predominantly grazing county the social framework was simple in terms of stratification. But with population growth and commercialization after mid-century, the diffusion of intensive grain production in the Suir valley, and the wealth derived therefrom, served to create new social categories in rural society, especially at the intermediate level of the farmer. This development led to a more stratified society in these areas and in consequence to a wide range of grievances in times of unrest. In this region unrest stemmed primarily from economic issues: for the peasant these were conacre rents, access to commons, potato tithe, and employment; and for the farmer rents, distraint, eviction, and tithe on cereal crops; while opposition to tithe in general was a unifying factor between classes in this region, it was only secondarily a class conflict.

Class conflict was the most obvious characteristic of unrest outside this region. Thus the intense grazing region centred on Cashel had a simple social structure, a point implicitly made in the

remarks of a local author in 1741 who identified in this region vast tracts of land held by 'single persons in their own hands' and on the other hand there were 'herdsmen and shepherds and a few, a very few cottiers'.[1] Lacking intermediate categories of tenants, this region witnessed the sharpest and most direct conflict between the grazier and the smallholder, because of the resistance to agricultural change in grazing districts. This context defined the narrow range of grievances in this region, and because unrest here involved direct confrontation it was less complex than in the more southerly parts.

1. Character

In chronological terms agrarian unrest is essentially a post-1760 phenomenon. Detailed analysis of agrarian movements here is not extended beyond 1805, a year which marked a departure from the older forms of rural agitation and the adoption of the more pronounced methods of factionalism. The most serious phases or outbreaks were in the years 1760–6, 1770–6, 1785–8, and 1799–1803. Within these periods outrages display an intensity in individual years namely 1763, 1775, 1786, 1800, and 1802. Within individual years there was a general absence of outrage between the months of June and September, a period during which the demands on peasant time and labour were high. The only significant departures from this rule occurred in 1775 and 1786 when the high summer months exhibited a sustained level of unrest, reflecting the seriousness of peasant demands in both years.

In the period 1760–6, forty-two cases of serious outbreaks were reported; the chief centres of unrest were in the south of the county being associated with the areas around Cashel, Clogheen, Clonmel, Fethard, and Mullinahone.[2] The unrest of these years

---

[1] Publicola, *A letter from a country gentleman*, 2.

[2] Statistics on the incidence of unrest in the various periods are derived from the following sources: (1) newspapers: *CEP, CG, CH, DG, FDJ, FJ, FLJ, HC, LJ, WC*, and *WM*; (2) other printed material: *Gentleman's and London Magazine, (Walker's) Hibernian Magazine,* D. Herbert, *Retrospections* (1929–30), and D. Trant, *Considerations* (Dublin, 1787); (3) manuscripts: NLI, MSS 8395 (2), 8917 (1), 11,422 and 17,728, Mount Melleray, Burke MS 31, PRO, HO, 100/17, NA, SCP, 1015/14, 1A 52 159.

derived primarily from the context of direct management by large graziers in areas where there had been no conversion to tillage and where stocking levels had increased sharply because of market attractions, leading to encroachments on commons. Though the earliest recorded incident was in Borrisoleigh in February 1760, the level of unrest in northern parts did not maintain itself to make a significant contribution to the movement as a whole in this period or later in the century.[3]

By the early 1770s expressions of rural outrage became more numerous and more concentrated. The number of serious cases recorded for the period 1770–6 was seventy-six, a figure which is almost double that for 1760–6. The epicentre of unrest shifted eastwards away from the Clogheen district and had its first serious manifestation in the Carrick area. It is in the triangle formed by Fethard–Cahir–Carrick that the unrest is concentrated in this period. This was the region in which the agrarian issues deriving from the spread of dairying and grain production found expression.

The third phase of unrest in 1785–8 shows a reversal in two respects. First, in terms of incidence the number of outrages recorded at thirty-three has fallen below even the level of the early 1760s, reflecting the more sophisticated methods of action employed by the Rightboys. Secondly, the previous concentration in the Fethard–Cahir–Carrick triangle is not repeated, with outrages being more scattered. This indicates a more broadly based concurrence with Rightboy aims, particularly in relation to tithes and church rates. The unrest of the 1780s is more diffuse, expressive of the more widely shared grievances of these years.

Finally, the years 1799–1803 witnessed a rise in the number of cases recorded and new concentrations in the levels of unrest. A total of fifty-eight incidents are on record placing this phase second only to the 1770s in terms of magnitude of agrarian crime. There is a bunching of incidents in areas adjoining the River Suir in its upper reaches north of Clonmel. The eastern and southeastern parts of the county are relatively free of major unrest at this time.

---

[3] For the Borrisoleigh incidents on the Damer estate: *FDJ*, 3–6 May, 26–9 June 1760; NA, Privy Council Office, index to proclamation books 1618–1875, *sub anno* 1760, calendar of presentments (1A 52 159), 264. In 1777 Young remarked that, 'No Whiteboys have ever arisen in these baronies [Upper and Lower Ormond], nor any riots that last longer than a drunken bout at a fair' (*Tour*, i. 437).

Two important locational factors influenced the spatial occurrence and spread of agrarian outrages. First, many of the incidents can be traced to areas in which the building of new turnpike roads was undertaken. During the course of the century there were eleven acts of parliament which promoted road building in different parts of the county. An upsurge in this activity is apparent from the early 1750s when a number of new or amending acts were passed.[4] The construction of these roads is an index of the growing commercialization of the county. However they could be a source of grievance on two counts. First, leases of land along the proposed routes were overridden, tenancy arrangements disturbed and, in consequence, tenants' holdings reduced. Secondly, the toll-houses and gates erected at various points along the turnpikes for the collection of tolls on produce and animals, represented an additional imposition. Such toll-houses or gates were built at Urlingford, Longford Pass, Ninemilehouse, Ballypatrick, Twomilebridge, Marlfield, Clogheen, Knockboy, and elsewhere. These became the focus of attack by agrarian groups, on occasion making them important in a locational sense. Also they often acted as a means whereby unrest was disseminated to wider areas. This was the case in the Whiteboy movement of 1760–6, when the outrages spread from Tipperary to Cork via the new Clogheen–Ballyporeen–Mitchelstown road.

A second locational influence accounting for the incidence of a different category of unrest was the fact that the eastern part of Tipperary, with its expanding commercial farming, attracted labourers from south-west Ireland. Competition for employment in the agricultural and textile sectors often led to rivalry between local and outside labourers. The issue of outside labour was most prominent in the 1770–6 and 1799–1803 phases of unrest. It found expression along the Tipperary–Kilkenny border, its flashpoints being Carrick, Ninemilehouse, Mullinahone, Fennor, Longford Pass, and Urlingford, some of which were also toll-gates in the turnpike system.

---

[4] Excluding amending and consolidating legislation these acts were: 7 Geo. II, c. 20; 9 Geo. II, c. 22; 11 Geo. II, c. 18; 13 Geo. II, cc. 14, 15, 16; 25 Geo. II, c. 17; 31 Geo. II, c. 18; 5 Geo. III, c. 26; 19, 20 Geo. III, cc. 45, 46. See also Taylor and Skinner, *Maps*, 111–17, 120–1, 162–3, 188–96, 208–9.

2. Organization and Methods

In terms of organization the post-1760 agrarian movements
adopted traditional practices then current in rural society, but also
used more innovatory strategies. This fusion of traditional and
new characterizes the movements of the 1760s and 1770s. The use
of traditional practices assumed a number of different forms. The
long inheritance of tory activity in the county may have provided
an imitative stimulus for the Whiteboys given the emphasis on
pillaging and the captaincy structure, the latter being a discernible
feature of the movements of 1760–6 and 1770–6. Figures of
authority with titles such as Captains Fearnot, Flint, Alcock,
Slasher, and Squib, and untitled individuals holding leadership
positions, are in evidence.[5]

The organization and size of the rural movements beneath the
level of captain, which in some instances could be shared by up to
six persons, was not uniform.[6] In March 1763 it was reported that
over 14,000 persons were involved in the Whiteboy movement in
the county, and individual assemblies could be large; that in 1772
at Clonoulty reportedly numbered 2,000 and it was said to have
gone through the exercises of a disciplined army.[7] The size of
individual parties could range from a handful up to 600, but was
more normally under 100 persons. There was also a borrowing
from the themes of contemporary poetry. Thus use of designations
like 'Joanna Meskil', which was equivalent to a female personifica-
tion of oppression, indicates that the rural groups sought to depict
themselves in a more symbolic guise as the redressers of more
general, perhaps semi-political grievances.[8] The use of white
dress, uniforms, and regalia to distinguish themselves appears to
have been borrowed by the Whiteboys from the contemporary
apparel of such groups as mummers, strawboys, and wrenboys.
Whiteboy parties were often accompanied by musicians and horn-

---

[5] For titled: *FDJ*, 26–9 Mar., 5–9 Apr., 31 May–4 June 1763; *FLJ*, 30 Dec.
1775–3 Jan. 1776; *Gentleman's and London Magazine*, 32 (1763), 232 (mis-
paginated, *recte* 175). For untitled: *FDJ*, 18–22 May 1762; *FLJ*, 12–16 Dec. 1778;
WC, 29 Dec. 1775–2 Jan. 1776; *WHM*, Feb. 1774, 115, Mar. 1777, 215.

[6] *FDJ*, 11–14 Jan. 1766.

[7] *FDJ*, 16–19 Apr. 1763; *FJ*, 11–14, 16–18 Jan. 1772; *WHM*, Feb. 1772, 112.

[8] *FDJ*, 26–9 Mar. 1763, 1–4 Sept. 1764.

sounding, and occasionally legitimate mummers were mistaken for Whiteboys, as at Clonmel in 1774.[9]

The post-1760 agrarian groups derived much of their discipline and cohesion from a system of oath-taking, marking a departure from earlier groups. This was to ensure adherence to the movement's objectives and secrecy, as the evidence of revenge actions taken against recalcitrant followers illustrates.[10] Oaths had a wider function as they were used to gain more extensive support in the rural community for the movement's aims. This strategy was widely and successfully used in 1785–8 as a means of winning popular concurrence with Rightboy aims. Thus in 1786 locations as far apart as Owning near Carrick, Cahir, Moycarkey, Knocking-temple, Newport, and Cashel were the scenes where Rightboys swore the local inhabitants.[11] This was one element of sophistication not discernible in the two previous phases of unrest when oath-taking was used as a means of control rather than as a device for disseminating aims.

In 1760–6 the chief Whiteboy grievances concerned the enclosure of commons, conacre rents, and tithe—especially that on potatoes. The levelling of ditches and stone walls around commons was a registering of Whiteboy disapproval of the enclosure of such lands for grazing purposes by the landlord, his agent, or by newly installed tenants. The aim was to have such lands revert to communal use. A threatening letter addressed to 'the gentlefolks of this county' and delivered to one tenant warned that the levellers had combined to 'level all walls and ditches yt have been mid (sic) to enclose [that] which is ordained for ye benefit of ye poor. We begin here tonight and will not cease till we level down all ye commonage in this county.'[12] Levelling activity was most widespread in the years 1761–4, and though it was the opinion of one contemporary writing from Clogheen in 1762 that 'all the damage they [the Whiteboys] ever did that way [i.e. levelling] is so very inconsiderable that it is not worth naming',[13] it is clear that in individual cases losses were not insignificant. The value of lands was reduced because of the destruction of improvements like

[9] *FJ*, 15–18 Jan. 1774; *FLJ*, 16–20 May 1778.
[10] *FDJ*, 6–9 Apr., 5–9 Nov. 1765; *FJ*, 2–6 Apr. 1765.
[11] *FLJ*, 1–5, 26–9 July, 5–9, 26–30 Aug., 9–13 Sept. 1786; *HC*, 3 July, 11 Sept. 1786; *CG*, 29 June–3 July, 7–11 Sept. 1786; *WHM*, July, 390, Aug. 1786, 446.
[12] Mount Melleray, Burke MS 31, p. [273].
[13] *FDJ*, 10–13 Apr. 1762.

enclosures. Levelling was also used at this time as a method for destroying walls erected around deer-parks, lands which the Whiteboys considered should be made available as potato ground. In March 1763 the deer-park of John Watson of Clonbrogan near Fethard was thrown down and four of his deer killed, and John McCarthy at Lisheen and John Carden had similar experiences at the hands of the Whiteboys.[14] Related to the issue of access to potato ground was that of tithe on potatoes, resentment over which was expressed by their being destroyed as at Clogheen in 1763.[15] The demolition of dwelling houses can be identified with the desire to eject new tenants introduced on to recently enclosed commons, as happened in 1762 near Fethard, near Cashel, and in 1763 near Clogheen.[16] Other types of destruction recorded include the cutting down of an orchard on the Damer estate at Borrisoleigh in 1760, the burning of turf at Newcastle and the scattering of grain stacks at Rossmore both on the Perry estate in 1765, and the burning of farm buildings in a number of areas.[17] Intimidation was sometimes a part of Whiteboy activity as in physical maiming, the whipping of tithe proctors and others, and the sending of threatening letters.[18] Despite all this there was a general absence of serious assault with only one case of agrarian murder on record.[19]

In the unrest of the early 1770s the main issues were tithe especially that on cereal crops, outside labour, and new tenants particularly dairymen. To gain redress of these grievances personal intimidation was used. In relation to tithe this took the form of beating tithe proctors, often allied with the administering of oaths connected with the collection of tithe as was the experience of Revd Nicholas Herbert in 1773 and Revd Edward Herbert a year later.[20] Beatings and oaths were also administered to outside labourers, while their employers were maimed.[21] So far as direct

[14] *FDJ*, 19–22 Mar., 25–8 June, 8–11 Oct. 1763.

[15] *FDJ*, 29 Oct.–1 Nov. 1763.

[16] *FDJ*, 29 June–3 July, 3–6 July 1762, 22–6 Nov. 1763.

[17] *FDJ*, 3–6 May 1760, 15–19 Oct. 1765; *DG*, 2–6 July 1765; Burke, *Clonmel*, 364; NA, 1A 52 159, pp. 264, 266.

[18] *FDJ*, 5–8 Oct. 1765, 11–14 Jan. 1766; *CEP*, 31 Mar. 1763; FJ, 18–22 Mar. 1766; *Gentleman's and London Magazine*, 35 (1765), 703.

[19] NA, 1A 52 159, pp. 264, 266; Burke, *Clonmel*, 365.

[20] Herbert, *Retrospections*, i. 22, the year should be 1773 (see *FLJ*, 22–6 Jan. 1774); *FLJ*, 3–6 Apr. 1776; FJ, 20–2 Sept. 1774.

[21] *FLJ*, 22–6 Oct., 9–12 Nov. 1774; *FJ*, 24–6 Oct. 1776.

intimidation of new tenants is concerned a dual approach is
evident. First, there was the standard formula of physical attack,
singly or often in association with the imposition of oaths. Thus in
1771 the dwellings of farmers and dairymen near Fethard were
attacked, their occupants whipped and sworn, and another
dairyman was buried in a grave and made to swear to return to Co.
Waterford.[22] The second approach was the issuing of threatening
notices to new tenants enjoining them to relinquish possession to
the former tenants or else violence would ensue.[23] Alternatively
the notices cautioned the landlord not to replace existing tenants
in favour of outsiders, instanced in 1775 in the case of Hugh
Daniel.[24] This level of intimidation extended itself in this period
into several murders of persons of status notably Ambrose Power
in November 1775, and in the attempted murders of Philip Going
in 1773 and John Bagwell in 1775.[25] A new form of intimidation
introduced at this time was the imposition of a levy on the better-
off farmers either to finance legal proceedings on behalf of the
Whiteboys, or more generally simply as protection money.[26]

The destruction of property in the 1770s was significant though
subsidiary in its incidence to acts of intimidation. Houses of new
tenants were demolished or broken, the dairy utensils of dairymen
from Co. Waterford were destroyed, and cereals collected as tithe
were either set on fire or scattered.[27] There was a residue of
levelling activity in areas where it had been to the fore in the early
1760s. But levelling as an instrument of redress declined in the
intervening period, a trend consistent with the fact that enclosure
of commons receded as a major issue. There was a marked
increase in attacks on houses to obtain firearms, a practice not
greatly evident in the 1760s. At least fifteen such attacks are on
record for the years 1771–6 mostly in 1775, a particularly violent
year.[28] This marks a departure from previous practice, and arms

[22] *WC*, 12–15 Feb. 1771; *FLJ*, 4–7 Dec. 1771.
[23] *FLJ*, 24–8 Apr. 1773.
[24] *WHM*, May 1775, 318.
[25] *WC*, 29 Dec. 1775–2 Jan. 1776; *FJ*, 17–19 Aug. 1773; *FLJ*, 10–14 Aug. 1776.
[26] *FJ*, 11–13 Jan. 1774; *FLJ*, 11–15 Sept. 1773.
[27] *WC*, 5–8 Nov. 1771; *FLJ*, 4–7 Dec. 1771, 17–21 Sept. 1774, 17–21 June, 29
July–2 Aug., 28 Sept.–2 Oct. 1775; *FJ*, 14–17 May 1774, 20–2 July 1775; *CEP*, 23
Aug. 1773.
[28] *WC*, 12–15 Feb. 1771; *FLJ*, 5–8, 8–12 Aug., 28–31 Oct. 1772, 16–20 Sept., 11–
14 Oct. 1775, 13–16 Mar., 13–17 Apr. 1776; *FJ*, 5–8 Aug. 1775.

attacks were associated with the stealing of horses which became more common in these years.[29]

The unrest of the mid-1780s is characterized by a general reduction in the level of serious violence as the strategies adopted by the Rightboys were more sophisticated. This development is partly explained by the nature of the grievances at this time: tithes, clerical dues and rates, church rates, and rent, which were less sectional than the objectives of the 1760s and 1770s. Because the grievances were more widely experienced the Rightboy aims received a degree of popular, communal sanction, making the need to resort to violence less contingent. The absence of serious violence can also be attributed to the highly effective leadership of the Rightboys, and also to the degree of upper-class support which the movement enjoyed. Although some cases of intimidation against clergymen are evident, the new strategy of swearing entire parishes to pay only certain prescribed amounts in tithe payments, proved to be more effective.[30] Threats and collective swearing sessions were employed to regulate rates and dues paid to Catholic clergy.[31] Rent and general tenancy arrangements as issues are reflected in the number of cases of forcible possession, refusals to pay rent, rescuing of distress, and a residue of resentment against outside tenants.[32] Of their nature many of these incidents involved a degree of confrontation, but that serious personal attacks had become less common is reinforced by the fact that there was a sharp decrease in the number of attacks seeking possession of firearms.[33]

In contrast, the violence in 1799–1803 was characterized by attacks on the person and various forms of intimidation, with the destruction of property less prominent. This level of personal violence arose out of the main grievances of these years, namely shortages created by the bad harvest and the failure of the potato

[29] *FLJ*, 29 Oct.–2 Nov. 1774, 30 Oct.–2 Nov. 1775; *FJ*, 1–3, 29 Apr.–2 May, 1–3 Aug. 1775.

[30] NLI, MS 8395 (2); Trant, *Considerations*, 67–72; *FLJ*, 3–6 Aug. 1785, 26–9 July 1786; *CG*, 10–14 Nov. 1785, 7–11 Sept. 1786.

[31] *CG*, 29 June–3 July 1786; *FLJ*, 26–9 July, 26–30 Aug., 9–13, 16–20 Sept. 1786; *WHM*, July 1786, 390.

[32] Hamilton to Sydney, 5 Nov. 1785 (PRO, HO, 100/17/171–171ᵛ); White, *Anthologia Tipperariensis*, 54; *FLJ*, 23–7 Oct., 3–6, 24–7 Nov. 1784; *WHM*, Sept. 1785, 501; *CG*, 14–17 Mar., 21–4 Nov. 1785.

[33] *CG*, 21–5 Dec. 1786, where its common occurrence between Urlingford, Thurles, Cashel, and Killenaule is reported.

crop, the displacement of estate employees and sitting tenants, and the employment of outside labourers. The chief means used to gain redress on these issues was by personal attack. New tenants or new estate employees were murdered as were a proctor, Lord Cahir's steward, a caretaker, and others.[34] Beatings and floggings were administered to new tenants, outside labourers and their employers, and estate employees.[35] Intimidation was employed as a method to regulate the price of potatoes, to obtain potatoes, and to enjoin the quitting of farms on new tenants.[36] Threatening notices were also circulated in relation to the quitting of farms and to potatoes.[37] Essential for the execution of these personal attacks was the availability of firearms the stealing of which displays an upturn in these and following years.[38]

3. Issues and Participants

The social composition of the agrarian movement was pyramidal in character: a large base of the labourer/cottier class with representation from other classes narrowing as one rose in the social scale. In the 1760s one observer labelled the Whiteboys of Tipperary as a 'parcell of wretches' and, more specifically, 'swineherds and cowboys'.[39] For the grand jury of the county in 1762 the agitators were 'low, idle, and disorderly persons', while the levellers referred to themselves as 'revengers for wrongs done the poor'.[40] These remarks refer to the labourers and cottiers, a class lacking uniformity, embracing as it did both those in the occupancy of small conacre plots and those in employment (whether casual or long term), or a combination of both. The issues of conacre and potato tithe which they advanced were also

---

[34] *FLJ*, 2–6 Mar. 1799; *WHM*, Mar. 1800, 190, Apr. 1800, 254, Sept. 1800, 188; *LJ*, 24–8 Apr. 1802; *FDJ*, 26 Aug. 1800; *CG*, 17–20 Nov. 1802; NA, RP, 620/57/64, SCP, 1020/39; NLI, MS 27,571, p. 286.

[35] *CH*, 10, 27 Nov. 1802; *LJ*, 18–22 Sept. 1800; *FDJ*, 16 Oct. 1800; *WM*, 28 Aug., 8 Nov. 1802; *CG*, 8–11 Sept. 1802; NA, RP, 620/9/97/8.

[36] *CH*, 27 Oct. 1802; *LJ*, 17–21 Sept. 1803; *WM*, 28 Nov. 1801, 19 May 1802; *CG*, 25–9 Dec. 1802; NA, RP, 620/57/49.

[37] *WM*, 11 Sept. 1802; Hare to Somerton, 2 Apr. 1801 (Agar papers, box 3).

[38] *FDJ*, 30 July 1801; *LJ*, 1–4 June, 6–9 July, 7–10 Sept., 16–19 Nov. 1803; *CH*, 8 June 1803.

[39] Sheffield City Library, Wentworth Woodhouse Muniments, Burke MS 8/9.

[40] Mount Melleray, Burke MS 31, pp. 273, 288.

ones which attracted support from artisans and craftsmen in the towns like Clonmel, Clogheen, and Carrick where textile workers held outlying plots.

Furthermore the movement attracted some other subsidiary elements who either acted in a supportive capacity or who were motivated by self-gain. Of the former category schoolmasters, of whom two cases (one a Whiteboy leader) are recorded for this time, were able to provide the necessary skill for writing threatening letters.[41] Some Catholic priests may have had an identity of interests with the agitators as the destruction or depopulation of village communities consequent on enclosure decimated a main source of clerical income. One commentator remarked in 1763 that 'very many of these priests who had villages with an hundred or two of cottages upon them, which paid them 6 pence or a 1s. a year each, are now deserted and their poor stipends dwindled to nothing'.[42] In this way Catholic priests like Revd Nicholas Sheehy of Shanrahan, Revd John Doyle of Ardfinnan, and Revd Pierce Daniel of Cahir may have seen fit to render some token but non-active support to the agrarian rebels.[43] Catholic gentlemen were seen by the Protestant gentry as playing an active role in promoting the disturbances. This was a mistaken view as many of them were the victims not the instigators of Whiteboy violence. Leading Catholics renounced any implication of involvement. Edmund Sheehy, a Catholic tenant, referred to 'those fools called Whiteboys', that he knew of no 'man in the light of a gentleman connected with them', and that 'I have endeavoured as much as was in my power to suppress this spirit of Whiteboys'.[44] The only Catholic of any standing involved in the Whiteboys was the Clogheen woollen manufacturer James Hyland who was described as 'a very wealthy man and [a] considerable dealer in wool', whose participation arose from motives of profit.[45]

Levelling activity over enclosure was directed at new grazier tenants such as Pierce Dwyer near Clonmel, Ferris at Newcastle, and Edward Hodgson at Kill; at landlords' stewards, as in the case of Edward Briscoe on the lands of John Bagwell near Clogheen; and at landlords themselves, as in the cases of Thomas Hackett of

[41] *FDJ*, 26–9 Mar., 31 May–4 June 1763.
[42] *Wilson's Dublin Magazine*, Apr. 1763, 199; cf. *FDJ*, 10–13 Apr. 1762.
[43] *FDJ*, 22–6 June 1762.
[44] TCD, MS 873/728.
[45] *FDJ*, 10–13 Apr. 1762.

Fethard, John Willington at Roanstown, and John Damer at Borrisoleigh.[46] Large graziers like John Watson of Clonbrogan, Richard Moore of Barne, John Carden, and John McCarthy of Lisheen who by creating new deer-parks reduced potential conacre lettings, were also victims.[47] So far as tithe is concerned the chief victims were the tithe farmers or jobbers, while one person attempting to obtain a valuation for tithe on cereal crops was intimidated and made to take oaths.[48] Labourers sent by Revd Richard Foulke to collect potato tithe near Clogheen were accosted and he himself was assaulted when he tried to collect his tithe.[49] Employees or labourers on estates were often the victims of attack largely by those displaced from such employment or those who had not secured it.[50] Thus the Whiteboy movement of the early 1760s was characterized by a conflict between, on the one hand a large body of marginal elements in rural society mainly labourers and cottiers, and on the other substantial tenant farmers, graziers, and tithe farmers.

In the early 1770s as the nature of the grievances altered so also did the related social composition of the agitators, accompanied by a shift in the make-up of the group against whom the violence was directed. In these years the issue of tithe on cereal crops was one which affected a broad section of rural society. Farmers, whose participation in the unrest of the early 1760s had been negligible, now became active because tithe on cereals became more onerous as a result of the recent expansion in cereal growing. This occurred mainly in the Suir valley in districts hitherto devoted to stock raising, and largely tithe-free as cattle were effectively exempt from tithe since 1735. In south Tipperary, where the transition to grain was most marked, farmers or their sons resisted.[51] Because of their social position there were attempts to press large farmers into leadership roles in the movement.[52] Their involvement is also apparent from the description of those who led the attack on the Grubb household at Anner mills in July 1775, when it was

---

[46] Mount Melleray, Burke MS 31, p. 273; NLI, MS 11,422 (deposition of 24 Feb. 1762); *FDJ*, 3–6 May, 26–9 June 1760, 3–6 May 1762, 8–12 Nov. 1763, 24–8 Sept., 15–19 Oct. 1765; *DG*, 2–6 July 1765.
[47] *FDJ*, 19–22 Mar., 25–8 June, 8–11 Oct., 22–6 Nov. 1763.
[48] Ibid. 5–8 Oct. 1765.   [49] Ibid. 29 Oct.–1 Nov. 1763.
[50] Ibid. 5–9 Nov. 1765.
[51] Herbert, *Retrospections*, i. 22 (for 1774 read 1773); *FLJ*, 22–6 Jan. 1774, 8–11 May 1775; *FJ*, 20–2 Sept. 1774.   [52] *FLJ*, 10–14 Aug. 1776.

remarked that they were 'far above the lower order of people, were decently dressed, and spoke the English language very well'.[53] Farmers and their sons were also concerned in rescuing goods distrained by their landlords in lieu of rent.[54]

Dairying was expanding in the county from mid-century, but the growth in Co. Waterford was relatively greater forcing dairymen there to seek extra ground across the River Suir in south Tipperary and Kilkenny. Relatively more prosperous than their Tipperary counterparts, the Waterford dairymen were able to offer higher rents for dairy land to those letting it locally. This had the consequence of bringing them into competition with local interests who resented their intrusion, as local dairymen were unable or unwilling to pay the high rents demanded by the dairymasters.[55] Local dairymen either tried to intimidate the dairymasters, not to dispossess them, but to continue them in tenancy in preference to the Co. Waterford men, or to destroy the dairying utensils of the latter, inflict beatings, or impose oaths.[56] Attacks on Waterford dairymen and their local landlords are recorded in the early 1770s for the vicinity of Fethard, Clonmel, and Carrick.[57] The spread of these locations testifies to the extent to which the outsiders had intruded. The purpose of such attacks was to intimidate the dairymen to quit their holdings and remove back to Waterford. Those who made land available to them were also intimidated. In a well-documented case in April 1775 (at the opening of the dairy season when lettings were entered into), Hugh Daniel of Poula-kerry near Carrick was served with a threatening notice not to dispossess his sitting dairyman in favour of one Power, an outsider whose surname suggests a Waterford origin. This conflict arose because Lonergan, the sitting dairyman, had refused a rent demand of £40 for part of the dairy which he held from Daniel, the implication being that Power was able to furnish an amount equal to or in excess of this.[58] These attacks demonstrate the developing sense among certain categories of tenant, in this case local dairymen, of the need to control the occupancy of land in their own favour.

[53] *FJ*, 1–3 Aug. 1775. [54] *FLJ*, 16–19 Aug. 1775.
[55] *WHM*, May 1775, 318. [56] Ibid.; *FLJ*, 17–20 May 1775.
[57] *FLJ*, 9–13, 16–20 Feb., 4–7 Dec. 1771, 17–20 May 1775; *FJ*, 20–2 Apr. 1773, 29 Apr.–2 May 1775; *WC*, 12–15 Feb., 21–4 May 1771; *WHM*, July 1775, 435.
[58] *WHM*, May 1775, 318.

The intrusion of outsiders, whereby they came to be a threat to their economic interests, was also a grievance among labourers and cottiers at this time. The expansion in cereal cultivation created a demand for extra labour at harvest time, a demand largely filled by the recruitment of migrants from south-west Ireland. Their arrival in large numbers became a threat to the employment prospects of the local labour force, as the outsiders worked for lower wages. Data on wage rates for a number of locations in Tipperary recorded in the years 1776–7 shows that rates were not uniform over the county as a whole, that they were lower than the national average, and that the rise in wage rates over the preceding twenty years had only been about 1*d.* per day.[59] Some of the activities engaged in by the Whiteboys imply that they sought to achieve an improvement in wage levels. Much of the vendetta waged against estate employees in the 1760s, such as herdsmen, shepherds, carriers, and limeburners, was because they had accepted such employment at existing or lower wages in defiance of Whiteboy orders.[60] The context for employment was changing mainly because the growth in commercial cereal cultivation which took off after 1770 created a new and expanded source of employment. The demand was sufficient to attract migrant labourers from Cork and Kerry as seasonal workers. Their arrival was a threat to the economic interests of local labourers because it tended to raise rents as well as undercut local wage rates. Attempts by local combinations to rectify these disadvantages took the form of direct action against the outsiders with a view to their expulsion. Such attacks are in evidence for the Clonmel and Cashel areas in 1774; while the employers of such workers were also the victims of attack, as near Cahir in 1776.[61]

Labourers, cottiers, and country people generally were also resentful of a number of financial and material impositions which they regarded as arbitrary. Tithe exactions were a unifying grievance which found expression in the destruction of stacks of wheat and barley, and the intimidation of proctors.[62] There was also resistance to church rates, notably in the Birdhill–Newport

[59] Young, *Tour*, ii. 50–1.
[60] *FDJ*, 5–9, 26–9 Mar. 1763, 24–8 Sept., 5–9 Nov. 1765, 11–14 June 1766; *CEP*, 29 Aug. 1763; *FJ*, 18–22 Mar. 1766; *FLJ*, 22–6 Oct. 1768.
[61] *FLJ*, 22–6 Oct., 9–12 Nov. 1774, 24–8 Dec. 1776; *FJ*, 24–6 Oct. 1776.
[62] *FJ*, 20–2 Sept. 1774; *FLJ*, 8–11 May 1776.

district where in 1774 it was reported that 'thousands' of country people defied their imposition.[63] The substantial role of labourers and cottiers is again emphasized in the number of attacks for firearms, and in the taking of horses and their accoutrements.[64] Many of the grievances were shared by artisans and craftsmen in the towns. Their participation accounts for the spread of serious unrest to the Carrick area in the early 1770s, coinciding as it did with difficulties in the textile industry there. At a time of economic difficulty textile workers sought to protect their interest by, for instance, trying to maintain tithe potato rates in the deer-park near the town at current rates, by destroying barley and wheat stacks, and by general acts of intimidation.[65] A number of town dwellers acted in a leadership capacity notably Patrick Hackett, a carrier from Carrick, and Richard Dooly, a weaver from the same town; while others such as schoolmasters and publicans acted in supportive roles.[66]

The agitation of the mid-1780s was preoccupied with the issues of tithe on cereals, clerical dues and rates, church rates, and rent. These issues, particularly tithe, cut right across rural social divisions. While the bulk of the membership of the Rightboys, as in previous movements, continued to be drawn from the lower orders in society, upper-class involvement was more general than previously. The sustained expansion in cereal growing after 1784, evident in the rise in the number of flour mills in the county from thirty-eight in 1778 to seventy in 1788, is indicative that agricultural employment at this time was good. It was of a sufficient scale to absorb the local and seasonal labour supply. As a result conflict between both groups over access to employment is not evident as one of the sources of unrest in the years 1785–8. Labourers, cottiers, servants, and artisans, however, were aggrieved because of the exaction of tithe on cereal crops as shown in the opposition to Revd Nicholas Herbert in 1782, and because of clerical impositions exemplified in nearby Cahir in 1787 when it was reported that 'the lower class of peasantry shut up the chapel every Sunday and would not permit the priest to say prayers'.[67]

[63] Revd M. Ormsby to A. Ormsby, 10 June 1774 (NLI, MS 17,728).
[64] *FJ*, 1–3 Aug. 1775; *FLJ*, 28–31 Oct. 1772, 28 Feb.–1 Mar. 1775.
[65] *FLJ*, 3–7 Nov. 1770, 17–21 Sept. 1774; *FJ*, 24–6 Aug. 1773.
[66] *FLJ*, 4–7 Dec. 1771, 16–20 May 1772, 24–8 Apr. 1773, 22–6 Oct. 1774, 2–6 Dec. 1775, 3–6 Apr. 1776; *WHM*, May 1775, 318, Jan. 1776, 68–9.
[67] *Parliamentary register*, vii (1787), 148.

Upper-class involvement was triggered off through resentment of tithe, the payment of which had implications for their own tenants' ability to meet rents. One peer reported to government in 1786 that 'Those who have risen in the county of Tipperary and indeed elsewhere declare that they are encouraged by people of consequence.'[68] Of Revd Herbert's parish of Knockgraffon in 1780 it was said that 'many of the head parishioners' were actively concerned in resisting tithe claims.[69] This must have been repeated in many of the adjoining cereal-growing parishes. The most eminent example of gentry participation is perhaps Samuel Middleton, a reported leader of the Rightboys in the Borrisoleigh area where he had property and distilling interests.[70] There were also attempts to involve socially prominent persons as leaders of Rightboy groups. Thus in July 1786 about 1,000 people met at Ninemilehouse and made James Connolly, an innholder, take oaths, and later threatened him to proceed to swear others which he refused to do, whereupon further intimidation ensued.[71] In the same month the Rightboys tried at Moycarkey to enforce oaths on John Mannin of Shanbally, gentleman, and attempted unsuccessfully to make him assume a leadership role in swearing other parishes.[72] Large farmers also became associated with the unrest. Richard English near Cullen took and retained forcible possession of lands for an extended period and others were involved in the rescuing of distress for rent arrears and acts of repression against new tenants.[73]

Those who were victims of Rightboy action are identified by the central issues. Regarding tithes, clergymen such as Revd William Ryan of Kilvemnon, Revd Samuel Riall of Ballingarry, and Revd Richard Lloyd of Clonoulty were personally threatened or had their property destroyed.[74] Others, whose duty it was to collect tithe, were also maltreated.[75] Catholic clergy such as Revd Francis Power, Revd William Lonergan of Carrick, and the parish priest

[68] HMC, *Rutland*, 330. [69] Herbert, *Retrospections*, i. 76.
[70] Lucas, *Directory, sub* Borrisoleigh. [71] *FLJ*, 6–10 Oct. 1787.
[72] *FLJ*, 26–9 July 1786; *CG*, 7–11 Sept. 1786.
[73] *FLJ*, 22–6 May, 16–20, 23–7 Oct., 3–6, 24–7 Nov. 1784, 7–11 May, 16–19 Nov., 17–21 Dec. 1785, 21–5 Jan., 15–18 Feb. 1786; *CG*, 16–20 May 1782, 20–3 Jan. 1783, 14–17 Mar. 1785.
[74] NLI, MS 8395 (2); Trant, *Considerations*, 67–72; *CG*, 10–14 Nov. 1785; *FDJ*, 4–6 June 1789.
[75] *FLJ*, 3–6 Aug. 1785, 15–18 Feb., 9–13, 16–20 Sept. 1786.

of Newport, were the objects of attack over dues and rates.[76] The rescuing of distress, the refusal to pay rent, and the forcible possession of lands were practices adopted largely in defiance of landowners or head-tenants.[77]

The unrest of the first decade of the nineteenth century was viewed by the landed élite of the county in more serious terms than previous phases of unrest, a view also influenced by the legacy of the 1798 rebellion. Indicative of upper-class responses to contemporary fears are the remarks made in the *Clonmel Herald* in 1802 when it commented that the object of the recent outrages was 'to acquire by physical strength a dominion over the landowners, and to regulate the prices of the acres by enhancing the difficulty of labour'. The attempted restriction on outsiders or 'strangers' taking lands on the expiry of a lease, which was a distinct feature of the unrest of these years, was contrary to landlord interests. The result would be the effective loss of control over the disposal of land by the landlord, because he would be forced to treat with the sitting tenant. The effect, as the *Clonmel Herald* warned, would be 'on the expiration of a term there can be no competition of bidding and the peasant becomes in fact the owner of the land which he can depreciate as he pleases'.[78] The unrest of the period after 1800 had serious implications for landlords, with their right to dispose of and fix the price of property as they thought appropriate being challenged by the sitting tenantry.

The transfer of land was also identified as critical by the judges of a special commission sent to try the disturbers in Tipperary, Limerick, and Waterford in 1803. They concluded that the source of the recent unrest was the attempt 'to join in a system of opposition to the introduction of strangers (by whom they meant persons of any other vicinity) from becoming the tenants of farms, and to compel the land[ed] proprietors to treat with, exclusively, the ancient occupiers'.[79] One of the magistrates for the county, Edmund Power, concurred in this view remarking that 'It is well known that the farmers who are nearly or out of lease are

[76] *FLJ*, 1–5 July, 9–13 Sept. 1786.

[77] Hamilton to Sydney, 5 Nov. 1785 (PRO, HO, 100/17/171–171ᵛ); *CG*, 21–4 Nov. 1785; *WHM*, Sept. 1785, p. 501.

[78] *CH*, 1 Sept. 1802; see also [Thomas Elrington], *Letters on tythes published in the Dublin Journal and Correspondent under the signature of N* (Dublin, 1808), 12.

[79] *Annual register 1803* (1805), 295.

principally the cause of all the disturbances and outrages, which are done to deter others from bidding for their farms and their landlords from raising their rents'.[80]

Clearly there was a conflict of interests, subsisting at a time of rising land values, between landlords who sought to obtain the best possible increase in rent when leases expired and those sitting tenants who, unable to meet such demands, sought to protect their interests by a resort to violence. So far as access to land was concerned the two key and interrelated issues which prompted the violence were new or outside tenants and rent demands. Attacks on new tenants or their landlords are recorded for locations around Cahir, Cashel, Clonmel, and on the Limerick border.[81] These attacks were executed by bands led by or including displaced tenants who did not have their tenancies renewed, those with leases running out, and a minority who contrived attacks in order to relinquish their lease commitments. These were largely tenant farmers who combined with labourers, artisans, and other associated elements who were pressing their own specific grievances.

The majority of attacks were directed at new tenants who had recently taken lands, with a view to making them surrender their farms and quit the area. The earliest and most serious of such attacks was in April 1801 on William Price, a tenant to lands near Cashel. He was shot as he inspected lands he had recently leased at Ballinree on the Smith-Barry estate near the town, and he later died of his wounds. The motive behind the attack was stated by a resident in the locality when he wrote that 'the alleged reason is that he [Price] took a farm from Smith-Barry Esqr., or rather from a Mr. Boys who held under Mr. Barry, which had been tenanted by the ruffians that perpetrated this horrid act'.[82] Price was the successful bidder in a recent auctioning of the lands, but it is significant that the unsuccessful bidders were reported to be the

[80] Power to Normanton, 25 Feb. 1809 (Agar papers, box 3); see also PRO, HO, 100/103/242; monthly report of Sir Charles Ross, Clonmel, 1 Mar. 1802 (ibid., 100/109/51); *Annual register* 1816 (1817), 404.

[81] NLI, MS 27,571, p. 286; NA, SCP, 1020/39; PRO, HO, 100/103/238, 100/109/67; *LJ*, 5–9 June, 6–10 Nov. 1802, 17–21 Sept. 1803, 7–11 Sept., 23–6 Oct. 1805; *CH*, 8 Sept., 10 Nov., 6 Apr. 1802; *CG*, 25–9 Dec. 1802.

[82] Hare to the archbishop of Cashel, 16 Apr. 1801 (Agar papers, box 2); see also NA, SCP, 1020/39; PRO, HO, 100/103/123ᵛ; *WM*, 16 May 1800.

intended targets of future attack.[83] The murder of Price was the manifestation of resentment by the former tenants in response to their dispossession on the termination of the lease of the previous head-tenant. The majority of the other assaults on new tenants were less extreme and were mainly intimidatory.[84]

Sitting tenants were also active in attempting to ensure their continuance in advance of their leases expiring. This activity took the form of issuing notices to their landlords and prospective bidders with the aim of deterring them from entering any arrangement detrimental to the occupier. In September 1802 William Bourke near Newpark was arrested for posting threatening letters to prevent persons taking a farm he held under Richard Moore of Clonmel, and he addressed a notice to Moore cautioning him against countenancing such dealings.[85] In November 1802 the houses of M. Reilly and J. Casey, tenants to Thomas Grubb near Clonmel, were attacked by forty or fifty men. Casey, by pre-arrangement with the attackers, was absent but Reilly was flogged because he was to succeed the following March to the old tenant.[86] This case points to the fact that some of these outrages may have been contrived or collusive: a sitting tenant arranged a mock attack in order that it might act as an excuse for giving up a farm, of which we only get notice when the attempt was unsuccessful.[87] Not all tenants, however, had the option of resorting to such novel tactics in order to forgo their lease obligations. Tenants unable to meet their rent payments had to face the normal sanctions of distraint or ejectment. The victims also included those who were acting in a caretaker capacity over certain lands, dairymen, and estate stewards because their functions included receiving and arbitrating on bids for farms, the removal of old tenants on the expiration of leases, and the installation of new tenants.[88] These functions made stewards figures of odium to the displaced tenantry. The most serious assault on an estate steward was in February 1800 when Alexander Mollison, Lord Cahir's steward, was murdered.[89]

[83] Hare to the Archbishop of Cashel, 16 Apr. 1801 (as n. 82).

[84] NA, 1020/42; *LJ*, 5–9 June 1802; *CH*, 8 Sept. 1802, 6 Apr. 1803; *CG*, 25–9 Dec. 1802.   [85] *CH*, 8 Sept. 1802.   [86] *WM*, 8 Nov. 1802.

[87] *LJ*, 17–21 Sept. 1803.

[88] NLI, MS 27,571, p. 286; *CH*, 10 Nov. 1802; *WM*, 4 Feb. 1804.

[89] *WHM*, Mar. 1800, p. 190; *CH*, 25 June 1803; NA, Privy Council Office, index to proclamations 1618–1875, *sub* 18 Feb. 1800.

The second major issue was rent. The public solicitation of bids for lands tended in effect to raise the rent beyond the reach of the sitting tenant. An instance of this process in practice can be seen in the reletting in 1806 of the lands of Tureenbrien on the Rous estate on the Tipperary–Limerick border. George Ryan the sitting tenant had died and the lands were advertised for reletting from 25 March 1806. Ryan's son, Ewer, offered £150 for the lands, but was prepared to go as high as £200. The other bids received, however, equalled or exceeded this latter sum as follows: T. Carpenter (£200), T. Frend (£200), G. Maher (£200), P. Ryan, who was another son (£220), T. O'Brien (£265), and M. Ryan (£270).[90] It is not recorded who was the successful bidder, but clearly the son of the former tenant was in a position of disadvantage. Tenants in such a position tried to protect their interests either by trying to maintain rents at their existing levels (i.e. below a competitive rate), or by forcibly staying on in their lands after their leases had fallen in. Both strategies were intended to force the landlord into an impossible situation where he was intimidated from proceeding with public auction of the lands, and by default was forced to treat with the existing tenantry.

The unrest of this period also involved the labouring class and the landless. One landlord writing from Cordangan near Tipperary in November 1802 described the rural disturbers in his area as consisting of 'labourers, mechanics, discharged militiamen, and farmers who are yearly tenants'.[91] A different perspective of their social composition is provided by a commentator from Clonmel who remarked in January 1803 that the unrest 'arose out of local prejudices and antipathies between the resident peasantry and those itinerant labourers commonly designated in the south by the name of Kerrymen'.[92] Conflict over access to land and employment arose because some of the essential means of support for the lower peasantry were undermined. Shortages were exacerbated by wartime inflation causing the price of basic food items to rise sharply. In addition, the bad harvest of 1799 and the failure of the potato crop in 1800 led to a shortage and consequent price rises in

[90] Ryan to Rous, 6 Mar. [1806], T. Carpenter, T. O'Brien, P. Ryan, M. Ryan, G. Maher, and T. Frend to Rous 7, 12, 17, 21 Mar., 4 Apr. 1806 (East Suffolk Record Office, Rous papers, HA/11/D8/4).

[91] Cooke to Marsden, 8 Nov. 1802 (NA, RP, 620/61/110).

[92] *LJ*, 22–6 Jan. 1803.

these commodities. An object of the unrest was to force a reduction in the prices of essential foodstuffs like potatoes and milk, and to regulate their supply and disposal. In May 1800 the Long family at Drumbane, Thurles, were sworn to sell as much of their potatoes as possible to the people of the area at 4s. 4d. per barrel and only to feed their pigs once with them; and other acts of intimidation with a similar intent occurred.[93] The price of grain also rose, a situation exacerbated by the fact that some farmers combined to keep their grain from disposal at market, and that such forestalling apparently went unchecked.[94] At this time also in the intensive grazing areas of the county, rents for potato ground were high and were not matched by the availability of employment, nor by wage levels which tended to be as low as 5d. or 6d. per day, much the same as thirty years previously.[95] It became an object of the unrest in grazing districts to undertake the breakup of grassland in order to reduce the price of potato ground.[96] This also accounts for the attacks on estate workers on the Massy-Dawson estate at Newforest engaged in erecting deer-park walls which would have kept the enclosed land from use as potato ground.[97]

The most serious violence was associated with potato ground which was let out at high rates in grazing areas especially in the rich grasslands west of Cashel running into Limerick. As employment on grazing farms was minimal compared with the labour-intensive nature of employment in tillage areas, wages were low, and the price of food (milk and potatoes particularly) was high, the demand for conacre was pressing for the cottier and labourer. They had an inherent interest in maintaining conacre rents at existing levels and in seeking an expansion in the area available as potato ground. Much digging activity was engaged in at this time to break up grassland and thereby gain a reduction in the price of conacre. Part of the lands of Ardmayle near Cashel were dug up and a notice sent to the proprietor threatening him with death unless he made a certain number of acres available.[98] In an attempt to counter such activities, Sir Charles Asgill, the active

[93] Sir C. Asgill to Littlehales, 4 Sept. 1800 (NA, RP, 620/57/49).
[94] Asgill to Littlehales, 1 Dec. 1802 (PRO, HO, 100/94/283–4); NA, RP, 620/57/64.   [95] Cooke to King, 12 Oct. 1800 (PRO, HO, 100/94/177–8).
[96] Duff to Littlehales, 1 Nov. 1800 (PRO, HO, 100/94/227–8).
[97] *LJ*, 18–22 Sept. 1801.
[98] NA, SCP, 1020/42; PRO, HO, 100/109/67–67ᵛ; NLI, MS 27,571, p. 292.

military commander for the Clonmel district, tried to make the residents of one area turn back the land again after it had been dug up in May 1801.[99] Though there was also the intimidation of those engaged in the erection of deer park walls, structures which were traditionally regarded by the peasantry as keeping suitable land from letting as conacre, the most effective means of controlling conacre rent was by direct action against farmers. In November 1801 farmers near Chancellorstown were made to swear not to accept more than a certain price for their potato ground and to refund whatever they had already accepted above that price, threats which they complied with.[100]

Conversely, unrest arose in the by now traditional arable areas of the south-east because of the selective reversion by certain landlords to pasture. Such a process raised fears among small-holders that they would be obliged to pay more for their tillage grounds than formerly. These fears were expressed in attacks on or intimidation of new employees like shepherds and herdsmen installed to oversee the new pasture lands.[101] Also there was a renewal of attacks on migrant labourers simply because their presence in the county frustrated efforts by local labourers to gain concessions in relation to wage rates and extra conacre.[102] The second most important social element were displaced farmers who were unable or unwilling to pay the new rent levels demanded when land fell out of lease at this time. They were prominent in leading attacks against new tenants with the intent of forcing them to surrender their recently taken farms and return them to their former occupiers.[103]

In the unrest of the period 1760–1803, the social status of the participants was determined by the grievances. The social composition of agrarian movements in Tipperary suggests that they derived their main support from landholding and landless labourers, cottiers, servants and artisans. Existing at a level of subsistence or just above it, this was the class which was largely affected by the issues of access to potato ground, conacre rents,

[99] PRO, HO, 100/103/238.   [100] *WM*, 28 Nov. 1801.

[101] *LJ*, 24–8 Apr., 15–19 May, 27–31 Nov. 1802; *CG*, 8–11 Sept. 1802.

[102] *LJ*, 16–20 Oct. 1802, 24–7 Apr. 1805; *FDJ*, 16 Oct. 1800; *CG*, 20–3 Oct. 1802; *WM*, 28 Oct. 1802.

[103] NA, SCP, 1020/39; Hare to Somerton, 2, 16 Apr. 1801 (Agar papers, box 3); *WM*, 11 Sept., 8 Nov. 1802; *CH*, 10 Nov. 1802, 6 Apr. 1803; *CG*, 25–9 Dec. 1802; *LJ*, 6–10 Nov. 1802, 17–21 Sept. 1803.

tithe (particularly that of potatoes), and employment. These issues survived with a certain consistency right through the period and so point to the lower peasantry as being the core group in the agrarian movement. It is at this level that the element of class conflict is most evident. The catalyst which widened out the movement to involve those higher up in the social scale was that of tithe which accounts for the association of the more substantial elements like large farmers with the unrest of the 1770s and 1780s. The latter group had issues peculiar to itself, especially in relation to tenancy arrangements and the introduction of new tenants in their place, as in the 1770s and 1799–1803. Those against whom the agitation was directed comprised those with a vested interest in tithes, migrant labourers and dairymen, local land speculators who took lands over the heads of sitting tenants, and large graziers who enclosed commons or refused conacre. The agitation was not simply one existing between different social groups, although this was substantially the case. It also entailed conflict within the labouring class for access to employment and within the tenant farmer and dairyman class for lease preferences.

4. Tithe

An array of charges on land, ranging from rent to parish cess, were included in the catalogue of grievances advanced by agrarian movements after 1760. Excepting rent, which was an issue more associated with the occupation of land, tithe was the main charge. The tithe system was inequitable because of two basic anomalies: since 1735 pastureland was effectively exempt from tithe, and in Munster (and parts of Leinster) potatoes were subject to tithe.

In 1735 some landlords petitioned parliament against recent novel exactions (at least outside the north of Ireland) made on them for tithe of agistment on their cattle. When parliament resolved that the demand was burdensome, the result was the effective exemption of pasture and grassland from tithe.[104] In a

---

[104] Boulter to Walpole, 9 Aug. 1737 (Boulter, *Letters*, ii. (1770), 181–3); J. Finlay, *A treatise on the law of tithes in Ireland and ecclesiastical law connected therewith* (Dublin, 1828), 91–103. Agistment referred to the feeding of cattle on pasture land, with tithe of agistment being the tithe taken on the feeding of such cattle (Finlay, *Tithes*, 90). The non-demand for tithe of agistment in the previous 65

county like Tipperary where the rural economy before 1770 was dominated by grazing, this decision favoured the large grazier and served to place the onus for paying the bulk of tithe on the tiller. The effect was aptly described by Revd Patrick Hare, vicar-general of Cashel, who in 1801 observed that the implication of the House of Commons resolution in 1735 was that it 'exonerated the grazier of tithes and left the burden on the tiller; the grazier grew rich, the tiller grew poor; the landlord preferred the rich grazier who could engage for large tracts, and dispossessed the poor tiller with his ragged family; the tiller was then under the necessity of contracting with the rich grazier for the worst parts of the land at most exorbitant rents with tithes superadded, the poor tiller with his family is reduced to beggary'.[105] This situation was worsened by the fact that in Tipperary, as well as other Munster counties and parts of Leinster, tithe rates were higher than elsewhere despite a narrower tithe base; and potatoes were subject to tithe, their rate being higher than that for other crops.[106] Those dependent on potatoes as a means of support, i.e. labourers and cottiers, thus became the main group in rural society from whom tithe payments were exacted.

The tithe system was also inequitable because of the inter-mediaries between tithe owner and tithe payer with a vested interest in the maintenance of the system. These functionaries arose because of the cumbersome nature of tithe collection and the difficult circumstances concerning parochial provision in the Established Church. The number of parishes per benefice per clergyman in Tipperary was too great to make the personal collection of tithes feasible. In 1791 the average size of a parish situated in the respective dioceses in Tipperary was: Cashel 2,881 acres, Emly 2,595 acres, Lismore 2,875 acres, and Killaloe 3,281 acres, with an overall average for the entire county of 2,908 acres per parish.[107] In terms of the number of parishes per benefice, the

---

years was the reason given for making any claims for it illegal after an act of 1800 (40 Geo. III, c. 23). For a general survey of the tithe issue see M. J. Bric, 'The tithe system in eighteenth-century Ireland', *PRIA*, 86 C (1986), 271–88.

[105] Hare to Somerton, 2 Apr. 1801 (Agar papers, box 3).

[106] Young, *Tour*, i. 437, 447, 457; ii. 108, 110; Power, 'Tipperary', Table LIV.

[107] Calculated from D. A. Beaufort, *Memoir of a map of Ireland* (Dublin, 1792), 123–4, 130. The calculations refer solely to those sections of the respective dioceses situated in county Tipperary.

ratios for those parts of the respective dioceses located in
Tipperary was: Cashel 3.5, Emly 3.3, Lismore 2.1, and Killaloe
2.7. This is equivalent to an overall average for the entire county
of parishes per benefice of 2.9 making it higher than the national
average which stood at about 2.[108] On average the size of a
benefice was 8,410 acres.

The existence of large benefices is further substantiated by the
trend towards the union of parishes, reflecting personnel and
income difficulties in the church locally. The union of parishes
occurred where tithes were insufficient to support a clergyman. A
number of unions were in existence at the start of the eighteenth
century, namely those which were attached to the cathedral
chapters of Cashel and Killaloe, and in those areas where tithes
were in the hands of lay owners.[109] The number of unions by mid-
century was about thirteen and their institution does not resume
until 1767, between which date and 1807 a further thirty-eight
were made.[110] The number was static up to 1767 but grew
markedly in the 40 years thereafter indicating that large and
extensive benefices were created for clerical support. In 1807 of
the twenty-nine unions whose total acreages can be determined,
seventeen were less than 7,000 acres each, and twelve were
between 7,000 and 14,000 acres. Individually the larger unions
were Fethard (10,987 acres), Tubbrid (10,211 acres), Shanrahan
(9,870 acres), Cullen (10,751 acres), Tipperary (8,835 acres);
while other large unions whose acreages are not forthcoming, but
which had a significant complement of parishes, included Carrick
and Clonmel.[111]

Given the existence of such extensive parishes, non-residence of
clergymen was common. In consequence there was a natural
resentment against paying a tax for which no equivalent service
was rendered; understandable among Protestants, it was doubly so

---

[108] D. A. Beaufort, *Memoir of a map of Ireland* (Dublin, 1792); D. H.
Akenson, *The Church of Ireland: Ecclesiastical reform and revolution 1800–1885*
(New Haven and London, 1971), 57. Calculations are based on dividing the number
of parishes per diocese by the number of benefices. The figures have been rounded
downward. Beaufort gives 189 parishes for the entire county and 63 benefices,
which is equal to 3 parishes per benefice.

[109] Information computed from N. Carlisle, *Topographical dictionary of Ireland*
(Dublin, 1810).

[110] Computed from ibid.; NA, Privy Council Office, Ecclesiastical index 1711–
1869, and 1A 52 147.

[111] Carlisle, *Topographical dictionary.*

for Catholics. Even where a minister was resident there was an intrinsic difficulty in getting a body of parishioners to co-operate in its payment, compounded where Catholics as the majority population were concerned. The incomes of Anglican clergy were low. In the mid-seventeenth century, of 167 parishes in the county for which figures are available, 133 were in the income range from tithes of £1–£40, 31 were between £41 and £100, and 3 in the range £100–£200.[112] Income from tithe was small and was obtained with difficulty. For example, the living of Clonmel in 1739 had an income of £100 but was declared to be 'one of the largest and yet poorest parish[es] in this kingdom'. Out of this amount a salary of £40 was paid to a curate, an indispensable person because of the extent of the living, and towards this tithes contributed £24 derived from 'very small pittances collected from a great number of [the] poorest people'.[113] The value of the tithes of Clonmel a century previously was £40,[114] so that at £24 there was a net decline of £16 in tithe revenue in the intervening period.

Given the inconvenience and cost of taking tithe in kind in such extensive parishes the tithe owner had two options. In the first place he could reach agreement with the tithe payers of the parish for a monetary composition (*modus decimandi*) in lieu of the tithes, an arrangement which had the sanction of custom, as opposed to statutory law. This method was one whereby the tithe payers effectively purchased their own tithes and agreed by written bond to meet the tithe owner's demand at a valuation to be arrived at between them and his proctor or valuator.[115] Secondly, in cases where such agreements could not be reached because the tithe payer considered the proctor's valuation unacceptable, the tithe owner could lease out the tithes of a parish or group of parishes to a tithe farmer (for short periods of seven to ten years), or in smaller lots within a single parish to tithe canters or middlemen.[116]

[112] *CS*, i, ii (tithe data).

[113] J. Swift to the earl of Arran [autumn 1739] (*The correspondence of Jonathan Swift*, ed. H. Williams ((Oxford, 1963–5), v. 170–1).   [114] *CS*, i, 386.

[115] PRO, HO, 100/21/390, 'Memorandums concerning Tythes etc.' [1787]; J. S. Donnelly, 'Irish agrarian rebellion: The Whiteboys of 1769–76', *PRIA*, 83 C (1983), 300.

[116] PRO, HO, 100/21/390; J. S. Donnelly, 'The Rightboy movement, 1785–8', *Studia Hibernica*, 17–18 (1977–8), 159–160; R. Woodward, *The present state of the Church of Ireland* (Dublin, 1787), 44–5; R. Bellew, *Thoughts and suggestions of the means towards improving the condition of the Irish peasantry* (2nd. edn., London, 1808), 16–17.

Such leasing of tithes could be resorted to where the parishioners proved troublesome over a period about agreeing to a composition. It could also be the most convenient option when litigation in the ecclesiastical courts (to which the tithe owner could resort when the tithe payers sought to pay tithes in kind, which was their legal right) proved to be costly, tedious, and ultimately ineffective.

The intrusion of these middlemen functionaries between tithe payer and tithe owner, while they were regarded as necessary by the latter, came to be viewed by the former as exploitive and arbitrary. This was because tithe farmers demanded an increased amount in tithe payments from the lower peasantry above the amount they passed on to the clergyman; while tithe proctors demanded a percentage for their work as collectors and valuators; and tithe canters were regarded as undermining the bargaining position of tithe payers when, compositions not having been arrived at, they leased small denominations from the clergyman.[117] There were, therefore, inequities in the tithe system because the burden of payment, due to the exemption of pasture and the liability of potatoes as tithable, fell on the gardens and plots of the peasantry. This position was made more exploitive by the existence of tithe middlemen who, from a profit-seeking motive and in varying degrees, had an interest in the system being perpetuated.

Unrest over tithe arose after 1760 because, on the one hand, the value of tithe increased commensurate with the growth in the economy; and because, on the other, the resources of the peasantry, in terms of potato ground, conacre rents, and wage rates, were not sufficient to meet outgoings of which tithes were regarded as particularly onerous as they were a tax on essential food items and on productivity. The main thrust of the agitation over tithe in the early 1760s was directed at achieving a more equitable dealing by restricting or eliminating the activities of tithe intermediaries and by refusals to pay potato tithe. It was the opinion of one gentleman writing from the county in 1766 that the Whiteboy disturbances had arisen from 'A parcell of wretches opprest with tithe farmers', while it was the view of James Buxton, a Catholic gentleman executed in 1766, that the troubles origin-

---

[117] PRO, HO, 100/21/390–390ᵛ; Woodward, *Present state*, 44–5.

ated from a desire to put 'a stop to the oppressive and arbitrary valuation of tithe jobbers'.[118]

Attempts were made to force the tithe farmers or jobbers to relinquish their agreements with clergymen for tithe, and to prevent such agreements being arrived at. These attempts were widespread if one is to judge from the statement made by the magistrates in July 1763 when they referred to 'several lawless persons [who] have illtreated several who dealt and threaten those who shall deal, with the proprietors of tithes in several parishes and have contemptuously posted up public advertisements to that purpose'.[119] Instances of such attacks are forthcoming for areas in the south-west of the county where parishes were extensive and where tithe farming was common. In October 1763 Timothy Loughnan of Clashavagha was seized by nearly one hundred persons and threatened to be buried alive if he did not promise to relinquish an agreement which he had since 1760 with Revd Richard Foulke and Revd William Downes for the tithes of Newcastle parish near Ardfinnan.[120] Loughnan would appear to have succumbed to these threats for a prospective successor, Edmund Wall, received a threatening notice shortly afterwards vowing his death if he closed the agreement with the two clergymen.[121] Revd Foulke of Tullaghorton, was also intimidated because he had taken a lease of the tithes of Derrygarth parish and as a result he gave up his lease to Revd Laurence Brodrick of Newcastle in 1763, being as it was said 'frightened by the Whiteboys'.[122]

The aim in all this was to deter actual and potential tithe farmers from carrying out their functions, the objective being to eliminate them and, as Buxton put it, 'to deal for tithes with none but the immediate proprietor'.[123] Accordingly surplus amounts going to the tithe farmer would be dispensed with and the amount actually paid by the parishioners reduced. The desire was not for a total abolition of tithe, rather it was for the elimination of the tithe middlemen and their excessive demands. Such a motivation

---

[118] Sheffield City Library, Burke MS 8/7, 9.
[119] *CEP*, 25 July 1763.
[120] Burke, *Clonmel*, 364; NA, 1A 52 159, p. 265.
[121] Mount Melleray, Burke MS 31, p. [269]; NA, 1A 52 159, p. 266.
[122] Burke, *Clonmel*, 365.
[123] Sheffield City Library, Burke MS 8/7.

accounts for the intimidation of proctors in 1765, as at Clonmel and Ardfinnan where one was whipped and made to swear not to deal any longer in tithes.[124]

The second area of tithe agitation at this time concerned potato tithe. In the early 1760s conacre lettings were being sold for four or five guineas, and in Tipperary the price of conacre was estimated at twice or three times that formerly paid.[125] Given this level of expense and the fact that income at a daily wage of 4d. for 300 working days brought in £5 annually, the peasant household budget was tight. Often, however, there were only 200 working days in the year which gave earnings of 4 guineas, leaving 9s. to spare which went towards hearth money (2s.), rent of a cabin (2s.), and tithe (5s.).[126] Thus, because it was such a substantial variable cost which could make the difference between solvency and beggary, potato tithe was particularly resented. Because the early 1760s witnessed a sharp rise in conacre rents without an accompanying rise in labourers' wages, there was a widespread campaign among this class to refuse payment of potato tithe. By late 1764 a large number of occupiers had refused to set out or pay potato tithe, with the consequent sharp decline in clerical incomes. There were calls for the total abolition of tithe on potatoes in certain districts, but the general emphasis was on hindering their collection, as with Revd Richard Foulke when he failed to gather his potato tithe in Clogheen.[127] The response to the tithe agitation was an act (7 Geo. III, c. 21) of 1767 which sought to provide for the better collection of tithe and to make more effective litigation in tithe disputes. However, as became evident no law could be devised to draw tithe effectively if those liable were uncooperative.

The emphasis on tithe shifts in the 1770s, for tithe on potatoes recedes in significance while that on cereals assumes a greater prominence, due to the recent expansion in cereal cultivation. The demands for tithe on cereals were viewed as punitive especially by those farmers who were just earning a good return after a large initial outlay on the conversion of pasture to tillage.[128] This

[124] *FDJ*, 1–5, 5–8 Oct. 1765.
[125] Sheffield City Library, Burke MS 8/9; *Wilson's Dublin Magazine*, Apr. 1762, 198.   [126] *Wilson's Dublin Magazine*, Apr. 1762, 198.
[127] *FDJ*, 29 Oct.–1 Nov. 1763, 1–4 Sept. 1764.
[128] E. J. Evans, *The contentious tithe: The tithe problem and English agriculture, 1750–1850* (London, 1976), 30–1.

situation was compounded by the economic depression of the early 1770s, this context accounting for the role of farmers and their sons in the unrest.

The methods used in an attempt to defeat the demands for tithe on cereals were threefold. First, the Whiteboys sought to force a departure from the customary form of tithe payment and bond in favour of a reversion to making the clergyman take it in kind. This was a strategy decided on in the knowledge that it would present major problems of organization and collection. But in cases where individual clergy became mobilized, the second strategy of the destruction of the tithed cereals and hay and the breaking-up of carriages intended for its conveyance was used. Instances of both happened at locations near Carrick, Clonmel, and Cahir.[129] Associated with the two preceding strategies was that of restricting the functions of tithe proctors whose basic duty of valuation would have been made redundant if tithe was paid in kind. A statement reportedly made by two Whiteboys before their execution in Clonmel in April 1776 suggests that the elimination of proctors was one of the main aims of the movement of the 1770s. It declared that 'we know of no design among the White Boys but the infatuated one of discouraging proctors and tythe jobbers'.[130] One such proctor, John Wharton who acted for Revd Nicholas Herbert, was severely maimed in October 1773 when he was at Knockgraffon to bring in tithe, and another of Revd Herbert's proctors was ill-treated on the same count the following year.[131] As to the tithe jobbers or farmers, it would appear that they lost heavily as a result of the unrest of these years with some having to surrender their contracts.[132]

Tithe on cereals came to be an especial focus of grievance for the Quakers as they were prominent in forwarding the transition into grain production locally. The community opposed the payment of tithes on conscientious grounds.[133] A clause in the tithe act (7 Geo. III, c. 21, s. 11) of 1767 enacted that Quakers refusing to pay tithe could be summoned by two justices of the

---

[129] NA, 1A 52 159, p. 267; *FLJ*, 28 Sept.–2 Oct. 1776; *CEP*, 23 Aug. 1773.

[130] *FLJ*, 27 Apr.–1 May 1776.

[131] *FLJ*, 22–6 Jan. 1774, 3–6 Apr. 1776; *FJ*, 2–4 Nov. 1773, 25–7 Jan., 20–2 Sept. 1774; Herbert, *Retrospections*, i. 22.

[132] J. Cooke to J. Galway, 4 Sept. 1775 (NLI, MS 2480, pp. 223–6).

[133] *Brief and serious reasons why the people called Quakers do not pay tithes. Published by said people in 1768* (Dublin, 1786), 4–6.

peace and payment ordered if the sums involved were not in excess of £10, and upon their refusal distress could be taken. However, there was a proviso whereby the decision of the justices could be appealed against at the assizes, and in the event of such an appeal being lodged no distress could be taken until the case was decided (s. 12). Previous experience of litigation indicates that the assize judges tended to favour the appellants.[134] Thus Quaker evasion of tithe was made more easy by the fact that decisions to take distress could be appealed with every likelihood of success. In addition the act itself was a temporary one only remaining in force for a period of two years from 24 June 1768, a clause which shows that, in the tradition of the resolution of 1735, parliament was not eager to facilitate greater efficiency in tithe collection. The Quaker case for non-payment was reinforced by the publication of tracts which outlined their objections and these were accepted as valid at the time.[135] In the context of the unrest of the 1770s there was some resentment against Quakers themselves for their reluctance to pay tithes. It is possible to view the attack by persons of comfortable standing on the house of Joseph Grubb of Anner mills in July 1775, in this light.[136]

Tithe on cereals continued to be the central issue in the Rightboy movement of the 1780s as the trend towards the conversion of pasture to arable accelerated. When pastureland was ploughed up and sown with seed it ceased to be tithe free so that from the harvests of 1785 new demands for tithe on wheat, oats, and barley were forthcoming. These were resented by those farmers and gentlemen who had undertaken the movement into cereals and out of this developed various strategies designed to defeat clerical expectations of increased income from this expanded tithe source. The agitation which ensued had four main objectives in relation to tithe payment. The first aim was to effect the payment of tithe in kind rather than agreeing on a valuation and composition with the tithe owner. If this occurred on a limited scale it might prove manageable, but it became Rightboy practice to universalize the method over a wide area, thereby making it untenable for the clergyman to consider drawing in kind. An early manifestation of the problems involved was in 1780 when Revd

[134] Society of Friends Library, Dublin, National sufferings no. 1, 1655–1693 (YMG I), *sub* 1687.
[135] *Brief and serious reasons*, 25.   [136] *FJ*, 1–3 Aug. 1775.

Nicholas Herbert of Knockgraffon, received fifty or sixty notices from his parishioners for his tithe to be drawn in kind on one particular day. In an effort to defy this challenge Herbert obtained the loan of the extra horses, carts, and labour required for the operation from friends. But the drawing of the tithe was carried out at great cost, effort, and risk, his daughter, Dorothea Herbert, remarking that 'Feeding and providing for such a number of men and horses was a dreadful expence and trouble'. As the tithe was drawn in there was the danger that efforts would be made to regain or destroy it. The rector's daughter reported graphically that her father 'stood out each night patrolling to see that all was safe and my mother sat out in the gravel walk with a candle and her account book till break of day. Whilst every individual amongst us had a station to guard [and] spies [were] scatter'd throughout the parishes to watch that none was subtracted by night. We had not a servant in the house the whole time and were in continual peril of our lives.'[137]

This practice of setting out tithe in kind was subsequently adopted by the Rightboys on a more universal scale. The inhabitants of Owning, Cahir, Moycarkey, Knockingtemple, Newport, and Cashel were sworn by Rightboy groups in 1786 in order to gain their compliance.[138] The aim was to create an impossible situation for clergymen and force them to comply with Rightboy demands. One landowner, Edward Moore of Mooresfort near Tipperary, was concerned about the effect the demand for tithe to be gathered in kind would have and about the inability of tithe owners to confront the challenge with any degree of effectiveness. Writing in late June 1786 Moore observed that the country people 'are under oath to leave their tythes in kind unless a small value be offered for them; I take it for granted this will be done upon the same day in the several parishes. How can these tythes be drawn? Where will be the horses got to draw them? After they are drawn may they not easily be destroyed?'[139]

When Revd Patrick Hare went in August 1786 to collect his tithes in the parish of Kilbragh near Cashel he found that the inhabitants were sworn not to sell them to him, which suggests that

[137] Herbert, *Retrospections*, i. 75–6.
[138] *CG*, 29 June–3 July 1786; *FLJ*, 26–9 July, 26–30 Aug., 9–13, 16–20 Sept. 1786; *WHM*, July 1786, 390.
[139] HMC, *Rutland*, 317.

they were being offered in kind only.[140] Even if the tithe was drawn away the Rightboy intention was not to allow consignments to remain intact, as Edward Moore feared and as Revd Hare experienced when his tithe was destroyed.[141] Similarly in December 1788 a considerable amount of wheat in a barn, and two stacks of wheat, and four of hay were maliciously set on fire near Clonoulty, the property of Revd Richard Lloyd.[142] Part of the strategy also was the intimidation of labourers who were employed to assist in the collection of tithe for the tithe owners; while those who undermined Rightboy rules by agreeing to pay tithe by monetary composition were avenged.[143]

The greater universal adherence to the offering of tithe in kind, the more effective it was in gaining the tithe owners' acceptance of reduced rates for tithe which was the second objective at this time. Evidence for tithe rates decreed for different crops by the vicars' court of Cashel between 1766 and 1785 in cases cited before it by clergy, shows that the average amounts decreed for the respective crops were: potatoes 5s. 3d., wheat 6s. 1½d., barley and bere 7s. 2d., oats 3s. 7d., meadow 6s. 6d., and rape 7s. 8d.[144] These relate to set tithe, i.e. the price agreed on directly between tithe owner and tithe payer. However, the real amount paid in tithe could be twice or three times the amount of set tithe, the difference being accounted for by supplementary demands made by tithe middlemen. The profit margins they obtained at a time of rising agricultural prices especially for grain crops, were deemed to be excessive. It became a Rightboy aim to prescribe schedules of tithe rates of their own and to gain the concurrence of clergy and tithe payers to them. The amount of these rates differed according to the level of compromise achievable in different parishes, but in general not only did the Rightboy schedules seek to eliminate the profiteering of tithe middlemen altogether, but also they sought to have the amount in set tithe reduced by up to half in the case of potatoes and barley and a greater fall in the case of oats and wheat.

The ability of the Rightboys to secure concurrence with their schedules of tithe rates by tithe owners was closely linked with

---

[140] Trant, *Considerations*, 75.　　　　[141] HMC, *Rutland*, 317.
[142] *CG*, 12–15 Jan. 1789.
[143] *CG*, 7–11 Sept. 1786; *FLJ*, 16–20 Sept. 1786.
[144] *Parliamentary register*, 8 (1788), 200–3.

their third objective which was the removal of the tithe inter-mediaries, particularly tithe farmers. Their elimination was pre-sented as desirous to the tithe owner as income would then accrue more readily to him, and to the tithe payer because as a consequence of direct dealing with the clergyman the amounts demanded in tithe would be more equitable. The farming-out of tithes of parishes or groups of parishes continued to be a widespread practice previous to the outbreak of unrest.[145] Persons who entered such leasing contracts were the group who made such heavy demands on occupiers and who reaped large profits for themselves. Their oppressiveness was recognized by govern-ment.[146] The Rightboy strategy of paying tithe in kind and of seeking adherence to schedules of tithe rates was designed to make the role of the tithe farmer redundant. Tithe farmers felt under threat at this time, for when Revd Patrick Hare demanded tithe composition for the produce of the farm of Garrane in Ballysheehan parish, north of Cashel, the agent refused unless Hare agreed to make a new lease of the tithes of the parish to him during his incumbency, which Hare declined to do.[147]

Despite Rightboy insistence on the taking of tithe in kind the essential function of another tithe middleman, the proctor, remained which was that of viewing and subtracting the appro-priate amount of the respective crops. Proctors thus became the focus of Rightboy attention largely with a view to dissuading them from executing their duty. In 1785 Thomas Hayden was compelled to take an oath not to come into Lismoylan on any tithe business; in January 1786 a proctor living at Kilmakil near Thurles on Sir William Barker's estate, was forcibly brought to Urlingford and there cropped and buried; and at Clonmel in September an attempt was made to make a proctor surrender his lease.[148] Similarly the proctors of Revd Patrick Hare, who were sent in June 1786 to view and value the tithes of the parish of Kilbragh, near Cashel, were beaten, robbed of their valuation books, and sworn to discontinue their duties.[149]

---

[145] *CG*, 26–9 Aug. 1782, 10–13 Feb., 20–4 Mar. 1783, 12–15 Jan., 5–9 Feb., 27–30 Dec. 1784, 12–16 May 1785, 23–6 Jan. 1786.
[146] HMC, *Rutland*, 319, 354.
[147] Trant, *Considerations*, 41–4; *Parliamentary register*, 8 (1788), 201–2.
[148] *FLJ*, 3–6 Aug. 1785, 15–18 Feb. 1786; *CG*, 7–11 Sept. 1786.
[149] Trant, *Considerations*, 73.

Rural unrest

The final aim of the Rightboys was to maximize the effect of offering tithe in kind, specifying tithe rates, and restricting tithe middlemen by direct action against the tithe owner himself. At least three major acts of personal intimidation against clergymen are on record. The first of these was directed at Revd Samuel Riall of Ballingarry, near Killenaule, in June 1783, when he received a notice threatening him with the fate of Ambrose Power (who was murdered in November 1775 for his opposition to the Whiteboys) if he persisted in making demands for tithes.[150] The tithes of the parish had been advertised for letting the previous year and opposition to their collection continued after the delivery of the note to Revd Riall at least until September 1783.[151] A more violent attack took place in October 1785 when it was reported that 'a great number of persons armed with clubs, poles, pitchforks, and firearms some of whom were covered with white shirts', broke into the house of Revd William Ryan of Kilvemnon near Mullinahone, violently assaulted him and tried to make him swear that he would dispense with his proctor and that he would value his own tithes and set them.[152] Finally in December 1788 a large quantity of tithed cereals belonging to Revd Richard Lloyd of Clonoulty, was set on fire and destroyed.[153]

The cumulative effect of the Rightboy campaign was to force a sharp reduction in the income from tithe for clergy in Tipperary in 1786 and 1787. By December 1786 the archbishop of Cashel was circulating a notice to his diocesan clergy seeking 'as accurate an estimate as you can make of your losses this year in consequence of the combinations or outrages of the Whiteboys'.[154] The clergy of Waterford and Lismore diocese, which included south Tipperary, lost one-quarter of their revenue in 1786, losses which had to be made up by emergency legislation in 1787 and 1788.[155] There may have been a temporary decline in tithe farming due to the success of the Rightboys. As early as 1787 an acreable tax in lieu of tithes was being implemented in certain parishes, and it became the policy on the Hely-Hutchinson estate to encourage a

[150] NLI, MS 8395 (2).
[151] NA, 1A 52 164, p. 153; *CG*, 26–9 Aug. 1782.
[152] *CG*, 10–14 Nov. 1785; Trant, *Considerations*, 69.
[153] NA, 1A 52 164, p. 105; *CG*, 12–15 Jan. 1789; *FDJ*, 4–6 June 1789.
[154] [Archbishop of] Cashel to diocesan clergy, 20 Dec. 1786 (Agar papers, box 3).
[155] NLI, MS 16,350/91–2; 27 Geo. III, c. 36, ss. 1–3, 28 Geo. III, c. 44.

commutation of tithes.[156] On the whole, however, the farming of tithes continued to be resorted to by tithe owners as a convenient if onerous and costly means of gaining income from tithe; and it may have contributed to an increase in non-residence among clergy. Proctors, though they may also have experienced a downturn in the short term, continued to be required for the purpose of valuation, for valuation as a method of tithe assessment continued, as a tithe survey of Ardmayle and Ballysheehan in 1791 shows.[157]

On the broader front tithe appears to have receded as a major issue in the catalogue of rural grievances after its high profile in 1785–8. The wartime inflation of 1793–1815 brought the more fundamental issues of land occupancy, rent, and employment into greater focus, relegating charges on land, like tithe, to a more subsidiary position. While it may have been less important in reality, tithe did remain as one of the elements in the general armoury of expressed grievances. In 1793, for example, the inhabitants of a parish in west Tipperary proceeded to an adjoining parish in Limerick and, reportedly, 'swore the people to pay no more rents, no tythes, and to go to the next parish to administer the same oath there'.[158] The politicization of the agrarian movement does not appear to have occurred in the county in the 1790s. Indeed in order to win support among the Munster peasantry in general it was reported of the United Irishmen that they had to 'dwell with peculiar energy on the supposed oppressiveness of tythes'.[159]

With a bad harvest in 1799 and a failure of the potato crop in the summer of 1800, the rising price of basic foodstuffs, static wages, and a rise in the acreable amount being demanded for tithe, incidental charges like tithe were brought into prominence again. Resentment was directed primarily against proctors. In March 1799 a proctor to the Revd A. Herbert of New Inn named Shortis and his wife were murdered.[160] In November 1800 Colonel Littlehales reported that one of the causes of the renewal of violence in his district of Cashel was the proctors 'who they state to

[156] *A letter from a Munster layman of the Established Church to his friend in Dublin* (Dublin, 1787), 28–9; TCD, Donoughmore, D75/1.

[157] Tipperary County Library, Thurles, tithe book for the parishes of Ardmayle and Ballysheehan, 1790–1801.

[158] *Proceedings of the parliament of Ireland* (Dublin, 1793), iii. 462.

[159] *Comms. Jnl. (Ire.)* xvii. pt. 2, p. dccxxx.

[160] *FLJ*, 2–6 Mar. 1799.

be oppressive in the collection of tithes'.[161] Proctors continued to be the object of serious attack in the years following, with the destruction of barns and crops in evidence also.[162] Under this type of pressure some tithe owners may have thought it wise to dispense with the services of their proctors at least temporarily and to issue public notices to that effect, as at Fethard in 1802.[163]

Though not on as extensive a scale as previously, the leasing out of tithes is apparent for this period also. In 1807 there were 653 actions tried at Tipperary quarter sessions involving tithe, while ten years later the figure stood at 1,084.[164] Tithe also became an important issue in county politics in 1807. In August of that year a meeting of the freeholders was held in Cashel for the purpose of instructing their representatives in parliament to introduce a bill to abolish tithes and devise some alternative means of support for the clergy.[165] Such radical proposals took over thirty years to come to fruition. In the interim the underlying inequities of the system persisted, entailing as they did the exemption of pasture, the existence of exacting tithe intermediaries, higher tithe rates in Munster counties like Tipperary despite a narrower tithe base, and the methods of enforcing payment being exploitive, cumbersome, and resented.

5. Other Charges

Tithe was the major incidental charge which provoked rural opposition. There were others which occasionally emerged in the catalogue of rural grievances: other payments to the Established Church; dues paid for the support of the Catholic clergy; and various civil payments.

Other payments due to the Established Church derived from the church rates agreed on at the local church vestry and applotted on all parishioners. This church tax was used for the maintenance and repair of churches, the employment of teachers and parish clerks,

[161] PRO, HO, 100/94/227–8; NA, RP, 620/61/110, 620/13/178/50.

[162] *LJ*, 9–13 June, 4–8 Sept., 3–6 Nov. 1802, 23–7 Aug. 1806; *WM*, 19 Sept. 1807.   [163] *CH*, 24 Nov. 1802.

[164] Wakefield, *An account of Ireland*, ii. 488–9 n.; *PP* 14 (1822) (304), 8.

[165] *Southern Reporter*, 15 Aug. 1807; *LJ*, 5–8 Aug., 29 Aug.–2 Sept. 1807; *Clare Journal*, 7, 10, Sept. 1807; NLI, MS 27571, p. 358; [Elrington], *Letters*, 4–15.

donations to the poor and the support of orphans and foundlings, supplies for church services, road repair, and latterly as payments for substitutes in the militia. Evidence for church rates in the parishes of Shanrahan, Ballysheehan, and Templetenny in south Tipperary for 1725–96 shows that the amount levied by the vestry increased over fourfold in the seventy-year period. Before 1760 the rate remained below £16 but in that year there was a sharp rise to over £40, the levying of which coincides with the outbreak of Whiteboy unrest in these parishes. A major refurbishment of Shanrahan church in 1778 led to a rise in the rate to £50, a level which was maintained in the early 1780s. In 1795 there was an extraordinary rate of £83 struck, accounted for by a sum of £54 which was to be paid for providing substitutes for nine men balloted on the parish under the militia act.[166] Evidence for Duntryleague, a union skirting the Tipperary–Limerick border, indicates that church rates rose from £26 in 1766 to £88 in 1811. The rate remained below £30 before 1771 but in that year shot up to £118 and stayed above £50 until 1775, coinciding with the unrest of the period. It rose sharply in 1781 to £81 but fell off thereafter and was not abnormally high in the years 1786–93. It only exceeded earlier levels in 1802 when it reached £118, a level maintained for three years. In 1808 the largest rate yet struck (£288) went to raise thirteen men from the union under the militia act.[167]

Apart from the cases of Shanrahan and Fethard (where in October 1762 there were reports of opposition to the collection of church dues),[168] the issue of church rates was not advanced as a major grievance by the Whiteboys. The lack of evidence regarding widespread resistance may be due to a general and traditional evasion of payment, and opposition may only have emerged when the local vestry made a concerted effort to enforce payment. As much is to be implied from the incidents at Newport in 1774, when the vestry struck a rate of 4*d*. per acre on the Protestants and 2*d*. per acre on the Catholics in the four parishes in the union of Newport, towards furnishing a new church. It was reported that the Catholics, 'who it appears have not paid any church rates for 15 years past, refused to pay it or anything at all, whereupon the

---

[166] RCB, MS P.79, vestry minutes Shanrahan, 1725–96.
[167] RCB, MS E.2–5, vestry minutes Duntryleague, 1766–1824.
[168] *DG*, 9–12 Oct. 1762.

church wardens attempted to distrain but were beat[en] back wherever they went'.[169] However, church rates were an important item in the catalogue of Rightboy grievances. The rate struck at Shanrahan was consistently high in the early 1780s. Hostility was expressed towards Revd Samuel Riall over parish cess in 1783, and much of the swearing activity outside chapels must have included provision for a curtailment in the general level of parish rates.[170] Evidence from two other parishes, Shronell and Relickmurry, shows that there were sharp increases in church rates in the early 1780s.[171] This period would seem to have been one when church rates were resisted most because of their rising level, the rise occurring at a time of widespread poverty.

Catholic clergy received voluntary payments for officiating at baptisms, marriages, and funerals in addition to Christmas and Easter dues. Priest's money, as one contemporary termed it, was one of the charges identified in the 1760s as being oppressive to the rural poor.[172] But it was not, apparently, until the 1780s that there was any movement as such advancing it as a grievance. In this the concentration was on enforcing certain rates which the clergy should be paid.[173] Attempts to impose such rates took two forms, the first of which was the intimidation of individual priests. In June 1786 between 400 and 500 Whiteboys made the priest of Newport swear to take only 5s. for a marriage and 1s. 6d. for a christening.[174] Other acts of violence or destruction directed at priests, or attempts to curtail them carrying out their functions at a number of centres in 1786–8, can be associated with regulation also.[175] The second method was to swear entire districts or towns to adhere to the rates laid down by the Rightboys. In late June 1786 up to 2,000 of them swore the people of Cahir regarding such

[169] Revd M. Ormsby to A. Ormsby, 10 June 1774 (NLI, MS 17,728).
[170] NA, 1A 52 164, p. 153.
[171] Cashel Deanery: vestry minute books, Shronell 1757–1832, Relickmurry 1770–1809. The rate for Shronell stood at £20 in 1758 and at £40 in 1800. During the 1760s and 1770s it did not exceed £20; in 1783 it rose sharply to £83; but in the years 1784–95 it fell again to within the range £20–£30. The rate for Relickmurry stood at £15 in 1770, and at £60 in 1809. It was static at the £15 mark during the 1770s; in 1781 there was a sharp rise to £86 and it remained high in ensuing years, but levelled off again to the £36 or £37 mark in 1788–1801.
[172] HMC, *12th report Charlemont*, app. x (1891), 21; J. Bush, *Hibernia curiosa*, 30.
[173] HMC, *Rutland*, 316.   [174] *CG*, 29 June–3 July 1786.
[175] HMC, *Rutland*, 310; NA, OP, 18/21; *Parliamentary register*, 7 (1787), 148; *FLJ*, 9–13 Sept. 1786; *WC*, 5–8 Sept. 1786.

rates, and the declared intention was to do the same at Clonmel.[176] The rates as prescribed by the Rightboys varied from parish to parish according to the degree to which existing or prevailing levels were considered excessive, and the assertiveness with which the new schedules were advanced.

Civil taxes took a number of forms. Most of these were unpopular with the peasantry, though agitation was largely directed at their reduction rather than their total abolition. The amount of county cess shows an overall upward trend from 1738 onwards. There was a sharp increase in the middle decades of the century from £200 in 1738, to £1,450 in 1750, to £7,300 in 1775. Rises in the county cess were most continuous in the 1780s and this contributed to demands for a reduction in a range of incidental charges in these years.[177] Resented by Catholics in particular was the rapparee tax levied on them to compensate for the destruction wrought by tories and rapparees. A rate was agreed on at the general sessions held at Fethard in October 1765 in order 'to reimburse the several persons [for] their losses sustained by their burning by papists'.[178] From the agreed rate a proportional amount was assigned on each barony, Kilnamanagh having a rate of ½d. per acre levied on every Catholic as its contribution to the total. A more universal tax, the hearth tax, was regarded as an unpopular imposition until its abolition in 1793. It was levied at the rate of 2s. per hearth and agitation was directed at gaining a reduction of half in this amount.

The increasingly defence-oriented nature of the local administration in the 1790s involved additional demands on inhabitants to support the military establishment. There was, for instance, considerable resistance to the raising of militia units locally in 1793.[179] In 1796 there was further hostility in several baronies to the levying of extra money intended for the augmentation of the militia. Thus in March the grand jury reported that 'a spirit of resistance has appeared in many of the baronies' against the

---

[176] *WHM*, July 1786, p. 390; *HC*, 18 Sept. 1786.
[177] For 1738: Dublin City Libraries, Pearse St., Gilbert MS 36, p. 370; for 1750: NLI, MS 8914; and for 1775 and the 1780s: Kennedy, *Digest*, ii. 1002–11. By 1789 the cess had increased to £14,462.
[178] NLI, MS 19,822, pp. 272–85.
[179] *CG*, 29 May–1 June 1793; PRO, HO, 100/44/. See also T. Bartlett, 'An end to moral economy: The Irish militia disturbances of 1793', *Past and Present*, 99 (1983), 41–64.

constables collecting the extra cess.[180] In the same year a proposal for the revaluation of houses in Clonmel for minister's money (the urban equivalent of tithes) was resisted unsuccessfully by the parishioners especially the Quakers.[181]

Turnpike gates could also be the source of complaint at times due to the tolls levied at them. In 1775 up to fifty Whiteboys paraded through the street of Twomilebridge near Clonmel having passed the turnpike gate there.[182] In 1786 the keeper of the turnpike gate at Longford Pass was attacked and robbed of money and arms and sworn not to remain in the area or to collect any further tolls.[183] What made all these incidental charges resented was that at times of rising rents for smallholders and of static wages (1760s), or economic difficulty (early 1770s, 1780s), they collectively represented a variable cost in outgoings which could make the difference between peasant solvency or impoverishment.

6. Control

When the local establishment was first confronted with unrest in 1761–6 the response progressed from one of a mixture of disbelief and lethargy and a reliance on traditional methods of repression, to one where the Whiteboys were suppressed by severe means. The reason ascribed by government as to why the movement had gone unchecked for so long was, as Halifax reported in April 1762, 'the want of spirit in the magistrates who have suffer'd the mischief to grow from small beginnings'.[184] The first recorded response to the unrest which began in October 1761 was five months later in March 1762 when the grand jury petitioned the lord-lieutenant to adopt effective measures.[185] This appeal was occasioned by their inability to obtain solid evidence on which to bring charges, reflecting the tight oath-bound nature of the agrarian organization. The government sent troops under the earl of Drogheda and Sir James Caldwell who, in co-operation with local gentry, had by

---

[180] NLI, MS 7331, p. 8.
[181] NA, OP, 18/48; Mount Melleray, Burke MS 71(v). For the background to the tax see Power, 'A minister's money', 183–200.
[182] *FLJ*, 1–5 Apr. 1775.
[183] *CG*, 21–5 Dec. 1786.
[184] PRO, SPI, 63/421/249.
[185] Mount Melleray, Burke MS 31, p. 288.

late May scoured the countryside and imprisoned many suspects.[186] However, this activity was not reflected in convictions at the proceedings of a special commission under judge Richard Aston sent down to try those charged in June. To the disappointment of the magistrates there were no capital convictions, only one person was found guilty of riot and he received a light sentence.[187] Despite some outrages committed during the summer there was no business of consequence at the autumn assizes of 1762, pointing to the continued inability of the gentry to check the unrest.[188] All the leaders of the movement remained uncaptured and for their apprehension a subscription was opened with the rewards increasing in amount from £130 to 300 guineas.[189]

Not until the spring assizes of 1763 were two capital convictions on Whiteboy charges obtained, six others were found guilty of riot, and forty others were to be tried by a special commission.[190] A third capital conviction was had in May when John Fogarty, alias Captain Fearnot, a schoolmaster and reputed Whiteboy leader, was found guilty of high treason and hanged in Clonmel.[191] However twenty others out of the forty facing charges were acquitted because of lack of evidence.[192] These proceedings were a mortal blow to the self-confidence of the gentry as forty Whiteboys went free and only three hangings were had after a year and a half of rural outrages.

To add to this setback the unrest continued unabated in late 1763 and 1764. There were no Whiteboy convictions at the summer assizes of 1763 nor at the spring assizes of 1764, while at the summer assizes of 1764 the trials of Whiteboy leaders were deferred because of a lack of evidence to prosecute.[193] All this occurred despite the appointment of extra justices of the peace, the passing of legislation in May 1764 indemnifying magistrates for their actions taken in quelling riots, and the reiteration of orders in

[186] HMC *15th report*, app. 8 *Ailesbury* (1898), 340; *DG*, 17–20 Apr. 1762; *FDJ*, 20–4 Apr. 1762.

[187] *Gentleman's and London Magazine*, 31(1762), 371; 32 (1763), 232 (*recte* 175).

[188] *FDJ*, 28 Sept.–2 Oct. 1762, 5–8 Mar. 1763; *CEP*, 10 Mar. 1763.

[189] *FDJ*, 26–9 Mar. 1763; *Gentleman's and London Magazine*, 32 (1763), 232 (*recte* 175).

[190] *FDJ*, 22–6, 26–9 Mar., 16–19 Apr. 1763; *CEP*, 31 Mar. 1763; *Gentleman's and London Magazine*, 32 (1763), 232 (*recte* 175), 238.

[191] *FDJ*, 25–8 June 1763.

[192] *FDJ*, 31 May–4 June 1763; *Gentleman's and London Magazine*, 32 (1763), 307. [193] *FDJ*, 26–30 July 1763, 7–10 Apr., 21–5 Aug. 1764.

August whereby the local magistrates were empowered to lead detachments of the military against the agitators.[194] The lack of success of these measures is implicit in the passage in 1765 of a comprehensive Whiteboy act (5 Geo. III, c. 8) which extended the list of capital felonies and made the giving of information more attractive. In its application the act was superficial for two reasons. First, the lessons of the years 1761-5 for the gentry were the role of oath-taking and intimidation by the Whiteboys in maintaining the silence of the populace at large, the harsh treatment of informers, and the unreliability of prosecution witnesses. Given this context, belief in the ability of the 1765 act to induce a greater co-operation among the rural community against the disturbers was mistaken, a point recognized by John Hely-Hutchinson.[195] Secondly, a downturn in economic conditions brought on by a severe drought beginning in April 1765 and continuing throughout the summer, resulted in poor harvests and depleted livestock numbers, leading to food shortages.[196] Coping with the effects of these disasters served to diminish the urgency of specific rural grievances, and thereby led to a decline in unrest, a result which the 1765 act of itself was unable to achieve.

The unrest of the early 1770s was a more serious threat to law and order in that it saw the wider acquisition and use of firearms, and there were for the first time serious personal attacks on members of the gentry. There was no effective response to these threats initially. Despite the extended catalogue of felonies prescribed under the act of 1765, convictions for Whiteboy crimes in 1771-5 were few, a situation due more to deficiencies in the processes of law than to lack of vigour among the gentry. A spirited exertion in May 1773 resulted in the taking of Thomas Rafter, a Whiteboy leader, near Carrick but this effort was frustrated by failure to secure his conviction, a situation worsened by Rafter's later escape from custody.[197] This lack of success made the magistrates fall back on the reward system to induce informers, which failed since the next major arrest did not

---

[194] Pearse Street Library, Robinson MS 34 (3), 181; NLI, Parker papers, appointment dated 4 Feb. 1764; NA, M2554, p. 134; 3 Geo. III, c. 19; *FJ*, 20-4 Mar., 17-21 Apr. 1764.

[195] J. Caldwell, *Debates in the Irish parliament in the years 1763 and 1764* (London, 1766), i. 85.

[196] Donnelly, 'Whiteboy movement', 52-3.

[197] *FLJ*, 25-8 Aug. 1773; *FJ*, 8-11, 11-13 May, 15-17 June, 10-12 Aug. 1773.

materialize until January 1774; and though a few other arrests followed in succeeding months these did not have a deterrent effect on the growing cycle of unrest.[198] To add to the low morale of the gentry, in May 1774 Rafter, who was convicted and was due to be executed, was granted a free pardon by the lord-lieutenant.[199]

As the level of violence increased in late 1774 and 1775 there were calls for greater resolution. Candidates intending to stand in the forthcoming general election were told pointedly to be in the forefront of such efforts.[200] Strong action did not come until August 1775 when the gentry in Clonmel resolved on greater effort. Committees were to be established in each barony to receive subscriptions for a central fund out of which payments of £50 were to be made to anyone who would inform on Whiteboy meetings in advance, and of £20 for information on the location of stolen firearms. A promise of protection and a pardon were offered to those who would inform on their colleagues, and in all cases an assurance was given that the names of the informers would be kept secret.[201] Thereafter the Fethard gentry notably William Barton, Matthew Jacob, and the ill-fated Ambrose Power were particularly active in tracking down offenders, but despite some success the overall level of violence remained.[202] In addition the new Catholic archbishop of Cashel, James Butler, in October 1775 issued a statement to be read in all chapels condemning the Whiteboys of the Fethard and Killenaule areas.[203] But since the incidents at Ballyragget, Co. Kilkenny in February 1775, in which Butler supported the action of his brother in openly resisting a Whiteboy attack on the town, clerical admonitions were less likely to meet the desired response.

With the reward system and clerical sanctions not succeeding, the situation seemed hopeless. In the end what induced a greater determination to quell the unrest was the brutal murder of Ambrose Power of Barrettstown in November 1775.[204] The event provoked a quick campaign of repression resulting in twenty-three arrests between December 1775 and January 1776, in which the

---

[198] *FLJ*, 7–11 Aug. 1773, 22–6 Jan., 12–16 Feb. 1774; *WHM*, Feb. 1774, p. 115.
[199] *FLJ*, 11–14 May 1774; *FJ*, 10–12 May 1774.
[200] *FJ*, 25–7 Oct. 1774.
[201] *FLJ*, 16–19 Aug. 1775.
[202] *FLJ*, 25–9 Nov. 1775.
[203] CDA, James Butler II papers, 1775/6.
[204] Donnelly, 'Irish agrarian rebellion', 307–8, 325.

Fethard gentry excelled.[205] A special commission in January 1776 produced four capital convictions and dramatic executions followed immediately after sentence, accompanied by full confessions.[206] In the following months two developments strengthened the resolve of the gentry. First, a revised and extended Whiteboy act (15 & 16 Geo. III, c. 21) passed which added to the list of felonies incurring the death penalty and increased the powers of the magistrates. Secondly, from February 1776 a number of volunteer corps were formed. Ironically the first of these were not in the disturbed area of the south-east, but in the north at Roscrea in an area free of unrest at this time.[207] By May two further corps under Benjamin Bunbury and Sir Cornwallis Maude were formed, in July another at Nenagh under Peter Holmes, and by the end of the year another under Sir John Carden at Templemore.[208] These corps, coupled with the determination of the gentry following Power's murder, served to quell Whiteboy agitation at this time.

Gentry concern with the threat of rural unrest remained evident in the early 1780s. As early as 1781 a meeting at Killenaule of the gentlemen from Slievardagh and Middlethird baronies passed resolutions for the suppression of the Whiteboys, the offering of rewards for information, and the giving of assurances that informers would not be obliged to prosecute nor would their identity be revealed.[209] It is also clear from these resolutions that the volunteer corps still had a function in policing at this time. But despite a number of committals, capital convictions in the early 1780s are conspicuous by their absence.[210] Indicative of local concern was a meeting of the gentry in late September 1784 at which they resolved to uphold and vindicate the law and recommended that the sheriff apply to government for military aid—which reflects the gravity of the situation.[211] The crisis became a more widespread threat to law and order with the arrival of the Rightboys in the autumn of 1785. The events which heralded a general extension of unrest from late September were

---

[205] *FLJ*, 6–9, 13–16, 20–3 Dec. 1775, 30 Dec.–3 Jan. 1776, 6–10, 13–17 Jan. 1776; *FJ*, 2–4, 4–6 Jan. 1776; *WC*, 29 Dec. 1775–2 Jan. 1776, 9–12, 16–19, 19–23 Jan. 1776.   [206] *WC*, 19–23 Jan. 1776.
[207] *WC*, 27 Feb.–1 Mar., 23–6 July 1776.
[208] *Munster volunteer registry* (Dublin, 1782), 18, 57.
[209] *WHM*, Nov. 1781, 614.
[210] *FLJ*, 13–17 Apr. 1782, 29 Sept.–2 Oct. 1784; *WHM*, Apr. 1785, 220–1.
[211] *FLJ*, 29 Sept.–2 Oct. 1784.

the murder of Lyons Cane and the assault on Revd William Ryan of Kilvemnon.[212] These personal attacks spurred the gentry into activity, just as the murder of Power had a decade earlier. A meeting was quickly convened at Fethard at which a revival of the volunteers was called for to act in co-operation with the military, and a county-wide subscription was opened for which a substantial sum of £1,000 was lodged with the Clonmel bank.[213] This renewed resolution produced the desired effect. During December some of Revd Ryan's attackers were taken, and at the assizes in April 1786 170 prisoners were held on capital charges in Clonmel jail. However, only one capital conviction for an agrarian-related crime was obtained.[214]

The response of the local establishment to the high phase of Rightboy agitation in 1786–7 can be characterized in two ways. The first was one of reform. Many of the gentry lent tacit approval to the Rightboy resistance to tithe with Edward Moore of Mooresfort, colonel of the Tipperary volunteers, in June 1786 advocating to government 'the abolition of the tythe laws and the substitution of some other mode in lieu thereof'.[215] Similar statements advocating reform of the tithe system through parliament were forthcoming during the summer of 1786 from the peasantry of Golden, the Catholics of Roscrea, sixty freeholders and Protestants of Roscrea, and the inhabitants of Carrick.[216] Some magistrates and landlords sought to dissuade the agitators from their course of action by persuasion.[217] This approach was to be ineffective because of Rightboy indifference to such appeals and because the Established Church resisted change; though the Catholic Church locally, headed by archbishop Butler, initiated reforms intended to mitigate the more blatant abuses among the clergy which the Rightboys complained of.[218]

Appeasement proved ineffective and advocates of reform and of social control by the church were overtaken by events so that the more established ways of dealing with the disturbers came to be invoked anew. Between July and September 1786 a number of

[212] PRO, HO, 100/17/171–171ᵛ; *CG*, 10–14 Nov. 1785.
[213] *FLJ*, 12–15 Oct. 1785.
[214] HMC, *Rutland*, 254, 262; NLI, MS 1008, pp. 51, 53, 64; *CG*, 21–4 Nov. 1785; *FLJ*, 23–6 Nov. 1785. [215] HMC, *Rutland*, 317.
[216] *CG*, 3–6 July 1786; *WC*, 5–8 Sept. 1786; *FLJ*, 30 Aug.–2 Sept. 1786.
[217] NLI, MS 50(O)/4; *CG*, 12–15 June 1786; Brady, *Press*, 239–40.
[218] CDA, James Butler II papers, 1786/4, 7; Brady, *Press*, 239–40.

Rightboy leaders were taken and there was a revival of volunteering.[219] There were calls by the bishop of Killaloe, and also at a
badly attended meeting at Cashel, for the gentry to become more
actively involved.[220] Nevertheless, eight persons were found guilty
at the September assizes with one execution.[221] One of the
controversial decisions of the assizes was the acquittal of Revd
Patrick Hare on a charge of murdering John Swiney of Kilcock
who had opposed his tithe demands, which Hare conceded were at
rates higher than those of other clergy.[222]

The year 1787 saw significant changes in confronting the
Rightboy problem. In late March a new act (27 Geo. III, c. 15)
came into force which increased the penalties for various types of
rural disorder. The likelihood that the application of this act would
be effective increased because a further measure (27 Geo. III, c.
40) in May 1787 provided for the division of specified counties,
including Tipperary, into districts for each of which a chief
constable and sixteen sub-constables were appointed with the
holding of general sessions eight times annually. The county was
divided into seven districts and Cashel, Clonmel, Thurles, and
Nenagh were designated for the sessions twice yearly.[223] The good
effects of these measures were seen in the number of committals
for Rightboy crimes in subsequent years for which the sub-
constables were primarily responsible, and in the busy sessions at
Cashel and Clonmel.[224] All this was consistent with the traditional
response of the local establishment to unrest since 1760, one
dictated by the expediency of the current situation, by a class
reaction to events, and by an over-reliance on the informer system
without any attempt to initiate reform.

[219] *CG*, 7–11, 28–31 Sept. 1786, 1–5 Feb. 1787; *FLJ*, 2–6, 9–13 Sept. 1786; *HC*, 7
Sept. 1786; *WHM*, Aug. 1786, 446.
[220] NLI, MS 13,047 (5); *CG*, 28–31 Aug. 1786.
[221] PRO, HO, 100/18/326–9; *WHM*, Sept. 1786, 501, Oct. 1786, 556; *Comms.
Jnl.(Ire.)*, xii. pt. 2, pp. dxxviii–dxxix.
[222] *WHM*, Oct. 1786, 556–7.
[223] *CG*, 29 Oct.–1 Nov. 1787; *HC*, 20 Sept. 1787; *FLJ*, 15–19 Sept. 1787.
[224] *CEP*, 24 Apr. 1788; *CG*, 28 June–2 July, 29 Oct.–1 Nov., 29 Nov.–3 Dec.,
27–31 Dec. 1787, 13–17 Nov. 1788; *FLJ*, 4–7 July, 22–6 Sept., 6–10 Oct., 24–8 Nov.
1787.

6

Sectarian Conflict

The decade of the 1760s saw the conjunction of a unique set of circumstances in the political legal, eçonomic, and religious spheres, and in time and place, which made Protestants feel threatened because of their own minority position in the county and, as they perceived it, because of a new assertiveness on the part of Catholics. The open sectarianism which resulted had implications for denominational and political relationships nationally. There were antecedents in terms of confessional composition and tensions in the county which provided the framework within which the events of the 1760s materialized. As a background to the events of the 1760s two questions can be considered initially: what were the political trends in the county, and what was the disposition of the different religious denominations before 1760?

1. Politics Before 1760

Land was the basis of political power. However, landownership changes on the Ormond, Everard, and Dunboyne estates and the fact that some estates, notably that of the Mathews, were still attaining their full extent or unified form, meant that before mid-century solid political interests were still evolving. Their emergence was influenced by the nature of the electoral system. Until the octennial act of 1768 which limited its life to eight years, parliament could only be dissolved by the death of a sovereign, which occasioned general elections in 1702, 1714, 1727, and 1761. Equally unpredictable were the deaths of sitting members which precipitated by-elections. Despite the fact that in practice elections of both types occurred in every decade before 1760, except the 1740s and 1750s, the expectation was that they would be infrequent.

Given the number of seats for the county (2) and its three

boroughs (6), the outlets for political representation in Tipperary were low compared with adjoining counties like Cork (28 seats) or Kilkenny (18 seats). Between 1692 and 1760 representation for the county constituency was shared by nine families, the majority of whom were New English of the post-1650 period. Politically the Mathew family was the only one to display continuity right through the century and beyond. In fact, acrimony at the level of the county constituency is closely associated with the Mathews. George Mathew's conversion and his association with the Tory duke of Ormond, facilitated his election in 1713, when he sat in the Tory interest with three other convert MPs associated with Tipperary.[1] The 1713 election was highly contentious for a pro-Tory sheriff and convert, Terence Magrath, was in office (an influential post since he acted as returning officer for the election), nationally many converts appeared as candidates, and there was widespread participation by Catholics.[2] One defeated Whig candidate protested that his successful opponent, Sir Redmond Everard, was a convert and that he was 'set up by a popish interest'.[3]

The participation of convert candidates and charges of Catholic influence were to be recurrent features of elections. In the contested general election of 1727 George Mathew was elected, but only on petition.[4] Though no explicit evidence regarding the participation or interference by Catholics is forthcoming, it is possible that it was the case for an act of 1728 (1 Geo. II, c. 9, s. 7) explicitly deprived Catholics of the parliamentary franchise.[5] In a disputed election in 1735 brought about by the death of Kingsmill Pennefather, George Mathew, the other sitting MP, in correspondence with Henry Otway in May 1735 referred to 'all ye

---

[1] Unless indicated otherwise references to elections and individuals returned are taken from the introductory sections of the respective volumes of the *Journals of the House of Commons of the kingdom of Ireland*, 3rd edn., ii–xx (Dublin, 1796–1800), abbr. as *Comms. Jnl. (Ire.)*. D. W. Hayton, 'The crisis in Ireland and the disintegration of Queen Anne's last ministry', *IHS*, 22 (1981), 202–3; J. G. Simms, 'The Irish parliament of 1713', *Historical Studies*, 4 (1963), 84. The four convert MPs were Cornelius O'Callaghan, Sir Redmond Everard (both Fethard), George Mathew (county Tipperary), and Derby Egan (Kilkenny City).

[2] Hayton, 'The crisis in Ireland', 202–3.

[3] Ibid. 203.

[4] *Dublin Journal*, 28–31 Oct. 1727; *Comms. Jnl. (Ire.)*, iii. pt. 1, 470, 501.

[5] J. G. Simms, 'Irish catholics and the parliamentary franchise 1692–1728', *IHS*, 12 (1960–1), 28–37.

schemes going forward towards a further division in our county'.[6] Mathew, Richard Pennefather, and others resolved to avoid a contest, but despite this the by-election developed into a contest between John Dawson and Joseph Damer. Damer, who was advanced in the Mathew interest, was returned and Dawson attributed his failure to the fact that the sheriff, Theobald Mathew (Annfield), among other irregularities, delayed the opening of the poll in order to facilitate the creation (much of it by Catholics) of freeholders who voted for Damer.[7] Thus in two key years, 1713 and 1735, two convert sheriffs influenced the outcome in favour of the Mathews, and even in 1727, when a sheriff favourable to Mathew was not in office, the decision still ultimately went in his favour. The year 1736 marks the end of the first phase of the Mathew involvement in the county representation. Mathew and Damer both died in 1736, and in the subsequent by-election Nehemiah Donnellan and Stephen Moore were returned, apparently unopposed, and both were to represent the county between 1737 and 1760.[8]

Tipperary's three boroughs—Cashel, Clonmel, and Fethard—were freeman boroughs, i.e. the right to return MPs was vested in the freemen, the mayor or sovereign, and the burgesses. During the course of the century dominant interests became established in each three. The crucial date in Cashel is 1733, when the death of Matthew Pennefather occasioned a by-election. In advance of it over 120 freemen were created, and the election was contested by Stephen Moore and Richard Pennefather who, despite Moore's charges of favouritism towards him on the part of the mayor, and of evidence of some freemen being married to Catholics, was elected.[9] This victory was attained at the expense of the archbishop of Cashel who supported Moore.[10]

It is significant that Henry Boyle, who was then establishing a political power-base in Munster, and who as future speaker of the House of Commons was to be the chief government opponent,

[6] G. Mathew to H. Otway, 18 May 1735 (NLI, MS 15,055 (i)).
[7] *Comms. Jnl. (Ire.)*, iv. pt. 1, 190.
[8] *Dublin Weekly Advertiser*, 22 Feb., 4 Mar. 1736–7.
[9] NLI, MS 5577, fos. 11–22ᵛ; *Comms. Jnl. (Ire.)*, iv. pt. 1, 124, 128–32.
[10] W. Moore to H. Boyle (n.d.). (PRONI, D2707/A1/2/106); *Comms. Jnl. (Ire.)*, iv. pt. 1, 127–32; A. P. W. Malcomson. 'The parliamentary traffic of this country', in T. Bartlett and D. W. Hayton (eds.), *Penal era and golden age: Essays in Irish history, 1690–1800* (Belfast, 1979), 145–6.

supported the Pennefathers in Cashel in 1733.[11] Thus on the one side was an alignment of Moore, the archbishop of Cashel and the government, and on the other Pennefather and Boyle. The outcome can be regarded as a defeat for government and a success for Boyle in his formation of a Munster block of MPs in the House of Commons. For the Pennefathers the victory meant that they exercised complete control of the borough subsequently, indicated by the fact that the number of freemen never grew to a large and therefore unmanageable size, falling to eighty by 1791.[12] One member of the family sat for Cashel from 1703 and two members from 1753. The only break in this pattern was in 1799 when Richard Bagwell was brought in for one of the seats. This was exceptional, however, for it was the normal practice of the family never to dispose of the borough seats by sale.[13]

The struggle for control of Clonmel borough was waged by the Moore family from at least 1700, and was to continue for over fifty years. During the mayoralty of Stephen Moore (1724–5) ninety-two freemen were created to act in the Moore interest.[14] This development was a prelude to rivalry over representation of the borough in parliament. Before the decline in influence of the duke of Ormond he was, as landowner, able to recommend candidates as MPs for the borough.[15] Between 1692 and 1726 Moore and Robert Hamerton (who represented the opposing faction in the corporation) represented the borough. The 1727 general election presented Stephen Moore with the opportunity to consolidate his victory of 1724 and to deprive Hamerton of the second seat. In the event however, though Moore and his co-candidate achieved a majority, this on petition was declared invalid as it had been obtained by virtue of the freemen created by Moore in 1724–5.[16] The rival candidates, Robert Hamerton and Robert Marshall, were accordingly elected. This was a significant defeat for the Moores and it was compounded by the removal of a Moore from the office of mayor in 1731 and by the failure of Guy Moore to achieve a by-election success on the death of Hamerton in 1733.[17] The successful candidate in that by-election, Sir Thomas Prender-

[11] K. Pennefather to H. Boyle, 11 June 1733 (PRONI, D2707/A1/2/104); E. Hewitt (ed.), *Lord Shannon's letters to his son* (Belfast, 1982), p. xxix.

[12] *FLJ*, 5–8 Jan. 1791.

[13] Falkland, *Parliamentary representation* (Dublin, 1790), 95.

[14] Burke, *Clonmel*, 115–16.   [15] BL, Add. MS 28,877, fos. 374–375ᵛ.

[16] Burke, *Clonmel*, 116.   [17] Ibid.; BL, Add. MS 46,984, 214–16.

gast, a convert, sat continuously with Marshall for Clonmel in the period 1733–55. In the wider context it is noteworthy that Prendergast owed his success in part to the influence of Henry Boyle.[18] The year 1733 was a key one for the extension of Boyle's interest into two Tipperary boroughs, and it marked the defeat of government-favoured candidates, the Moores, in both centres.

Excluded from the borough representation, the Moores continued to dominate the corporation until 1747, when an unexplained break was seized upon by the opposing group to install its own mayor, Jeremiah Morgan, during whose mayoralty an important set of by-laws was enacted in an attempt by the Moore opponents to ensure a perpetual influence over the corporation and the return of members to parliament.[19] The main instigation behind these by-laws was the Quaker merchant interest, mainly the Bagwell and Riall families, indicative of a shift in the composition of the group opposed to the Moores. Despite the success of the Moores in regaining the mayoralty in 1748 the by-laws of that year were confirmed and extended in 1750.[20]

While the Moores retained virtual control of the corporation, the parliamentary representation of the borough was since 1733 in the hands of their opponents. In 1754, however, a by-election was occasioned by the promotion of Marshall to a judgeship and the Moores seized the opportunity to fill the vacancy. The mayor, William Kellett, supported the Moores, the by-laws of 1748 and 1750 were repealed and all powers, including the selection of freemen, were vested in the common council alone.[21] The candidates for the vacancy were Guy Moore and William Bagwell who was successful on petition but who died soon after, allowing the seat to devolve on Moore.[22] Significantly the House of Commons divided evenly (106 to 106) on the petition, and it was only with the casting vote of the Speaker, Henry Boyle, that victory went to Bagwell.[23] This decision was consistent with Boyle's support of Prendergast in 1733 and therefore with the anti-Moore group now represented by Bagwell.

The Moore family remained supreme in Clonmel thereafter for two members of the family represented it continuously from 1761

---

[18] Earl of Meath to H. Boyle (n.d. [*c.*1732/1733]) (PRONI, D2707/A1/2/102).
[19] Burke, *Clonmel*, 117–18.   [20] Ibid. 118–19.   [21] Ibid. 119.
[22] *Comms. Jnl. (Ire.)*, v. 240, 332–44, 357; NLI, MS 8019 (3).
[23] *Comms. Jnl. (Ire.)*, v. 357.

to 1799, when ironically the patronage was sold by Lord Mount Cashell to John Bagwell, a descendant of the opposing party in the 1750s. Although it was observed of Clonmel in 1775 that 'Lord Mount Cashell at present has the sole dominion over this borough',[24] the non-residence of its MPs was regarded as detrimental to their interest and popularity, and one observer remarked in 1773 that 'this borough is very open and if any person attended to it and resided in the town he would probably succeed'.[25] This situation operated to the advantage of the Bagwells who, being resident and popular merchants, took advantage of the Moores' neglect. In 1782 a committee under John Bagwell, and dominated by Quaker merchants, attempted to break the monopoly held by the Moores over the creation of freemen.[26] Encouraged by the current preoccupations of constitutional agitation and, in particular, the demand for parliamentary reform, this attempt was directed with the general election of 1783 in view. It was unsuccessful as Stephen and William Moore were returned without difficulty. Yet in the years that followed Bagwell accumulated much wealth (in 1780 he had purchased Moore's flour mill at Marlfield), office, and influence locally, making his purchase of the borough in 1799 a popular and not unexpected event. In the interim the universal hold of the Moores remained, indicated by the fact that the number of freemen was static or rose only slightly from sixty in 1705 to eighty in 1754, and fell to seventy-two in 1783; and by the fact that they, like the Pennefathers at Cashel, never disposed of their seats by sale.[27] The Moore family had engaged in a struggle stretching over fifty years before its control over Clonmel was finally made secure in 1756.

At Fethard the Everard family came to have an influence over the borough from an early period, and in 1713 Sir Redmond Everard and Cornelius O'Callaghan, both converts, were its MPs. But it was more usually represented by local families like Sankey, Jacob, and Cleere, particularly when Everard's Jacobite sym-

---

[24] *AH*, 12 (1943), 137.
[25] M. Bodkin, 'Notes on the Irish parliament in 1773', *PRIA*, 48 C (1942–3), 214.
[26] *CG*, 24–7 June 1782.
[27] *The case of the protestant freemen of Clonmell* (n.p. [1705]); NLI, MS 8019 (3); H. Grattan, *Memoirs of the life and times of the Rt Hon Henry Grattan* (London, 1841), iii. 484; *PP Corporations (Ire.)*, 28 (1835), 479–89; Falkland, *Parliamentary representation*, 95.

pathies entailed his absence from the locality. Just as in Clonmel, the year 1754 in Fethard witnessed some crucial developments. A by-election in 1754 allowed Robert O'Callaghan to enter parliament for Fethard. The O'Callaghans had built up an influence in the corporation by virtue of their association with Everard in 1713, and because they had acquired part of the encumbered Everard estate in the 1720s. As with Pennefather at Cashel and Moore at Clonmel, O'Callaghan's emergence at Fethard was aided by the creation of ninety-eight new freemen in 1754.[28] Already a rival to the O'Callaghan claims had arisen following the purchase by Thomas Barton of the remnant of the Everard estate in 1750, yet the Bartons found it difficult initially to achieve any solid influence in the borough. The final agreement on the division of the corporation and the borough representation came only in 1787. By it an equal division was agreed on whereby the nomination of one of the MPs was to lie with O'Callaghan, the other with Barton. To complement this it was proposed to reduce the number of freemen so that the influence of both parties could be exercised more effectively. Thus the 900 freemen of 1783 had by 1790 been reduced to 300, and by the 1830s to a nominal 13 or 14.[29] This pattern of a reduction in the number of freemen, once a dominant interest had become established, accords with that at Cashel and Clonmel.

The pattern of political behaviour before 1760 was one where, with the decline of the Ormond political presence, at the level of the county constituency there was a tradition of contest focused on the Mathews; convert MPs sat for the county and at Clonmel and Fethard; there were expressions of Catholic influence at elections; and new patrons emerged with the Pennefathers at Cashel, and the Moores at Clonmel, while the O'Callaghan and Barton families came to share the patronage of Fethard. The absence of the Mathews from the county representation after 1736, was to make more marked the opposition to them when they revived their aspirations to represent the county in 1761.

[28] NLI, MS 5858 (second part), 45–6, 130–7.
[29] NLI, PC, 46 (ii) Barton papers, folder entitled 'Fethard Corporation (ii)', document headed 'Copy of a paper given by Lord Lismore to Edwd. Collins about the corporation, the 29 April [17]87'; *FLJ*, 5–8 Jan. 1791; Grattan, *Memoirs*, iii. 484; *PP Corporations (Ire.)*, 502.

2. The 1761 Election

The 1761 general election in Tipperary was controversial because of the candidature of Thomas Mathew. He had converted in 1755 but the sincerity of this conversion was questioned especially by Sir Thomas Maude of Dundrum, his opponent, an evangelical Protestant and noted estate improver, who later charged that he objected to Mathew on the grounds that he had 'professed the popish religion many years after the age of twelve and had not conformed to the Protestant religion, or educated his children as required by the several acts of parliament'.[30] Further, a member of the Mathew family had married Sir James Cotter, the chief advocate of the Stuart cause in Ireland in the early eighteenth century, for which he was executed in 1720.[31] This association may have been recalled in the context of the election given the contemporary threat from France. More significantly, after the death of George Mathew (d. 1760), the Thomastown and Thurles estates devolved on Thomas Mathew of Annfield thereby uniting for the first time the hitherto separate estates of the family under the ownership of one individual. This made Mathew one of the county's largest proprietors, a fact which had its implications in terms of the election and which made him seem a threat to other political interests. Given the family's absence from the county representation since 1736, Mathew may have sought to use his recent accretion of property to re-establish the family's political interest.

It is possible that Mathew's position as head of the freemasons—an egalitarian and non-sectarian body at this time[32]—is indicative of his wider standing in the county. The majority of lodges active in the county in the 1760s were founded after 1756, the exception being one of the two Thurles lodges which was established in 1735. Thomas Mathew formed a second lodge in Thurles in 1757 with an initial membership of twenty-three.[33] The two Thurles lodges had

[30] *Comms. Jnl. (Ire.)*, vii. 71.

[31] W. Hogan and L. O'Buachalla, 'Letters and papers of James Cotter junior, 1689–1720', *JCHAS*, 68 (1963), 68.

[32] T. de Vere White, 'The Freemasons', in T. D. Williams (ed.), *Secret societies in Ireland* (Dublin, 1973), 49, 53.

[33] Grand Lodge of Freemasons of Ireland, Dublin: registers of lodges for the eighteenth century; P. Crossle, *Irish masonic records* (n.p., 1973).

the largest membership of all lodges in the county by the 1760s and their patron, Mathew, was elected provincial grand master of Munster in 1757, and was grand master of England in 1766–70.[34] But apart from this possible indicator of wider support, Mathew was suspect on a number of grounds: the sincerity of his conversion, his large landed estate, the former Jacobite associations of his family, and especially the overt Catholic support in his favour.

Mathew was advanced in the Catholic interest, for it was said that the Catholics of Tipperary 'imprudently at that time made great exertions at a contested election in favour of a gentleman whose mild principles conciliated their affections', and this they did 'through resentment to some intolerant gentlemen who were in opposition to their favourite and avowed enemies of their profession'.[35] Though Catholics could not vote or be elected they could bring their influence to bear in three ways: nominal conversion in order to qualify to vote; influencing Protestant freeholders, some of whom were their tenants, to vote in a certain way; and attempting to vote when unqualified. Catholic assertiveness did not go unchallenged, for the 1761 election turned out to be an intense sectarian affair. During the course of polling, Maude's election agent, Daniel Gahan, questioned the qualifications of freeholders, whether they were born of Catholic parents, educated as Catholics, or if converts to produce their certificates of conversion.[36] Gahan challenged Mathew's election agent, Thomas Prendergast, with the assertion that his wife was Catholic and that therefore he was disqualified from voting; a duel ensued resulting in Prendergast's death.[37]

The fact that three candidates, Maude, Mathew, and Henry Prittie of Kilboy, went forward in the election meant that a contest was inevitable. When polling closed on 8 May 1761 the poll stood thus: Prittie 924 votes, Mathew 532, and Maude 486, with Prittie being elected (marking the successful entry of the family to the county representation) and a double return made in respect of the other two, because of which both candidates were obliged to

---

[34] J. P. Lepper and P. Crossle, *History of the grand lodge of free and accepted masons of Ireland* (n.p., 1925), i. 85, 275.
[35] A. Griffith, *Miscellaneous tracts* (Dublin, 1788), 240.
[36] Burke, *Clonmel*, 365–6.
[37] Ibid.; [Lidwell], *Lidwill's life*, 20–1.

petition.[38] This was unusual as it was more normal for only the defeated candidate to petition and Mathew's supporters insisted that this should be the case, and the requirement that Mathew should also petition was obviously a diminution of his success in the poll, suggesting that parliament was giving Maude an advantage.[39]

Maude's petition indicates how sectarian the election was. He had already made his objections to Mathew's candidature known to him before the election on the basis that he was not a fully qualified Protestant. Maude claimed that during the election a great number of Mathew's voters refused to show their certificates of conversion; that most of them 'admitted themselves to have been born of popish parents and educated in the popish religion'; and that 'great mobs of Irish papists' crowded the election hall and intimidated him. After the close of polling Maude demanded a scrutiny because, as he claimed, a 'very great' many of the votes cast for Mathew were invalid, those concerned being 'papists or born of popish parents and not having duly conformed and having married popish wives'.[40] Thus the charge made by Maude was that Catholics not merely influenced the election but that they actually voted or attempted to do so. Had their votes been excluded, Maude claimed that he would have achieved a majority over Mathew.

In his petition Mathew, in contrast, concentrated on the partial way in which the sheriff, Richard Waller, conducted the election. Mathew claimed that Waller acted 'illegally, arbitrarily, and partially in prejudice of the petitioner and in favour of Sir Thomas Maude'.[41] The result was that though Mathew gained a majority of thirty-six votes in the gross poll, the sheriff refused to return him as duly elected. Mathew clearly did not dwell on the sectarian nature of the election as this would have had no advantage in parliament. In the event parliament came out strongly in favour of Maude. A report by a Dublin lawyer writing to a friend in county Cork in November 1761, recorded that 'When one of the friends of Mr. Mathew attempted to speak there was such a coughing and snorting that 'twas impossible to hear, but when one of the friends of Sir Thomas did so it was all silence.'[42] Mathew could only rely

---

[38] King's Inns MS, 39 D, fo. 127ᵛ.   [39] *AH*, 15 (1944), 28.
[40] *Comms. Jnl. (Ire.)*, vii. 71–2.   [41] Ibid. 72.
[42] R. Chester to H. Cole-Bowen, 14 Nov. 1761 (*AH*, 15 (1944), 28).

on about twenty supporters in the house, whereas the majority were in favour of Maude. In January 1762 the house voted by sixty-seven to seventeen votes that Mathew be obliged to withdraw his petition, and Maude was declared duly elected and returned as the second member for county Tipperary.[43]

The 1761 election in Tipperary was unique in the history of parliamentary politics as it is the only instance of an attempt to disqualify a member on the grounds that he was a Catholic. It displayed the ability of the substantial Catholic landholding and gentry class to mobilize in favour of a convert of large landed estate and to achieve an initial victory. Though Mathew's victory was later overturned this was only to be a short-term setback. The long-term effect of the 1761 election was to establish a pattern whereby county electoral politics became divisive, centring on the status, sympathies, and associations of the Mathews. In the short term the local Protestant consciousness was informed by a range of other fears and concerns, the articulation of which was to galvanize a section of the gentry into a course of action leading to the traumatic events of 1765–6.

3. Churches and Denominations

The Catholic Church enjoyed a wide toleration in the county by the 1750s, despite statutory provisions to the contrary. Although disorganized initially due to the penal legislation passed between 1690 and 1710, the church continued to exist largely unhindered and was to re-emerge in a renewed state by mid-century. It experienced a resurgence in the late seventeenth century under John Brennan, bishop of Waterford and Lismore (1671–93) and archbishop of Cashel (1677–93). In the period 1712–91 the leading church office in Munster, i.e. the archbishopric of Cashel, was held by prominent members of the Butler family. Although he had to remain itinerant due to the political situation in the 1710s, because of his episcopal status and his connection with the attainted duke of Ormond, Christopher Butler (archbishop 1711–57) remained generally resident in the region and during his long episcopate was able to attend to church organization unimpeded.

[43] *Comms. Jnl. (Ire.)*, vii. 102–5.

In terms of clerical personnel, in 1704 a total of sixty-two persons registered as priests in the county.[44] About half of them were aged fifty or under so that there was a fair prospect of long years of service remaining. In 1731 there were sixty-two priests many of them officiating in Cashel diocese, in addition to itinerant clerics.[45] A seminary was established in Cashel by archbishop Butler for the education of clerical aspirants. In 1731 there were forty mass houses of varying quality known to the authorities to be in use.[46] One private chapel is mentioned, that of Justin McCarthy at his residence near Tipperary, and possibly another in the Kearney household at Killusty, Fethard, and there may have been others in existence unknown to the authorities. Of the forty structures, six were newly built or then building including an impressive new structure at Tipperary measuring 92 feet by 76 feet in cruciform design. The structure was cited by local Protestants as an instance of the vibrancy of the Catholic Church, but it can also be viewed as part of the overall redevelopment of the town then being sponsored by its landlord, Smith.[47]

By the 1750s the Catholic church though materially poor was well organized. The diocesan visitations undertaken by James Butler, appointed coadjutor to archbishop Christopher Butler in 1750 and his successor in the See from 1757 to 1774, show that church buildings were modest in terms of size and furnishings. In the visitations of the 1750s and early 1760s numerous chapels were visited at locations spread across the diocese of Cashel. Newly built chapels or those under construction were evident at eight centres in these years, many of them receiving financial assistance from local Catholic families who also made donations of furnishings as in the case of Fogarty, Purcell, Mathew, and Butler (Dunboyne). Protestant families like Lidwell also made gifts of this kind.[48]

Though the church was lacking in material resources it was becoming better organized with a wider parochial structure well established by the 1750s. Clerical numbers were maintained with

---

[44] *Irish Ecclesiastical Record*, 12 (1876), 516–27.
[45] *Arch. Hib.*, 4 (1915), 175.
[46] The full report covering dioceses in Tipperary is in *Arch. Hib.*, 2 (1913), 112–17, 146–7, 150, 154–5.   [47] Loveday, *Diary of a tour*, 43.
[48] The foregoing and what follows is based on the reports edited in *Arch. Hib.*, 33 (1975), 1–90, 34 (1976–7), 1–49.

fifty-seven secular and six regular clergy in the archdiocese in 1752, and synods and conferences were regularly held, mostly in Thurles at which regulations on the conduct of the clergy and on their pastoral functions were formulated.[49] Appointments to parishes were under the strict control of the archbishop and many priests were required to produce evidence of their title on visitation. Indeed the dangers regarding the proper functioning of clergy derived more from interloping clerics than from local justices of the peace.

A work of clerical discipline, the so-called 'Psalter of Cashel', originally produced by archbishop Butler in 1731, was in 1750 rewritten and made available as the *Constitutions of the Dioceses of Cashel and Emly great and small*. This work, which was unique for Catholic Ireland at the time, laid down a strict code of conduct for priests and was reinforced by the diocesan synods and conferences where individual pastoral incidents requiring resolution were also dealt with. As part of a greater administrative efficiency priests were required to maintain registers of baptisms, marriages, and deaths, and this duty appears to have been adhered to in about half of the parishes visited. Particular attention was paid to the preparation of candidates for the priesthood and regular ordinations took place, mostly at Thurles.[50] In the realm of education seventy-three teachers are identifiable as functioning in the period 1752–60. This evidence is witness to the extent of toleration, reinforced by the fact that such thoroughgoing visitations took place without interference, that the archbishop could socialize freely during his perambulations, and that cases of persecution were few.

Apart from the north of the county, where durable Protestant rural communities developed as a result of the seventeenth-century land settlement, Protestants elsewhere were concentrated in the towns and thin on the ground in rural areas. A series of censuses was compiled at times when Protestants felt insecure. In 1691 during the Williamite campaigns a listing of the Protestant and Catholic inhabitants of Cashel was ordered by the corporation to be compiled.[51] In 1731 at a time of fear a national religious census was taken. The return for Tipperary gives an enumeration

---

[49] Ibid. 33 (1975), 17–37, 58–9.
[50] Ibid. 6, 46; vol. 34, 18–22.
[51] NLI, MS 5575, fo. 92ᵛ.

of 1,627 Protestant and 16,465 Catholic families, a ratio of 1 : 10.[52] Similar circumstances, in the form of a Jacobite invasion scare, operated in 1745 to influence the making of a return by Col. Pennefather of all Catholics and Protestants aged between sixteen and sixty who were capable of bearing arms, which shows that there were 2,600 Protestants and 18,000 Catholics, equal to a ratio of 1 : 7.[53] At the outbreak of war in 1756 the array of Protestants in Munster was 11,863, of which Tipperary accounted for 2,300 or nearly 20 per cent.[54] A further religious census was compiled in 1766, some of the best surviving returns being from the southern half of Tipperary. They indicate that the overall ratio of Protestants to Catholics at that date was 1 : 9.[55] This numerical inferiority clearly influenced the attitude of Protestants in Tipperary, a factor recognized by a visitor to the county in 1760 when he remarked that 'The Protestants here are what we should call in England red-hot Protestants, the smallness of their number makes it necessary for them politically to be so'.[56] Yet significantly, the 1760s saw a greater expression of activity in the Established Church locally. For instance, the archbishop of Cashel, Michael Cox, held triennial visitations of the dioceses under his control in 1763, 1766, and 1769 at Cashel, Clonmel and other centres.[57] The building of a new cathedral at Cashel was reinitiated in 1763, supported by local and parliamentary grants.[58]

There was a Presbyterian presence in the county from the mid-seventeenth century. The Commonwealth had supported Independent or Baptist ministers at Clonmel, Carrick, Cashel, Thurles, Fethard, and Cullen.[59] The Sankey family of St. Johnstown advanced the appointment of a minister at Clonmel in 1673 and ministers continued to be provided for. One of them,

[52] Lambeth Palace Library, MS 1742, fos. 43–8 (PRONI, Mic.310).
[53] BL, Add. MS 29,252, 40.
[54] Brady, *Press*, 202.
[55] NA, 1766 census for Cashel and Emly; W. H. Rennison, *Succession list of the bishops, cathedral, and parochial clergy of Waterford and Lismore* (n.p. [c.1920]), 233–4.
[56] BL, Add. MS 29,252, 38–9.
[57] *FDJ*, 26–30 July 1763, 19–22 July 1766; *FLJ*, 3–7 June 1769.
[58] *FDJ*, 12–15 Feb. 1763; *Comms. Jnl. (Ire.)*, vii. 209–10, 218; viii. pt. 1, 180–1, 194–5, 201, app. clxx.
[59] J. M. Barkley, *A short history of the Presbyterian church in Ireland* (Belfast, 1959), 17; J. S. Reid, *History of the Presbyterian church in Ireland* (Belfast, 1867), ii. 558.

Revd William Campbell, was tutor to the Bagwells in 1750.[60] A continuing Presbyterian presence was maintained at Fethard and Tipperary.[61] These Dissenter groups were small and were ultimately dependent on the patronage of local families like Sankey at Fethard, Bagwell at Clonmel, and Roe at Tipperary. Nevertheless the grouping of such prominent individuals into a sect was important enough to gain political notice, for in 1775 Matthew Jacob of Mobernan near Fethard was said to be the leader of the Presbyterians in the county.[62]

From the mid-seventeenth century Quaker groups were functioning at Cashel, Clonmel, Tipperary, Kilcommon near Clogheen based on the Fennell household, and near Roscrea based on the Hutchinsons.[63] French Protestant Huguenot families were settled by the duke of Ormond at Clonmel and Carrick in the Restoration period as part of his schemes to promote the textile industry.[64] Methodism arose in the mid-eighteenth century at a number of centres, like Shronell near Tipperary under the Damers, following the many visits of John Wesley to the region.[65]

Dissenters were concentrated in the south of the county particularly in and around Clonmel, for they came late to the northern part of the county. Because of the seventeenth-century settlement, the attractions of the better lands and the towns of the south, and the preferences of local families, Dissenters struck deepest roots in the southern half. The 1831 census shows that in the civil parishes of north Tipperary covered by the diocese of Killaloe the total number in the category 'other denominations', which included Methodists and Quakers, was 84 divided between

[60] *A history of congregations in the Presbyterian church in Ireland 1610–1982* (Belfast, 1982), 309–11.

[61] Ibid. 480–1, 777–8; diary of Revd John Cooke, minister at Tipperary 1701–5 (GO, MS 544, esp. pp. 12–13, 22).

[62] *AH*, 12 (1943), 141.

[63] Society of Friends Library, Dublin: National sufferings 1655–93 (YMG, I) *passim*; NLI, MS 5575 (unfoliated) *sub* 11 Aug. 1703; W. Penn, *My Irish journal 1669–1670*, ed. I. Grubb (London, 1952), 27, 37–8, 66–7; W. Edmundson, *Journal* (Dublin, 1833), 298–9; G. W. Grubb, *The Grubbs of Tipperary: Studies in heredity and character* (Cork, 1972), 19–70; I. Grubb, *The Quakers in Ireland 1654–1900* (London, 1927), 32, 42, 102, 113.

[64] G. L. Lee, *The Huguenot settlements in Ireland* (London, 1936), 117–18; S. J. Knox, *Ireland's debt to the Huguenots* (Dublin, 1959), 13, 37, 56.

[65] NLI, MS 11,887, entry for Feb. 1752; *Journal of John Wesley*, ed. N. Curnock (London [1912–17]), iii. 399, 476, 482; iv. 42, 161, 277, 398–9, 401, 507–8, 510; v. 208, 319; Marnane, *Land and violence*, 25.

Roscrea (38), Borrisokane (37), and Templederry (9). There were no Presbyterians returned for north Tipperary. In contrast the southern half, covered by Cashel and Lismore dioceses, returned a total of 157 Presbyterians with 370 others. The largest Presbyterian congregations were in Inislounaght (57) based on the Bagwells, Clonmel (44), and the parishes around Fethard (39). Other Dissenters, mainly Quakers and Methodists, were present in the 'other' category, notably at Clonmel (202), Shanrahan (47), and Cahir (68).[66] The main centre of Protestantism, Anglican and Dissenter, was Clonmel itself which was the hub of the sectarian events of the 1760s.

Attempts to redress the numerical imbalance between Protestants and Catholics took two forms: the promotion of Protestant settlement in areas where it was sparse, and conversion schemes. Colonization schemes were an integral part of the strategy to revitalize the Ormond estate in the 1690s, but were unsuccessful as sales were to local interests and there was no substantial influx of Protestant tenants, who at any rate were in short supply. The Damer family were engaged in introducing Protestant textile workers on to their estate at Shronell in the 1740s. In 1766 eighty-two Protestant families were in Shronell and five adjoining rural parishes equivalent to 451 persons (if a family size multiplier of 5.5 is assumed), but by 1831 this figure had fallen to ninety-seven.[67] O'Callaghan was engaged in similar colonization schemes at Clogheen also in the 1740s, drawing on social categories ranging from the artisan to the large tenant. Following twenty-two conversions on the estate in 1747 an interesting social and religious mix emerged. The head-tenantry came to include Catholics like Walter Woulfe, Bryan and Roger Sheehy, converts like Prendergast and McGrath, the Quaker Fennell, and new Anglican leaseholders of the 1740s like Bagnell and Beer. In 1766 there were twenty-three Protestant families in Shanrahan parish and if the figures for six adjoining parishes are added, then the total reaches 301 individuals.[68] By 1831 these parishes had a total of 599

---

[66] *PP, Public instruction*, 33 (1835).

[67] A household size of 5.5 is used as a multiplier in computations from the 1766 census where the number of families only is given (for the contemporary validity of this figure see PRO, SPI, 63/420/162). NA, 1766 census for Shronell; *PP, Public instruction*, 33 (1835).

[68] Rennison, *Succession list*, 233.

indicating a doubling in the Protestant population in the 65-year period after 1766.[69]

A greater growth rate is apparent on the Maude estate at Ballintemple where, stimulated by the events of the 1760s, the landlord began to promote Protestant settlement from 1767. In 1766 there were eight Protestant families, or forty-four individuals, in Ballintemple.[70] By 1831 the figure stood at 158 persons representing a threefold rise from 1766.[71] Thus the ratio of Catholics to Protestants on the estate was reduced from 10 : 1 in 1766 to 4 : 1 in 1831. In fact Ballintemple and Shanrahan with their improving landlords, and Templemore with a new military barracks, were the only centres outside the established Protestant concentrations to display an increase in settler populations over the period. There was also a successful colonization of the Kilcooley estate with Palatine settlers sponsored in the 1770s by Sir William Barker, who was also a participant in the events of the 1760s. The 1766 return for Kilcooley does not survive, but by 1831 there were 532 Protestants there.[72] Significantly, the most successful experiments in Protestant colonization were sponsored by individuals or families who had a close connection with the purge of the 1760s.

The other means of reducing the numerical superiority of Catholics was by an active policy of conversion. It cannot be said that the 600 or so conversions recorded for the county in the eighteenth century resulted from any evangelical or missionary endeavour on the part of the Established Church. These were largely the result of legal, family, social, and occupational circumstances. The only area in which any formal structure for active conversion existed was in the charter schools. The background to the foundation in 1733 of the Incorporated Society for Promoting English Protestant Schools in Ireland was the strength of catholicism as revealed in the House of Lords report of 1731 and the desire of prominent clergymen to promote the Established Church. It was perceived that the decaying state of the Church of Ireland and the vitality of catholicism could be reversed by an educational process through the establishment of charter schools which would also serve as vehicles for improvement and inculcate

[69] PP, *Public instruction*, 33 (1835).
[71] PP, *Public instruction*, 33 (1835).
[70] NA, 1766 census Ballintemple.
[72] Ibid.

loyalty to the state. The purpose of the schools was therefore many-faceted—educational, religious, political, agricultural, and industrial—many of their leading promoters being also members of the Linen Board (founded 1711) and the Dublin Society (founded 1731).[73]

Locally three charter schools were founded in the 1740s: Clonmel, whose main supporters were the Moores and Bagwell; Cashel, supported by the corporation, the archbishop and local families; and Newport, promoted by Lord Jocelyn as part of the development of that estate village.[74] These schools did not achieve their object of acting as agents for the advancement of the state religion through the attainment of large-scale conversions. They were conducted at considerable expense, and reports on their condition in the 1780s were generally unfavourable.[75] Nevertheless they are significant as an index of local gentry preoccupations and perceptions, because of the landed families involved in their promotion, and their location in the south. Both endeavours of colonization and conversion failed to markedly increase Protestant numbers relative to Catholic. Their numerical inferiority contributed to the sense of vulnerability felt by Protestants locally, and this was to be a motivating factor for their actions in the 1760s.

4. Clerical

The actions of a section of the Protestant gentry in the county in the 1760s derived in part from the character of the local enforcement of the penal laws against Catholics in the previous half-century. The prevailing attitude, at the time of the passing of the penal legislation, was that Catholic clergy represented a

---

[73] K. Milne, 'Irish charter schools', *Irish Journal of Education*, 8 (1974), 3–29.
[74] For Clonmel: TCD, MS 5789 (lease of 23 Apr. 1747; will of 16 Jan. 1743); *A sermon preached before the society corresponding with the Incorporated Society in Dublin* (London, 1752), 19–20; for Cashel: TCD, MS 5789 (leases of 24 Sept. 1745, 2 Aug. 1749); NLI, MS 5578, 64; *A sermon* (1749), 88; *A sermon* (1757), 58; for Newport: TCD, MS 5789 (lease of 9 July 1747); *A sermon* (1757), 59. A fourth school was proposed for Fethard, but was never built: *Report of the Incorporated Society* (Dublin, 1766) *sub* Fethard; NLI, MS 5858 (second book), 16; RD, 154/239/103585.
[75] *Comms. Jnl. (Ire.)*, xii, pt. 2, pp. dcccxii, dcccxiii, dcccxxi, dcccxxii, dcccxxxi, dcccxxxii; xiv. pp. cvii–cviii.

foreign jurisdiction (papal and Stuart) and hence were a challenge to the state, thus necessitating their banishment or registration and the regulation of Catholic religious practice. However, the 1731 report revealed an unsubdued church in which 'the parish priests even unregistered ones appear everywhere with little reserve and the papists frequent their mass houses as openly as Protestants do their churches'.[76] Fears were further heightened in 1732 when an alleged scheme involving archbishop Christopher Butler, whereby funds were to be raised to aid the cause of the Pretender, was revealed.[77] Although the evidence adduced was of dubious authenticity, the episode made government recognize and admit the existence of an ecclesiastical jurisdiction in Munster in the form of an archbishop and suffragan bishops.

The mid-1740s, which had as its context the Jacobite invasion of Britain, saw renewed enforcement of the penal laws against Catholic religious practice. In response to a government directive to the justices in 1744 the chief Catholic residents of Thurles and Cashel had to appear before magistrates to give information on clergy.[78] At Clonmel the mayor enquired into the clergy but they were found to have fled, yet he had the large mass-house locked up along with the friary.[79] Following the Jacobite success in Scotland in September 1745 the Anglican archbishop of Cashel instructed his clergy to remind Catholics of the leniency with which they had been treated and 'how far their future ease may depend on their peaceable behaviour at this time'.[80] Despite this warning, as we have seen, the open functioning of the Catholic Church is evident from the visitations of the 1750s and early 1760s. In the 1750s however, the widespread toleration hitherto enjoyed by the church was challenged because of belligerent activity on the part of priests and their communities which had the effect of sharpening local Protestant sensibilities.

The first of these concerned the attempt by Revd John Haly to

[76] *A report made by his grace the lord primate from the lords committees appointed to enquire into the present state of popery in this kingdom* (Dublin, 1732), 5.

[77] *Comms. Jnl. (Ire.),* iv. pt. 1, 106; iv. pt. 2, pp. xlvi–xlvii.

[78] W. P. Burke, *The Irish priests in the penal times, 1660–1760* (Waterford, 1914; repr. Shannon, 1969), 358–61; NA, 1A 52 159, p. 256.

[79] Burke, *Clonmel*, 357–8; RIA, MS 24 G. 9, p. 277.

[80] Brady, *Press*, 72; see also F. J. McLynn, ' "Good behaviour": Irish catholics and the Jacobite rising of 1745', *Eire–Ireland*, 16 (1981), 43–58.

convert Charles Moore, a Protestant, and for this he was presented at the assizes of 1750.[81] He was charged under the tory acts and those who presented him for trial included Sir Thomas Maude, Stephen Moore, Sir William Barker, and Matthew Bunbury, individuals who were to figure prominently in the events of the 1760s. The significance of being charged under the tory acts was that the amounts decreed in damages were to be recovered from Catholics only. Interestingly the two accounts of such a tax that survive date to this period and relate to the half-barony of Ikerrin (1750) and the barony of Kilnamanagh (1765), where the Maude estate lay.[82]

The second incident concerned Revd Daniel O'Neill (or Neale) of Cullen. In 1753 a reward was issued for his capture following the marriage ceremony he had performed for Henry Grady who had abducted Susanna Grove. Following his arrest and while being conveyed from Clonmel to Limerick for trial, he was in April 1754 rescued by a large mob from the under-sheriff and army near Cashel.[83] The high sheriff, Jonathan Lovett, reported that a crowd of 'at least 3,000 men and women' participated in the rescue.[84] The incident led to concern among justices about the size of such rescue parties. Joseph Damer remarked to government that 'the common papists are insolent and provide themselves with arms'.[85] As a consequence of the tide of apprehension which the whole affair unleashed, Lovett had to abandon his country mansion and take refuge in Tipperary. A government reward of £100 for O'Neill's recapture was to no avail for by 1766 he was still openly officiating in Cullen, a fact which was given particular notice in the census of the parish in that year.[86] The incident represented an open challenge to local law and order; it witnessed the mobilization of a Catholic mob, the use of violence, and the subsequent renewal of his clerical functions by O'Neill. In all it was a clear overriding of the authority of the justices.

The third incident was more serious and was to provide the context for the hostility towards Catholic clergy in the early 1760s. In September 1758 Lord Kingston published a notice offering a reward for bishop John O'Brien of Cloyne who had imposed an

[81] Burke, *Irish priests*, 360; NA, 1A 52 159, p. 261.
[82] NLI, MSS 8913, 19,822, 272–85.   [83] Brady, *Press*, 83, 85.
[84] Quoted in Marnane, *Land and violence*, 26.
[85] Quoted in ibid. 27.   [86] NA, 1766 census for Cullen, p. 7.

edict of excommunication on the town of Mitchelstown. The background to this lay in archbishop James Butler's determination to retain the revenues of Mitchelstown parish and O'Brien's design to remove them from him. Added to this was the fact that both had been rival candidates for the See of Cloyne in 1748 with O'Brien being successful, and there was a dispute between the two about the encroachment of the Franciscan friars into Mitchelstown. The result of this rivalry was twofold: there was a confusion of authority in relation to church matters in Mitchelstown, and the conflict gave clergy a high public profile which brought them to the attention of the authorities. Far from achieving a resolution, the conflict became more fully public in the late 1750s, culminating in the assault on Pierce Creagh, bishop of Waterford, when he came to the town in 1758 to meet Butler. In response, Creagh suggested to O'Brien that the town be placed under interdict for six months, which accordingly was announced in all surrounding parishes.[87] This was a serious situation and Kingston, then an absentee, clearly viewed the incident as a threat to his authority and therefore issued his reward for O'Brien. In this way a quarrel between two bishops, who by law were not supposed to be in the country at all, was transferred to the public stage thereby bringing them into direct confrontation with the authority of the landlord.

The Mitchelstown affair served to bring Revd Nicholas Sheehy, parish priest of Ballyporeen, to the notice of the gentry of south Tipperary since priests in adjoining parishes were obliged by O'Brien to publicize the edict he had imposed on the town.[88] Because of his gentry status and the coincidence in time and place of the Whiteboy outbreaks in his parish, Sheehy became marked out for destruction. From situation or sympathy or both, Sheehy became involved in issues of social concern in his area. He openly declared his opposition to tithes and encouraged people not to pay them, and he opposed the abolition of commonages.[89] He advocated the non-payment of church rates and for this reason abolished them in the parish of Newcastle on the grounds that it

---

[87] The foregoing is based on J. Coombes, *A bishop of the penal times: The life and times of John O'Brien, bishop of Cloyne and Ross, 1701–1769* (Cork, 1981); and for summaries: *Arch. Hib.*, 33 (1975), 3; C. Costello, *In quest of an heir: The life and times of John Butler* (Cork, 1978), 31.

[88] Brady, *Press*, 94–5.

[89] TCD, MS 873/717, 723, 725.

had no Protestant community or church.[90] From situation and inclination Sheehy was predisposed to favour the demands of the Whiteboys when their agitation over commons and tithes broke out in late 1761 in the district where he ministered. Even a contemporary Catholic apologist conceded the fact of Sheehy's 'unavoidable connection with those rioters several hundred of whom were his parishioners'.[91] Doubt, however, has been cast on the credibility of his one overt Whiteboy act and he may only have associated himself with the movement in its early stages, distancing himself from its proceedings once it became more violent.[92] By that stage, however, Protestants in the area had become alarmed and came to identify Sheehy and others as the fomenters of the agrarian violence.

5. Land and Economic Issues

In 1762 and 1764 three legislative measures were passed in the Irish parliament to give Protestants greater security of title. The first and more immediately relevant act (1 Geo. III, c. 13) enacted that the title of Protestants to lands held under converts was not to be affected by the failure of such converts to fulfil the full legal requirements of conversion. Any deficiencies in this regard had to be rectified before 25 March 1763, though this date was later extended.[93] The second act (1 Geo. III, c. 12) sought to secure Protestant purchasers of estates which formerly belonged to Catholics or persons in foreign service. No sales of land or interests therein made to Protestant purchasers were to be called into question and their recovery sued for by virtue of provisions in the penal laws. In effect the act gave Protestant purchasers immunity from proceedings under the penal legislation.

The insecurity of title which these acts sought to mitigate derived from litigation under the penal laws and from deficiencies in the registration of converts, both of which served to undermine Protestant land titles. The need for the act to protect Protestants

[90] TCD, MS 873/723, 725; cf. Rennison, *Succession list*, which gives three Protestants in the parish of Newcastle.
[91] Burke, *Clonmel*, 368.   [92] Ibid. 369.
[93] The act was later extended to 1 Dec. 1767 (5 Geo. III, c. 5), 1 Dec. 1768 (7 Geo. III, c. 20, s. 7), 24 June 1790 (17, 18 Geo. III, c. 36, s. 9), and to 1791 (19, 20 Geo. III, c. 14, s. 2).

holding under converts arose from decisions in the cases of *Tomlinson* v. *O'Farrell* (1759) and *Nugent* v. *Nugent and Howth* (1762). The judgments in these two cases questioned the legal status of existing converts and the title of Protestants holding under them. In the former case the plaintiff was decreed as a Protestant discoverer to the defendant's estate in county Longford on the grounds that he could prove that Edward O'Farrell, a nominal Protestant, had not completed the full legal requirements of conversion, i.e. filing his certificate of conversion within six lunar months as opposed to six calendar months, and as a consequence was still legally a Catholic. As a result of this difference of a few days his conversion was declared to be invalid and the estate was decreed to the discoverer, a decision upheld on appeal to the English House of Lords in 1761.[94] In the Howth case, in an amazing decision consistent with the judge's interpretation of the letter rather than the spirit of the penal laws on land, the property was awarded to a nominal Protestant against one who was born and bred as one.[95]

Existing statutory requirements were repeated in the 1762 act with an extension of time for qualifying. Existing converts were required to perform the full legal requisites of conversion which consisted of taking and receiving the sacrament, subscribing the declaration, taking the oath of abjuration, and filing a bishop's certificate to this effect within six (lunar) months following conversion (8 Anne c. 1, s. 11). It was O'Farrell's failure to fulfil the latter provision which allowed the decision to go against him. Thus Catholics who had converted before 1762 and who were still living were obliged to convert again in order that their status as Protestants might be legally validated and the title of Protestants holding under them made secure. This requirement accounts for the rise in conversions in the early 1760s.[96]

For this reason there was considerable pressure to convert in these years, and the act would appear to have been used by the ultra-Protestant gentry in Tipperary as an instrument to get comfortable Catholics to convert for the first time. Between 1762

---

[94] G. E. Howard, *Several special cases on the laws against the further growth of popery in Ireland* (Dublin, 1775), 121–39.　　　　[95] Ibid. 136 n.

[96] T. P. Power, 'Converts', in Power and Whelan (eds.), *Endurance and emergence*, 102, 116–20; id., 'Conversions among the legal profession', in Hogan and Osborough (eds.), *Brehons, serjeants and attorneys*, 164–5.

and 1765 inclusive, there were ninety conversions recorded of Tipperary persons.[97] This number included Thomas Mathew of Thomastown (a convert of 1755), Francis Mathew his son and heir, Richard Lalor, gentleman, James Mandeville of Ballydine, and James Hackett of Orchardstown. When the act was further extended to 1 December 1768 the number of converts for the years 1766–8 inclusive was seventy, half of this number being for 1768, an election year. Among the converts of these years were Milo Burke of Rapla (a large middleman near Newport), William Kissane of Scalliheen (a large grazier on the Damer estate), Thomas Mandeville of Ballydine, and James Nagle of Garnvella. Those landowners in fee, like Mathew and Mandeville, and middlemen like Kissane and Burke, made themselves secure by virtue of their full legal conversion against the hostility of their Protestant tenants at least on the issue of title. It was known Catholics and converts who were large landholders who failed to comply with the provisions of the 1762 act who became the objects of Protestant gentry hostility in south Tipperary in the early 1760s. This is the key to understanding why certain individuals and not others became implicated in the purge of 1765–6. It was not persons like Mathew and Mandeville or other legal converts who were identified as victims of the purge, rather it was Catholics particularly middlemen on the Butler (Cahir) estate—James Farrell, Edmund Sheehy, James Buxton, James Nagle (who only had his certificate of conversion enrolled on 28 December 1765), and Richard Keating—who held out against complying with the act, who became the objects of a purge.

The third piece of legislation was an act of 1764 (3 Geo. III, c. 26) which confirmed Protestants who had purchased Catholic lands in their title and secured them against any proceedings at law which might undermine that title. The act is relevant in the Tipperary context, particularly in relation to John Bagwell. His grandfather had in 1729, and in the early 1730s, purchased about 2,700 acres most of it from two Catholics, Lord Dunboyne and John Slattery. In 1761 Bagwell was seeking legal opinion on the validity of his title to these lands particularly those of Dunboyne.[98]

---

[97] Compiled from O'Byrne, *The convert rolls*, from which information on all individual converts is derived.
[98] NLI, PC, 260–1 Riall, folder marked 'Lord Dunboyne' containing a legal opinion of George Cole copied by J. Bagwell, 12 Mar. 1761.

This uncertainty in relation to the Dunboyne title was added to by the fact that the then current holder of the title, Pierce Butler, was an idiot and in consequence it was said that he 'could not acquire the positive merit of being a Protestant'.[99] This made his status suspect and created apprehensions in Bagwell that proceedings against Dunboyne under the penal laws might result in an undermining of his title and the loss of his estate. Dunboyne was arrested in Waterford in 1762 under warrant from the lord-lieutenant but was later released.[100] Only with the act of 1764 were fears like those of Bagwell's diminished.

A further manifestation of Protestant fears about land title in the early 1760s concerned the attempts to introduce legislation which would allow Catholics to invest money in mortgages on land. These attempts were stimulated by the credit crisis of 1759–60, of which the failure of banks and merchant houses in Cork and Dublin was symptomatic, and the smaller banks in Clonmel and Waterford must have been affected as well.[101] Indicative of the effects of the restriction on credit locally is the remark made by William Perry, a landowner near Clonmel, to Simon Newport, a Waterford banker, in May 1761 that 'Altho' money perhaps may be a little scarce now, yet within these few years it might have been had on land[ed] security I know at 4½ p[er] c[ent], very large sums and perhaps shortly may again'.[102] Apart from the direct evidence it gives of the scarcity of credit in south Tipperary, there is also made explicit in Perry's remark the existence of considerable funds locally and the expectation that they might be availed of in future. Many of these funds were in the hands of large Catholic middlemen, and it was from a desire to release such funds in the form of mortgages on land that the movement in parliament from 1761 to formulate legislation arose.

As things stood, large Catholic tenants and merchants who had accumulated surplus funds as a result of the economic upturn of mid-century were at a serious disadvantage. By law they could not obtain any interest in land beyond a lease for 31 years, which

---

[99] Howard, *Cases*, 275; see also NA, Miscellaneous letters and papers, 1A 52 167, p. 3; *FDJ*, 27 Apr.–1 May, 24–8 Dec. 1762.

[100] [Dunboyne (?)] to T. Kavanagh, 31 Aug. 1766 (Kavanagh correspondence, NLI, Mic.P.7155).

[101] Cullen, *Economic history*, 73; id., *Merchants, ships and trade 1660–1830* (Dublin, 1971), 43.   [102] Burke, *Clonmel*, 188 n.

provision excluded them from holding mortgages on other people's land. In this situation rich Catholics wishing to lend money had to do so on the more precarious security of bonds or legally enforceable IOUs. An instance of such a transaction was in 1763 when James Nagle, the Catholic middleman, loaned Ambrose Congreve £500 repayable in 6 months at 5 per cent interest, conditional on a bond of £1,000.[103] It was partly in an attempt to eliminate the necessity of Catholics having recourse to the risky and insecure practice of loans by bond, that the proposal for mortgages on land was advanced. Already the right of Catholics to lend money on the security of the borrower, whereby the lender could receive the profits of the estate though not enter into possession of it, was being questioned in law in the 1750s with the result that such arrangements became discoverable.[104]

Advocates of the measure argued that the fact that Catholics were confined to taking personal security only for loans was a restriction both on them and on Protestants who wished to borrow more extensively.[105] In addition, it was argued that if a suitable outlet was not obtained for half of the money then in circulation held by Catholics, then they would be obliged to invest in foreign securities which would be detrimental to the country economically and politically.[106] At a time when land values were rising and when there was a demand for extra land to cater for the growing market for livestock products, these were very strong arguments in favour of liberalizing the access of Catholics to mortgage facilities. The proposal received the support initially of over fifty members in the Commons, particularly those with a legal background who saw the concession as desirable on grounds of equity.[107]

Opponents of the measure judged it in political rather than economic terms, seeing it as a device to obtain a liberalization of the penal laws. By increasing the number of Protestant debtors to Catholic creditors the proposal would allow Catholics an undue advantage over Protestants. It would permit Catholic creditors to come into the actual possession of lands by virtue of default in repayments by debtors unable to redeem their lands. It was fears

---

[103] NA, Acc.1079/2/3/9.
[104] L. M. Cullen (ed.), *The formation of the Irish economy* (Cork, 1969), 39 n.
[105] Caldwell, *Debates*, ii. 511–13.
[106] M. O'Conor, *The history of the Irish Catholics from the settlement in 1691* (Dublin, 1813), 306.   [107] PRO, SPI, 423/29–30; O'Conor, *History*, 306–9.

that this would lead to a sharp growth in the Catholic landed interest that prompted the defeat of the bill. It also led to a later motion seeking to allow Catholics to take securities on land without interfering with its management or possession, but this was also defeated.[108] Once Catholics had obtained possession of the lands of their Protestant debtors, it was argued, Catholic tenants would be introduced in place of Protestants. Lands so possessed would not be subject to the penal laws on Catholic landholding.[109] The measure was seen to have a more direct political implication in that, if it passed, it would allow Catholic creditors to influence tenants on appropriated estates at elections and would also give them an undue influence over members of parliament who were their debtors. It was recognized that many MPs were already heavily dependent on Catholic moneylenders on the basis of personal security, Lord Charlemont referring to 'a sort of Popish patronage in both houses of parliament, where the members were deeply indebted to Papists'.[110] To extend this influence by granting Catholics the right to lend on landed security was judged to be politically inexpedient. Thus what was advanced by its proposers as an economically desirable and legally consistent measure, was opposed by its detractors as being detrimental politically.

Amongst those who resisted the measure in parliament was Sir William Osborne the owner of a large estate east of Clonmel, and other reaction locally was also hostile.[111] An important figure who influenced public opinion was Sir James Caldwell who published a pamphlet before the bill was introduced in 1764 outlining his opposition.[112] Of a military background, having experience of suppressing rural disturbers in the north of Ireland, possessing a strong religious sense, and being an improver, Caldwell is of importance in the Tipperary context.[113] His arrival in the county to

---

[108] *Comms. Jnl. (Ire.),* vii. 280–1.

[109] J. Caldwell, *A brief examination of the question whether it is expedient either in a religious or political view to pass an act to enable papists to take real securities for money which they may lend* (Dublin, 1764), 16–18.

[110] Quoted in PRONI, Education Facsimiles, *The penal laws* (Belfast, 1975), 109.

[111] C. Musgrave to Grandison, 3 Feb. 1764 (PRONI, T3131/C/14); O'Conor, *History*, 130. [112] Caldwell, *Brief examination.*

[113] W. H. G. Bagshawe, *The Bagshawes of Ford: A biographical pedigree* (London, 1886), 260, 281, 292, 297–8; TCD, MS 3860/1.

suppress the Whiteboys brought him into contact with kindred spirits locally, notably Maude, an improver; Bagwell, a strong Unitarian; Jacob, a staunch Presbyterian; and Revd John Hewetson. His local contacts in 1762–3 provided Caldwell with material and insights on the strength of wealthy Catholics which he utilized in his publication which ran to two Dublin editions during 1764. Caldwell provides direct evidence of the existing strength of Catholic creditors in the county and how they used their position there to negate the operation of the penal laws. He cites Justin McCarthy of Springhouse, an extensive Catholic middleman of 9,000 acres between Tipperary and Golden, who, Caldwell says 'merely by the number of Protestants that were his debtors, kept all persons of that religion in awe throughout the whole county and effectively prevented them by mere intimidation from putting any of the popish laws in execution for many years'.[114] From the perspective of the Protestant political nation, the land settlement, law enforcement, and of the individual business concerns of people like Bagwell, it was vital that the mortgage bill be defeated as it was. Though the precise implications of the measure at national level are unclear, locally it was of decisive importance.

In the wider context of the conflict of the 1760s the choice of McCarthy as a prime exemplar of the power and influence of Catholic creditors is important in three respects. First, it accounts for the inclusion of Catholic merchants in the port of Waterford, who were related to or connected with Tipperary families, in the purge of the 1760s. The Justin McCarthy cited by Caldwell died in 1756 and his heir, Denis, died in 1761 leaving the estate and fortune to his son Justin, a minor.[115] These events received public notice in the press at the time.[116] Because of the minority, the estate came to John McCarthy, second son of Justin (d. 1756), who married Anne, daughter of Thomas Wyse a wealthy merchant in Waterford. Wyse participated at the meeting of leading Catholics in 1760 at which the Catholic Committee was founded.[117] Waterford also had other Catholic merchants with ties in

---

[114] Caldwell, *Brief examination*, 13.

[115] Will of Justin McCarthy, Springhouse, gent., 18 July 1752 (in NLI, MS 11,422).

[116] *FDJ*, 17–20 Oct. 1761.

[117] T. Wyse, *Historical sketch of the late Catholic Association of Ireland* (London, 1829), i. 62–3, 68, 79, 82–4, 89.

Tipperary: Martin Murphy, agent for Lord Cahir, Philip Long, and Bartholemew Rivers. Complementary to this were the ties between Protestants in the port and the hinterland. The banking connection between Bagwell and Newport existed, the latter being in correspondence with people like Perry on the issue, and no doubt being aware of the position of Wyse in the port.

Secondly, the McCarthys had important overseas interests in Bordeaux where they were leading merchants.[118] Given the context of the Seven Years War with France and the re-emergence of Pretender invasion scares in the early 1760s, the French factor was to be a vital catalyst in making Tipperary Protestants believe that the Whiteboys were led by French officers and financed and armed by French funds channelled in through Catholic merchants in Waterford. Catholics in the ports were therefore doubly suspect because of their French connections and because of the links with prominent Catholics in the hinterland. Finally, the McCarthys were head-tenants to about 1,000 acres on the estate of Thomas Mathew of Thomastown.[119] Mathew's participation in the 1761 election had provoked Protestant resistance, and this now became further consolidated because of the mortgage bill debate in which one of his large head-tenants was cited by opponents of the measure.

In the economic and social sphere rivalries developed over competition for land and over quarterage. In the period 1760–7 over 2,640 acres came up for reletting on the Butler (Cahir) estate.[120] Most of these lands were in the region from which most of the Catholics implicated in 1765–6 were drawn. The early 1760s was a period of rising land values and of increasing demand for extra land required for stocking. The lands on the Cahir estate were eminently suitable for pasture and had the added convenience of large mountain commons. The large sitting tenants on the Cahir estate: Nagle, Keating, and Baldwin, who were Catholic midddlemen, had their interests renewed at this time and remained undisturbed as the dominant social group. This group

---

[118] P. Butel, *Les négociants Bordelais: l'Europe et les Iles au XVIIIᵉ siècle* (Paris, 1974), 161–2, 292, 345; L. M. Cullen, *The emergence of modern Ireland 1600–1900* (London, 1981), 119.

[119] TCD, Barker Ponsonby papers, P5/45.

[120] *FDJ*, 5–8 Jan. 1760, 24–8 Feb., 25–8 Apr., 7–10 Nov. 1761, 11–15, 15–18 Jan., 22–6 Nov. 1763, 9–13 July 1765, 6–10, 10–13 Jan., 1–4 Aug. 1767.

appears to have been more socially acceptable to Protestants, despite the minority status of the latter in the district and the extensive acreages held by the former. A report on the trials in 1766 remarks of them that they were 'very respectable as they lived in affluence and with reputation, associated with the gentlemen of their neighbourhood with whom they lived in the highest hospitality, frequently receiving and returning visits'.[121] On the other hand, however, other lands were taken up by more minor Catholics such as Edmund Sheehy, James Buxton, and James Farrell. Their success in securing leases, at a time of expanding demand for livestock, caused resentment among Protestants who had failed in their bids. Thus it was said that the cause of hostility towards Sheehy was his taking of a farm near Clogheen which one of the Bagwells was bidding for.[122] At a time of general scarcity of money, these Catholics possessed the capital to bid successfully for leases and thereby take on extra ground at an economically favourable time.

The upward social and economic mobility displayed by this group of minor Catholic gentry, consequent on their gaining leasing preferences, their relative status being indicated by Sheehy's income of £300–£400, operated to give them an appearance of pretentiousness. This was epitomized in the designation 'buck' being applied to Farrell and Sheehy. In 1766 Farrell was described as 'a young man of genteel appearance', while Sheehy was 33 years of age at the time of his execution in 1766.[123] The appellation 'buck' and the youth of those concerned suggests that they were indiscreetly assertive of their new-found status. This is the basic reason why these parvenus in local Catholic society, flaunting their new prestige, were proceeded against with such vigour by an interested group of gentlemen, many of whom had failed to obtain leases. This also accounts for the hostility towards Lord Cahir's agent, the Waterford-based Martin Murphy, who was responsible for deciding on new tenants.

Catholic merchants in the towns became suspect because of suspicions that they were channelling French money. Contemporaneous with this, Catholic demands for the removal of quarterage were being advanced. From the late seventeenth

---

[121] *Gentleman's and London Magazine* (Apr. 1766), 248.
[122] TCD, MS 873/724.
[123] *Gentleman's and London Magazine* (Apr. 1766), 246.

century (in Clonmel from about 1680) Catholics were allowed second-class guild membership on payment of a fine on entry to a town or upon opening a house, and on payment of quarterage every quarter which allowed them to trade openly. In Clonmel, where there were three guilds of merchants, cordwainers, and brewers, fines varied in amount from 5*s.* to half a guinea or more, quarterage from 6*d.* to 3*s.,* but more commonly not more than 12*d.* per quarter by the early 1760s.[124] These sums were not unduly severe but they were resented by Catholics since they conveyed no real or lasting privileges, and because they had no legal basis. There was intermittent resistance to the tax and this received an impetus when a judgment in the case of *Mahony* v. *The mayor of Cork* decreed damages against the mayor for imprisoning Catholics who had refused to pay the tax. The judgment also found that quarterage had no statutory basis.[125]

In 1764 anti-quarterage agitation arose in Clonmel but the reaction of the local authorities to it ensured that it acquired local sectarian significance. By February 1765 in Clonmel Catholic opposition to quarterage was equated with disloyalty, complicity with the Whiteboys, and by extension, treason. Clonmel Catholics, summoned to take the oath of abjuration, appeared but refused in conscience taking it and were fined £2 per man as a result.[126] In their defence the Catholics declared that they had willingly taken the oath of allegiance when requested to do so, and admitted that they had protested over quarterage but only on the ground that it was illegal. The attempt to enforce quarterage payments by means of a summons to take the oath of abjuration was, in their view, a perversion of the original intention of that oath, and they dismissed any suggestion of being associated with the Whiteboys.[127] The corporation of the town, seeking to have its position on the issue made more secure, petitioned parliament soliciting legislation which would confirm its role in relation to guild membership and quarterage. The petition from Clonmel Corporation in January 1766 would appear to be exceptional among towns in tending to buttress its case by linking refusal to pay quarterage with sympathy for whiteboyism. It declared that 'within these two or three years last past and particularly since these deluded

---

[124] Burke, *Clonmel*, 146.
[125] Cullen, *Formation*, 43–4.   [126] *FDJ*, 16–19 Feb. 1765.
[127] Ibid. 2–5 Mar. 1765; *FJ*, 19–23 Feb. 1765.

insurgents called White Boys have intruded themselves in this county, sundry of these Quarter Brothers countenanced by those, under the specious pretence of redressing grievances, have refused to pay quarterage'.[128] The Catholics countered this with a petition of their own in which they stressed the illegality of the tax.[129] In this case, as with the mortgage legislation and the land transactions on the Cahir estate, sectarian criteria were applied to an essentially economic issue.

6. Defence

The circumstances of the 1760s engendered renewed fears among Protestants as to their security, and there was a concern that defence measures be taken. Already there was a long tradition of local defence in the form of the militia, and to this was added a large military contingent for the suppression of the Whiteboys. This was led by Lord Drogheda and Sir James Caldwell, whom one source claims was introduced to the county to lead irregularly raised local forces.[130] Under orders approved by government in March 1763 and renewed in August 1764, the regular forces were required to assist in Tipperary against the Whiteboys, and justices of the peace were empowered to lead parties of the military for this purpose.[131] The justices had, therefore, considerable forces at their disposal to be used at their discretion. Their powers were further extended by an act (3 Geo. III, c. 19) which came into force in May 1764, whereby magistrates were indemnified for actions taken by them in the course of suppressing unrest. The arbitrary use of this privilege of immunity was evident in the extreme course of action adopted by the justices in 1765–6.

As a practical expression of local defence needs there was a concerted effort in the early 1760s, as part of the process of reimposing the penal laws, to disarm Catholics. The need to do so was sanctioned by the superiority in numbers of Catholics over Protestants, by the open evasion of the laws on arms by Catholics, and by the security threat created by the wartime situation. In

---

[128] Burke, *Clonmel*, 146.   [129] Ibid. 147.
[130] *FDJ*, 18–22 Mar. 1766; T. Corcoran, *Some lists of Catholic lay teachers and their illegal schools in the later penal times* (Dublin, 1932), 38.
[131] NA, M2554, 2, 134.

response to this the restrictions on Catholics carrying arms were reinvoked because of the fear that they would be used in favour of the French should they invade. Such fears had a long history in the minds of Protestants. The possession of arms by Catholics was a major cause of concern to the authorities in the early part of the century when sympathy for the Stuarts was still strong. These fears were especially real in Tipperary because of the connection with the duke of Ormond who was a main supporter of the Jacobite cause. A system of licences was introduced, and in 1704 nine Catholics including Col. Thomas Butler and George Mathew of Thurles were so licensed.[132] Many of these licensees were imprisoned in 1714–15 when there were fears of a Jacobite invasion. There was a keen local response to a government directive ordering the enforcement of the laws against Catholics. The main Catholics of Clanwilliam were summoned to appear before the magistrates at Tipperary in June but failed to do so, as did new converts whom the justices suspected 'were not sincere Protestants'.[133] The justices of the peace in Lower Ormond were more successful in making Catholics there take the oath of abjuration, while justices at Killenaule and Cashel were active at this time also.[134] A government proclamation of July 1715 ordered the seizure of arms and horses in the possession of Catholics, and following this there were systematic arms searches by the magistrates, as at Cashel where prominent Catholics like Nicholas Purcell, George Mathew and his son, and John Ryan (Inch), were taken up.[135] Despite some resistance, one magistrate admitted in 1715 that 'I don't find any arms worth speaking of in possession of the papists'.[136]

Protestant fears of support for the Stuart cause sharpened when there was the threat of a foreign invasion. In 1722 evidence was sworn that a large number of gentlemen in west Tipperary were involved in treasonable meetings in favour of the Pretender. While government ordered the enforcement of the laws, it is unlikely that these claims had any substance, but they reveal the perceptions of local magistrates at a time of insecurity.[137] In normal times Protestants in the county were apathetic towards the enforcement of the penal laws, at least those relating to security, and indeed

---

[132] *Arch. Hib.*, 4 (1915), 59–63.   [133] Burke, *Irish priests*, 355–6.
[134] Ibid. 356–7; NA, 1A 52 159, p. 250.   [135] Burke, *Irish priests*, 209, 349.
[136] Quoted in ibid. 349.   [137] Brady, *Press,* 36; PRONI, D104/5/3/86.

appear to have been intimidated from the normal process of law enforcement by the numerical superiority of Catholics. In 1729 one magistrate admitted that 'the number of papists is so great that it is hazardous for the civil power to put the laws in execution'.[138]

The early 1730s was a time of insecurity when the laws on Catholics bearing arms were tightened and when there were arrests of persons suspected of recruiting for France.[139] The invasion scare of 1739–40 prompted legislation providing for the delivery of arms by Catholics to magistrates, and in 1744–5 there were local searches for arms and arrests on suspicion of enlisting for the Pretender.[140] The official view during the Seven Years War was that there was little likelihood of a threat from Irish Catholics. In May 1759 the archbishop of Armagh informed the duke of Bedford that 'the Roman Catholics of property, whether landed or monied, would not assist' the French enemy.[141] Such assurances were officially accepted despite the shock of Thurot's landing at Carrickfergus in February 1760. Hostilities with France ceased in 1762, though a formal peace was not signed until February 1763. This chronology is important in relation to local circumstances. It was only after war had concluded that charges of demobilized French and Irish officers leading the Whiteboys emerged in Munster, though they were not credited by government.[142] It is against this background that the retrospective participation of individual Catholics in south Tipperary as leaders of the Whiteboys favouring the French was formulated by a group of Protestant gentry. It provided the framework for charges brought against a section of leading Catholics.

Local opposition to Catholics bearing arms received an early manifestation in the scheme of 1762 to raise a Catholic legion in Ireland for service under the king of Portugal, on Britain's side in the war against Spain. Traditionally the British government, though it regretted the fact that the penal laws precluded Catholics joining the British army, thereby forcing a large recruitment to the

---

[138] Burke, *Irish priests*, 349.
[139] Chavigny to Newcastle, 20 June 1733 (PRO, SPI, 63/396/38); Boulter, *Letters*, ii. 56.
[140] Burke, *Irish priests*, 350, 357–8.
[141] *Correspondence of John fourth duke of Bedford*, ed. J. Russell (London, 1842–6), iii. 379–80.
[142] Halifax to Egremont, [?] Feb. 1762, 13, 17 Apr. 1762 (PRO, SPI, 63/421/76^v, 245–7, 253–253^v); Bagshawe, *Bagshawes of Ford*, 281.

foreign brigades of countries hostile to Britain, had tacitly accepted this trend as it tended to rid Ireland of truculent elements. Accordingly the plan for the recruitment of Catholics for the king of Portugal received official sanction, Egremont specifying that those Catholics chosen were 'to be selected as, from their suspected religious principles, are least to be trusted with the defence of Ireland'.[143] Rumours of the scheme caused a furore in the Irish parliament, but one of those who spoke in favour of the proposal in the Lords was Lord Carrick who became associated with the extreme party in Tipperary.[144]

Symptomatic of local opinion were the sentiments of a Protestant author writing from Clonmel in March 1762 who advocated resistance to the scheme.[145] In his view it would only serve to aid Britain's enemies as Catholics were subjects of the pope and any oath of theirs to serve king George III's ally would therefore be venal and their implicit loyalty was to France. If Catholics were armed as suggested then they could with easy facility act in unison with the Whiteboys who were already threatening wide areas of Munster. Replying to the objection that Catholic peers leading the legion would be responsible for those under them, the Clonmel author asks whether such leaders can 'answer for their own tenants who it is notorious here are the ringleaders of these Levellers?'.[146] This was a reference to tenants on Lord Cahir's estate, identifying them as the instigators of the rural unrest who would be presented with the opportunity of extending their influence through the projected legion plan. More pointedly the tract evinces a deep mistrust of the intentions both of the Dublin government and Britain in relation to the whole legion plan. The author declares his surprise that 'the Protestant interest of this kingdom is so little regarded by ourselves or our neighbours, that our lives and properties are to be trifled with, and so fair an open[ing] given for an invasion on both by either foreign or domestic foes'.[147] It was credited that the French were assisting the Whiteboys and the legion scheme would further reinforce this alliance.[148]

[143] *Calendar of Home Office papers, 1760–1765* (London, 1878–99), 159.

[144] Halifax to Egremont, [?] Feb., 8 Apr. 1762 (PRO, SPI, 63/421/227–227ᵛ); *Comms. Jnl.(Ire.)*, vii. 154–5; *Lords Jnl.(Ire.)*, iv. 243.

[145] Hibernicus, *Some reasons against raising an army of Roman Catholicks in Ireland in a letter to a member of parliament* (Dublin, 1762).

[146] Ibid. 6.   [147] Ibid. 4.

[148] C. Musgrave to Grandison, 6 Apr. 1766 (PRONI, T3131/C/14).

However, none of this was given any credence at government level and Halifax, the lord-lieutenant, rejected charges of French involvement, recognizing that the charge was contrived by an interested faction.[149] In the event the legion failed to materialize but the episode stands out as important in the development of local Protestant perceptions about their own security and in their attitude to the motives of government. In the immediate term following the legion controversy, at the summer assizes the grand jury made available rewards of £20 (additional to the sum stipulated in the penal legislation), for the first three Catholics found guilty of carrying arms.[150] Thus a law, which had only been periodically enforced previously and which it was recognized was openly flaunted in normal times, was enforced with an added incentive.

The invocation of an historical dimension by the Clonmel author was duplicated shortly afterwards by the republication of a number of works which served to reinforce the position and arguments of the militant gentry in Tipperary. Prominent in promoting this were the Cork merchants Phineas and George Bagnell, whose brother William Bagnell of Marlhill was an active member of the Tipperary grand jury and a distinguished Whiteboy hunter. In 1763 the Bagnells claimed to have spent £1,148 fitting out a paper mill near Cork.[151] In 1766 they republished Sir John Temple's *The Irish rebellion or the history of the beginning and first progress of the general rebellion raised within the kingdom of Ireland upon the three and twentieth day of October 1641*, which was first issued in a London edition in 1646. In 1767 a new edition of William King's *State of the Protestants of Ireland under the late King James's government* (first edition, London, 1691), was published.

The importance of the reissuing of these publications was threefold. First, originally issued following attacks by Catholic forces on Protestant colonists, they retrospectively provided the intellectual and historical justification for the actions of the Tipperary gentry in 1765–6. Secondly, the publications were available for public purchase in Clonmel indicating that there was demand for such works.[152] Thirdly, the works were subscribed to by those members of the gentry who were closely associated with

---

[149] Halifax to Egremont, 17 Apr. 1762 (PRO, SPI, 63/421/253–253ᵛ).
[150] *FDJ*, 19–22 June 1762.
[151] *Comms. Jnl. (Ire.)*, vii. 209.
[152] *CEP*, 26 Jan., 23 Mar. 1767.

the course of events in the 1760s. The subscribers included William Bagnell of Marlhill, Matthew Bunbury of Kilfeacle, John Bagwell of Kilmore, and Matthew Jacob of Mobarnan, all grand jurors. In the context of the historical perspective portrayed by these works it is also relevant that, following the events of 1765–6, the anniversary of the battle of the Boyne was celebrated in flamboyant fashion in July 1767, an event which had not been marked to such a degree hitherto.[153]

There were also a number of defences of the Catholic position published in the 1760. Already in the 1750s Charles O'Conor had published several works, notably the *Case of the Roman Catholics of Ireland* (1755), which expressed the loyalty of Catholics to the existing order and sought means whereby this could be given expression. In 1761 appeared Henry Brooke's *The trial of the cause of the Roman Catholics* which went into a fourth edition in 1762, and in 1766 an apologetic work by Viscount Taaffe, a member of the Catholic Committee, appeared.[154] Another member of that committee, and a correspondent of Edmund Burke and O'Conor, was John Curry who published a work disassociating respectable Catholics from the Whiteboys in Munster.[155] Curry also brought out a collection of historical memoirs on the Irish rebellion, a controversial work in which he sought to clarify the role of Catholics in relation to the events of 1641, and with which Burke was associated in the publication of London editions.[156]

7. Penal Laws: Reassertion

The occurrence of a unique set of circumstances in time and place made the local establishment feel threatened. On the one hand, Tipperary gentry were mistrustful about the motives of government on the Catholic issue, exemplified by local resistance to the

[153] *FJ*, 4–7 July 1767.

[154] Viscount Taaffe, *Observations on affairs in Ireland* (Dublin, 1766).

[155] J. Curry, *A candid enquiry into the causes and motives of the late riots in Munster together with a brief narrative of the proceedings against those rioters anno 1766 in a letter to a noble lord in England* (London, 1766).

[156] J. Curry, *An historiographical and critical review of the civil wars in Ireland from the reign of Queen Elizabeth to the settlement under King William* (Dublin, 1775); *The correspondence of Edmund Burke*, ed. T. W. Copeland *et al.* (Cambridge and Chicago, 1958–78), i. 201–2.

Catholic legion proposal. In consequence they felt alienated from the administration, a situation not aided by the fact that the early 1760s saw a succession of lack-lustre and irresolute lord-lieutenants. On the other hand, the Tipperary Protestant gentry had to contend with what they perceived as a new truculent assertiveness on the part of Catholics, as demonstrated in the 1761 election, the existence of a group of parvenu gentry on the Butler (Cahir) estate, the struggle for the removal of quarterage, the threat to authority shown in the Mitchelstown affair, and the aggressive behaviour of Fr Sheehy. Added to this was the threat to land titles as expressed in a series of adverse legal decisions and in the proposal that Catholics be allowed to lend money on landed security. Fears over land title were deepened by further apprehensions that lands would be overrun by a foreign enemy in league with an internal Whiteboy force led by prominent Catholics. To compound matters the local gentry were experiencing psychological paranoia as a result of their failure to gain convictions for whiteboyism, in particular the leniency with which justice Richard Aston treated suspected Whiteboys at the trials in Clonmel in 1762 increased the local gentry's lack of confidence in the will of the Dublin administration to suppress the rioters. All this was reinforced by the minority position of Protestants in the region. Presented with the spectre of resurgent catholicism in its manifold forms, and a lack of confidence in the motives of government, the nerve of the Protestant gentry broke, leading to a heightening of hysteria and inevitable sectarian conflict. The outcome was a frequent reassertion of the penal laws, and the presentation of the Whiteboys as a treasonable force in league with the French intent on the overthrow of the state. The reputation of the Tipperary gentry in the eyes of the country would, it was assumed, be enhanced for their public spirit in uncovering and quelling an insurrection by rebels designed to subvert the state. It was the need to vindicate themselves in this regard which drove the gentry relentlessly onward towards their course of action.

Indicative of the arbitrary construction placed on events, and of a greater fixity of purpose, was a shift in the nature of appointments made to the office of sheriff and justice of the peace. The persons appointed as sheriff successively after 1762 were those who identified closely with the more extreme interpretation of events. They were John Bagwell, Kilmore (1763), Sir William

Barker (1764), Sir Thomas Maude (1765), and Daniel Toler (1766).[157] To complement this there were some notable appointments as justices of the peace. There were ninety-nine justices in the county in 1760, the third largest per county in Ireland after Cork and Limerick.[158] Despite this large number the quality and distribution of justices varied enormously. It was recognized that where the Whiteboys were most active, i.e. in the Cahir–Clogheen–Ardfinnan district, justices were thin on the ground; but this deficiency was soon rectified with the appointment of William Bagnell of Marlhill, John Miles of Rochestown, and Cornelius O'Callaghan, junior.[159] Bagnell and Miles were head-tenants on the O'Callaghan estate, and Bagnell is important in a wider context because of his relatives in the Cork publishing trade. Bagnell was to distinguish himself against the Whiteboys, being publicly commended by the grand jury in 1766.[160] Another prominent grand juror was John Bagwell. He was a head-tenant on the O'Callaghan and Butler (Cahir) estates, and so like Bagnell and Miles would have had direct experience of the Whiteboys. He was concerned about his title to the Dunboyne lands purchased in 1729, and the success of the upstart Sheehys in gaining a lease advantage over him. He was also a supporter of the charter schools. In 1765 he was appointed to a parliamentary committee enquiring into the disturbances in Munster, and in 1767 he was a member of a Commons group discharged with the duty of preparing a revision of the 1766 Whiteboy act.[161]

Sir Thomas Maude's involvement arose from the challenge made by Thomas Mathew in the 1761 election and this extended itself into a desire to suppress any expressions of Catholic assertiveness. Barton of Fethard, with other purchasers of the Everard property like O'Callaghan, was apprehensive over title. They were all members of the grand jury of April 1766. The role of O'Callaghan may seem incongruous. There was a tradition of conversion in the family, and in its first generation as landowners in the county it identified strongly with the ethos of Anglicanism

---

[157] GO, MS 570, 73.

[158] Dublin City Library, Pearse St., Robinson MS 34 (3), 181.

[159] Burke, *Clonmel*, 364; *FJ*, 20–4 Mar. 1764; *FDJ*, 17–21 Apr. 1764; *CEP*, 10 Mar. 1763. [160] *FDJ*, 22–6 Aug. 1766.

[161] *Proceedings of the Incorporated Society* (1742), 39; *Comms. Jnl. (Ire.)*, viii. pt. 1, 61, 209.

introducing Protestants on to the estate in the 1740s. The need for a closer identification became more apparent in the 1760s because of the presence of whiteboyism on the estate, the role of Fr Sheehy whose relatives were found among O'Callaghan's tenantry, and O'Callaghan's fears over his own title because of the original purchase from Everard. Of the rest, although not a justice for Tipperary, Revd John Hewetson of Suirville, Co. Kilkenny, was closely associated with proceedings there, so much so that he has been distinguished by later generations with the title 'Whiteboy Hewetson'. A lowly curate in the Established Church, he was keen to gain advancement, and his desire to ingratiate himself with the authorities by a firm display of loyal activity against the Whiteboys and Catholic gentry is clearly evident from the construction he imposed on the events of the early 1760s.[162] Subsequently, he was reminding government of the need to promote him as a reward.[163] The grand jury of 1766, the most useful index of those who formed the right-wing grouping, also included Richard Perry, William Perry, John Walsh, Thomas Hackett, Richard Moore, and William Chadwick, who themselves or their tenants suffered from Whiteboy outrages or were active in their suppression. John and Daniel Toler were also members.

Through the frequent inclusion of these individuals in grand juries, the penal laws were enforced in a number of areas. A curb was placed on the open conduct of schools by Catholics, especially in Clonmel, for in October 1765 a notice appeared to the effect that 'a stop is now put to teaching by popish schoolmasters and that it is determined to put the law in force against any such who shall presume to teach in said town', and this decision had been arrived at by 'the fixed resolution of the magistrates and principal inhabitants'.[164] Encouragement was to be given to additional Protestant schoolmasters to open schools in the town.[165] There were suspicions that schoolmasters were instrumental in aiding the Whiteboys (e.g. they wrote threatening notices for them), and such suspicions were now reinforced.

More ominous was the enforcement of the 1704 act against unregistered clergy. In June 1762 Fr Sheehy, Revd Doyle of

---

[162] National Army Museum, London, Townshend MS 6808/7/6/1 (n.d. [c. 1790]).

[163] Hewetson to [Townshend], 1 July 1771, 25 July 1772 (RCB, MS A.3.140, 141).

[164] *FDJ*, 22–6 Oct., 5–9 Nov. 1765.   [165] Ibid.

Ardfinnan, and Revd Daniel of Cahir were presented by the grand jury at the summer assizes as unregistered priests, thus renewing a provision which had long fallen into disuse.[166] It was followed in 1763 by an indictment against Fr Sheehy for Whiteboy involvement but he was, in the event, bailed for £2,000.[167] This particular charge followed the first two major capital convictions made by the previously embarrassed Tipperary magistrates of Whiteboys who up until then had evaded conviction. In the ensuing period up to 1766 only one other capital conviction on a charge of whiteboyism was obtained, which explains why a section of the gentry became so militant after 1763. Since the common people, labourers and cottiers, who constituted the Whiteboy movement were anonymous to the authorities and so could avoid detection, gentry efforts at obtaining arrests became directed at the leaders of the community. Thus Revd John Hewetson was subsequently to refer to Sheehy as 'a very capital ringleader of those insurgents and the very life and soul of those deluded people'.[168] The process whereby the magistrates linked the agrarian crimes to the priests was made explicit in a grand jury statement of July 1763 endorsed by John Bagwell. It refers to the ill-treatment and threats accorded to the owners of tithes and the suspicion that such acts were encouraged by priests illegally officiating in the parishes concerned. The grand jury resolved to prosecute such priests to the utmost and requested aggrieved parties to apply to them with information.[169]

Such information was to be vital in formulating a prosecution case, but nothing further is heard of Sheehy until the spring assizes of 1764. This lapse marked a period when material information was compiled on Sheehy and others, and it was a stage when more serious charges were devised. The paucity of capital convictions for whiteboyism meant that the position of the justices of the peace in relation to the agrarian movement was critical. Given what had happened in 1763–4, the charge of whiteboyism was projected on to a wider plane, that of high treason. Doing so had three advantages for the justices of the peace: it would serve to restore their reputation previously tarnished, due to the acquittals

---

[166] Brady, *Press*, 105; *Gentleman's and London Magazine* 31 (1762), 371.
[167] TCD, MS 873/729.
[168] National Army Museum, London, Townshend MS 6806/7/6/1/13.
[169] *FDJ*, 26–30 July 1763.

of Whiteboys; it would help to convince government of the seriousness of affairs in the county; and it would allow them to proceed with impunity and vigour against persons who were regarded as traitors. This represented a crucial transformation in perceptions as a right-wing group took matters into its own hands. This precedent was facilitated by an act (3 Geo. III, c. 19) which came into force in May 1764 whereby magistrates were indemnified for their actions taken in the course of suppressing rural unrest. At the March assizes of 1764 Sheehy and three others had already been indicted for intending to raise a rebellion at Clogheen and for being armed for that purpose with 200 others dressed in white apparel, which coincidentally was also the colour of the Jacobite Pretender.[170] These proceedings were of sufficient gravity to cause Sheehy to flee to his relatives in county Limerick for shelter.[171] As late as November 1764 government was unconvinced as to the charge of treason which was advanced particularly by Lord Carrick. Government encouraged him to seek further evidence and was reluctant at that stage to issue a proclamation against Sheehy but favoured his private apprehension by Cornelius O'Callaghan.[172] However, the knowledge of Sheehy's disappearance, the renewal of Whiteboy outrages, and the pressure from local justices resulted in the issuing of a proclamation in February 1765 offering a reward of £300.[173] This action shows the ability of the Tipperary gentry to secure a government proclamation against Sheehy.

The subsequent facts of the case are well documented and do not require detailed repetition.[174] A number of points pertinent to the case, however, necessitate a certain emphasis. First, the fact that Sheehy voluntarily surrendered within a month of the proclamation being issued implies a degree of innocence on his part. Secondly, the fact that his surrender was made privately to O'Callaghan, as had been the original intention in November 1764, and that a condition of that surrender was that his trial be held in Dublin, suggests a recognition by government that the local gentry could not be trusted to administer justice impartially. As

---

[170] Burke, *Clonmel*, 369–70.

[171] M. Lenihan, *Limerick: Its history and antiquities* (Limerick, 1866), 357, n. 2.

[172] Shannon and Ponsonby to [Halifax ?], 10 Nov. 1764 (Mount Melleray Abbey, Burke MS 47 (unpaginated), *sub* P. Creagh.

[173] *FDJ*, 19–23 Feb. 1765.   [174] Burke, *Clonmel*, 372–9, 385–92.

much was stated by Sheehy himself in his hope for impartial justice in Dublin which, he said, 'was more than he could expect in the county Tipperary'.[175] Thirdly, there was a long delay in bringing a prosecution case against him. Following a four-month confinement in Dublin, Sheehy was admitted to bail of £4,000 in July on condition that he stand trial in November following.[176] Yet when November arrived no prosecution case was forthcoming which made Sheehy, fearing that witnesses would be interfered with, petition that the trial be held as agreed. Not until February 1766, however, eleven months after the original surrender, did Sheehy stand trial in Dublin where he was acquitted following the discrediting of the prosecution evidence.

The long delay involved in the assembling of their case by the Tipperary right-wing justices of the peace and its failure in the event to stand up in court, meant that the prosecution charge of treason was entirely undermined. Once again the Tipperary justices were frustrated but on this occasion, having been disappointed in their attempts over five years to gain substantial convictions on Whiteboy and associated charges, they were determined to obtain Sheehy's conviction at any cost. For this purpose Sheehy, after his acquittal in Dublin, was charged with the murder of John Bridge and was conveyed to Clonmel where he stood trial, was found guilty, and executed on 15 March 1766. This event created shock and comparisons were made with the only other event of similar gravity in the century, the execution of James Cotter in 1720.

At the time of Sheehy's surrender in March 1765 the grand jury began to proceed against a group of Catholic gentlemen and farmers. At the assizes of that month bills of indictment for high treason were found against thirty-two persons who were described as 'mostly men of good circumstances and considerable influence', and three were allowed bail of £500 each.[177] Something of the geographical diffusion of this group is indicated in the remark of Buxton that Revd John Hewetson's list of people to be purged included 'every man gentle and simple that is worth speaking to from Clonmell to Mitchelstown', including Catholic middlemen on

---

[175] Quoted in ibid. 373. [176] *FDJ*, 6–9 July 1765.
[177] TCD, MS 873/732; *FJ*, 30 Mar.–2 Apr. 1765; R. R. Madden, *The literary life and correspondence of Marguerite Gardiner, Countess of Blessington* (London, 1855), i. 394.

the Butler (Cahir) and O'Callaghan estates.[178] A number of them, subsequent to the indictments, applied to the grand jury for bail but this was refused. Conscious of their innocence, at least twelve of them issued public notices in June outlining the circumstances and declaring their willingness to surrender and, if indicted, to stand trial.[179] Those concerned were John Bourke of Rouska, James Hickey of Frehans, James and Thomas Coughlan, James Hilan, Lisfunchion, all farmers; John Baldwin, Cahir, Robert Keating, Knockagh, James Nagle, Garnvella, Edmond Doherty, Roxborough, Edmund Sheehy, Lodge, and Thomas Beer, Burgess (a Protestant), all gentlemen, and John Coughlan, Crana, MD. The most important figures in the group (Sheehy, Nagle, Keating, Baldwin, Doherty, and Hickey), gave public notice of their surrender and of being in actual custody in Clonmel jail.[180]

Three aspects of these developments are worth noting. First, the refusal to grant bail was very serious. In common law a person accused or indicted of high treason was bailable upon good surety until he was convicted, and refusal to grant bail where the party ought to be bailed was a misdemeanour, punishable not only by suit of the party concerned but also by indictment.[181] Refusal of bail by the justices of the peace showed their concern that there might be interference with witnesses, that further offences might be committed, or that the accused might not, despite assurances, turn up for trial. In any event, they did not observe due process of law, something which later stirred government to seek a reform of the grand jury system. Secondly, the group of Catholic gentry and farmers who were indicted stated that they were unaware of who their prosecutors were. This implies, as with Fr Sheehy, that the right-wing faction had not yet put together a proper prosecution case, which again casts doubt on the legality of the entire proceeding. Thirdly, again like Fr Sheehy, those who voluntarily surrendered in the summer of 1765 had to undergo a long confinement of eight months before their trials came in March 1766. It was not merely the convictions and executions which

---

[178] Sheffield City Library, Fitzwilliam Muniments, Burke MS 8/8.

[179] *DG*, 25–9 June, 16–20 July 1765; *FDJ*, 6–9 July 1765.

[180] *DG*, 20–3 July 1765; *FDJ*, 30 July–3 Aug. 1765.

[181] E. Bullingbrooke, *The duty and authority of the justices of the peace and parish officers for Ireland* (Dublin, 1766), 73, 76.

astounded public opinion, but also the arbitrary methods outside the law by which they were achieved.

Early in 1766 further persons, 'some of them farmers of substance', were imprisoned in Clonmel on a murder charge and, at the time of Fr Sheehy's trial in March, John Purcell of Thurles, 'a man of considerable property', was charged with high treason, and James Buxton believed to be Fr Sheehy's deputy was captured at this time also.[182] At the assizes held in March six persons including Edmund Sheehy, James Farrell, and Robert Keating were ordered to stand trial in Kilkenny for their involvement in the Newmarket affray in 1764. They were acquitted, but were then returned to Clonmel where a special commission to try all those charged was to sit in April. At these trials the convictions of Sheehy, Farrell, and Buxton were obtained on a murder charge, while eight others though acquitted of that charge were allowed bail to appear to answer the further charge of high treason. Despite the appeals and petitions made by them in which they declared their innocence, Sheehy, Buxton, and Farrell were executed in Clogheen on 3 May 1766. This was the culmination of the hysteria, for at the March 1767 assizes the remainder of the chief Catholics like Doherty, Keating, and Nagle were acquitted and passions abated thereafter.[183]

8. Aftermath

The executions and terror in south Tipperary generated widespread fears both within the area itself and in east Munster generally. Because of the charges made that Catholic merchants in the ports were supplying funds for the advancement of the plot, they also came under suspicion. Evidence from the dying declarations of Farrell and Buxton shows that attempts were made to make them turn approver by swearing against Catholic merchants and clergy in Waterford particularly, but in Cork also. They included Martin Murphy, Philip Long, Thomas Wyse,

---

[182] *FDJ*, 1–4 Feb., 15–18, 22–5 Mar., 1–5 Apr. 1765; *DG*, 1–5 Apr. 1765.
[183] For these proceedings: Sheffield City Library, Burke MS 8/3–9; *FDJ*, 29 Mar.–1 Apr., 5–8, 8–12, 12–15, 15–19, 19–22 Apr., 6–10 May 1766, 24–8, 28–31 Mar., 5–8 Sept. 1767; *Gentleman's and London Magazine* (1766), 244–8.

bishop Pierce Creagh, and Dominick Farrell.[184] This was a clear attempt by the extreme party to extend the purge outside the county.

Catholic apologists viewed the events of 1765–6 as catastrophic, and parallels were drawn with previous acts of persecution. Curry and Griffith likened the episode to the popish plot in 1678, however O'Conor felt that a movement towards concession could result from the events, especially if liberal Protestant MPs could be canvassed.[185] In June 1766 he wrote to Curry that 'The Tipperary affair is I find become a very important one, not only to our people in general but to some *patriots* in particular.'[186] He encouraged Curry to assemble material on the events and to publish them which he did in a Cork edition of 1767. While O'Conor's purpose was as much to dissociate the Catholic gentry from the Whiteboys as to rehabilitate catholicism in general, this publication was one element in opening the way for Catholic relief.

Another element which aided in that process was the fact that, as a result of the purge, militant protestantism was discredited. The charges of treason and murder were not widely credited outside the region. The only formal approval came from the grand jury of county Dublin in 1767 which gave credence to the charges of rebellion and congratulated Maude, Carrick, Bagwell, and Bagnell for their public service.[187] Indicative of government reaction was the payment of £227 to Hewetson for his efforts, but a request from the grand jury that the two prosecution witnesses be rewarded in the amount of £600 was not conceded.[188] Local reaction to the right-wing party was displayed by assaults on its members, threats to the lives of Bagwell and Maude, and the stoning to death of Fr Sheehy's executioner in 1770.[189] By that

[184] Burke, *Clonmel*, 402–5; Sheffield City Library, Burke MS 8/9.

[185] A. Griffith, *A letter to Daniel Toler esq. relative to the death of Rev. Nicholas Sheehy*, in *Miscellaneous tracts* (Dublin, 1788), 240; [J. Curry], *A parallel between the pretended plot in 1762 and the forgery of Titus Oates in 1679* (Cork, 1767), 6.

[186] C. G. Ward and R. E. Ward, *The letters of Charles O'Conor of Belangare* (Ann Arbor, Mich., 1980), i. no. 148.

[187] J. Hewetson, *Memoirs of the house of Hewetson or Hewson of Ireland* (London, 1901), 126; Mount Melleray Abbey, Burke MS, Clonmel, ii. 349–50; see also F. Blackburne, *Considerations on the present state of the controversy between the Protestants and Papists of Great Britain and Ireland* (London, 1768), 187; *FLJ*, 22–5 Apr. 1767.

[188] Mount Melleray Abbey, Burke MS 31, pp. 288–9; Burke, *Clonmel*, 496–7.

[189] NA, Proclamations, 5 Oct. 1770; TCD, MS 873/730–1; *FLJ*, 31 Jan.–4 Feb. 1767.

stage the entire prosecution case based on the murder of Bridge was totally undermined when in 1768 one of the prosecution witnesses retracted his testimony.[190] Despite the discredit engendered by the episode much of the truculent attitude displayed was perpetuated in reactions to later political events. Hewetson about 1790 wrote a long memorandum to Lord Townshend in which he traced the origins and implications of the rural unrest, and advanced the view that the Rightboys were associated with the revolutionaries in France. He also advocated union with Britain if the franchise was extended to Catholics.[191]

Moderate opinion at the time was shocked at the events of 1766. One of the patriots to whom O'Conor referred, Lord Charlemont, reacted sharply to the proceedings declaring that 'The furious and bigoted zeal with which some Protestants were activated was shocking to humanity and a disgrace to our mild religion.'[192] Religious zeal, he claimed, had been used to advance schemes of a more devious kind and the notion of a French plot was conceived in order to support them. Another contemporary, Charles O'Hara of county Sligo, believed that Fr Sheehy was guilty of murder but doubted whether proofs of a rebellion would be forthcoming and suspended judgment on the validity of the treason charge.[193] O'Hara's correspondent, Edmund Burke, was interested in the episode from a personal and a political viewpoint. Burke's assistance was sought on behalf of a distant relative, James Nagle of Garnvella, who converted in December 1765, reflecting the fears current following his declaration of innocence in June 1765. Though convinced of his and the others' innocence, Burke was reluctant to take the matter outside the course of law.[194] Nevertheless Burke, whose three visits to Ireland between 1760 and 1767 provided him with direct knowledge of the events of the period, was interested in the wider aspects of the case, shown by the survival among his papers of copies of the petitions and dying declarations of Sheehy, Buxton, and Farrell.[195] Burke castigated

[190] Burke, *Clonmel*, 395.
[191] Townshend MS, 6806/7/6/1/18, *et seq.*
[192] HMC, *12th report, Charlemont*, app. 10 (1891), 20 n.
[193] *Edmund Burke, New York agent*, ed. R. J. S. Hoffman (Philadelphia, 1956), 340–1.
[194] *Correspondence of Edmund Burke*, i. 277.
[195] Sheffield City Library, Burke MS 8/1, 3, 5–8; *Correspondence of Edmund Burke*, iv. 409.

the self-interest of the gentry who promoted the violence, and expressed his incredulity at the charges advanced by them.[196]

Out of the excesses of the 1760s, arose on the one hand, a greater readiness by Catholics to identify openly with the establishment and, on the other, a Protestant willingness to make concessions to Catholics. Already from the 1750s a movement was taking place among Catholics to devise an acceptable means of expressing their allegiance to the sovereign. The refusal of the pope to recognize Charles Edward as the legitimate sovereign of Britain, after the death of the Old Pretender in 1766, encouraged a renewal of these attempts whereby Catholics could attest their loyalty which had just been brought into question in Tipperary. These efforts came to nothing as a draft formula for an oath was rejected by Rome in 1768. This decision was conveyed through the nuncio in Brussels who instructed the archbishops of Armagh and Dublin to inform the other bishops of the decision, which they failed to do. However, the verdict was published by Thomas Burke, bishop of Ossory, as a supplement to a new edition in 1772 of his *Hibernia Dominicana*, originally published in 1762.[197] This caused a sensation among those Catholics who had been working for a compromise, yet it quickened their resolve to devise an acceptable oath, in which process the Anglican bishop of Derry, Frederick Hervey, played a leading role.[198] An oath was embodied in an act of 1774 (13 & 14 Geo. III, c. 35), which formally denied the more extreme papal claim to exercise temporal power and to excommunicate rulers and have them deposed or murdered by subjects.

Significantly the movement to advance acceptance of the oath was foremost in Munster. In September 1774 James Butler assumed office as the new Catholic archbishop of Cashel. He represented a new generation of bishops. He viewed the oath as legitimate and in this was supported by his suffragan bishops. What hastened Butler's support for the oath was the background

[196] Ibid.; NLI, MS 2714, 190; *Correspondence of Edmund Burke*, i. 249, 255–6; see also C. C. O'Brien, *The great melody: A thematic biography of Edmund Burke* (London, 1992), 54–5.
[197] M. Wall, 'Catholic loyalty to king and pope in eighteenth-century Ireland', *Proc. Irish Catholic Hist. Comm.* (1961), 20–1; introduction by T. Wall to the 1970 edn. of T. Burke, *Hibernia Dominicana* (Kilkenny, 1762).
[198] J. R. Walsh, *Frederick Augustus Hervey, 1730–1803, fourth earl of Bristol, bishop of Derry, 'Le bienfaiteur des Catholiques'* (Maynooth, 1972), 11–22.

of sectarian tension in the 1760s and the renewal of Whiteboy violence in the early 1770s, particularly during 1775. Such events created the context out of which the tensions of the 1760s might be repeated so that Butler was keen to attest Catholic loyalty openly. Indicative of this is his staunch defence of his brother Robert Butler's spirited action in organizing resistance to the Whiteboys at Ballyragget, Co. Kilkenny, in February 1775, which served to allay government suspicions of Catholic complicity or apathy.[199] That the attack was led by the local priest, Fr Cahill, was significant, for it contrasted sharply with the perceived reverse role which Fr Sheehy had played in the early 1760s. Although Butler's attempt to use his office to quell whiteboyism in his archdiocese was of little effect, it was sufficient to make government well disposed towards him.

While maintaining his campaign against whiteboyism, in the course of the following months Butler took steps to establish the acceptability of taking the oath of allegiance. First, he submitted the oath for scrutiny by theologians at the Sorbonne who declared that it could be taken by Irish Catholics without danger to their religion.[200] Secondly, having obtained this clarification Butler convened a meeting of the Munster bishops at Cork where on 15 July 1775 they adjudged the oath as containing nothing contrary to the Catholic religion.[201] This unprecedented declaration was later to bring Butler into conflict with Rome. In his defence he argued that the particular situation in Munster, where government implicated the clergy in the rural unrest, required that they prove their loyalty. The necessary delay in getting Rome's decision in the matter could have proven fatal.[202] Butler's action was a critical move as it showed the willingness, indeed urgency, with which the southern bishops wished to advance the taking of the oath, even without the consent of the other bishops and without Rome's prior approval. The third action taken by Butler was to arrest the damage done as a result of the reissuing of *Hibernia Dominicana*. The Munster bishops took the radical step of entering Burke's Ossory diocese in order to make him retract, but he protested at

---

[199] CDA, James Butler II papers, 1775/5.
[200] M. Tierney, 'A short title calendar of the papers of Archbishop James Butler in Archbishop's House, Thurles', *Coll. Hib.*, 18–19 (1976–7), 108–9.
[201] CDA, James Butler II papers, 1775/2.
[202] Ibid. 1776/6, 1777/1.

this intrusion and they withdrew.[203] They reassembled at Thurles where they issued a strong condemnation of Burke's work as tending to weaken the allegiance due to the king, as causing controversy among Catholics, and as providing an instrument to ascribe disloyalty to Catholics.[204] These actions by Butler opened the way for Catholics to accept the oath at least in Munster. In August 1775 a group of Tipperary Catholics said to be 'most respectable' took the oath in Clonmel.[205] Such an open display of loyalty when the American war of independence was beginning and when the Irish parliament was due to reassemble, was timely. The entire episode of the oath saw Butler assuming the initiative in its acceptance by the general body of Catholics in his archdiocese, but at the cost of division with the majority of other Catholic bishops outside Cashel archdiocese.

Despite these initiatives the rural unrest in the region continued unabated. Archbishop Butler issued an instruction to the people and clergy in October 1775 condemning the Whiteboys, declaring excommunicate all those who assisted them, and ordering all stolen arms to be returned.[206] This appeal was to no avail for in late November occurred the atrocious murder of Ambrose Power of Barrettstown. Power was a member of the grand jury which had convicted Fr Sheehy in 1766, and his murder caused alarm. A report from Clonmel to Sir Edward Newenham (who was foreman of the county Dublin grand jury which sent the congratulatory address to the Tipperary gentry in 1766) in the wake of the murder shows that some persons viewed the Whiteboys as a cover movement to arm Catholics and feared a massacre of Protestants.[207] This context provided the stimulus for the widespread taking of the oath at Clonmel, Carrick, Cahir, Cashel, Fethard, and Thurles in the first three weeks of December.[208] With 368 subscribers including gentry, clergy, farmers, and the mercantile

[203] T. Wall introduction to the 1970 edn. of T. Burke, *Hibernia Dominicana*.

[204] CDA, James Butler II papers, 1775/4; E. O'Flaherty, 'Ecclesiastical politics and the dismantling of the penal laws in Ireland, 1774–82', *IHS*, 26 (1988), 34–7, 41. The contrasting experience in Wexford and Kilkenny is apparent: P. J. Corish, 'Two centuries of catholicism in Wexford', in Whelan and Nolan (eds.), *Wexford*, 240; F. O'Fearghail, 'The Catholic church in county Kilkenny, 1600–1800', in Nolan and Whelan (eds.), *Kilkenny*, 236.

[205] *FLJ*, 19–23 Aug. 1775.

[202] *Coll. Hib.*, 18–19 (1976–7), 110.

[207] NLI, MS 8395 (3).   [208] *FLJ*, 6–9, 9–13, 16–20, 23–7 Dec. 1775.

class, Tipperary had the largest number in any county in Ireland.[209] The oath-takers came from about sixty locations throughout the county but were concentrated in a region from south of Cahir to north of Thurles, the region where the Catholic interest was strongest. Together the landed interest and the Catholic commercial interest in the towns were emerging as a middle class which was to be the most articulate group outside parliament in the furtherance of Catholic relief.

The taking of the oath by Catholics, though voluntary, was seen as an expression of loyalty. While no formal relaxation of the penal laws resulted from its taking, and while papal disapproval delayed its universal acceptance, it created a favourable climate for concessions, a development influenced by political trends locally. The 1768 county election was closely contested, the candidates being Sir Thomas Maude (the sitting member), Francis Mathew (son of Thomas Mathew, defeated in 1761), Henry Prittie the younger (son of the deceased sitting member who died in 1768), and John Bagwell. Mathew and Prittie, Maude and Bagwell went forward as joint runners. It is evident that Catholic influence was again brought to bear in favour of Mathew and Prittie in 1768. Following Mathew's success it was said that he 'Came in by the papist int[ere]st of this Co[unty]'.[210] Catholic landlords influenced Protestant freeholders to vote in a certain way, and prominent Catholics were well placed to act as canvassing agents. Walter Woulfe, a wealthy Carrick merchant, recommended persons whom Mathew and Prittie could usefully approach with a view to obtaining their favour.[211] Nationally there were a large number of conversions in advance of the election in order that such persons might qualify to vote.[212] In 1768, thirty-two conversions are officially enrolled for the county representing one-seventh of the national total for that year, and the largest annual figure for the county in any year in the 1760s. In contrast to the pattern in other counties the majority of these conversions took place before the election in July. This figure may seem low in isolation, but it must be viewed in the context of the total number of conversions for 1760–7 of 127 persons who also would have had the right to vote in

---

[209] *Fifty–ninth report of the deputy keeper.*
[210] Bodkin, 'Notes', 213.
[211] Woulfe to F. Mathew, 24 Feb. 1768, same to H. Prittie, 13 July 1768 (NLI, MS 9630, unfoliated).   [212] Brady, *Press*, 131.

1768. The figure is also significant because of the slim margin of twenty-five votes by which Mathew was returned.

The juncture between Prittie and Mathew may have been an attempt to allow moderate opinion to express itself in the wake of the events of 1766, thereby halting Maude's return for a second term. Certainly it was unusual in the context of eighteenth-century politics to have a coalition between two major political interests stated so publicly as it was and sealed privately by a bond of £1,000. Yet it is indicative of the strength of feeling produced by the events of the early 1760s that the need for it arose. Bagwell's implicit juncture with Maude arose out of the same context, but for the opposite motives. In the poll Maude's vote of 696 over Mathew (621) gave him a majority for the first seat, while Mathew's majority of 25 votes over Prittie (596) was sufficient to give him the second seat.[213] The election was divisive, a point stressed in an assessment of Mathew that he was 'Sir Thomas [Maude]'s antagonist in Tipperary'.[214] In 1768 the legacy of defeat in 1761 was overturned by Mathew's success, but the pattern of opposition to the family was maintained through Maude's return.

The divisions at local level were reflected in attitudes towards government. Following the 1768 election Maude came in as a government supporter having been made a privy councillor by Townshend, while Mathew opposed government.[215] The political issues current in the early 1770s stemmed partly from the policy of direct control by a resident viceroy, inaugurated by Townshend and continued by his successors, and partly from the concerns of the political community itself. Maude's advancement as a privy councillor was an expression of the new policy enunciated by Townshend of creating a strong 'Castle' party dependent on the lord-lieutenant and rendering him a majority in parliament in return for patronage.[216] But most Tipperary gentlemen entering parliament in 1768 opposed government, with Maude and Guy Moore Coote (MP for Clonmel, 1761–82) the only committed government supporters. This is not altogether surprising for it was to the advantage of most MPs, particularly new members like

---

[213] King's Inns Library, MS 39 D, fo. 127ᵛ.

[214] NA, M734 (1).

[215] D. Large, 'The Irish house of commons in 1769', *IHS*, 11 (1958), 37.

[216] T. Bartlett, 'The Townshend viceroyalty, 1767–72', in Bartlett and Hayton (eds.), *Penal era*, 88–112.

Cornelius O'Callaghan and Francis Mathew entering on a parliamentary career, to adopt a distant stance and thereby obtain the best terms possible from government. The fluid nature of much of their opposition is exemplified by the fact that by 1773 the Pennefathers, Holmes (Banagher), Croker (Fethard), and Prittie had been won over to support, while Mathew and O'Callaghan were still in opposition.[217] These positions of a pro- and anti-government line were to be tested by the current political issues as Townshend and his successor, Harcourt, grappled with a resilient parliamentary opposition articulating the grievances emanating from the economic difficulties and political concerns of the early 1770s.

In November 1773 an address formulated by freeholders at Nenagh expressed concern among other issues about the appointment of pensioners, placemen, and members of parliament to office.[218] This concern arose out of the means adopted by Townshend to win support after 1768, exemplified by Maude's advancement. It was the strong belief that acceptance of such places and offices necessarily involved a compromise of independence, and the freeholders wished their MPs to support a bill to limit their number. Their MPs were informed that their constant attendance in parliament exerting themselves on the above issues was expected, and they were told that 'it is our determined resolution that parliamentary conduct shall be the invariable rule of our future choice'.[219] Maude's response to the address reflects his commitment as a government supporter and, at the same time, his anxiety to maintain popularity among the freeholders. Attempting to reconcile the two purposes probably accounts for the description of him in 1775 that 'he supports pretty steadily, but upon two occasions last session opposed and *affected* independence, but seeing his seat in the [Privy] Council and Peerage in danger he returned to government'.[220] Maude was rewarded for his support by being elevated to the peerage in 1776 as Lord De Montalt. He was one of twenty-two new peers created in that year as part of the government's winning of support for delicate measures, notably the despatching of 4,000 troops to America.

---

[217] Bodkin, 'Notes', 183, 198, 200, 213–14; T. Bartlett, *Macartney in Ireland 1768–72* (Belfast, 1980), 11.
[218] *FJ*, 30 Nov.–2 Dec. 1773.   [219] Ibid.
[220] W. Hunt (ed.), *The Irish parliament in 1775* (1907), 35 (my emphasis).

Yet his attempt to benefit from both freeholder support and government patronage was increasingly incompatible in the context of the 1770s.

In contrast, Mathew remained in opposition, a stance which was more likely to prove beneficial in the election of 1776 and in terms of popularity, given the trend of constitutional agitation during the 1770s. By 1775 the other MPs connected with the county and supporting government were Guy Moore Coote, the Pennefathers, John Damer (Swords), Peter Holmes, and John Hely-Hutchinson; those in opposition with Mathew were Cornelius O'Callaghan, Henry Prittie, and Sir William Osborne; while Colvill Moore was absent and John Croker could not be depended on.[221] Thus by 1776 a majority of MPs associated with Tipperary supported government, while only Mathew and O'Callaghan remained consistent in their opposition.

The role of Prittie in the 1768 contest was decisive and he was again to have a crucial influence in 1776. In 1768 Prittie had agreed to give his interest to Mathew conditional on a bond of £1,000. Payment on the bond was not subsequently demanded, Mathew presumed that the understanding with Prittie was to be binding in the 1776 election also, and on this basis Prittie was applied to for his interest on Mathew's behalf. Disavowing any obligation to be bound, Prittie declared his intention of standing singly and unconnected, and at this stage Mathew offered to honour payment of the bond. Prittie remained uncompromising in his neutrality but conceded that his second preference votes should be equally divided between Mathew and Daniel Toler, another candidate, a proposal which Prittie contended freed him from the obligation of the bond.[222] In a closely contested election with a gross poll of 1,470, Prittie was elected with a majority of 104 votes as also was Mathew with a margin of 66 votes over Toler.[223] Given the narrowness of the margin and, in contrast to 1768, the absence of an alliance, Toler proceeded to petition but this was unsuccessful.[224] As a result Mathew was returned a second time for the county and

[221] W. Hunt (ed.), *The Irish parliament in 1775*, 14–16, 26, 38, 39, 40, 42, 45.
[222] The foregoing is derived from *Minutes of evidence taken before the select committee on the Tipperary election* (n.d. [1777]), *passim*.
[223] King's Inns Library, MS 39 D, fo. 127ᵛ.
[224] *Minutes of evidence*, 119; *Comms. Jnl. (Ire.)*, ix. pt. 1, 297, 312, 320.

Prittie achieved the prestige of attaining a first-time victory at county level.

A list of the main political interests in the county in 1775 and the poll book for the 1776 election, indicate that the bulk of the support for Prittie and Toler came from the leading landowners and freeholders of the north of the county.[225] Prittie's support came from ninety-five freeholders on his estate, supplemented by marriage links and connections. His brothers-in-law, Thomas Otway, Peter Holmes, Michael Head, and Matthew Bunbury were important landowners who could vouch for the votes of their freeholders, it being remarked of Holmes that he 'has a good interest (as to freeholders) in this county', a remark also made about Francis Sadlier of Sopwell Hall, who was Prittie's father-in-law.[226] In this way the votes of freeholders in one barony, Lower Ormond, where in 1784 there were 400 freeholders (equivalent to one quarter of the county total at that date), were accounted for.[227] Prittie had the support of his relative the earl of Clanwilliam, one of the county's leading landowners, who could render a large freeholder support for Prittie which extended his support base beyond its northern stronghold (see Fig. 2). Thus family ties, combined with a strong freeholder base, ensured Prittie of a strong real and personal interest. The Toler interest in terms of freeholders was less extensive than that of Prittie, rather his political interest derived from the fact that he was a relative of Prittie's. This connection was all-important for, deficient in wealth and freeholders, Toler became dependent on the second prefer-ence votes of Prittie and his connections. This strong alignment ensured that Prittie would top the poll. On a broader canvas Prittie's main political connection outside the county was Sir Henry Cavendish, his uncle by marriage. By virtue of this link Prittie became associated with the Devonshire interest and, by extension, the Ponsonby interest which, from the 1760s, was making successful encroachments on the Boyle power base in Munster.[228]

The pattern of support for Mathew was quite different. He had

---

[225] *AH*, 12 (1943), 137–44; 1776 poll book: RIA, MS 12. D.36. Unless otherwise stated this section is based on an interpretation of both these sources.

[226] *AH*, 12 (1943), 138.

[227] *Minutes of evidence*, 54; *CG*, 8–12 Jan. 1784.

[228] Hewitt (ed.), *Shannon*, pp. xxxiii, xxxix.

some advantage in that he was a sitting MP for the county. Against this, however, was the fact that he had few direct connections by marriage with the Protestant political community in the county, indeed nothing on a scale comparable to that of Prittie (see Fig. 1(c)). Lacking local support through marriage links, Mathew became dependent on freeholders on his estate and the backing of other interests sympathetic politically. The majority margins attained by the Mathews in earlier elections were narrow: 36 votes in 1761, 25 in 1768. Conscious of this narrow margin, lacking in political support, and unable to avail himself of a pre-arrangement as in 1768, Mathew was concerned to maximize the potential of his freeholder vote and thus granted to sixty or seventy persons, who were rent chargers, the status of freeholders on the Thurles estate.[229] Thus a large proportion of the 467 freeholders (representing about one-third of the gross poll) who voted singly for Mathew, were freeholders on the Mathew estate. Mathew had government support in the election since his nominee was John Scott, the recently appointed solicitor-general who was Mathew's brother-in-law and a supporter of Catholic relief. Scott had recently been won over to the administration and had staunchly defended it against the patriots' most vociferous spokesmen, the Floods, who had opposed Thomas Mathew in the Callan election of 1768. Scott may have been influential in winning Mathew to the government side. Certainly after 1776 Mathew was in support and this was to favour his elevation to the peerage (1783) and his advancement of Catholic relief. This emphasizes a general point that those in parliament who favoured Catholic demands were generally government supporters and rarely patriots, whereas those who supported patriot demands were generally inimical to Catholic relief.

The 1776 election marked a decided shift in the political character of the county in two respects. First, Mathew turned from opposition to standing as a government nominee in opposition to Prittie whose loyalties lay with Ponsonby, a government opponent. In this sense Mathew, ironically, may be seen as replacing Maude (who had been raised to the peerage) as the pro-government choice in the county representation. This transition was to be of

[229] M. Callanan, A history of the barony of Eliogarty (NLI, Mic.P.4546, 204); St Patrick's College, Thurles, Skehan notebooks, parish of Thurles, ii. 88; *Minutes of evidence*, 36–42.

great significance subsequently because the enfranchisement of the Catholic 40s. freeholders after the act of 1793 increased the number of voters the Mathews could mobilize. Yet in 1776 this was far in the future and Mathew was still dependent on a narrow electoral majority. Although he could marshal an impressive number of freeholders and could get support from a range of other interests, his inability to achieve a more decisive majority was a reflection of his isolation in the county's landed class. Yet it was the Mathews' championing of the Catholic cause, in alliance with the Catholic interest and a group of liberal Protestants, which was to characterize political development locally for the remainder of the century and beyond. Secondly, Prittie's victory and Toler's good showing signalled a shift in the leadership of the Protestant political community compared to the 1760s. At that time the gentry around Clonmel with Maude were prominent leaders and grand jurors, a pattern influenced by the location and emphasis of sectarian tension in that decade. Prittie's victory in 1776 saw the transfer of political leadership to the north. The disposition of interests implicit in the 1776 election result with one member for the government, the other against, was to be tested in the constitutional and political issues which arose in following years.

Its first relevant manifestation was on the Catholic issue. Already the first concession had come with an act of 1772 (11 & 12 Geo. III, c. 21) which allowed Catholics to take 61-year leases of bogland. In the 1770s despite continued agitation over quarterage and quarterage bills, the tax never received the legislative sanction which had been sought by the corporations. Clonmel petitioned in 1768 and 1774 seeking confirmation in law of the tax, and support for quarterage was stipulated in an address by the freeholders to the two county MPs in 1773.[230] The Clonmel petitions continued to associate the agitation over quarterage with sympathy for whiteboyism. The ultimate success of the Catholic mercantile lobby on the issue was a significant milestone.

The lessons of the American war had parallels in Ireland particularly in relation to Catholics. The government came to accept that concessions to Catholics would be desirable from a security viewpoint, and public opinion was moving in this direction

---

[230] *Comms. Jnl. (Ire.)*, viii. pt. 1, 270; ix. pt. 1, 91–2; *FJ*, 30 Nov.–2 Dec. 1773; see also D. Dickson, 'Catholics and trade in eighteenth-century Ireland: An old debate revisited', in Power and Whelan (eds.), *Catholics in Ireland*, 98.

also.[231] Archbishop Butler and four of his bishops supported an address of loyalty in 1778, though no bishops from the other three archdioceses did so.[232] Those who supported the bill included Mathew, O'Callaghan, Sir William Osborne (who argued that the repeal of the laws would likely lead to an increase in conversions to the Established Church), John Hely-Hutchinson, and John Scott; while its opponents included the Pennefathers, Prittie, John Toler, and G. M. Coote.[233] The act's passage vindicated the approach adopted by archbishop Butler, for subsequently the opposition of the other bishops to the oath of allegiance collapsed.[234]

The act of 1778 (17 & 18 Geo. III, c. 49) removed the most severe of the restrictions imposed by the acts of 1703 and 1709 on leasing and inheritance. The 31-year stricture on leases was repealed as was the requirement of descent in gavelkind, and also the method whereby the conversion of the eldest son made the parent tenant for life. Only those who took the oath of allegiance could benefit from the act and, as in 1775, Tipperary Catholics subscribed enthusiastically. At Clonmel it was reported that 'upwards of 600' persons took it in one day at the assizes; while nationally within the first year of the act's operation over 6,500 persons took the oath, and in the period 1778–92 the national total exceeded 12,000.[235] Apart from Dublin city, those qualifying under the act were most numerous in Munster. The official returns put the total of oath-takers in Tipperary in 1778–92 at 730, but if those with addresses in the county who took it elsewhere are included the figure was over 900.[236] Occupational or social status is not ascribed in over half (455) of this total, but included were Lord Cahir, and gentlemen and esquires like John Baldwin (Cahir), Peter Dalton (Grenanstown), Count Christopher Dalton (Grenanstown), Thomas McCarthy (Springhouse), Edward Mandeville, Richard Doherty (Loughloher), John Galway

[231] *Correspondence of Edmund Burke*, iii. 387; Howard, *Cases*, v–vii; T. Bartlett, 'The origins and progress of the Catholic question in Ireland, 1690–1800', in Power and Whelan (eds.), *Catholics in Ireland*, 9–10.

[232] O'Flaherty, 'Ecclesiastical politics', 38.

[233] RIA, MS B.1.2; R. E. Burns, 'The Catholic relief act in Ireland, 1778', *Church History*, 32 (1963), 192.

[234] O'Flaherty, 'Ecclesiastical politics', 39–40.

[235] *FJ*, 24–6 Sept. 1778; *Comms. Jnl. (Ire.)*, xv. pt. 2, p. clxxxvii.

[236] NA, Catholic qualification rolls, 1778–91 (1A 52 10); *Comms. Jnl. (Ire.)*, xv. pt. 1, p. clxxxv.

(Carrick), Denis and George Ryan (Inch), and several Scullys and Sheehys. The large number of farmers (190) who took the oath is to be noted as it was the group within the Catholic middle interest which would benefit from the relaxation of the 31-year lease restriction. Farmers were earliest to subscribe to the act with thirty-three recorded in 1778–9 alone and there must have been many more in the unspecified category. To the wealthy and numerous Catholic landed class was added the articulate clergy (23) under archbishop Butler's leadership, and the mercantile and service sectors in the towns. These classes together constituted those who would gain most from the 1778 act. They formed the politically conscious grouping in Catholic society pressing for social and economic advantages.

The new climate created by the taking of the oath of allegiance (1774) and the 1778 act was manifested in 1779 when there was fear of a French invasion, an event which formerly had led to apprehension. On this occasion Catholic gentlemen offered their services for defence to the magistrates which was accepted and publicly acknowledged.[237] This development was in sharp contrast to the early 1760s when a similar invasion threat had produced a contrary reaction among Protestants. Once the political climate seemed favourable Catholics pressed their advantage. Archbishop Butler was in contact with the Speaker of the House of Commons, Edmund Sexton Pery, on the issue of further concessions, and he received assurances from government that Catholic claims would be favourably entertained.[238] Amid the conclusion of the American war in late 1781, with declarations from MPs like Peter Holmes, John Hely-Hutchinson, and David Walshe in favour of a further relaxation of the penal laws and with government support, two further acts giving relief received the royal assent in 1782.[239] The first of these (21 & 22 Geo. III c. 24) enabled Catholics who took the oath of allegiance to acquire land (except in parliamentary boroughs) on the same terms as Protestants. It also recognized *de jure* what was already in existence *de facto*, i.e. the open practice of the Catholic religion, and the validity and legality of Catholic marriages. The second act (21 & 22 Geo. III, c. 62)

[237] *HC*, 7–10, 10–14 June 1779.
[238] Butler to Pery, 28 Jan. 1780 (NLI, Mic.P. 1561); O'Flaherty, 'Ecclesiastical politics', 45–6.
[239] *Parliamentary register* (1782), i. 172, 239, 248–51, 286–8.

freed Catholic education from its former legal constraints and also repealed laws relating to the guardianship of children.

These concessions were important gains for Catholics. Yet the forward manner in which Catholics advanced their demands was productive of some hostility locally in 1780. Archbishop Butler was charged with using his position and family influence to advance the interests of the Catholic Church in the diocese to the detriment of the Established Church. It was reported to him that 'the established church appeared in your diocese scarcely tolerated, whilst the Church of Rome assumed uncommon usurpations in show as well as in substance'.[240] This charge proceeded in large measure from particular grievances of Revd Francis Garnett, rector of Thurles, relating to circumstances there. His attempt to present them in more general and seditious terms failed to convince government in the person of John Scott, attorney-general, who was sympathetic to the opposite view.[241] This again is in marked contrast to the situation in the 1760s when claims by people like Revd John Hewetson seemed to command credence. In the immediate context of the controversy of 1780, relations between Butler and the new Anglican archbishop of Cashel, Charles Agar (1779–1802) were good. This good relationship appears to have continued despite the involvement of Butler in public controversy with Agar's fellow bishop, Richard Woodward of Cloyne, in the 1780s over the latter's charge that little trust could be placed on the oath of allegiance taken by Catholics.[242]

As a result of the 1782 measures the activities of priests became less restricted. Thus Revd Marnane openly advertised the establishment of his school in Tipperary in 1786, and the deaths of priests were given more regular notice in the newspapers indicating public recognition of their status in local society.[243] Organizational improvement in the church continued with a general visitation held in a Cashel diocese in 1776 and a synod in 1782, while the

[240] L. H. Renehan, *Collections on Irish church history*, ed. D. McCarthy (Dublin, 1861), i. 339.

[241] Ibid. 339–42.

[242] Thomas [Bernard, bishop of] Killaloe to Buckinghamshire, 22 Feb. 1787 (NLI, MS 13,047/5); R. Woodward, *The present state of the Church of Ireland*, and J. Butler, *A justification of the tenets of the Roman Catholic religion and a refutation of the charges brought against its clergy by the lord bishop of Cloyne* (Dublin, 1786).

[243] *CG*, 14–18 Dec. 1786; *FLJ*, 8–11 Sept. 1790; Brady, *Press*, 221, 229, 232, 259, 273, 276.

Tridentine decrees were published in Cashel in 1777.[244] The most serious problem faced by the church in the 1780s was that of the Rightboys. Butler was active in disciplining those priests who had caused much of the Rightboy resentment by exacting exorbitant fees. Firm measures were adopted at a meeting of the bishops in June 1786 to eliminate such abuses, while Butler visited two parishes to personally dissuade the parishioners from associating with the Rightboys.[245] All this activity was consistent with Butler's position, held since the early 1770s, a position which emerged out of the divisive and tragic events of the 1760s, events which were to rebound to the advantage of Catholics and which, in the process, were to alter the disposition of political forces in the county and beyond.

[244] CDA, James Butler II papers 1771/4, 1776/1, 1782/6, and see also 1778/7, 1789/6.
[245] Brady, *Press*, 239–40.

7

The 1790s: Prelude, Course, and Aftermath

The 1790s was a decade of crisis in Irish society. Changes in legislation and in the political order occurred rapidly; traditional alignments and loyalties between classes and individuals and within the upper class became less assured; and the growth of radicalism, deriving its intellectual basis from French revolutionary ideas, found its ultimate expression in the 1798 rebellion. Contemporaneous with these developments was the challenge presented by Catholics for admission to the political nation. Why the divisive nature of these developments nationally was not duplicated locally can only be understood first, in the light of the events of the 1760s and their aftermath, and secondly, of the political developments of the late 1770s and 1780s.

1. Political Developments, 1776–1790

The issues of the period up to 1783 were dominated by the achievement of concessions in trade and politics, due in part to the pressure brought to bear by the Volunteer movement. The origins of this body locally lie in the emergence in early 1776 of small groups joining for mutual self-defence against the Whiteboys. Their more formal association came in May 1776 with two corps under Benjamin Bunbury and Sir Cornwallis Maude, followed by another at Templemore under John Carden before the end of the year.[1] The real stimulus to volunteering came with the defence needs of the country consequent on the withdrawal of troops to engage the American colonists then in revolt, and in 1778 the declaration of war with France. By 1779 eighteen Volunteer corps had been formed, all in 1779; two further corps were formed in

---

[1] *Munster volunteer registry* (1782), 18, 57.

1781; and the eighteen functioning corps in the county in 1782 represented about one-quarter of the provincial total.[2]

The formation of these corps is expressive of the *esprit de corps* of Protestants in the county. This was particularly so in the north where the leading interests (Prittie, Toler, Carden, Holmes, Stoney, Jocelyn, and Parsons) participated and where the complement of officers in each corps was more impressive. This northern prominence apart, significantly Francis Mathew was able to sponsor three corps. The one Catholic corps was that under Pierce Butler, brother to Lord Cahir, though individual Catholics were included in other corps. In 1782, of the eighteen corps then functioning, eleven were led by landowners who were or who had recently been members of parliament either for the county, its boroughs, or boroughs outside, or as members of the House of Lords: Henry Prittie, Francis Mathew (3), Cornelius O'Callaghan, Richard Pennefather, Peter Holmes, Lawrence Parsons, the earls of Clanwilliam and Tyrone, and Lord Jocelyn. Each corps was composed of about forty rank and file members drawn from the head-tenantry or from friends or political associates of the colonel.

The Volunteers as an extra-parliamentary body extracted the concession of free trade in 1779–80. This success was followed by renewed constitutional agitation in the years 1780–3 over legal provisions which appeared to bind Ireland unfairly to Britain and which came to be a source of resentment among the political community in Ireland. Expressive of the range of constitutional issues articulated was an address issued after a meeting in February 1780 of the Slievardagh Light Dragoons at Killenaule presided over by Jacob Sankey. In it they resolved not to support candidates at any future election unless they gave assurances of advocating 'the real constitutional interest and rights of the Kingdom'. In particular they expected that their present county and borough MPs would support the repeal of Poynings' law. Also expressed was abhorrence at the act of 6 Geo. I (1720) which had asserted the British parliament's claim to legislate for Ireland, and which denied the appellate jurisdiction of the Irish House of Lords.[3] Following this, in late March 1780 an assembly of the freeholders in Clonmel presided over by Lord Kingsborough (a

[2] Ibid. 20–1, 23, 57–66.
[3] *FJ*, 22–4 Feb. 1780, also printed in C. H. Wilson, *A compleat collection of the resolutions of the volunteers, grand juries etc. of Ireland* (1782), i. 278.

large county Cork landowner whose estate extended over the Tipperary border) moved several resolutions advocating that unless parliament asserted its independence then the recently won commercial concessions would be endangered.[4] Those present included John Bagwell (Belgrove), John Bagwell (Kilmore), Daniel Toler, Sir Edward Newenham, and Counsellor Fitzgerald (probably Gamaliel Fitzgerald-Magrath). In advance of the new session of parliament in late 1781, where these issues were to be debated, an assembly of the freeholders and borough electors was called for to instruct MPs on what line of conduct to follow.[5]

The resolutions adopted at the Dungannon Volunteer convention in February 1782 asserted the legislative independence of Ireland, demanded an amendment to Poynings' law, a limited mutiny bill, a modification of the penal laws, and a bill to secure the independence of the judiciary.[6] In March and April at least seven volunteer corps in Tipperary passed resolutions specifically approving of the proceedings at Dungannon.[7] All agreed to press for the redress of their grievances by constitutional means and defended their action by claiming that any freeholder who learned the use of arms did not abandon his civil rights. Of the two county MPs, Henry Prittie came out strongly in favour of the resolutions. His parliamentary conduct on the matters in question was commended by the Borrisokane and Roscrea corps, and at a meeting of delegates from all the county's corps at Clonmel on 14 March, at which Prittie as the county's chief Volunteer presided, his 'meritorious' stance was noted.[8] In contrast, Francis Mathew was more cautious in respect of his support of the Volunteers engaging in radical constitutional politics. Only one of his corps is recorded as formulating an address in response to the Dungannon resolutions, and this was moderate in tone.[9]

The different emphases placed by the two MPs on the constitutional issues was reflected in a grand jury address in March 1782. The division arose because of Mathew's support for government on some key matters. As foreman of the grand jury he took the unprecedented step of authorizing but not personally

---

[4] Burke, *Clonmel*, 159.   [5] *FJ*, 17–19 July 1781.
[6] P. D. H. Smyth, 'The volunteers and parliament 1779–84', in Bartlett and Hayton (eds.), *Penal era*, 122–4.
[7] Wilson, *A compleat collection*, i. 24, 69–70, 80–1, 157, 169–70, 180, 185–6.
[8] Ibid. 269–70.   [9] Ibid. 219–20.

concurring in the resolutions arrived at by the grand jury. A total of seven resolutions were agreed on by sixteen members of the grand jury. They were as follows: first, that members of parliament were representatives of and derived their power solely from the people; secondly, that the king, lords, and commons of Ireland was the only body competent to make laws for the kingdom and attempts to usurp this function were unconstitutional and illegal; thirdly, that the power exercised by Poynings' law was unconstitutional; fourthly, that the ports of the country should remain open to all foreign nations not at war with the king; fifthly, that a mutiny bill not limited from session to session might be dangerous to the constitution; sixthly, that the independence of the judges in Ireland was essential for the administration of justice; and finally, that all constitutional means would be used to seek redress of these grievances.[10] The grand jurors who subscribed to these declarations were John Bagwell (Marlfield), John Bagwell (Kilmore), Wray Palliser, Henry Prittie, Daniel Gahan, Anthony Parker, William Perry, Samuel Jacob, Gamaliel Fitzgerald-Magrath, Robert Nicholson, Edward Moore, John Power, Minchin Carden, William Baker, Samuel Alleyn, and John Lapp Judkin. A majority of these were voters for Prittie and Toler in the 1776 election, and most of them were leaders or officers in Volunteer corps.

Though he was unsuccessful, Mathew strongly resisted the adoption of these resolutions. He refused to accept the majority decision in the matter, and instead published a separate notice explaining the points at issue. While his refusal was unprecedented, Mathew was careful to stress that 'the difference of opinion was not on the great or essential articles', being one of degree rather than of substance.[11] Accordingly Mathew with six other grand jurors—Cornelius O'Callaghan, Richard Pennefather, Richard Hely-Hutchinson, Theobald Butler, William Armstrong, and James Fogarty—declared their agreement with all the resolutions except those relating to Poynings' law and the mutiny bill. These last they felt were too strong and in their stead they substituted a more general and moderate statement expressing their wish to support any measures which their parliamentary representatives

[10] *FJ*, 23–6 Mar. 1782 (also printed in Wilson, *A compleat collection*, i. 144–7, and in *CG*, 30 June–3 July 1783).
[11] *FJ*, 23–6 Mar. 1782.

deemed necessary in order to prevent any encroachment on the constitution. The Mathew group was in a minority for radical expressions were the order of the day. What Mathew later depicted as a 'patriotic frenzy' had, he said, 'seized upon everybody and the strictest ties of friendship gave way to this frantic zeal of passing resolutions'.[12] In consequence, normally reliable allies to Mathew such as Samuel Alleyn, Anthony Parker, William Baker, and John Power changed their allegiance influenced by the patriotic fervour of 1782. This division within the grand jury over the constitutional issues illustrates the inability of Mathew, a government supporter, to stem the tide of local fervour at a critical point. The local Volunteer movement led by Prittie gained a singular success by its influence over the majority of the grand jurors. Nevertheless Mathew benefited from his efforts on behalf of government for in April he was recommended for the peerage, and the resultant vacancy in the county representation was to provide the context for the 1783 county election.[13]

These developments coincided with the pace of constitutional agitation nationally. In April 1782 Grattan's motion for a declaration of rights was carried by the House. In June success was achieved when the British act for repeal of the declaratory act (6 Geo. I, c. 5) passed, and finally in July Poynings' law was amended to fulfil Irish demands coupled with a measure to secure the independence of the judiciary and limiting the duration of the mutiny act. For this granting of legislative independence there was a loyal address of gratitude from the sheriff, gentlemen, and freeholders of Tipperary.[14]

From this success the reform movement proceeded in 1783–4 to formulate demands for a reform in the system of parliamentary representation. Their purpose was to reduce the influence of the crown on parliament by limiting its disposal of patronage, to make representatives more responsible to the views of their constituents, and to make the franchise more equitable by a reduction in the influence of the great interests.[15] For this purpose, in advance of

[12] Mathew to Carlisle, 19 Mar. 1782 (PRO, HO, 100/1/5–6).
[13] Carlisle to Shelburne, 13 Apr. 1782 (PRO, HO, 100/1/60); North to Northington, 2 July 1783 (BL. Add. MS 33,100, fos. 189, 194).
[14] Address of the sheriff, clergy, and freeholders of Co. Tipperary to the king (n.d. [c. July 1782]) (PRO, HO, 100/2/231).
[15] R. B. McDowell, *Ireland in the age of imperialism and revolution, 1760–1801* (Oxford, 1979), 293–326: Smyth, 'Volunteers', 130–5.

the election in July 1783, a body designated as the 'Constitutional Associating Freeholders' was formed in Clonmel in April to promote the demand for parliamentary reform. Using the opportunity of Mathew's elevation to the peerage and the forthcoming election, the association sought to mobilize independent freeholder opinion based on the ideas of the Volunteer movement. Its aims were to maintain the independence of the county and to restore a proper connection between representative and elector. A test oath was formulated and candidates taking it would be assured of support in the election. By the oath the candidate agreed to be bound by the instructions of the freeholders expressed at a properly convened meeting, and undertook not to accept title, place, or emolument without their approval. Prospective candidates were requested to state their position in relation to the taking of the oath.[16] This was a clear challenge to the major interests, though it was less so to Prittie and Toler who were already closely linked to the more forward demands of the Volunteers and who readily expressed their acceptance of the test oath.[17]

The promoters of the association were Lord Kingsborough, Edward Moore, Sir William Barker, John Bagwell (Marlfield), Robert Nicholson, John Bloomfield, John Congreve, Richard Biggs, and Samuel Jacob. They were prominent in the Volunteer movement locally and had supported the resolutions on parliamentary independence in March 1780, and in March 1782 five of them were among the sixteen grand jurors who had forwarded the seven declarations against the consent of the foreman, Mathew. The association's aims received initial support from 300 persons, including the Quaker merchant interest in Clonmel which Bagwell was moulding in his favour against the Moore monopoly of the borough, and David Walshe candidate for Fethard. Neither the Moores of Clonmel nor the Pennefathers of Cashel lent their support, not surprisingly since to do so would have endangered their respective borough interests. Similarly with Fethard, as neither Thomas Barton nor Cornelius O'Callaghan appear as subscribers. Mathew's followers in the county, particularly those grand jurors who dissented from the majority in March 1782, are absent though some Mathew head-tenants like the Smithwicks

---

[16] *CG*, 14–17 Apr. 1783.
[17] Ibid. 15–19 May, 5–9 June, 30 June–3 July 1783.

subscribed. Peter Holmes, swayed possibly by his borough interest in Banagher, was not present among the initial subscribers. The formation of the association indicates how the issue of parliamentary reform acted as a focus for the emergence locally of an independent interest opposed to the large electoral interests.

One of the promoters of the association, Sir William Barker, put himself forward as a candidate in August 1782 as did Sir Cornwallis Maude, brother of the late Sir Thomas Maude (d. 1777).[18] Mathew's advancement to the peerage precluded his candidature, his eldest son Francis James was too young to stand in the family interest, and because of the political volatility of the times Mathew could not trust someone like Samuel Alleyn to go forward to hold the seat until his eldest son was old enough to stand. In January 1783 Barker withdrew as a candidate, while Maude declined to accept the test oath devised by the association and withdrew as a candidate in June 1783.[19] This left the field open and Prittie and Daniel Toler were returned without a contest marking a notable success for the association and a singular defeat for the major interests of Mathew and Maude, though the association had no influence on the borough returns. As the new parliamentary session opened in October 1783 the two county MPs were in opposition, Clonmel and Fethard were each divided, and both Cashel members were in support.[20]

In the new session pressure for reform proceeded apace. There were five Tipperary delegates at the national convention of the Volunteers which sat in Dublin in November to discuss parliamentary reform: Samuel Alleyn, Daniel Toler, Edward Moore, Sir William Barker, and Thomas Hackett.[21] The major obstacle to the advancement of the reform proposals was the House of Commons itself, and in late November it rejected the Volunteers bill on the matter by a large majority.[22] Votes of thanks were later passed to Toler, Prittie, and Thomas Barton (Fethard) for voting with the minority.[23] From this it is clear that only a minority of the county's MPs backed reform, though it is important to stress that this minority included the two county representatives. The major

---

[18] *HC*, 12 Sept. 1782; *CEP*, 12 Aug., 12 Sept. 1782; *FLJ*, 21–4 Aug 1782.

[19] *FLJ*, 15–18 Jan., 14–18 June 1783; *CG*, 5–9 June 1783.

[20] E. M. Johnston, 'Members of the Irish parliament, 1784–7', *PRIA,* 70 C (1971), 226–7.   [21] Grattan, *Memoirs*, iii. 471.

[22] McDowell, *Ireland*, 306–9.   [23] *CG*, 12–15 Jan. 1784.

borough interests of the Moores at Clonmel, the Pennefathers at Cashel, and O'Callaghan at Fethard opposed. Undaunted by this fact and by the Commons vote, forty-five freeholders requested the sheriff in December 1783 to convene a meeting of all the freeholders to consider instructions to their representatives on the subject of reform.[24] The sheriff James Fogarty, a convert, who had supported Mathew, his patron, on the issue of the declaration in March 1782, refused but the freeholders proceeded to plan a meeting regardless.[25] Very likely it was at this meeting that a lengthy petition on reform was decided on and later forwarded to parliament. This petition addressed itself to some of the main deficiencies in the electoral system as identified by the independent freeholders. The petition sought to define in practical terms the nature of the elective franchise in relation to residence, polling, and qualification; it advocated a limit of three years to the length of parliament; and it sought to restrict places and pensions.[26] Such reforms were a direct assault on the power and privilege of the borough owners, a majority of whom composed the House of Commons which for this reason, and because government was hostile to the measure, again rejected the proposals for reform in March 1784.

The matter did not rest there for in July the sheriff was addressed by Napper Tandy, on behalf of the Dublin radicals, seeking a meeting of the Tipperary inhabitants to choose delegates to attend a national congress where reform would be debated.[27] The sheriff, Richard Moore of Chancellorstown, who was colonel of the Clonmel Independents and who was also related to the proprietors of Clonmel borough, the undermining of whose position was implicit in the reform proposals, declined assembling the county.[28] Despite this refusal 120 freeholders (representing 7.5 per cent of the total electorate of 1,600) met in Clonmel in mid-August and voted by a narrow majority of sixty-five to fifty-five in favour of general resolutions on reform which were to be presented by the two county MPs and sent to the king, but against

---

[24] Ibid. 8–12 Jan. 1784.
[25] Ibid.; cf. *CG*, 14–17 Apr. 1783, where the Constitutional Association advocated that freeholders should assemble on issues without the consent of the sheriff.
[26] *Comms. Jnl. (Ire.)*, xi. pt. 1, 219.   [27] *CEP*, 22 July 1784.
[28] Ibid.; cf. G. Ponsonby to Bolton (n.d. [1784?]) (NLI, MS 16,350(26)).

electing delegates for the national congress.[29] While Moore authorized the resolutions by adding his signature, it is significant that the freeholders and independents were unable to secure a grand jury resolution on the issue, as in March 1782. Though the congress was held in October it was evident by then that the impetus had fallen out of the reform movement as it had with the Volunteers.

The proposals formulated by Pitt for a commercial treaty between Ireland and Britain were introduced into the Irish House of Commons in February 1785. They sought to regulate trade between the two countries and they were accepted by both houses.[30] Due to opposition from manufacturing interests in Britain however, the proposals had to be modified subsequently to such an extent as to make them less attractive to Ireland and in this modified form they were perceived to undermine the legislative independence achieved in 1782. The local response to the proposals first became apparent in late June when forty-three freeholders, mainly from the Tipperary town and Cashel area, requested the sheriff to convene a meeting of the county in order to instruct their representatives on the issue. The sheriff, Thomas Barton, who was a supporter of reform and who as MP for Fethard opposed the commercial treaty, fixed the meeting for Cashel.[31] It is not apparent whether anything of substance emanated from the meeting, but in late August the Commons by a slim majority granted leave to introduce a bill based on Pitt's proposals, but this was not proceeded with largely because a majority in the Irish parliament was no longer assured. At a meeting of the freeholders at Cashel in November the measures were condemned outright as tending to further the interests of Britain at the expense of Irish prosperity, that they would be subversive of commercial rights, and would prove destructive of Ireland's trades and manufactures.[32] The conduct of Henry Prittie and Daniel Toler, who had voted with the minority in August in opposing the introduction of the revised proposals in bill form, was commended and a

[29] Rutland to Sydney, 20 Sept.1784, enclosing petition of the freeholders of Co. Tipperary, 19 Aug. 1784 (PRO, HO, 100/14/108–10); NLI, MS 52 (P)/19; *FLJ*, 21–5 Aug. 1784.

[30] McDowell, *Ireland*, 327–38; A. P. W. Malcomson, *John Foster: The politics of the Anglo-Irish ascendancy* (Oxford, 1978), 49–58.

[31] *CG*, 27–30 June; *FLJ*, 25–9 June 1785.

[32] *CG*, 10–14 Nov. 1785; *FLJ*, 12–15 Oct. 1785.

public declaration of their position on the matter was solicited from the freemen and burgesses of Cashel, Clonmel, and Fethard.[33]

This last was clearly intended to be an embarrassment to the five borough representatives who supported government on the issue. One of them, Cornelius O'Callaghan, progressed to the peerage in 1785 as Lord Lismore as a result of government's disposal of patronage to the Ponsonbys to whom O'Callaghan was allied and whose threatened defection forced government to drop the commercial propositions.[34] It is not evident how much freeholder support the meeting enjoyed, but presumably it would have included the members of the Constitutional Association and those who had met in July in Cashel. Significantly, the two county MPs and Barton opposed the proposals thereby maintaining their position as government opponents, but the five others did not and no grand jury resolution on the matter was forthcoming. As the experience of March 1782 had shown, the position of the grand jury on any particular issue was to be the influential factor. In the absence of any movement by the grand jury on the issue the efforts of a section of the freeholders on the commercial proposals were likely to be ineffective. Greater unanimity was evident locally in the years 1785–8 in confronting the more pressing issue of the challenge to law and order presented by the Rightboys. Agrarian disturbance in the 1780s did not act as a backdrop to sectarian tension as it had in the 1760s. Though Daniel Toler resurrected the Fr Sheehy affair in a parliamentary debate in 1787, and a more hardened attitude persisted among the gentry around Clonmel, sectarian animosities were dormant at this time.[35] The other constitutional issue of the decade i.e. the regency crisis, produced by the temporary insanity of George III in 1788–9, did not produce any major political reaction locally other than a congratulatory address from the grand jury on the king's return to health.[36]

Thus the period of political and constitutional agitation between 1776 and 1785 saw Tipperary shift from having a majority of its MPs on the opposition side to a majority in favour of government in 1785. This transformation materialized because of the nature of

[33] *CG*, 5–9 Nov. 1785.   [34] Hewitt (ed.), *Shannon*, p. xlii.
[35] L. M. Cullen, 'The 1798 rebellion in its eighteenth-century context', in P. J. Corish (ed.), *Radicals, rebels, and establishments* (Belfast, 1985), 101, 112 n. 27.
[36] Address dated 27 Mar. 1789 (PRO, HO, 100/5/386).

the local response to parliamentary reform and the commercial proposals. In the process the 1776 election was a turning point as it marked Mathew's parting of the ways with Prittie and his association with government thereafter. After 1776 political agitation locally became more radical, reflected in the popularity of volunteering, the majority grand jury address of March 1782, and the inauguration of the Constitutional Association in April 1783. The return of Prittie and Toler in the 1783 election marked the emergence of two strong political families in the north of the county and signalled the transfer in the leadership of the Protestant political community from its 1760s southern emphasis. This concentration of political influence in the hands of two northern, anti-government MPs, and the absence of Mathew as a government supporter, seemed to seal the fate of Tipperary politics indefinitely. The experience of the 1790s, particularly on the Catholic issue, was to show how short-lived the achievement of the 1780s was.

2. The Catholic Issue

Given the problems of the 1790s it is striking how Tipperary avoided the tensions evident elsewhere. The chief issue of the early years of the decade was Catholic relief. The Catholic Committee, which had gone into abeyance since the early 1780s, experienced a revival in its fortunes and the towns of Cashel, Carrick, Clonmel, Nenagh, and Thurles came to have representatives on the general committee; George Ryan of Inch played an active part; and there was a network locally for the collection of funds.[37] Following the secession of the aristocratic elements from the committee in late 1791 in protest against the adoption of a more radical programme by the merchant interest led by Edward Byrne (who was related to the Mathews, see Fig. 1) and John Keogh, its aims in 1792 were to attain the elective franchise and grand jury representation for Catholics. For this purpose county delegates were chosen for a Catholic convention to be held in late 1792. In July 1792 Keogh met the Munster bishops in Tipperary

---

[37] *Arch. Hib.*, 9 (1942), 119–20, 160–1; addresses to Westmoreland, 27 Dec. 1791, 2 May 1792 (PRO, HO, 100/36/1–4, 100/37/108–11).

town and received their support for the committee's aims.[38] The clergy played an important role in building up support locally for the committee. Arrangements were later made with the new archbishop of Cashel, Thomas Bray, to have two persons from each parish appointed to choose county delegates for the general committee, and bishop William Egan of Clonmel helped to obtain signatures.[39] Protestants fearfully saw a parallel between the proposed Catholic convention and the contemporary French revolutionary assembly. During the summer of 1792 many county meetings were convened at which the proposed convention was condemned, but it is significant that Tipperary was not among these.[40]

Only from October 1792 does any element of discord enter into the progress of the Catholic issue locally. On 2 October the Catholics of the county met at Thurles where a cautiously worded declaration signed by fifty-seven of those present was issued.[41] It was at this meeting that delegates (Laurence Smith, a Carrick merchant, John Lalor of Long Orchard, and James Scully of Kilfeacle) for the convention were chosen.[42] Significantly a day after the Thurles meeting (on 3 October) a 'very numerous' meeting of the Protestant gentry, clergy, and freeholders took place at Nenagh. The meeting formulated a declaration to the two county MPs, Daniel Toler and John Bagwell, to support the constitution and to 'vigorously oppose all attempts at innovation or alteration in Church and State'. The address was signed by sixty of the principal gentry, and provision was made for obtaining further signatures.[43] By report 'near 600 freeholders', equal to about two-fifths of the entire body of the county's freeholders, signed the address.[44] The Nenagh meeting shows the quick response of the Protestant gentry to the proceedings at Thurles. The initiative taken by the northern gentry reflects the shift which had taken place in the political leadership of the county in the 1780s.

There was a division of opinion among Tipperary Protestants on the issue of concessions to Catholics. On the one hand, a minority including Prittie and Toler opposed it vigorously. On the other

[38] NLI, MS 27,571, 222.
[39] CDA, Bray papers 1792/10.
[40] *FDJ*, 30 Aug.–1 Sept., 6–8 Sept. 1792.
[41] PRO, HO, 100/38/273.
[42] Ibid.
[43] PRO, HO, 100/38/356.
[44] PRO, HO, 100/38/357; *FDJ*, 22 Dec. 1792.

hand, an influential group of liberal Protestants like Lord
Donoughmore and families with a background of conversion, like
Lords Lismore and Llandaff, favoured a relaxation. When the
petition of the Irish Catholics was prepared in December 1792
Lord Donoughmore, who was the chief spokesman in favour of
relief in the House of Lords, played an important role in making
its contents acceptable to the convention and the British side.[45]
Finally, there were others who were unsure how to respond,
remained apathetic, and accepted the reforms passively when they
came. Given the background of sectarianism in the early 1760s a
concerted campaign by Protestants to resist change at this time
might have been expected. But the issues in the early 1790s had a
different context from thirty years previously, in particular the
conjunction of interest between Catholics (who were making
considerable advances in their own right) and liberal Protestants
had strengthened in the intervening period. The result was that
Catholics were proceeding from a position of strength rather than
weakness in the early 1790s, in contrast, for instance, to Wexford
where the Catholic and liberal interest proceeded from a position
of weakness in the 1790s. The balance between signatories to the
address (two-fifths of the county's freeholders) and non-signatories
(three-fifths) may loosely represent the alignment of Protestant
opinion in the county.

Indicative of the transfer of political leadership from south to
north since the 1760s is the way Tipperary MPs responded to the
bills for Catholic relief. In February 1792 Daniel Toler (county
MP), John Toler (solicitor-general), and Peter Holmes
(Kilmallock), all northern landowners, spoke against the measure
of relief introduced in that month; whereas those who welcomed
the measure in varying degrees included Sir Thomas Osborne
(Carysfort), Francis Hely-Hutchinson (University of Dublin), and
John Bagwell of Marlfield (county MP), whose estates were in
south Tipperary.[46] Resistance to Catholic claims intensified in late
1792. In November it was reported that a number of large

---

[45] *A report of the debates in both houses of the parliament of Ireland in the
Roman Catholic bill passed in the session of 1792* (1792), 251, *et seq.*; E. O'Flaherty,
'The Catholic convention and Anglo-Irish politics, 1791–3', *Arch. Hib.*, 40 (1985),
26–7.
[46] *Parliamentary register*, 12 (1792), 116, 133, 179, 187, 204–9, 220; *A report of
the debates of 1792*, 23, 99, 124, 148, 176–84.

landowners in Lower Ormond, including Toler and Prittie, were forcing their Catholic tenants to sign the Nenagh address.[47]

This local opposition did not influence the outcome at national level. The British government was determined to have a relief measure for Catholics pushed through the Irish parliament for security reasons. In the debates in February 1793, following the introduction of the relief bill, Bagwell and Holmes, though they had reservations about extending the elective franchise to Catholics, sided with Osborne and Hely-Hutchinson in favouring the measure.[48] The act (33 Geo. III, c. 21) as passed represented a major concession to Catholics as it made the oath of allegiance more acceptable; it repealed the abjuration oath and test; it restored Catholic 40s. freeholders to the franchise; and it opened a wide range of civil and military offices, local and national, to Catholics. The passage of the act was marked by celebrations in Tipperary and by expressions of thanks from local delegates and towns.[49]

The relative absence of upper-class conflict in the county in the 1790s can be ascribed in large degree to the success with which local Catholics became active in obtaining concessions without provoking a serious Protestant backlash comparable in scale to the 1760s. The opportunist conversion from at least 1792 of John Bagwell (county MP 1790–6) in favour of Catholic relief, which was consistent with a similar shift in attitude among the parliamentary opposition, contributed to the ease with which the new measures were implemented locally.[50] This is most evident in relation to Catholic representation on the grand jury, which was a particularly sensitive index of local influence and attitudes. In March 1793 the first Catholic in the county was chosen as a justice of the peace, and one of the county's chief Catholics, James Scully of Kilfeacle, was made a magistrate through Bagwell's recom-

---

[47] W. T. W. Tone (ed.), *Life of Theobald Wolfe Tone* (Washington, 1826), i. 206.
[48] *Parliamentary register* 13 (1793), 140, 268, 346–52; *A full and accurate report of the debates in the parliament of Ireland in the session of 1793* (1793), 144–5, 215; *FLJ*, 2–6 Mar. 1793.
[49] *FLJ*, 17–20, 20–4 Apr. 1793; *Waterford Herald*, 25 Apr. 1793; PRO, HO, 100/43/229–31.
[50] J.R. Hill, 'The meaning and significance of "Protestant Ascendancy", 1787–1840', in *Ireland after the Union* (Oxford, 1989), 13.

mendation and two other appointments as justices followed.[51] At the summer assizes of 1793 four Catholics, Ulick Allen, Laurence Smith, Denis Meagher, and James Scully, were on the grand jury with Scully remarking that 'Mr. Bagwell [of Kilmore, high sheriff] paid me a great compliment' by so choosing him.[52] Catholic representation on the grand jury after 1793 continued to be substantial. It was drawn from a group of six individuals: Ulick Allen, James Scully, Laurence Smith, Denis Meagher, Denis McCarthy, and Thomas Lalor. The admission of Catholics to positions of responsibility after 1793, achieved as it was by the consent of the Bagwell interest (John Bagwell of Kilmore being sheriff in the vital year of 1793) with opposition evident only in the north of the county, served to recognize the influence they had in local affairs. This process gave greater cohesion to the landed class as a whole as it faced the difficulties of the decade. It also meant that leading Catholics, having received recognition of their status, did not feel alienated from the *status quo* and as a result were less receptive to radicalism than was the case with their counterparts in Wexford.

All who sought to qualify under the 1793 act had to subscribe to an oath and the first opportunity to do so was at Clonmel in June 1793.[53] Previous experience of oath-taking in 1775 and 1778–91 indicted a high response rate among Tipperary Catholics. A total of 534 subscribed to the oath in the period 1793–6, the majority (525) in the first two years (1793–4) of the act's operation.[54] The high profile of rural Catholics of substance especially farmers (312), esquires (12), and gentlemen (40) reflects a prosperous and numerous Catholic landed and middle interest in rural society. Urban middle-class Catholics in the towns of Carrick, Clonmel, Thurles, Nenagh, Cashel, Borrisoleigh, and Tipperary were also to the fore with merchants (23), shopkeepers (13), and a whole range of craftsmen and tradesmen with those in the textile, provisioning, and alcohol branches prominent. Accompanying these were persons from the professional and service sectors. The large number of farmers taking the oath is striking. The earlier act

---

[51] NLI, MS 27,571, pp. 230, 232; *FDJ*, 7 Mar., 3–6 July 1793.
[52] NLI, MS 27,571, p. 233; *CG*, 23 July 1793.
[53] *CG*, 15–18 May 1793.
[54] The Catholic qualification rolls 1793–6 for Munster and Leinster (NA, 1A 52 76,78), from which the following figures have been computed.

of 1778 had benefited them by conceding greater rights in relation to the granting and receiving of leases and to the disposal of lands, while the act of 1782 allowed Catholics to take and dispose of lands on the same terms as Protestants. The main significance of the 1793 act was political in that it conferred on Catholics who registered their freeholds as being worth at least 40*s*. per annum, the right to vote in elections. Already, before the act had passed, the political advantages to be gained by a restoration of the franchise were recognized locally. In January 1793 Nicholas Maher of Thurles, a tenant on the Ryan of Inch estate, was requesting his landlord to change his term of years into a freehold with a view to availing of the revived franchise, and there are other cases.[55] One of the effects of the renewal of the electoral franchise to Catholics was to assist in the restoration of the Mathew family to political prominence in the county.

The next phase of Catholic pressure for relief from the remaining disabilities began in 1795. In January of that year Catholics from a number of Tipperary towns and parishes petitioned parliament.[56] This petition sought to take advantage of the declared preference of the new lord-lieutenant, Lord Fitzwilliam, in favour of full concessions to Catholics. The main focus of attention on the issue locally was the calling of a meeting of freeholders in Cashel in April in order to devise the best method of advancing Catholic demands. The fact that an open meeting for this purpose was held is instructive as it indicates Catholics mobilizing their influence behind a major issue at county level for the first time after 1793. The mixed meeting agreed unanimously to petition for the removal of the remaining restrictive statutes on Catholics which placed them 'beneath the rank of citizens', and by doing so to disclaim 'on the part of the Protestants of the county of Tipperary any wish for distinction in consequence of their religion'.[57] This petition was presented to the House of Commons and to the king.[58]

County meetings had traditionally been divisive and in the context of the 1790s they were avoided by many Protestants particularly when the matter of concessions to Catholics was under

---

[55] N. Maher to G. Ryan, 23 Jan. 1793 (Ryan papers).
[56] *Comms. Jnl. (Ire.)*, xvi. 30–2; *Parliamentary register*, 15 (1795), 51–2, 55.
[57] *Parliamentary register*, 15 (1795), 164.
[58] Ibid.; Camden to Portland, 27 Apr. 1795 (PRO, HO, 100/57).

discussion. The Cashel meeting was badly attended by Protestants, especially by those from the north of the county. By 1795 Protestants were divided on how to proceed with the Catholic issue in the light of the act of 1793. Some were in favour of further relief, like Revd Anthony Armstrong of Emly who, writing to Charles Agar, archbishop of Cashel, in advance of the Cashel meeting, expressed his wish that 'no man s[houl]d be deprived of his civil liberty on acc[oun]t of his religious persuasion', and that it was his intention to 'promote Catholic emancipation as far as can be done consistent with Protestant security'.[59] Others, however, like Revd Patrick Hare of Cashel and Lord Kingsborough, opposed any advance in Catholic claims. At the Cashel meeting both were prominent in speaking out on the issue, but found themselves in a minority on the day.[60] In between these two extremes were those who were undecided on the matter and did not know how to react. To the regret of some Protestants this group included the high sheriff in 1795, Peter Holmes. Significantly, Holmes unlike sheriffs in some other counties, seemed reluctant to oppose outright the holding of such a meeting. He sought advice from Agar who had been involved in making direct representations to the king that the admission of Catholics to parliament would be contrary to his coronation oath, and who opposed further relief.[61] The experience of 1795 showed Protestants to be in disarray on the Catholic question, there was no evident reaction from the northern gentry which had been so marked in October 1792, and the voice of hard-line Protestant opinion was passing to people like Revd Patrick Hare, possibly under Agar's tutelage, and Kingsborough. Despite carrying the issue locally, at national level Grattan's bill advocating complete emancipation was defeated in May with the minority, including John Bagwell, John and Francis Hely-Hutchinson, Thomas Barton, and Sir Thomas Osborne, voting in its favour.[62]

Concessions to Catholics in 1792 and 1793 were carried through

[59] Armstrong to the archbishop of Cashel, 28 Mar. 1795 (Agar papers, 21 m 57, box 2).

[60] Revd P. Hare to the archbishop of Cashel, 8 Apr. 1795 (Agar papers).

[61] P. Holmes to [the archbishop of Cashel], 27 Mar., 6 Apr. 1795 (Agar papers). Agar supported the lord chancellor, John Fitzgibbon, earl of Clare, in his direct representations to the king that the admission of Catholics to parliament would be contrary to his coronation oath (Malcomson, *Foster*, 424–7, esp. 427).

[62] *FLJ*, 16–20 May 1795.

without widespread sectarian hostility. In fact sectarianism was not a major component in upper-class or popular relationships in the 1790s in Tipperary. What resistance to change there was came from the northern half of the county where there was denser rural Protestant settlement. The 1831 census returns show that Protestants formed less than 5 per cent of the total county population. In only twelve parishes did the percentage range between 5–10 per cent; in seven between 11–20 per cent; and in only two cases (Borrisokane and Cloghjordan) did it exceed 20 per cent.[63] Numerically Protestants were strongest in the towns of Clonmel, Cashel, Nenagh, Roscrea, Thurles, and Tipperary; and they had a substantial though smaller presence in Cahir, Carrick, Fethard, Killenaule, Newport, and Templemore. Protestant rural communities were most in evidence in the parishes in the north. Thus out of twenty-six parishes (including urban parishes) containing over 200 Protestants, fifteen were situated in the northern baronies. Outside the northern half of the county Protestant rural communities were few, the main ones being at Kilcooley, Ballintemple, and Shanrahan.

It is in the northern area that sectarianism emerges. In 1797 some appearance of sympathy with orangeism among Protestant craftsmen in Nenagh manifested itself, and in 1798 fear of an Orange attack drove Catholics from their homes near Templemore.[64] However, such sympathy did not develop into a more radically politicized stance as it did in north Wexford. Certainly orangeism received no cognizance among the major political interests in the county. The high sheriff, Thomas Judkin Fitzgerald, was determined to discourage the emergence of an Orange faction in the county and, in the context of 1798 and the individual concerned, such a determination counted for a good deal.[65] No massacre of Protestants took place despite retrospective reports that this had been the intention at Ballintemple in 1797 and 1798, and at Kilcooley in 1798.[66] This was also despite the claim by Musgrave that the conspiracy in the county was promoted by

---

[63] 1831 census, tabulated from Nolan (ed.), *Tipperary*, 283–7.
[64] NA, RP, 620/33/104; SCP, 1017/52.
[65] NA, RP, 620/41/53.
[66] Ibid. 620/47/126; Hawarden to the archbishop of Cashel, 23 Mar. 1799 (Agar papers); TCD, Barker Ponsonby papers, P1/11/28.

propertied Catholics and clergy and that it had been frustrated by the exertions of the sheriff.[67]

The Catholic issue emerged in the county's electoral politics in the 1790s. Prior to the 1790 election predictions were that Prittie would be returned and a keen contest was expected for the second seat between Daniel Toler, the other sitting member, and Francis James Mathew, Lord Llandaff's eldest son.[68] In the event, however, Prittie declined going forward and instead sponsored John Bagwell as a candidate.[69] At the close of the poll on 26 May Toler had 1,491 votes, Mathew 845, and Bagwell 776 with the first two declared elected.[70] Bagwell, although he was assured of a seat in parliament by virtue of his election for Doneraile borough, petitioned against the Tipperary return.[71] In January 1792, after a long delay in disposing of the petition, Mathew's original majority of 69 was eliminated and Bagwell was given a majority of nineteen, thereby returning him in Mathew's stead.[72] This was a major setback for the pro-Catholic Mathews, for at the opening of the 1790s two ultra-Protestants represented the county. It also represented a personal failure for the Mathew family for they proved unable to retake one of the county seats last held by them in 1782. The result in 1790 was reminiscent of that in 1761 when a Mathew victory was overturned. To add insult to injury Bagwell was appointed to the prestigious position of colonel of the new county militia, as constituted in 1793, much to the declared annoyance of the Mathews who had made their strong preference for the position known to government.[73]

The exclusion of the Mathews from the county representation was temporary however, for in August 1796 Francis Mathew was elected without opposition to fill the vacancy occasioned by the death of Daniel Toler.[74] This development was fortuitous as it restored the balance to county politics and ensured that no contest

---

[67] R. Musgrave, *Memoirs of the different rebellions in Ireland from the arrival of the English* (Dublin, 1801), 52–3.

[68] Falkland, *Parliamentary representation* (Dublin, 1790), 93–4; *FLJ*, 27 Feb.–3 Mar. 1790.   [69] *LC*, 26 Apr. 1790; *EC*, 10 May 1790.

[70] King's Inns Library, MS 39 D, fo. 127ᵛ; *FLJ*, 5–8, 12–15, 19–22, 22–6, 26–9 May 1790; *FDJ*, 11–13, 13–15, 18–20, 20–2 May, 1–3 June 1790; *EC*, 17, 20, 27, 31 May 1790; *CEP*, 20, 24, 31 May 1790.

[71] *Comms. Jnl. (Ire.)*, xiv. 12, 32–3.

[72] *Comms. Jnl. (Ire.)*, xiv. 98; xv. pt. 1, 11; *FLJ*, 12–16 Feb. 1791.

[73] PRO, HO, 100/44/151–9; *FLJ*, 24–7 Apr. 1793.

[74] *FLJ*, 29 June–2 July, 10–13 Aug. 1796.

occurred in the general election of 1797 when Bagwell and Mathew were returned unopposed.[75] By the mid-1790s the harmonization of county politics which this outcome reflects can be attributed to national and local factors. Nationally the gentry as a whole, given the context of an attempted French invasion in 1796, were anxious to exhibit their patriotism, and therefore with the major exception of Wexford, shunned possible electoral contests in 1797 which might appear anti-patriotic.[76] Locally, Bagwell's espousal of the Catholic cause since 1792 won him much favour among Catholics and liberal Protestants. Of mercantile background, Bagwell operated from a narrow electoral base in the south of the county, and had little influence among the majority Protestant freeholders of the north whose interest went either for Prittie or Toler. Hoping to expand his influence Bagwell opportunely backed the Catholic cause in the hope of extending his political interest, though as a Dissenter he may have been influenced by contemporary Presbyterian radicalism which advocated Catholic rights. This flirtation with the Catholic cause did not outlast the Union debate, but while it persisted in the 1790s it served to reduce the prospect of contest and division. In contrast to Wexford, where the liberals were displaced and the initiative was in the hands of the ultra-Protestants in county politics as a result of the 1797 election, in Tipperary a balance of the two was achieved.

3. Radicalism

In the absence of major agrarian disturbances, in the absence of serious division over the granting of concessions to Catholics, and because politics in the county remained cohesive, what then is the context in relation to the development of political radicalism in the county in the 1790s?

It has been a common assertion of Irish historical writing that there was no rebellion in Tipperary in 1798 comparable to that in

[75] NLI, MS 27,571, 270; King's Inns Library, MS 39 D, fo. 127ᵛ.
[76] G. C. Bolton, *The passing of the Irish act of union* (Oxford, 1966), 27–30; K. Whelan, 'The religious factor in the 1798 rebellion in county Wexford', in P. O'Flanagan, P. Ferguson, and K. Whelan (eds.), *Rural Ireland 1600–1900: Modernisation and change* (Cork, 1987), 65–6; Cullen, 'The 1798 rebellion', 104–5.

Leinster and elsewhere.[77] Traditionally Tipperary has been regarded as an anomaly in the 1790s. The fact that no rebellion of serious proportions manifested itself there in 1798 has seemed peculiar, given the county's earlier experience of rural unrest. The degree to which Catholics could promote their claims and benefit from their results when achieved, without provoking a concerted Protestant backlash comparable in scale to the early 1760s, was vital. The ease with which Catholics received official recognition of their social and economic status, reflected in a high grand-jury membership, was instrumental in creating cohesion among the landed class during a period when new influences were intruding from outside. It meant that Catholics were not alienated from the *status quo* and thus were not predisposed to recruitment into leadership positions in the United Irishmen as happened else-where. Rather, Catholic sympathies at a broader level were successfully channelled into the realm of traditional politics whereby the liberal Protestant interest, epitomized by the Mathews, utilized the increased enfranchisement of the Catholics to consolidate and extend its alignment with that body.

The absence of sectarian rivalry in the 1790s becomes explicable when one considers that the concessions to Catholics achieved in that decade represented not a beginning but a continuation and part culmination of a process which had begun in mid-century. In the interim the extent of ultra-Protestant resistance to concessions had diminished considerably, shown by the absence of an active junta around Clonmel in the 1790s and by the conversion of the Bagwells to Catholic relief, though admittedly this was in expectation of short-term political advantage. Additionally during the decade there was no pattern of the falling-in of leases among Protestant middlemen, the non-renewal of which in Wexford contributed to a sharpening of attitudes among that class there.[78] Rather, resistance came to manifest itself in the north where the Protestant population was higher than the county average. Despite evidence of the advance of Defender ideas from the midlands, of the expression of United Irishman ideas transported from the

[77] C. Dickson, *The Wexford rising in 1798, its causes and its course* (Tralee, 1955), 4; Cullen, 'The 1798 rebellion', 93.

[78] K. Whelan, 'Politicisation in county Wexford and the origin of the 1798 rebellion', in H. Gough and D. Dickson (eds.), *Ireland and the French Revolution* (Dublin, 1990), 160–1.

north of Ireland, of only one United leader in the region, Harvey Morris, and of some Orange sympathies in one or two centres, nevertheless all these elements did not coalesce to produce a conflagration comparable to the Leinster experience.

Four factors contributed to this situation. First, whatever the retrospective claims of the sheriff, Thomas Judkin Fitzgerald, the Nenagh gentry and others, Defender and United Irishman organization in the region does not appear to have been elaborate. Secondly, Harvey Morris in north Tipperary was exceptional for Protestants there did not experience the rivalry of Catholic middlemen which in Wexford presaged disaster. Large Catholic middlemen were concentrated in the centre and south of the county where rural Protestant settlement was sparse, so that the pre-conditions for conflict at this level were absent. Thirdly, orangeism was not subscribed to extensively by Protestants who felt themselves threatened and it was actively discouraged by the sheriff where it appeared. Finally, the north of the county was not as strongly involved in cereal cultivation at this time as were the areas adjoining the River Suir, especially around Clonmel. It therefore did not experience the downturn in prices after the withdrawal of the subsidies in 1797 as did regions in the south. Had the north had a closer involvement in commercial grain production and a greater presence of Catholic middlemen, then the events of 1798 might have been different.

Despite the fact that no outright large-scale rebellion material- ized it is evident that there was some initial sympathy for republican objectives in the early 1790s. In July 1791, for instance, a numerous and respectable number of gentry from the Tipperary town district met there to mark the anniversary of the French revolution.[79] After the formation of the United Irishmen in October 1791 in Belfast, it remained strongest there and in Dublin. Attempts were made, however, to contact and encourage radical groups in the provinces. By January 1792 contact had been made with such a group in Nenagh and in March the Tipperary United Irishmen met in Clonmel where, according to Leonard McNally who was present, it 'promised to become extremely numerous'.[80] In June 1792 the secretary of the local society was

---

[79] *FLJ*, 20–4 July 1791.
[80] *AH*, 17 (1949), 8, 20, 40; NA, RP, 620/19/44.

written to from Dublin 'encouraging them in a pursuit of the grand object as that body, it is supposed, will consist of many hundreds in a very short time'.[81] Clonmel and Nenagh were the two centres where radical groups receptive to United Irish ideas developed earliest.

Some prominent Catholics were associated with the movement at this early stage. Such involvement is explicable, as Maureen Wall has demonstrated, because Catholics in addition to pressing their demands at a constitutional level with the government, were also responsive to the prospects for promoting claims through the United Irishman organization, at least in 1792.[82] This dual involvement accounts for the presence of some Catholics from Tipperary in the United Irishmen in the early 1790s. It is known that three such persons took the oath and joined the Society at a meeting in Dublin on 15 December 1792: Mr Lidwell, Mr Lew (Lowe ?), and Laurence Smith of Carrick.[83] Smith was a wealthy merchant, prominent locally in the advancement of Catholic claims, being one of the county delegates selected for the Catholic convention in 1792, and he was also one of the first four Catholics to be chosen for grand jury membership in 1793. Mr Lidwell is very likely George Lidwell of Dromard, a large Protestant head-tenant on the Mathew estate, a liberal in politics, who belonged to a family intermarried with the Lalor, Scully, and O'Brien-Butler families, members of which were closely involved in the promotion of the Catholic cause.[84] The identity and status of Mr Lew or Lowe has not been determined. These three were introduced to the meeting by Thomas Addis Emmet whose association with them probably derived from family and landed connections in Tipperary, and because of his contacts with prominent Catholics there through correspondence.[85] The Emmet connection was an important one and the three persons concerned were of some standing. But there is no evidence to suggest that their involvement in the United movement persisted after the achievement of major concessions for Catholics in 1793.

[81] *AH*, 17 (1949), 26.
[82] M. Wall, 'The United Irish movement', *Historical Studies*, 5 (1965), 130.
[83] *AH*, 17 (1949), 47, 49.
[84] NLI, MS 19,822, 78–84; Burke's, *Irish family records* (London, 1976), 726.
[85] NLI, MS 10,752; NA, RP, 620/15/2/1; T. A. Emmet, *The Emmet family* (New York, 1898), 6–7, 9.

The progress of radical ideas among the rural classes in Tipperary was far less advanced in the early 1790s than elsewhere. A government report on the spread of defenderism compiled in July 1795 excludes Tipperary from the list of counties affected.[86] Only with the repressive legislation introduced in early 1796 and the dissemination of radical ideas brought by Catholics fleeing the northern counties, does radicalism begin to infiltrate the county. According to Lord Waterford, writing in September 1796, the upper class, the middle class, the merchants and farmers were loyal, but the shopkeepers of Carrick and other towns were the most likely to prove disaffected.[87] The towns apart, it was in north Tipperary that the new ideas infiltrated most, largely as a spill-over from the spread of defenderism into the midlands in 1792–3. Northerners from Antrim were reported to have passed through Nenagh in September 1796 on their way to Cork via Cashel.[88] Oath-taking became more common in the Nenagh and Roscrea districts in the months following and by April 1797 confirmation of the spread of United activities to the county was forthcoming from government.[89]

Such radical ideas, which were millenarian in tone, stressed non-payment of rents and tithes, the prospect of French aid, and equal division of land.[90] These separatist notions were introduced into the county from two sources. The Tipperary militia, which was on duty in Derry in 1797, picked up treasonable notions there, with one Derry magistrate remarking that 'great numbers' of them had acknowledged themselves as Unitedmen.[91] As there was little attempt to purge militia regiments of treason before they departed from Ulster, the Tipperary militiamen on their return home carried the separatist message back.[92] Printed papers contained the oath and promises to make the people 'all rich and happy' were distributed in the county by persons from the north of Ireland dressed as pedlars.[93] Despite the infiltration of ideas by means of

[86] PRO, HO, 100/58/198.
[87] Kent RO, Pratt papers, U 840/174/12.   [88] NA, RP, 620/25/123.
[89] PRO, HO, 100/69/199; NA, RP, 620/29/28; *FLJ*, 1–5 Apr. 1797.
[90] NA, RP, 620/30/257.   [91] NA, RP, 620/23/190.
[92] M. Elliott, *Partners in revolution: The United Irishmen and France* (New Haven and London, 1982), 129.
[93] NA, RP, 620/30/257; Cooke to the archbishop of Cashel, 3 June 1797 (Agar papers); see also J. S. Donnelly, 'Propagating the cause of the United Irishmen', *Studies*, 69 (1980), 5–23.

these two sources and some evidence from the Clonmel area of swearing activity, the Defender and United movements were weak organizationally in the county in mid-1797. In May 1798 Camden, the lord-lieutenant, could confidently report of Tipperary that 'as the system was not organized there, so it has been more easily checked'.[94] The fundamental cause was the general absence of major agrarian issues, like tithes, which would have provided an essential layer of grievance upon which a more separatist political movement could have thrived. Indeed it was reported that the United Irishmen had 'to dwell with peculiar energy on the supposed oppressiveness of tythes' and had to contrive a series of agrarian outrages such as the burning of cereal crops and the houghing of cattle in order to win support among the peasantry in Munster.[95] In this sense much of the violence which occurred may have been artificially created having no other purpose than to win over the peasantry to a greater political commitment.

The pre-conditions necessary for a radical political movement to develop locally did not emerge. Before 1799 the county was comparatively free of serious economic upset, though there were years of difficulty in 1793 and 1797 for instance. Harvests were generally good, and the land market was stable. Serious and organized agrarian unrest was in abeyance. Rent was not a major source of grievance. The unsettled state of the country from late spring to late summer 1798 was used as an excuse by some tenants to delay paying their rents, and some agents like Peter Walsh on the Barker estate at Kilcooley had difficulty getting rents in. In July Walsh remarked to Barker that 'the rents came in very slowly'.[96] However, Walsh's appreciation of the novelty of the situation and his stressing that rents were paid punctually for many years back, points to the fact that prompt rent payment was the general norm for most of the decade. Evidence of opposition to tithes appeared in the summer of 1793 but it seems to have been part of a general agitation lacking specific direction and stemmed from the militia riots of the period.[97] Serious resistance to tithes did not re-emerge until after 1798 when less favourable economic prospects made them appear onerous. There was a rise in the amount of parish and county cess in the 1790s. Yet despite this rise

[94] PRO, HO, 100/76/173.   [95] *Comms. Jnl. (Ire.)*, xvii. pt. 2, p. dcccxxx.
[96] TCD, Barker Ponsonby papers, P2/3/4–6.
[97] *Proceedings of the parliament of Ireland* (1793), iii. 462.

neither was prominent as declared grievances, the implication being that rising incomes were sufficient to absorb these incidental charges.

With the traditional forms of local taxation (tithe, parish, and county cess) not constituting an issue of grievance, what provoked such expressions of discontent as occurred? Apparently novel forms of taxation (or the fear of such being imposed) and their associated obligations, provoked some hostility. The most innovative new imposition was that legislated for by the militia act of 1793 (33 Geo. III, c. 22). A specific number of men were to be raised by ballot in each parish and the whole to form the county regiment. In May 1793 a meeting at Cashel decided on the allocation of 560 men to the 140 parishes in eleven baronies based on the proportion of houses in each barony and parish.[98] An average of four men were recruited from each parish which was not unduly onerous. Rather it was the compulsory nature of enlistment which provoked popular resistance, though its scale in Tipperary was nothing compared to elsewhere in Ireland.[99] There were also fears that the militia when embodied would be obliged to serve outside Ireland and this contributed to resistance.[100] A further indication of hostility to the measure was the formation of a company in Clonmel in late May which offered insurance for those who wished to avoid service, if chosen by ballot, by providing substitutes in their stead at prescribed rates.[101] In the face of this opposition the government dropped the ballot method of enlistment, following which recruitment proceeded apace without opposition in June and July at locations like Carrick, Roscrea, and Tipperary.[102] Thus, despite some initial resistance to its compulsory character, the militia act was successfully implemented.

At another level the formation of the militia, because its membership was largely Catholic, was to pose problems with regard to public worship. In 1795 one Hyland, a private in the Irish Light Dragoons, was court-martialled at Carrick-on-Suir to receive 200 lashes because, on the advice of his priest, he had

[98] *CG*, 15–18 May 1793.
[99] Ibid. 29 May–1 June 1793; T. Bartlett, 'An end to moral economy', *Past and Present*, 99 (1983), 41–2, 59. [100] *CG*, 8–12 June 1793.
[101] Ibid. 29 May–1 June 1793.
[102] Ibid. 12–15 June 1793; *FDJ*, 16 July 1793.

refused to attend Protestant services. This acted as a prelude to
another case in November 1796 when controversy arose because of
an allegation that Catholics in the militia stationed at Ardfinnan
were being forced to attend Protestant services.[103] The allegation
had no substance, and despite the attempt of the new Catholic
bishop of Waterford and Lismore, Thomas Hussey, to project the
issue into a more general cause by embodying the episode into his
controversial pamphlet of 1797, *A pastoral letter to the Catholic
clergy of the united dioceses of Waterford and Lismore*, sectarian
conflict did not ensue. Similarly, Hussey's attack on the Established
Church of Ireland did not lead to a repetition of attitudes similar to
the 1760s.[104] This is indicative of the maturity of attitude which had
taken place locally since the 1760s.

The cost of maintaining the militia was borne by central funds so
that the localities did not have to bear a direct burden in this
respect. The larger cost of maintenance to the county only became
a reality with an additional act of 1795 (35 Geo. III, c. 8) which
augmented the militia by about one-third and which specified that
parishes failing to meet the quota of men had to pay £10 per man
short in lieu. In addition, by a further act of the same year (35
Geo. III, c. 2), counties were obliged to defray the cost of
maintaining the immediate family of the recruit during service
outside the county. In later years the amount levied on the county
for this purpose of family maintenance increased fourfold in four
years from £190 in 1795–6 to £889 in 1798–9.[105]

So far as the levying of a cess on parishes where the quota of
men was deficient is concerned, by early March 1796 it is clear that
there was extensive resistance, spread over several baronies.[106] As
Dickson has indicated the militia-maintenance cess was one
element in the growing burden of taxation in the 1790s with the
Munster counties to the fore in their resistance to the tax.[107]

---

[103] *Correspondence of Edmund Burke*, ix. 140–3.

[104] Thomas Hussey, *A pastoral letter to the Catholic clergy of the united dioceses of Waterford and Lismore* (Waterford, 1797), 9–10; see also D. Keogh, 'Thomas Hussey, Bishop of Waterford and Lismore, 1797–1803 and the rebellion of 1798', in W. Nolan and Thomas P. Power (eds.), *Waterford: history and society* (Dublin, 1992), 410–15.   [105] *Comms. Jnl. (Ire.)*, pp. xvii, ccxx.

[106] NLI, MS 7331, 8.

[107] D. Dickson, 'Taxation and disaffection in late eighteenth century Ireland', in S. Clark and J. S. Donnelly (eds.), *Irish peasants, violence and political unrest* (Madison and Manchester, 1983), 50–1, 54–5.

Opposed on the grounds that it was an innovative and novel measure and occurring in a year (1796) which was difficult in other respects, resistance did not repeat itself in later years. Ironically it was after the disbanding of the Tipperary militia in May 1802 that the unemployed militia recruits contributed to the violence and disturbances then becoming more serious again. The summer of 1793 when agitation over the militia arose also witnessed the expression of local fears that parliament had passed a land tax and a tax on cattle, fears which had to be countered by public statements from the gentry.[108] Further local hostility to taxation became evident in 1796 in Clonmel over attempts by the rector to gain a re-evaluation of the amounts paid by householders for 'minister's money', the urban equivalent to tithes.[109]

More serious in its local implications was the withdrawal of the subsidy scheme for the carriage of grain and flour to Dublin. By an act of 1797 (37 Geo. III, c. 24), from September 1797 the subsidies were to cease and be replaced by an export bounty through Dublin as already applied to other Irish ports. This alteration had a material effect on the malt trade in Wexford where production was closely dependent on the subsidies and on the demands of the Dublin alcohol industry.[110] The cessation of the subsidies had some of the effects in Tipperary they had in Wexford, where the resultant dislocation to economic activity in the spring of 1798 contributed to unrest there. The fact that Dublin was no longer available as a ready market meant that farmers were more dependent on the local market which was depressed. Revd John Garnett, writing from Thurles in early March 1798, commented that 'the stoppage of the bounty for the land carriage for corn, meal, and malt to Dublin lays them under a necessity of selling their grain at home for whatever pittance they can get'.[111] In addition, a prospective rise in the amount of duty on bere and barley from 12s. 9d. to 16s. per barrel, to come into effect after 25 March 1798, was having an equally bad effect in the county. This was because with barley prices to the producer depressed at 5s. to

[108] *CG*, 27–31 July 1793.
[109] Burke MS (Mount Melleray) 71 (v); NA, OP, 18/48; and for the background to the tax see Power, 'A minister's money', 183–200.
[110] T. Powell,'An economic factor in the Wexford rebellion of 1798', *Studia Hibernica*, 16 (1976), 145–53.
[111] Garnett to the archbishop of Cashel, 7 [March] 1798 (Agar papers).

6s., farmers were finding it hard to make up their rents.[112] It was this conjunction of detrimental circumstances in the spring of 1798 which made sections of the rural community more receptive to radical ideas. This abrupt alteration was noted by Revd Garnett when he reported that 'till lately this union [Thurles] was well effected, but now such a change has taken place that most of the lower order of people and several who were a year or two ago in a comfortable way have been infected with defenderism'.[113] Thus the withdrawal of the bounty and the imposition of the extra duty on bere and barley were the ultimate causes of this.

So serious was the economic situation that in April in Carrick, a textile town affected by the credit crisis of 1797, the grain merchant Matthew Scott gave over 1,000 barrels of oats to be sold in meal under the market price to the poverty-stricken of the district, and in June he was arranging to raise a large sum of money to be distributed in small loans to the textile workers of the town.[114] With the exception of a few minor outbreaks, the county was quiet during the summer. With a good harvest in prospect large numbers of countrymen in south Tipperary and around Callan accepted amnesty and surrendered their arms in order to take employment in saving it.[115] The brief association of local elements with a more radical agitation in February and March 1798 was not permanent. It took two successive bad years in 1799 and 1800 to produce a renewal of widespread rural agitation.

In Tipperary, as elsewhere in Ireland, concern with the issues of the loyalty of the inhabitants and of law and order were increasingly to the fore in 1797. Raids for arms became more common in March 1798 when houses of the gentry were attacked, notably around Cashel, Templemore, and in the Slievardagh Hills.[116] The effect of these arms raids was to heighten the sense of insecurity among the gentry displayed in their different attempts to

---

[112] Garnett to the archbishop of Cashel, 7 [March] 1798 (Agar papers).
[113] Ibid.   [114] *Comms. Jnl. (Ire.)*, xvii. 116.
[115] NA, SCP, 1017/49; cf. *FLJ*, 4–8 Aug. 1798.
[116] Only three arms attacks are on record for 1793–7 (*FLJ*, 4–8, 25–9 May 1793; *CG*, 22–5 Nov. 1797; resolution dated at Cashel, 21 Dec. 1796, Agar papers). In March and April 1798, however, fifteen attacks are recorded (*FLJ*, 31 Mar.–1 Apr. 1798; NLI, MS 27,571, 275–6; Camden to Portland, 7 Apr. 1798, PRO, HO, 100/76/43–4, Camden to Portland, 28 Mar. 1798, PRO, HO, 100/80; Revd Patrick Hare to the archbishop of Cashel, 4, 21 Mar. 1798, Samuel Alleyn to same, 28 Mar. 1798, Revd Francis Garnett to same, 7 Mar. 1798, all in Agar papers).

deal with the situation. A successful policy of disarming the peasantry was pursued by some with great effect, while in other instances the oath of allegiance was successfully administered by the gentry. In much of the south and south-west of the county order was maintained by Lord Donoughmore. In November 1797 the gentlemen of the area assembled in Clonmel at Donoughmore's request and resolved to keep the disturbances from spreading from adjoining Waterford by the creation of a fund nearing £1,000 to reward those giving information.[117] By late December 1797 he could report to government that 'we are perfectly quiet in this neighbourhood and I have no doubt will continue so'.[118] Gentlemen in other areas of the county also exerted themselves during 1797 to disarm and arrest suspected persons. In north Tipperary the gentry reacted quickly in March 1797 to disturbances around Nenagh by entering into a subscription for the purpose of obtaining information, and the voluntary taking of the oath of allegiance was proposed.[119] By April 1797 Peter Holmes of Nenagh reported to government that 'all appearances of ferment in this district have subsided'.[120] His optimism was justified for as late as February 1798, despite the spread of unrest to other areas in the interim, he could report of the baronies of Upper and Lower Ormond that they were as yet 'untainted with that turbulent and unruly spirit'.[121] In Slievardagh the officers of one of the two yeomanry units operating in the barony resolved in November 1797 to resist the spread of disturbances into their area and for this purpose established a fund of £500 for obtaining information; in December 1797 the gentry of Clanwilliam and Middlethird baronies planned to meet in Cashel for the purpose of adopting the best measures to prevent an appearance of outrages in their area; and in January 1798 Lord Mathew administered the oath of allegiance to over 1,000 people at Golden chapel and others continued to come to him for a similar purpose.[122] The cumulative effect of these gentry exertions was that the county was relatively quiet and subdued at the opening of the auspicious year of 1798.

The events of 1798 in the county were closely influenced by the appointment as high sheriff of Thomas Judkin Fitzgerald. He was

[117] NA, RP, 620/33/90. [118] Ibid. 174; see also *FLJ*, 20–3 Dec. 1797.
[119] NA, RP, 620/29/117. [120] Ibid. 208. [121] NA, SCP, 1017/46.
[122] NA, OP, 43/15/6; TCD, Donoughmore D23 fo. 1; *FLJ*, 15–18 Nov. 1797.

later to claim that had he not adopted severe methods against suspected persons then there would have been a rising to equal that elsewhere. These claims were made after the event to justify his actions, but even impartial evidence indicates that no rebellion of serious proportions occurred. The amount claimed for losses shows how little Tipperary was affected compared to other counties. One source gives five claims amounting to £1,223, and another gives twenty claims totalling £1,577. Yet despite these differing totals the amount for the county was infinitesimal compared to the £306,630 claimed for Wexford, or even the £33,454 claimed in neighbouring Kilkenny. Even the magnitude of this small amount is further reduced when one considers that half of the losses for which Tipperary persons claimed compensation, related to losses sustained outside the county.[123] These figures indicate that there was no rebellion of any magnitude. What is more decisive is the retrospective construction put on events by the sheriff. It was the bizarre, eccentric, and ruthless nature of the sheriff's methods which brought his motives into question, provoked resentment, and left a bitter legacy. His perception of and attitude to popular violence was influenced by the fact that in February 1798 a relative was brutally murdered by rebels.[124] Fitzgerald was recommended for the office of sheriff by the earl of Llandaff with the concurrence of John Bagwell. Fitzgerald accepted the position on condition that government 'enable me to execute the office with spirit in case of invasion', and that he be allowed to return the juries without interference, conditions which were agreed to.[125]

The course of action pursued by the sheriff is easier to appreciate if other factors are considered. March 1798 witnessed an upsurge in attacks for arms and the common opinion was that large sections of the rural community were ready and equipped to rise. The arms attacks stretched in a broad arc from Newport round to Templemore and were directed at gentry houses. Some gentlemen surrendered their arms readily out of fear, one Cashel clergyman remarking that: 'It is said some of them invited the insurgents to come and take their arms.'[121] Others, after resistance,

[123] *Comms. Jnl. (Ire.)*, xviii. pp. ccccvi–ccccvii; xix. pt. i, pp. cccxiv–cccxv.
[124] T. Pakenham, *The year of liberty* (London, 1978), 40–1; Burke, *Irish family records*, 1149.   [125] NA, OP, 43/15/6.
[126] Revd P. Hare to the archbishop of Cashel, 21 Mar. 1798 (Agar papers).

surrendered; while a few successfully repelled the intruders.[127] The quantity of arms taken was considerable. After the event the sheriff put the number of arms surrendered to him in the county at 9,500 pikes and 1,500 stand of arms, figures which he later inflated to thirty-six cart-loads of pikes and 22,000 stand of arms.[128] The gentry of Nenagh claimed that ten cart-loads of pike heads were seized in the baronies of Upper and Lower Ormond, and Owney and Arra.[129] By the end of March it was the sheriff's estimate that the total number of firearms in the possession of the disturbers stood at between 300 and 400 stand.[130] The consequences of this activity were twofold. First, gentlemen robbed of arms could no longer participate in their local yeomanry corps whose role was in consequence either curtailed or eliminated.[131] Secondly, gentlemen over a wide area were left defenceless, a situation which left them no option but to flee to the towns for security.[132] A vacuum of authority in certain areas resulted which had the effect of encouraging the disturbers in their purpose. The absence of their social superiors meant that a traditional deterrent to violence was forgone and one of the constraints of the 'moral economy' became redundant.

There was an upsurge in serious violence during and after March, and at least two important pitched battles were fought at Dundrum and at Toberadora near Holy Cross.[133] At Cahir 800 insurgents were reported to have entered the town, plundered houses, and paraded the streets 'as a regular army', while near Clogheen they attacked the military and yeomanry.[134] However, the commander-in-chief of the army, Sir Ralph Abercromby, who toured the disturbed areas in the south in April, put the figure for those who entered Cahir at 300.[135] Nevertheless, because of the

---

[127] S. Alleyn to same, 28 Mar. 1798 (Agar papers).
[128] *FDJ*, 18 Apr. 1799; *Report of an interesting case in which Mr Francis Doyle was plaintiff* (Dublin, 1808), 35.
[129] *FDJ*, 18 Apr. 1799.
[130] PRO, HO, 100/80/156; *FLJ*, 31 Mar.–4 Apr. 1798.
[131] PRO, HO, 100/80/156–7; S. Alleyn to the archbishop of Cashel, 31 Mar. 1798 (Agar papers).
[132] Revd P. Hare to the archbishop of Cashel, 4, 21 Mar. 1798 (Agar papers).
[133] Garnett to Cashel, 7 [Mar. 1798] (Agar papers); Hare to same, 21 Mar. 1798 (ibid.); Alleyn to same, 28 Mar. 1798 (ibid.); PRO, HO, 100/80/157. For Dundrum: *FLJ*, 30 Mar.–1 Apr. 1798; for Toberadora: *FLJ*, 30 Mar.–1 Apr. 1798; *WHM*, Apr. 1798, 381; Alleyn to Cashel, 31 Mar. 1798 (Agar papers); NA, OP, 78/10.   [134] PRO, HO, 100/76/43–4.   [135] Ibid. 125–6.

serious dimensions of the situation the entire county was proclaimed on 2 April, thereby making it subject to the provisions of
the insurrection act.[136] This provided for the death penalty for
administering illegal oaths and for the imposition of a curfew and
arms searches in proclaimed districts. Following on this a notice
issued from Cashel on 6 April to the inhabitants of the county
through the military commander of the district, Sir James Duff,
had an important influence. It required those who had robbed
arms to surrender them within ten days, or else troops would be
authorized to live by free quarter among the people until the arms
were given up.[137] An indication of the public response to this order
was when William Latham made 900 men in his parish of
Ballysheehan assemble and lay down their arms, ask forgiveness,
and take the oath of allegiance, and the parish was quiet
thereafter; by early May Sir John Carden had nearly all the stolen
arms and pikes in the Templemore area delivered up; and the
inhabitants of the parish of Templetenny (which was very
disturbed), under the influence of their priest, voluntarily surrendered their arms.[138]

The consequence of this campaign of disarming was that
potential rebels were rendered inactive in many areas, and the
arrest of the suspected leaders of the disturbances further tended
to defeat the prospect of outright insurrection.[139] By mid-May the
consensus locally and at government level was that stable
conditions were restored. So much did Lord Llandaff and the
sheriff feel this to be the case that they were recommending that
the army might in large measure be withdrawn, and the sheriff
confidently issued a proclamation requiring all those who had fled
to the towns to return to their rural domiciles.[140] The only trouble
spots to remain were in Upper and Lower Ormond and it was to
these areas that the sheriff directed his energies for the remainder
of May. This was the area which had proven receptive to the
spread of defenderism from the midlands. It was also the area in
which United sympathies were strongest, with Harvey Morris
being regularly chosen as the county representative from May 1796

---

[136] 36 Geo. III, c. 20; PRO, HO, 100/76/125–6, 100/79/348–9.
[137] TCD, *Proclamations* (Press A7 18, no. 11).
[138] NA, OP, 78/10; RP, 620/37/26; see also *FLJ*, 4–7 Apr., 19–23 May 1798.
[139] NA, RP, 620/36/122.
[140] NA, RP, 620/37/26; PRO, HO, 100/76/173.

and having command of a Nenagh group of rebels.[141] In addition great quantities of arms remained unsurrendered around Nenagh, but as a result of the sheriff's activities in north Tipperary large numbers of persons surrendered arms and gave information against those who swore them, who made their pikes, and who their leaders were.[142] This successful disarming of the north of the county was timely for after the rebellion began in Leinster on 23–4 May and emissaries were sent from Offaly into Ormond to get it to rise, no support was forthcoming.[143] Tipperary remained quiet all through June into late July, with emissaries trying to provoke revolt being handed over to the sheriff, and with an absence of reports of persons leaving the county to join in the main theatre of action in Leinster.[144]

Ironically the two most serious events in Tipperary occurred long after the rebellion elsewhere was suppressed. The first of these was on 16 July when, according to one witness, 2,000 persons from the Glen of Aherlow, Cahir, and other parishes were to assemble for an attack on Cashel, but the numbers actually assembling were deemed insufficient so they dispersed.[145] The other major incident was on 23 July at Slievnamon when a party of rebels led by John Power of Ballinaclogh, farmer, were routed by a party of the military.[146] Plans to attack a number of towns in the south of the county and Roscrea in the north were uncovered.[147] In late August the appearance of the French in Mayo provided the stimulus for some renewed activity. The most serious was the appearance of the United leader Harvey Morris in the county, but any plan of his to lead the disaffected towards a conjunction with the rebels in Connacht was forestalled.[148] Thus despite the traumatic events elsewhere between May and August, Tipperary did not participate in the general conflagration. What marks Tipperary off is that the peak of law and order activity was reached in June after, not before, the rebellion began.

[141] *Castlereagh memoirs and correspondence*, ed. C. Vane (London, 1848–53), ii. 94–6.
[142] W. Knox, bishop of Killaloe to the archbishop of Cashel, 6 May 1798 (Agar papers); NA, RP, 620/37/106, SCP, 1017/68. [143] NA, SCP, 1017/47.
[144] NA, RP, 620/38/147, SCP, 1017/48. [145] NA, RP, 620/3/22/1.
[146] TCD, MS 7311/1; PRO, HO, 100/77/303; J. Maher, *Romantic Slievenamon in history, folklore, and song* (Mullinahone, 1954), 102–11; *Duanaire Thiobraid Árann* (Dublin, 1981), ed. D. ÓhÓgáin, 63, 93–4; *Cornwallis correspondence*, ed. C. Ross (London, 1859), iii. 374.
[147] NA, SCP, 1017/49–51. [148] NA, RP, 620/3/51/25, 29.

However, the wide powers conveyed under the insurrection act were abused by the sheriff in particular, and because of the low military presence in the county during the summer months, much of the law enforcement was delegated to him. His arbitrary practice of accusing innocent persons of complicity, and his widespread use of flogging for obtaining confessions, provoked a strong reaction from some gentlemen and fear and resentment among the peasantry. His methods at the very least were unorthodox. In May 1798 while at Templemore he made a speech partly in Irish lasting three hours explaining the potential threat which the French posed to the peasantry, and made suspects kneel down before him and pray for the king and then forgave them all their past offences![149] The speech was apparently later published, and because of a misinterpretation of its Irish contents the view became widespread that it contained a declaration of a general massacre of the inhabitants of Clonmel.[150] More unusual still was his scheme to raise a personal corps of 100 men, each one of whom was to be a former United Irishman.[151] Such methods, however novel, were regarded as being a necessary requirement at a critical time. But when some of the sheriff's actions became directed against some of the loyal and well-affected inhabitants, then his tact and motives were called into question.

In an amazing episode in late June the sheriff concurred in the arrest by Col. Deering of Cashel of seven Catholic and four Protestant gentlemen, and in their being charged with being captains and officers of the United Irishmen.[152] This development was extremely serious not merely because those concerned were innocent, but because it displayed the sheriff's willingness to go against the wishes of his patrons the Mathews who did not wish the charges to be proceeded with and who vouched for the integrity of those implicated. It was also recognized by some as an anti-Catholic gesture. This was more obviously the case in respect of Fitzgerald's proceedings in June 1798 against two wealthy Catholic merchants in Carrick: Matthew Scott, grain merchant and Francis Doyle, cloth manufacturer. The former was charged with supplying the Wexford insurgents with pikes hidden in his grain boats,

[149] NA, RP, 620/37/26.
[150] P. De Brún, 'Scriptural instruction in Irish: A controversy of 1830–31', in P. De Brún, S. ÓCoileáin, and P. ÓRiain (eds.), *Folia Gadelica* (Cork, 1983), 150.
[151] NA, RP, 620/37/26.   [152] NA, RP, 620/3/47/1–3.

and the latter also with supplying pikes and being a rebel.[153] The charges had no foundation, but legal actions initiated by both against Fitzgerald for recovery of damages failed because the sheriff was able to resort to the provisions of the indemnity act (39 Geo. III, c. 3) which conferred retrospective legal sanction on actions done outside common law. Not only did the sheriff's actions offend Catholics, but he also antagonized Protestants. The flogging of a Clonmel teacher of French and editor of the *Clonmel Gazette* (the politics of which were pro-Catholic and which served the political interests of the Mathews), Bernard Wright, on suspicion of treason was a case in point for many Clonmel Protestants vouched for Wright's loyalty.[154] Equally serious was the sheriff's burning down in early May of two houses on Lord Hawarden's estate at Dundrum, one of which was owned by a Protestant who had been clerk of the parish; and he issued a warning to the rest of the tenantry that they would be treated in like manner if all arms were not given up within a specified period.[155] Lord Hawarden found the sheriff's behaviour inexplicable and on this basis would no doubt have agreed with Revd Patrick Hare's assessment of Fitzgerald as being 'absolutely a madman'.[156]

Much of this kind of activity served to promote division rather than cohesion among the upper class at a period of crisis. The sheriff's contrasting of the stout resistance offered by Mrs Bunbury in warding off rebels, aided by only two man servants, with the timid behaviour of those gentlemen who fled to the towns, was a challenge to gentry sensibilities and self-respect.[157] His proposal to levy the amount of £137, calculated to be the cost of damage caused in the Ormond baronies, on the rich absentees of the area was also provocative.[158] His attitude and actions were therefore unhelpful and lacked discrimination. It was widely recognized that hitherto quiet areas, like Carrick or Clonmel, with little or no indication of disaffection were plunged into that state in June after the sheriff visited those centres. This was certainly the view both of

---

[153] *The trial of T. J. Fitzgerald esq with proceedings in parliament on his petition* (Dublin, 1799); *A report of an interesting case in which Mr Francis Doyle was plaintiff*; *Comms. Jnl. (Ire.)*, xviii. 116–17.

[154] *The trial of T. J. Fitzgerald*, 5–13; Madden, *Countess of Blessington*, i. 20.

[155] Hawarden to Cashel, 13 May 1798 (Agar papers).

[156] Hare to same, 19 July 1798 (ibid.).

[157] NA, RP, 620/36/26.   [158] NA, RP, 620/37/151.

outside observers and of impartial locals.[159] The cumulative effect of these arbitrary activities was to alienate many influential sections of the loyal community, both Protestant and Catholic.

It is clear that Fitzgerald had at best minority support, for only the Nenagh gentry made a public statement defending his actions. This defence was issued only in February 1799 and was made in the context of the legal actions then being brought against the sheriff for his behaviour.[160] As part of that defence Fitzgerald found it necessary to construe retrospectively the existence of a rebellion in Tipperary in 1798 as a cover for his actions. He was supported by the northern gentry who were the most active in resisting Catholic claims in the early 1790s, but without any ultimate effect.

4. Union and Aftermath

The weight of opinion locally came out strongly in favour of the union in 1799 and 1800. This outcome was achieved despite an inauspicious prelude whereby the two county members, Lord Mathew and John Bagwell, voted against the measure on its first introduction in parliament.[161] An anti-union petition from the county was before the house by 5 February 1799 and Clonmel published resolutions hostile to the proposal.[162] With the anti-unionists earliest in the field the initiative was clearly theirs. Opposition was led by Lord Lismore and Hon. Francis Mathew (commonly called Lord Mathew), Lord Llandaff's son, who with forty-eight others on 14 March, during assize week, requested the sheriff to call a county meeting to consider the matter.[163] This request was successfully resisted by a counter-requisition signed by 192 persons with Catholic support.[164] There was some concern about the desirability of publishing the proceedings of the foregoing request as it was feared by the sheriff, Francis Hely-Hutchinson, that doing so would formally commit those who made a declaration against the measure from altering their opinion

---

[159] A. P. W. Malcomson, *Eighteenth-century Irish official papers in Great Britain* (Belfast, 1973), 186–7; *The trial of T. J. Fitzgerald*, 6, 8; *A report of an interesting case in which Mr Francis Doyle was plaintiff*, 5, 9, 15.

[160] *FDJ*, 18 Apr. 1799.   [161] Bolton, *Union*, 128 n. 1.

[162] *FDJ*, 21 Feb. 1799.   [163] TCD, Donoughmore papers, D6/7.

[164] Ibid., D6/11–14; PRO, HO, 100/86/201–6.

subsequently.[165] However, the government view that publication in the newspapers should ensue prevailed, as it would indicate the weight of property in favour of the measure and that it would have a good effect on influencing the outcome elsewhere in Munster.[166] The result was that the minority anti-unionists appeared discredited by their failure, and their ranks were depleted thereafter.[167] Thus in the first phase of the debate on the issue the pro-unionists carried the day strategically out-manoeuvring their opponents by not acceding to the demand for a county meeting.

The next phase in the debate took place in the summer of 1799. Although government was satisfied with obtaining pro-union signatures, it felt that a timely chosen and carefully managed county meeting productive of a pro-union address would be instrumental in converting the two county MPs away from their opposition stance.[168] Once government received assurances of a successful outcome, a county meeting was called for Clonmel on 10 August. At it Lord Donoughmore spoke in favour of union and proposed that an address be drawn up, in which he was seconded by Lord Ormond. The meeting instructed its two county representatives to support union and both duly made a commitment accordingly.[169] The address expressed the sentiments of the leading propertied interests (calculated at £300,000 per annum), excepting Lords Lismore and Mount Cashell. The Tipperary address was the first sign of support following the initial defeat of the measure in parliament. This was largely because of the support given to it by propertied Catholics in the county. Catholics declared in favour with Thomas Bray, archbishop of Cashel, assuring John Troy of Dublin that he would use his influence for that purpose, and with individual pro-union addresses forthcoming from the Catholics of Tipperary town and Cahir.[170] Clonmel, influenced by Bagwell's enforced conversion, sent up a pro-union address thereby forgoing its previous opposition.[171] The successful outcome of this phase of the debate was due in large measure to Lords Donoughmore and Llandaff. The episode

---

[165] Donoughmore, D48/5.   [166] Ibid., D6/9.
[167] Ibid., D6/17.   [168] *Castlereagh memoirs and correspondence*, ii. 354–5.
[169] PRO, HO, 100/89/142–3; *FLJ*, 24–8 Aug. 1799.
[170] *Castlereagh memoirs and correspondence*, ii. 344–5; *FLJ*, 7–10, 28–31 Aug. 1799; *CA*, 24 Aug. 1799; and for other Catholic pro-union declarations, see *FDJ*, 13 Sept. 1800.   [171] *FLJ*, 14–18 Sept. 1799.

was an embarrassing defeat for the opposition (whose strength in the county has been overstated), led by Lismore who was unwisely egged into this role by his connection with the Ponsonbys.[172] The event bore witness to the ability of Donoughmore and Llandaff to harness the newly enfranchised body of Catholics in their favour on a major political issue, which in essence was intended to be a further concession to Catholics in the expectation of which they had rendered their support. So far as government was concerned the formal accession of the county to the unionist camp deprived the opposition of five votes.[173]

The final phase in the debate took place in April 1800. The intervening period was marked by vacillation on the part of the Bagwell party. Richard Bagwell, John Bagwell's younger son and MP for Cashel (1799–1801), spoke in favour of union in January 1800.[174] In February, however, Bagwell senior, on the instructions of his constituents (some of whom he claimed had formerly supported but now opposed), and encouraged by the expectations held out to him by the opposition leaders, changed sides, declared his opposition, and brought his two sons with him.[175] Following this an attempt was made by Lismore in April to have the county reassemble to debate the matter anew, but this request was successfully countered by Donoughmore on the basis that the issue had already been unanimously decided on in August 1799.[176] This was the final show of opposition to the measure locally.

The county received a high proportion of new peerages for its support of the union: Donoughmore was made an earl, John Toler was created Lord Norbury, and Henry Prittie made Lord Dunalley; and among the peers to represent Ireland in the imperial House of Lords were Donoughmore, Llandaff, and Cahir.[177] The ease with which the strong pro-union lobby carried the issue locally reflects the effectiveness of the identity of interests between liberal Protestants and Catholics responding to a central political issue. In particular, the favoured position enjoyed by Lord Donoughmore among the county's Catholics and clergy

---

[172] Bolton, *Union*, 146, 148–50.
[173] *Cornwallis correspondence*, iii. 125.   [174] Ibid. iii. 163.
[175] Ibid. iii. 180; *Parliamentary register*, 17 (1800), 143; PRO, HO, 100/93/84; Clonmel Museum, Acc. 1985/60a.
[176] Donoughmore, D23, fos. 3–4.
[177] PRO, HO, 100/96/234, 100/97/79; *Cornwallis correspondence*, iii. 256, 286, 318–19.

allowed him to harness their considerable support on an issue which he championed. In contrast, opponents of the measure were a fragmented group made up of disparate elements namely: Bagwell whose position was dictated by motives of personal advancement rather than consistency of policy; Lismore who was influenced by his Ponsonby connection and who on other issues would have sided with the majority view; and Hon. Francis Mathew (Lord Mathew) who was a maverick politically.

The role of Catholics in the union issue particularly, and in Tipperary politics generally, shows that our definition of the parameters of the political nation in the eighteenth century needs to be redefined. The excesses of the 1760s created the context out of which concessions were made, and their achievement contributed to relatively harmonious upper-class relationships in the 1790s. There was a sharp increase in the number of freeholders following the act of 1793, and by 1807 out of 6,500 registered freeholders, 5,500 were Catholic.[178] They held a substantial propertied interest which served to transform Tipperary into a monolithically Catholic county in voting terms, the effects of which were to be seen even before full emancipation in 1829. In the general election of 1802 the two sitting members, Mathew and Bagwell, were returned unopposed with Francis A. Prittie, the other prospective candidate, declining a contest.[179] In the election of 1806, caused by the vacancy created by Mathew's elevation to the peerage consequent on the death of the first earl of Llandaff in August 1806, the Catholic vote was organized with clerical support in favour of Montague Mathew and Francis A. Prittie, which conjunction deterred Bagwell from standing.[180] This was to remain the pattern in the two following contested general elections in 1807 and 1812 with Mathew and Prittie joining to ward off the Bagwell challenge on both occasions.[181]

This pattern is significant because first, it shows that the family best positioned to benefit from the enfranchisement of the Catholics, i.e. the Mathews, used that development to establish a

---

[178] *Southern Reporter* (Cork), 6 June 1807.
[179] *CH*, 14 July 1802.
[180] CDA, Bray papers 1806/8,9 (iii); P. J. Jupp, 'Irish parliamentary elections and the influence of the Catholic vote', *Historical Journal*, 10 (1967), 183–96.
[181] CDA, Bray papers 1807/5; Donoughmore, D31/1; *WM*, 4 May, 8 June 1807; *LJ*, 23–7 May, 30 May–3 June 1807; *Southern Reporter*, 6 June 1807; G. Grace, *A letter to his grace the duke of Richmond* (Clonmel, 1813), app.

prominence in county politics. Previously the family, because of its narrow freeholder base, commanded slim electoral margins but this deficiency was eliminated by the rise of the Catholic vote. This natural sympathy was decisive in the elections of 1807 and 1812. After the 1807 election a meeting of the Catholics at Clonmel acknowledged the 'firm attachment' that subsisted between them and the Mathews, and Mathew in reply declared that it was the 'principle' of his family 'to maintain the most cordial good understanding' with them.[182] In 1808 it was declared at a large meeting of Catholics in Clonmel that the Mathews had 'long and uniformly espoused the cause of Catholic freedom'.[183] Secondly, the position established by the Mathews was such that they were able to return one member for the county, and also to assist in the return of another. In sum this clearly substantiates the view expressed by Wakefield that Lord Llandaff possessed 'an un-bounded influence' in Tipperary.[184] Given the substantial increase in Catholic freeholders making them a majority of the electorate, it was in the interest of families other than the Mathews to espouse the Catholic cause in varying degrees. That the Pritties, who had a large political interest based on family connection in the north, came to ally with the Mathews in county politics and to be pro-Catholic, is a measure of the shift in attitude which took place. The result was political and religious harmony, a point referred to in a motion passed at the meeting of 1808 which acknowledged the 'general liberality' of the Protestant gentry and nobility of the county as contributing to its 'happy exemption from religious dissentions'.[185]

Much of the support for Prittie derived from his opposition to Bagwell. The latter had espoused the Catholic cause in 1792 for political advantage, but his opposition to the union, which held out the prospect of further concessions for Catholics, marked a decline in his popularity among that body and his turnabout was not forgotten by Catholics subsequently.[186] With this loss of support among Catholics and Prittie's shift to a pro-Catholic stance, Bagwell's electoral base narrowed again to the Clonmel vicinity where an ultra-Protestant rump came to prevail.[187] The

---

[182] *LJ*, 20–4 June 1807.   [183] Ibid. 16–19 Mar. 1808.
[184] Wakefield, *Account*, i. 277.   [185] *LJ*, 16–19 Mar. 1808.
[186] Clonmel Museum, Acc. 1985/60a; Wakefield, *Account*, ii. 309, 312.
[187] Wakefield, *Account*, ii. 622.

movement towards Catholic relief sharpened the truculence of the gentry around Clonmel, thus making comprehensible the observation made of them in 1809 that 'The bigoted class of Protestants are exceedingly unruly and troublesome. They have no idea of subordination and are as regardless of the law as of the rights of their fellow citizens.'[188] The advent of the mass Catholic vote thus served to unite two major political interests, Mathew and Prittie, and to isolate Protestant ultraism electorally. With two pro-Catholic members representing the county from 1806 the Catholic issue was brought into the forefront of county politics, and a number of resolutions were adopted calling for the complete abolition of the remaining penal disabilities.[189] The conjunction between Prittie and Mathew ensured that the debate was conducted without disharmony, epitomized by the large number of Protestants who signed a petition in favour of Catholic emancipation in 1813.[190] The tradition of gaining concessions for Catholics, established at an early stage in Tipperary, was maintained in the nineteenth century by the strong nationalist spirit evident in the county at various stages and by the vibrancy of the Catholic Church.

[188] Ibid. 623.
[189] *LJ* 16–19 Mar.1808; CDA, Bray papers 1808/4, 14; in 1810: *WM*, 9 Apr. 1810; and in 1812: *LJ*, 21–5 Mar. 1812, BL Add. MS 59,257/22–3 (also in *WM*, 23 Mar. 1812), *WM*, 24 Aug. 1812.
[190] NLI, MS 11,422.

8

Conclusion

This study has focused on the particular experience of one locality in Ireland during the eighteenth century. The evolution and development of local concerns not merely illustrate the application of national themes, but they also show how uniquely local developments had an impact on concerns at national level. Such themes derive from the related areas of economy, land, and politics, and in this treatment the advantages of a composite regional study have been highlighted.

It has been shown that as part of Ireland's pre-industrial economy, Tipperary in the seventeenth and early eighteenth century was underdeveloped. However in time, as the region was drawn more fully into the market economy, its agricultural sector experienced growing diversification and commercialization. Eighteenth-century Ireland had a number of identifiable regional economies. But unlike the linen-based Ulster economy, Wexford's barley economy which focused on Dublin, Meath's mixed economy, or Mayo's weak and fitful response due to less well-endowed lands, Tipperary's strategic and accessible inland situation allowed it to respond to the needs of various markets.[1] This was because it comprised part of the respective hinterlands of the ports of Waterford, Cork, Limerick, and even Dublin. Thus it serviced the provisions trade through the Munster ports, its woollen goods met a demand in the domestic market, its cereals helped fulfil the needs of the capital and later formed a valuable export though Waterford, and its sheep meat was available in

---

[1] W. H. Crawford, 'Change in Ulster in the late eighteenth century', in Bartlett and Hayton (eds.), *Penal era*, 186–203; id., 'The evolution of the linen trade in Ulster before industrialization', *IESH*, 15 (1988), 32–53; id., 'Development of the county Mayo economy, 1700–1850', in R. Gillespie and G. Moran (eds.), *'A various country': Essays in Mayo history, 1500–1900* (Westport, 1987), 67–90; P. Lennon (*recte*, Connell), 'An economic geography of Co. Meath, 1770–1870', *IESH*, 8 (1981), 103–5.

Dublin. Producers in the county benefited from geographic accessibility to the market, demand leading to an intensification in agricultural production. In this respect, Tipperary had much in common with neighbouring Cork and Kilkenny.[2] Woollen manufacturing and flour milling were successively the vital areas of industrial activity, while other industries though small scale, were significant in terms of diffusion.

The dominant social group in local society was the land-owning class. This class was not a static one where number and personnel are concerned. There has been, on the one hand, an overemphasis on the notion of an uninterrupted stability in the Protestant land-owning class in the eighteenth century, and of a massive depletion in the Catholic landed interest on the other.[3] Such views fail to take account of the changes in ownership which took place and who benefited from them, and also fail to appreciate the nature and resilience of the Catholic propertied interest in specific regions. In Tipperary change in the structure and personnel of the landed class in the century was in two directions: a levelling at the top and a rise from the base which operated to change the essentially semi-feudal character of society still evident in the seventeenth century.

The landed class was not a homogeneous one. This was so at the outset of the eighteenth century and it was more so at its close. Members of the landed class were distinguished by differences in religion, race, and income. These differences, resulting from the seventeenth-century land settlement, were compounded in the course of the eighteenth by structural and personnel changes. In the former case this occurred through displacement at the top and emergence from below of more capitalized persons into the ranks of the farmer class; and in the latter by the persistence of a pervasive Catholic head-tenantry, by the survival of a residue of Catholic owners, and by the emergence of a hybrid group of converts.

Change in the landed class resulting from the disposal of property, notably on the Ormond, Everard, and Dunboyne estates, was a less marked feature of the late eighteenth century,

[2] Dickson, 'Cork'; id., 'Inland city: Reflections on eighteenth-century Kilkenny', in Nolan and Whelan (eds.), *Kilkenny*, 333–44; L. M. Cullen, 'The social and economic evolution of Kilkenny in the seventeenth and eighteenth centuries', in ibid., 273–88.

[3] E. M. Johnston, *Ireland in the eighteenth century* (Dublin, 1974), 1, 13, 18.

largely due to the fact that the scale in the rise of incomes allowed landlords to absorb greater expenditure without becoming insolvent. Good financial management was the general norm of landed families in this period. The breakup of the Mathew and Meade estates transformed a number of existing head-tenants, notably the Catholic Scullys and McCarthys, into landowners. Such a transition may be only of legal significance since such persons, even as head-tenants, had a recognized status within landed society. Nevertheless the change was important because it was of general occurrence, because of their position as Catholics, the amount of purchase money involved, and because it was resented.[4] Here were large middlemen availing of the difficulties of their landlords to transform their status to that of owners in fee.

If these changes are considered cumulatively with those in the early part of the century then a levelling at the top of the landed class occurred during the course of the century, a trend already apparent from the 1775 list of political interests. There was a significant movement upward into the lower and middle income groups, a trend later extended to the farmer class as is evident from the number of wealthy freeholders in the first decade of the nineteenth century. This rise was the most marked transition within the landed class because it was so pervasive.

The number of Catholic landowners in fee was reduced. The fact that the descent of only two estates in fee can be documented in detail may point to their exceptional status. More representative of the position of Catholic proprietors was their experience as converts and as large head-tenants. Conversion was the chief method whereby landed Catholics retained their patrimonies. It manifested itself at different times in different families according to circumstance, usually at critical stages in the evolution of such families. For the majority of those examined the critical point appears to have been reached in the 1730s and 1740s when either a generation of Catholic owners whose succession pre-dated the enactment of the penal legislation, or a succession of single male heirs, no longer obtained. The alternative for Catholic landowning families was conversion. One can view conversion either as a process in the decline of families or of their survival which applies in most of the cases examined. Catholic landowners who

---

[4] Wakefield, *Account*, ii. 544–5.

converted came to constitute a hybrid group within landed society. Their assimilation to the Protestant landed class could be difficult, as the situation of the Mathews exemplifies and as the experience of the 1760s shows. But ultimately it was these converts or their descendants, in association with the large group of Catholics at head-tenant and farmer level, and liberal Protestants, who were to triumph in the political leadership of the county particularly on the critical issue of Catholic relief.

The landed class secured their economic, social, and political position primarily out of the ownership of land, and the status and wealth derived therefrom. The context out of which land tenure in the eighteenth century evolved was established in the 1690s by the impoverishment of estates, scarcity of tenants, and depressed land values, and the landlord response to this situation. That response took the form of the granting of long leases at low or moderate rents for large holdings. Entrenched interests became established across the county as a result and there was a lessening of bonds between landlord and tenant. The position of existing interests was reinforced in the 1780s. At a time when the upward movement in land values temporarily lost momentum, as rent arrears accumulated, and when much land came on the market, large tenants benefited from the tenancy act of 1780, with Catholics additionally advancing due to the 1778 relief act. Large interests were confirmed in the 1780s and after, despite the efforts of landlords to reassert their control through the appointment of professional agents and the revival of manor courts. Given the loss of control conceded by landlords in the early eighteenth century and its confirmation in the 1780s, the leasing structure did not permit an advanced improvement policy except by a minority.

The rural disturbances which were to provide the county with a reputation of notoriety in the nineteenth century had their origin in the eighteenth. Agrarian unrest was not monolithically uniform over time in terms of its participants, victims, spatial occurrence, nor in its range of grievances. The broad framework was provided by commercialization, but unrest arose not merely in times of economic difficulty (early 1770s, 1799–1803) but also at periods of prosperity (early 1760s), and it was underpinned by sustained population change. Both factors, economic and demographic, influenced the social make-up of the agrarian movements over the different phases of unrest. The most persistent issue was that of

access to land and employment of the peasantry, particularly in 1799–1803 at a time of shortages and wartime inflation, which exacerbated conditions. The demand for labour increased over the period, but labourers were in a more vulnerable position because conacre rents soared, and subsidiary rights such as commonage either disappeared or were now charged for. The decline in spinning and combing also reduced rural supplements to income. Thus the labourer's and smallholder's economic position depended more exclusively on the issues of rent and employment than in the less commercialized, recent past.

Three factors in relation to unrest can be distinguished: smallholders and labourers were concerned with conacre plots, employment, wages, and commonage; rent and occupancy, though it could affect all classes, was a particular issue among the somewhat better-off in the conditions of the 1770s and 1780s; and the special problem of the dispossession of head-tenants, could affect them or their sub-tenants, and was a distinctive feature of the 1780s, exacerbating other tensions. Agrarian movements in Tipperary were dominated numerically by labourers, cottiers, and artisans who in times of economic prosperity sought to protect their position by attempts to control conacre rents, wage rates, and food prices, and to restrict graziers and large farmers in their appropriation of commons and in their creation of deer-parks. This involved them in conflict with their superiors (most sharply in the traditional grazing areas), but later also with those of their own social level (particularly in the developing grain-producing areas) as agriculture became more intensive. In times of economic difficulty this basic social stratum of the movement was supplemented by those higher up in the social hierarchy, particularly when tithe became a prominent issue. At periods of economic prosperity unrest was more definitely a conflict between social classes, while at times of economic downturn it was additionally a conflict within certain social classes. The combination of an exceptionally large proportion of marginal figures (i.e. labourers, cottiers), reflecting unequal access to land, and of threatened head tenants, itself a reflection of the inegalitarian social structure, if allied with grievances experienced by other groups such as dairymen and tenants, meant that Tipperary had a persistent and complex pattern of unrest which was to endure long into the nineteenth century.

The locality was also the scene of intense sectarian animosities in the 1760s which were unique for this period. The events of the 1760s are important because of their implications for the way in which Catholic relief occurred subsequently, and because of the role of the Mathew family in county politics before, during, and after those events. The 1760s mark a transition from a period when catholicism was informally tolerated to one when its status was recognized. Prior to 1760 the laws against catholicism were generally only sporadically enforced, a situation sanctioned by the minority status of Protestants in the county. But the early 1760s witnessed a dramatic turn around in the perceptions of Protestants locally. To them all the evidence suggested that Catholics were no longer accepting of mere toleration, rather there was a new assertiveness on their part in the political, economic, religious, and popular spheres which represented a serious threat to the stability of the establishment in church and state. That threat derived in its essentials from local circumstances and experiences, but it was the local gentry's ability to articulate that threat as having critical implications for national security which proved crucial. The identification of prominent local Catholics as the instigators of an internal and external security threat to the country led to the trials of 1765–6, the result of which was that Protestant extremism was discredited thereby opening the way for concessions to Catholics. The initiatives of archbishop Butler and the switch by Francis Mathew to government support in the 1770s, provided the context out of which such concessions materialized, a development also made possible by the role of Edmund Burke and the changing attitude of the British government due to its experience with the American rebellion.

There were significant parallels between the 1760s and the 1790s, the common factors being a general Protestant-gentry disaffection with government, the prominence of the Catholic issue, and the fear of a French rapprochement with local elements. The coalescence of these forces could have occasioned a repetition of the events of the 1760s, the more so because in the 1790s the French threat was more serious, given the dissemination of revolutionary ideas, the additional fear of a Catholic alliance with the Dissenters, and because the issue of Catholic relief was more divisive. That such a coalescence did not occur is primarily due to the absence of an active agrarian movement in the county in the

1790s, which elsewhere proved crucial as a catalyst in the development of radicalism and which in the 1760s had acted as the canvas upon which the events of that decade were delineated. By the 1790s also the political geography of the county had altered considerably with the reactionary leadership of the 1760s being replaced in the interim. A repetition of the events of the 1760s was also precluded because of the real advances made by Catholics by the early 1790s. Clearly a select group of Catholics became integrated into positions of status locally, and thus in the 1790s did not experience along with their Galway counterparts, for instance, the alienation so evident elsewhere.[5] The accepted view that Catholics were excluded from the political nation requires revision. On the one hand, it is clear that for long periods families who had a background of conversion sat in parliament and favoured the Catholic interest; and on the other, even before 1793 Catholics could influence the outcome of elections, something which was accentuated after 1793. Such advances could be made in the context that Catholic loyalty had been proven, for instance in the voluntary taking of the 1774 oath and the oath to qualify under the various relief acts.

[5] L. M. Cullen, 'Galway merchants and the outside world, 1650–1800', in D. O'Cearbhaill (ed.), *Galway, Town and Gown, 1484–1984* (Dublin, 1984), 71–2.

Genealogies

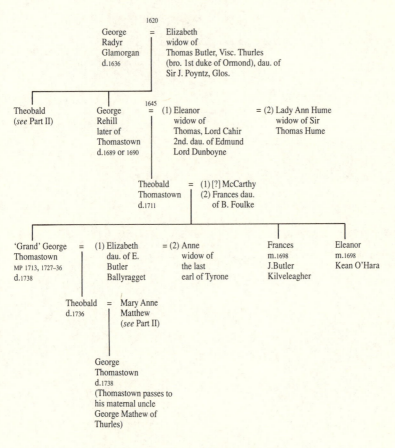

FIG. 1(a) Genealogy of Mathew (Part I)

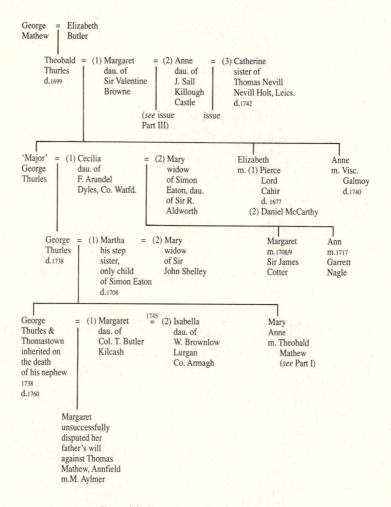

FIG. 1(b) Genealogy of Mathew (Part II)

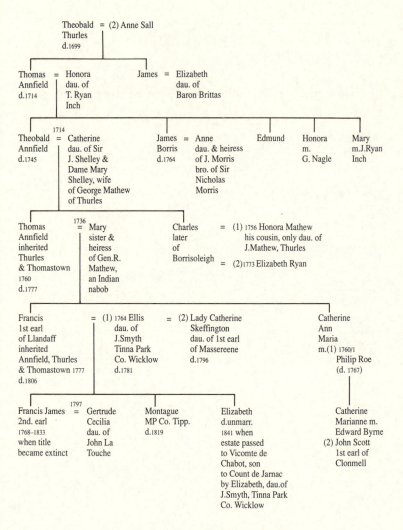

Theobald Thurles d.1699 = (2) Anne Sall

Thomas Annfield d.1714 = Honora dau. of T. Ryan Inch

James = Elizabeth dau. of Baron Brittas

1714
Theobald Annfield d.1745 = Catherine dau. of Sir J. Shelley & Dame Mary Shelley, wife of George Mathew of Thurles

James Borris d.1764 = Anne dau. & heiress of J. Morris bro. of Sir Nicholas Morris

Edmund

Honora m. G. Nagle

Mary m.J.Ryan Inch

Thomas Annfield inherited Thurles & Thomastown 1760 d.1777

1736
= Mary sister & heiress of Gen.R. Mathew, an Indian nabob

Charles later of Borrisoleigh = (1) 1756 Honora Mathew his cousin, only dau. of J.Mathew, Thurles

= (2)1773 Elizabeth Ryan

Francis 1st earl of Llandaff inherited Annfield, Thurles & Thomastown 1777 d.1806

= (1) 1764 Ellis dau. of J.Smyth Tinna Park Co. Wicklow d.1781

= (2) Lady Catherine Skeffington dau. of 1st earl of Massereene d.1796

Catherine Ann Maria m.(1) 1760/1 Philip Roe (d. 1767)

Francis James 2nd. earl 1768–1833 when title became extinct

1797
= Gertrude Cecilia dau. of John La Touche

Montague MP Co. Tipp. d.1819

Elizabeth d.unmarr. 1841 when estate passed to Vicomte de Chabot, son to Count de Jarnac by Elizabeth, dau.of J.Smyth, Tinna Park Co. Wicklow

Catherine Marianne m. Edward Byrne (2) John Scott 1st earl of Clonmell

FIG. 1(c) Genealogy of Mathew (Part III)

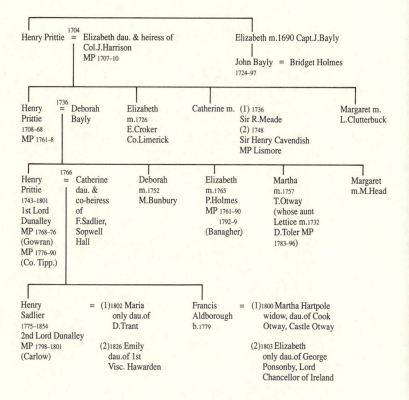

```
                              1704
Henry Prittie  =  Elizabeth dau. & heiress of          Elizabeth m.1690 Capt.J.Bayly
                  Col.J.Harrison
                  MP 1707–10                           John Bayly  =  Bridget Holmes
                                                       1724–97
```

```
Henry      1736   Deborah    Elizabeth      Catherine m.  (1) 1736              Margaret m.
Prittie    =      Bayly      m.1726                       Sir R.Meade           L.Clutterbuck
1708–68                      E.Croker                     (2) 1748
MP 1761–8                    Co.Limerick                  Sir Henry Cavendish
                                                          MP Lismore
```

```
Henry      1766   Catherine   Deborah     Elizabeth      Martha           Margaret
Prittie    =      dau. &      m.1752      m.1765         m.1757           m.M.Head
1743–1801         co-heiress  M.Bunbury   P.Holmes       T.Otway
1st Lord          of                      MP 1761–90     (whose aunt
Dunalley          F.Sadlier,              1792–9         Lettice m.1732
MP 1768–76        Sopwell                 (Banagher)     D.Toler MP
(Gowran)          Hall                                   1783–96)
MP 1776–90
(Co. Tipp.)
```

```
Henry            =  (1)1802 Maria       Francis      =  (1)1800 Martha Hartpole
Sadlier             only dau.of         Aldborough          widow, dau.of Cook
1775–1854           D.Trant             b.1779              Otway, Castle Otway
2nd Lord Dunalley
MP 1798–1801        (2)1826 Emily                    (2)1803 Elizabeth
(Carlow)            dau.of 1st                               only dau.of George
                    Visc. Hawarden                           Ponsonby, Lord
                                                             Chancellor of Ireland
```

FIG. 2 Genealogy of Prittie of Kilboy

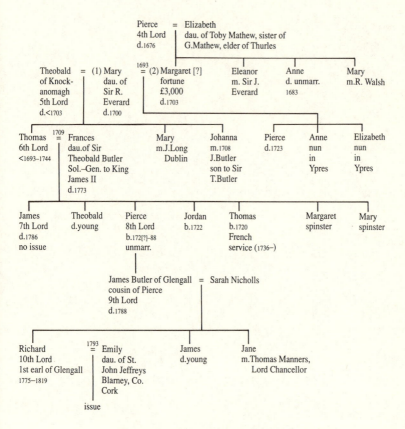

Fɪɢ. 3 Genealogy of Butler (Cahir)

Bibliography

GUIDES

BLACK, R. D. C., *A catalogue of pamphlets on economic subjects published between 1760 and 1900 in Irish libraries* (Belfast, 1969).

BUTTERFIELD, SIR H., 'Eighteenth-century Ireland, 1702–1800', in T. W. Moody (ed.), *Irish historiography 1936–70* (Dublin, 1971), 55–70.

CROSSLE, P., *Irish masonic records* (n.p., 1973).

CULLEN, L. M., 'The value of contemporary printed sources for Irish economic and social history in the eighteenth century', *IHS*, 14 (1964), 142–55.

ENGLEFIELD, D., *The printed records of the parliament of Ireland: A survey and bibliographical guide* (London, 1978).

GOODBODY, O. M., *Guide to Irish Quaker records, 1654–1860* (Dublin, 1967).

HANSON, L. W., *Contemporary printed sources for British and Irish economic history, 1701–1750* (Cambridge, 1963).

HAYES, R. J., *Manuscript sources for the history of Irish civilisation*, 11 vols. (Boston, Mass., 1965), 1st suppl., 1965–75, 3 vols. (Boston, Mass., 1979).

MCGUIRE, J. J., 'Ireland, 1660–1800', in J. Lee (ed.), *Irish historiography, 1970–79* (Cork, 1981), 56–85.

MUNTER, R. L., *A hand list of Irish newspapers, 1685–1750* (London, 1960).

ROEBUCK, P., 'The Irish registry of deeds: A comparative study', *IHS*, 18 (1972), 61–73.

MANUSCRIPTS

Belfast

Public Record Office of Northern Ireland (PRONI):
D104, D207, D354, D562, D572, D2707
T2368, T3131

Cashel, Co. Tipperary

Cashel Deanery:
  Vestry minute books for Shronell, 1757–1832; Relickmurry, 1770–1809;
  and St. Patrick's Rock and St. John's, 1786 to date

Chester

Cheshire Record Office:
  Smith-Barry papers (DCN series)

Clonmel, Co. Tipperary

County Museum:
  O'Callaghan papers
  Minister's money account for Clonmel, 1703
Bagwell Estate Office:
  Bagwell papers

Dublin

Church of Ireland College of Education:
  Purser–Griffith deeds
City Library, Pearse St.:
  Gilbert MS 36
  Robinson MS 34 (3)
Genealogical Office (GO):
  MSS 103, 160–2, 165, 171, 544, 570, 576, 814 (3, 8)
Grand Lodge of Freemasons:
  Registers of lodges
High School, Rathgar:
  Erasmus Smith Schools papers
  Registry book, i. 1674–1732; ii. 1732–92 (abstracted in NLI MSS
  16,929–30)
King's Inns Library:
  Prendergast MSS
  MS D39
  House of Lords appeals 4a: *Barton* v. *Barton*, 1765
National Archives (NA):
  M series 734 (1), 1418, 2197, 2547, 2578, 3391, 3957, 4917, 5259, 5302,
  5306, 5330–1, 6862.
  D series 16,339, 17,539, 20,786–8a, b.
  Acc. 976, 1079/1/2/1

BR/CAV/17/21
Lodge MS (i) records of the rolls; (ii) calendar of convert rolls, 1703–1838; (iii) alphabetical list of converts; (iv) fairs and markets
W. Betham's abstracts of prerogative wills
Catholic qualification rolls, 1778–96
E. Thompson's report on the revenue, 1733
Proclamations
1766 census for Cashel and Emly
Miscellaneous letters and papers (1A 52 167)
Index to chancery proceedings in the palatinate, 1662–90 (SP Press A2/3/18)
Official papers (OP)
Privy Council Office papers
Rebellion papers (RP)
State of the country papers (SCP)

National Library Of Ireland (NLI):
MSS 50 (0)/4, 133, 498, 772 (4), 1007, 2043, 2340, 2350, 2357–8, 2360, 2368, 2394, 2404, 2410, 2443, 2445–7, 2451, 2480, 2503–4, 2561, 2714, 2735, 2785, 4908–9, 5575–6, 5578, 5797, 5857–9, 7331, 8019, 8395, 8913–14, 8917, 8924, 9629–30, 10,752, 10,947, 11,044, 11,051, 11,416, 11,421–2, 11,887, 13,047(5), 13,794, 14,157, 15,055(1), 16,350, 16,929–30, 17,728, 19,822, 19,904, 23,787, 27,479–80, 27,485, 27,488, 27,490–2, 27,494, 27,571, 27,580

D series 3786, 4505, 4813, 4816, 4838, 4883, 5027, 5061, 5070–1, 5235, 5246, 5248, 5255–7, 5261–3, 5269, 5273, 5279, 5281, 5317, 5416, 5492, 7404, 11,314

Private Collections:
Bagwell (PC, 12,674 i–iii), Barton (PC, 46 i–ii), Byrne, Dunalley (PC, 870), Ormond (PC, 12,501), Ormond (unsorted), Parker, Riall (PC, 260–1), Trant (PC 564).

Reports on private collections:
Mansfield (11), Riall (48), Byrne (109)

Special Lists: Ormond 165 (covering D3579–5573):
Maps:
21.F.46 (15), 21.F.113 (24), 21.F.129 (4)

Microfilm Material:
M. Callanan, A history of the barony of Eliogarty (P.4546)
Cooke papers (P.1560)
Ledger of Courtenay and Ridgeway (P.4036)
Kavanagh papers (P.7155)
Minchin papers (P.5701)
Ryan papers (P.5489)

Registry of Deeds (RD):
  Memorials of registered deeds
  Memorials of deeds of partnership

Representative Church Body Library (RCB):
  MSS E.2–5, O.9, P.78–80

Royal Irish Academy:
  MSS B.1.1.1a, 2, G.1.2, H.3.2, H.4.2, 4.A.42, 12.D.36, 24.G.9
  Upton papers

Society of Friends Library:
  National sufferings, 1655–93
  Fennell papers
  Grubb papers
  Jacob correspondence

Trinity College Library:
  MSS 744, 749, 821, 847, 869, 873, 883/2, 750, 1729, 3577/2, 71, 3788,
    3860/1, 4879/1, 5789, 9865
  Barker Ponsonby papers
  Donoughmore papers
  College muniments: Mun/Me 4, Mun D series, Mun V 80–1, Mun P22,
    23

Ipswich

East Suffolk Record Office:
  Rous papers HA, 11/D8 (PRONI, Mic.253)

Leicester

Leicester City Archives:
  Braye of Stanford papers 23 D 57 (abstracted in the National Register
    of Archives list, no. 9254)

Limerick

City Library:
  Vere Hunt letterbooks and diaries (NLI, Mic.P.5527)

London

British Library (BL):
  Add. MSS 11,722, 18,022, 18,387, 19,829, 28,876–8, 28,939, 29,252,
    33,100, 35,892, 46,984, 59,253
  C 21 f 12 (14)
  Egerton MS 77

Guildhall Library:
  Christ's Hospital papers (Erasmus Smith material)

Lambeth Palace Library:
  MS 1742

National Army Museum:
  Townshend MS 6806/7/6/1

Public Record Office (PRO):
  Customs Office papers (CO)
  Forfeited Estates Commission (FEC) I, O.99
  Home Office (HO) 100 series
  State Papers Ireland (SPI)

Society of Friends Library:
  Gurney correspondence

Maidstone

Kent Record Office:
  Pratt papers U840

Nenagh, Co. Tipperary

James O'Brien & Co., solicitors:
  Bayly papers

Oxford

Bodleian Library:
  Carte MS 161

Paris

Bibliothèque Nationale:
  MS 20099: Coquebert de Montbret, Carnets des Voyages

Petworth House

Thomond papers

Preston

Lancashire Record Office:
  Derby papers (DDK series)

Bibliography

Private Custody

O'Callaghan papers (formerly in the custody of the late Mr Tim Looney,
   Cahir)
Phillips papers (C. O. R. Phillips)
Ryan of Inch papers (formerly in the custody of Mr J. Condon, Thurles)

Roscrea, Co. Tipperary

Heritage Centre:
   Mathew deeds (Chabot collection)
   Maxwell papers

Sheffield

City Library:
Wentworth Woodhouse muniments: Burke MS

Thurles, Co. Tipperary

Archbishop's House, Cashel Diocesan Archives (CDA):
   Archbishop James Butler I papers
   Archbishop James Butler II papers
   Archbishop Thomas Bray papers (All NLI Microfilm P.5998 *et seq.*)
County Library:
   Tithe book for Ardmayle and Ballysheehan parishes, 1790–1801
   Draft pedigree of the Cooper family
   P. Leahy, *Reference and rental to the map and survey now taken of the
      Thurles estate, 1818* (Dublin, 1819)
   Rentals of the Cole-Bowen estate, 1788, 1805
   Rental of the Damer estate, Roscrea 1770
   Rentals of the Damer estate 1787–98
   Rental of the Mathew estate at Thurles, 1744
St. Patrick's College:
   Notebooks of Revd W. Skehan
Moyaliffe Castle:
   Armstrong papers (in the custody of Mr R. Armstrong).

Waterford

City Library:
   Carrickman's diary, 1787–1810

Mount Melleray Abbey, Cappoquin:
  Revd W. P. Burke papers

Winchester

Hampshire Record Office:
  Agar papers (21 m 57)

PRINTED SOURCES

Records

AIRY, O. (ed.), *Essex papers*, 2 vols. (London, 1890).

ANON., 'Mallow and its neighbourhood in 1775', *JCHAS*, 27 (1921), 1–10,
  78–86.

BARTLETT, T., *Macartney in Ireland 1768–72* (Belfast, 1980).

BEDFORD, DUKE OF, *The correspondence of John fourth duke of Bedford*,
  ed. J. Russell, 3 vols. (London, 1842–6).

BIRCH, T., *A collection of state papers of John Thurloe*, 7 vols. (London,
  1742).

BODKIN, M., 'Notes on the Irish parliament in 1773', *PRIA*, 48 C (1942),
  145–232.

BOULTER, H., *Letters written by his excellency Hugh Boulter, D.D. lord
  primate of all Ireland*, 2 vols. (Dublin, 1770).

BRADY, J., *Catholics and Catholicism in the eighteenth century press*
  (Maynooth, 1965).

BURKE, EDMUND, *The correspondence of Edmund Burke*, ed. T. W.
  Copeland *et al.*, 10 vols. (Cambridge and Chicago, 1958–78).

BURKE, W. P., *The Irish priests in the penal times, 1660–1760* (Waterford,
  1914; repr. Shannon, 1969).

Calendar of Home Office papers, 1760–75, 4 vols. (London, 1878–99).

Calendar of the state papers relating to Ireland 1611–14 (London, 1877);
  1633–47 (1901); *1647–60* (1903); *1660–2* (1905); *1663–5* (1907); *1666–9*
  (1908); *1669–70* (1910).

CALLANAN, M., *Records of four Tipperary septs* (Dublin, 1938).

CASTLEREAGH, VISCOUNT, *Memoirs and correspondence*, ed. C. Vane, 12
  vols. (London, 1848–53).

*The charter of King Charles the second empowering Erasmus Smith
  esquire to found grammar schools in Ireland* (Dublin, 1897).

CORCORAN, T., *Some lists of Catholic lay teachers and their illegal schools in
  the later penal times* (Dublin, 1932).

CORNWALLIS, MARQUIS, *Correspondence of Charles first marquis Cornwallis*,
  ed. C. Ross, 3 vols. (London, 1859).

CRAWFORD, W. H., and TRAINOR, B. (eds.), *Aspects of Irish social history, 1750–1800* (Belfast, 1975).

D'ALTON, J., *Illustrations historical and genealogical of King James's Irish army list (1689)* (Dublin, 1855).

DUNLEAVY, G. W., and DUNLEAVY, J. (eds.), *The O'Conor papers: A descriptive catalog and surname register of the materials at Clonalis House* (Madison, Wis. and London, 1977).

EDMUNDSON, W., *Journal* (Dublin, 1833).

EDWARDS, R. D.,'The minute book of the Catholic Committee 1773–92', *Arch. Hib.*, 9 (1942), 3–172.

FALKINER, C. L., *Illustrations of Irish history and topography* (London, 1904).

GREGORY, [A.] (ed.), *Mr. Gregory's letter box 1813–30* (London, 1898).

HARDINGE, W. H., 'On circumstances attending the outbreak of the civil war in Ireland on 23rd October, 1641', *Trans. of Royal Irish Academy*, 24 (1873), 3–118, 265–313.

HERBERT, D., *Retrospections 1770–1806*, 2 vols. (London, 1929–30).

Historical Manuscripts Commission: *Egmont*, pt. 1 (1905), *Ormond*, ii–iv. (1902–6), *Stuart*, v. (1912), *Rutland*, iii. (1894), *12th report Charlemont* (1891); *15th report*, app. 8, *Ailesbury* (1898).

HOFFMAN, R. J. S., *Edmund Burke, New York agent, with his letters to the New York assembly and intimate correspondence with Charles O'Hara 1761–76* (Philadelphia, 1956).

HOGAN, W., and O'BUACHALLA, L., 'Letters and papers of James Cotter junior 1689–1720', *JCHAS*, 68 (1963), 66–95.

HUNT, W., *The Irish parliament in 1775* (Dublin, 1907).

JOHNSTON, E. M., 'Members of the Irish parliament 1784–7', *PRIA*, 70 C (1971), 157–68.

LAFFAN. T., *Tipperary's families: Being the hearth money records for 1665–6–7* (Dublin, 1911).

LARGE, D., 'The Irish House of Commons in 1769', *IHS*, 11 (1958), 18–45.

LOVEDAY, JOHN (ed.), *Diary of a tour in 1732 through parts of England, Wales, Ireland, and Scotland made by John Loveday of Caversham*, ed. J. F. T. Loveday (Edinburgh, 1890).

MACDERMOT, B. C. (ed.), *The catholic question in Ireland and England, 1798–1822: The papers of Denys Scully* (Dublin, 1988).

McDOWELL, R. B., 'Proceedings of the Dublin Society of United Irishmen', *AH*, 17 (1949), 1–144.

MALCOMSON, A. P. W., *Eighteenth-century Irish official papers in Great Britain* (Belfast, 1973).

O'BYRNE, E., *The convert rolls* (Dublin, 1981).

O'CONOR, CHARLES, *The letters of Charles O'Conor of Belangare*, ed. C. C. Ward and R. E. Ward, 2 vols. (Ann Arbor, Mich., 1980).

O'Dwyer, C. (ed.), 'Archbishop Butler's visitation book', *Arch. Hib.*, 33 (1975), 1–90; 34 (1976), 3–49.

Ó HÓGÁIN, D. (ed.), *Duanaire Thiobraid Árann* (Baile Átha Cliath (Dublin), 1981).

Ordnance Survey name book, vol. 122, Co. Tipperary (NLI typescript).

Pender, S., *A census of Ireland c.1659* (Dublin, 1939).

Penn, W., *My Irish journal 1669–1670*, ed. I. Grubb (London, 1952).

Power, P. (ed.), 'Carrickman's diary 1787–1810', *JWSEIAS*, 14 (1911), 97–102, 145–50; 15 (1912), 30–7, 62–70, 124–37; 16 (1913), 18–27, 74–85, 176–82; 17 (1914), 4–16, 120–7.

—— (ed.), *A bishop of the penal times being letters and reports of John Brenan, bishop of Waterford (1671–93) and archbishop of Cashel (1677–93)* (Cork, 1932).

Power, T. P., 'A minister's money account for Clonmel, 1703', *AH*, 34 (1987), 183–200.

Price, L. (ed.), *An eighteenth-century antiquary: The sketches, notes, and diaries of Austin Cooper 1759–1830* (Dublin, 1942).

Proclamations relating to 1798 (TCD, Press A.7.18. no. 11).

Public Record Office of Northern Ireland, Education facsimiles: 21–40, *Irish elections 1750–1832* (1973); 41–60, *The Act of Union* (1973); 61–80, *The United Irishmen* (1974); 81–100, *The '98 Rebellion* (1976); 101–20, *The Penal Laws* (1975); 141–60, *The Volunteers 1778–84* (1974); 221–40, *Ireland after the Glorious Revolution* (1976); 241–60, *Catholic Emancipation* (1976), all published in Belfast.

Renehan, L. H., *Collections on Irish church history*, ed. D. McCarthy, 2 vols. (Dublin, 1861).

Report of the deputy keeper of the Public Record Office of Ireland: fifth (Dublin, 1873), *sixth* (Dublin, 1874), *fifty-ninth* (Dublin, 1956).

Sadlier, T. U., 'Manuscripts at Kilboy', *AH*, 12 (1943), 129–54.

—— 'Co. Kilkenny in 1775', *AH*, 12 (1943), 144–7.

—— 'The county of Waterford in 1775', *JWSEIAS*, 16 (1913), 49–55.

Shannon, Lord, *Lord Shannon's letters to his son: A calendar of the letters written by the 2nd earl of Shannon to his son, viscount Boyle 1790–1802*, ed. E. Hewitt (Belfast, 1982).

Simington, R. C., *The civil survey 1654–1656 Co. Tipperary*, i: *Eastern and southern baronies* (Dublin, 1931); ii: *Western and northern baronies* (Dublin, 1934).

—— *The transplantation to Connacht 1654–1656* (Dublin, 1970).

Simms, J. G., 'Irish Jacobites', *AH*, 22 (1960), 11–230.

Skehan, W., 'Extracts from the minutes of the corporation of Fethard, Co. Tipperary', *Irish Genealogist*, 4 (1963–73), 81–92, 183–93, 308–22, 616–24; 5 (1974–9), 72–86, 201–15, 370–82.

Stokes, G. T. (ed.), *Pococke's tour in Ireland in 1752* (Dublin and London, 1891).

Swift, Jonathan, *The correspondence of Jonathan Swift*, ed. H. Williams, 5 vols. (Oxford, 1963–5).

Tierney, M. (ed.), 'A short title calendar of the papers of Archbishop James Butler in Archbishop's House, Thurles', *Coll. Hib.*, 18–19 (1976–7), 105–31; 20 (1978), 89–103.

Wesley, John, *The journal of John Wesley*, ed. N. Curnock, 8 vols. (London [1912–17]).

Parliamentary: Various

A bill for vesting certain lands in the King's County part of the estate of Peter Holmes (n.p., 1784).

A bill for vesting certain parts of the real estates devised by the will of Thomas Otway esquire (n.p., 1803).

A full and accurate report of the debates in the parliament of Ireland in the session 1793 (Dublin, 1793).

An act for enabling Charles earl of Arran to purchase the forfeited estate of James Butler late duke of Ormond (n.p., 1721).

An act for the establishing a purchase of certain fee farmes, lands, and hereditaments in Ireland made by Sir Alexander Cairnes (n.p. [c.1711]).

An act for the more speedy payment of the creditors of James late duke of Ormond and of the present duke of Ormond (Dublin, 1701).

An act for the sale of certain town, lands etc. in the County of Tipperary the estates of the Rt. Hon. John, earl of Clanwilliam and the Hon. Richard Meade (n.p. [1795]).

An act for the sale of part of the estates of the Rt. Hon. Robert, earl of Roden (n.p. [1803]).

An act for vesting certain manors, lands, and hereditaments the estate of Sir Redmond Everard, bart. in trustees (n.p. [1727]).

An act for vesting in trustees certain lands the estate of Francis Mathew (n.p. [1780]).

An act to explain and amend an act for vesting in trustees the estate of Francis Mathew of Thomastown (n.p., 1784).

A report made by his grace the lord primate from the lords committees appointed to enquire into the present state of popery in this kingdom (Dublin, 1732).

A report of the debates in both houses of parliament of Ireland in the Roman Catholic bill passed in the session of 1792 (Dublin, 1792).

Caldwell, J., *Debates in the Irish parliament in the years 1763 and 1764*, 2 vols. (London, 1766).

Journals of the House of Commons of the kingdom of Ireland, 3rd. edn., ii–xx. (Dublin, 1796–1800).

Journals of the House of Lords of the kingdom of Ireland, 8 vols. (Dublin, 1779–1800).

KENNEDY, J. P., *Digest of evidence taken before Her Majesty's commissioners of inquiry*, 2 vols. (Dublin, 1847–8).

Minutes of evidence taken before the select committee on the Tipperary election (n.p. [1777]).

Proceedings of the parliament of Ireland, 3 vols. (Dublin, 1793).

Report from the committee on the circulating paper, the specie, and the current coin of Ireland (1804), repr. as *PP*, 5 (407) (1826).

The parliamentary register or history of the proceedings and debates of the House of Commons of Ireland, 17 vols. (Dublin, 1781–1800).

The statutes at large passed in the parliaments held in Ireland, iii–xx. (Dublin, 1786–1801).

Parliamentary Papers

Butter report (Ire.), 5 (1826)

Census of population 1831, 39 (1833) (23)

Census of population 1841, 24 (1843)

Fairs and markets (Ire.), 41 (1852–3)

Manor courts, 15 (1837) (494); 17 (1837–8) (648)

Municipal corporations (Ire.), 28 (1835) (27)

Occupation of land (Ire.), 20–1 (pt. III) (1845) (616, 657)

Public instruction, 33 (1836)

Railway commissioners (Ire.), 35 (1837–8) (145)

Stock, 57 (1847–8)

Contemporary Works

General

A congratulatory address to his majesty from the peasantry of Ireland vulgarly denominated White Boys or Right Boys (Dublin, 1786).

A description of the collieries of Killenaule now to be let the estate of E. W. Newenham (Dublin, 1814).

A description of the silver and lead mines of Shallee (Dublin, 1814).

A letter from a Munster layman of the Established Church to his friend in Dublin (Dublin, 1787).

A list of the estates in Ireland of the Hollow Swords Blades with acres in each (Dublin, 1709).

An account of Mr Thomas Johnston's improvement of the livestock of the kingdom of Ireland (Dublin, 1777).

A sermon preached before the society corresponding with the Incorporated Society (London, 1749, 1752, 1757).

A state of the value of the forfeited estate of James, late duke of Ormonde (n.p. [*c.*1720]).

BEAUFORT, D. A., *Memoir of a map of Ireland* (Dublin, 1792).

BELLEW, R., *Thoughts and suggestions of the means towards improving the condition of the Irish peasantry*, 2nd. edn. (London, 1808).

BLACKBURNE, F., *Considerations on the present state of the controversy between the Protestants and Papists of Great Britain and Ireland* (London, 1768).

Bourke's, *Almanack* (Dublin, 1685).

BOWDEN, C. T., *A tour through Ireland* (Dublin, 1791).

Brief and serious reasons why the people called Quakers do not pay tithes, published by said people in 1768 (Dublin, 1786).

BULLINGBROOKE, E., *The duty and authority of the justices of the peace and parish officers for Ireland* (Dublin, 1766).

BURKE, T., *Hibernia Dominicana, sive historia provinciae Hiberniae ordinis praedicatorum* (Kilkenny, 1762); new introduction by T. Wall (Farnborough, 1970).

BUSH, J., *Hibernia curiosa* (London, 1769).

BUTLER, J., *A justification of the tenets of the Roman Catholic religion and a refutation of the charges brought against its clergy by the lord bishop of Cloyne* (Dublin, 1786).

CALDWELL, J., *A brief examination of the question whether it is expedient either in a religious or political view to pass an act to enable Papists to take real securities for money which they may lend* (Dublin, 1764).

CARLISLE, N., *Topographical dictionary of Ireland* (Dublin, 1810).

CAMDEN, W., *Britannia* (London, 1695).

COOTE, C., *General view of the agriculture and manufactures of the King's County* (Dublin, 1801).

CROSBY, T., *The history of the English Baptists from the reformation to the beginning of the reign of King George I*, 4 vols. (London, 1740).

CURRY, J., *A candid enquiry into the causes and motives of the late riots in Munster together with a brief narrative of the proceedings against those rioters anno 1766 in a letter to a noble lord in England* (London, 1766).

—— *A parallel between the pretended plot in 1762 and the forgery of Titus Oates in 1679* (Cork, 1767).

—— *An historiographical and critical review of the civil wars in Ireland from the reign of Queen Elizabeth to the settlement under King William* (Dublin, 1775).

DEIGHAN, P., *A complete treatise on the geography of Ireland on a new plan* (Dublin [1810]).

DODD, J. S., *The traveller's director through Ireland* (Dublin, 1801).

EACHARD, L., *An exact description of Ireland* (London, 1691).

[ELRINGTON, T.], *Letters on tythes published in the Dublin Journal and Correspondent under the signature of N* (Dublin, 1808).

FALKLAND, *Parliamentary representation* (Dublin, 1790).

FINLAY, J., *A treatise on the law of tithes in Ireland and ecclesiastical law connected therewith* (Dublin, 1828).

—— *A treatise on the law of renewals in respect to leases for lives renewable forever in Ireland* (Dublin, 1829).

GRACE, G., *A letter to his grace the duke of Richmond, lord lieutenant of Ireland concerning certain exertions of power and certain dispensations of patronage supposed to have originated in the late election for the county of Tipperary* (Clonmel, 1813).

GRIFFITH, A., *Miscellaneous tracts* (Dublin, 1788).

HALL, J., *Tour through Ireland*, 2 vols. (London, 1813).

HARRIS, W., *The history of the life and reign of William Henry, prince of Nassau and Orange, stadholder of the United Provinces, king of England, in which the affairs of Ireland are more particularly handled* (Dublin, 1749).

[HIBERNICUS], *Some reasons against raising an army of Roman Catholicks in Ireland in a letter to a member of parliament* (Dublin, 1762).

HOARE, R. C., *Journal of a tour in Ireland AD 1806* (London and Dublin, 1807).

HOLMES, G., *Sketches of some of the southern counties of Ireland collected during a tour in the autumn of 1797* (n.p., 1801).

House of Lords appeals (TCD, 202 r 32–4).

HOWARD, G. E., *Several special cases on the laws against the further growth of popery in Ireland* (Dublin, 1775).

HUSSEY, T., *A pastoral letter to the Catholic clergy of the united dioceses of Waterford and Lismore* (Waterford, 1797).

KING, W., *The state of the Protestants of Ireland under the late King James's government* (London, 1691).

LEWIS, S., *Topographical dictionary of Ireland*, 2 vols. (London, 1837).

[LIDWELL, J.], *Lidwill's life: The history of the life and adventures of John Lidwill from his birth to his present age of near sixty years written and selling by himself* (Dublin, 1804).

LODGE, J., *The peerage of Ireland* (rev. by M. Archdall), 7 vols. (Dublin, 1789).

LONG, J., *The golden fleece* (Dublin, 1762).

LUCAS, R., *A general directory of the kingdom of Ireland* (Dublin, 1788).

MASON, W. S., *A statistical account or parochial survey of Ireland*, 3 vols. (Dublin, 1814–19).

MOLL, H., *A set of twenty new and correct maps of Ireland with the great roads and principal cross roads* (London, 1728).

Munster volunteer registry (Dublin, 1782).

MUSGRAVE, R., *Memoirs of the different rebellions in Ireland from the arrival of the English with a particular detail of that which broke out 23 May 1798* (Dublin, 1801).

O'CONOR, M., *The history of the Irish Catholics from the settlement in 1691* (Dublin, 1813).

PATTERSON, W., *Observations on the climate of Ireland* (Dublin, 1804).

(PIGOT), *The commercial directory of Ireland, Scotland and the four most northern counties of England for 1820–21 & 22* (Manchester, 1820).

[PITT, W. M.], *A letter from Major Pitt of the Dorset regiment to the society for promoting the comforts of the poor established at Carrick-on-Suir in the county of Tipperary* (Dublin, 1800).

PUBLICOLA, *A letter from a country gentleman in the province of Munster to his grace the lord primate of all Ireland* (Dublin, 1741).

RADCLIFF, T., *Reports on the fine wooled flocks of Lord Viscount Lismore* (Dublin, 1820).

Reasons humbly offer'd for the maintaining a clause in the bill to prevent the further growth of popery in Ireland notwithstanding the endeavours and objections of George Mathews esq. against it (n.p. [c.1703]).

Report and observations of Robert Stephenson (Dublin, 1764).

Report of an interesting case in which Mr. Francis Doyle was plaintiff and Sir Thomas J. Fitzgerald was defendant (Dublin, 1808).

Report of the Incorporated Society (Dublin, 1766).

RIDGEWAY, W., *Reports of cases on appeals and writs of error in the high court of parliament in Ireland since the restoration of the appellate jurisdiction*, 3 vols. (Dublin, 1795–8).

RUTTY, J., *A chronological history of the weather and seasons and of the prevailing diseases in Dublin* (London, 1770).

SANDBY, P., *The virtuosi's museum containing select views in England, Scotland and Ireland* (n.p., 1781).

SCOTT, J., *Private diary of John Scott, Lord Earlsfort*, (n.p., n.d.).

SEWARD, W. W., *Collectanea politicia or the political transactions of Ireland from George III to the present time*, 3 vols. (Dublin, 1801–4).

—— *The Hibernian gazetteer* (Dublin, 1789).

SHERIDAN, T., *The life of the Rev. Dr. Jonathan Swift* (Dublin, 1785).

SMITH, C., *Antient and present state of the city and county of Waterford* (Dublin, 1746).

STORY, G., *A true and impartial history of the last two years* (London, 1691).

TAAFFE, VISCOUNT, *Observations on affairs in Ireland* (Dublin, 1766).

TAYLOR, G., and SKINNER, A., *Maps of the roads of Ireland surveyed 1777* (Dublin and London, 1778; rep. Shannon, 1969).

The case of George Mathew esq. (n.p., n.d.).

The case of George Mathew jun. esq. (n.p. [c.1711]).

The case of the Protestant freemen of Clonmell (n.p. [1705]).

The case of Thomas Butler of Kilcash esq., John Butler of Garryricken esq., and James Butler of Kilveleagher esq. (n.p. [c.1720]).

The compleat Irish traveller, 2 vols. (London, 1788).

The trial of Thomas Judkin Fitzgerald esq. late high sheriff of the Co. Tipperary before baron Yelverton and judge Chamberlain at the Clonmell assizes, March 18, 1799, on an action for damages brought

against him by Mr Wright, teacher of the French language, for having received by his order one hundred and fifty lashes on the 29th of May 1798. With the proceedings in parliament on his petition praying indemnification, and the debate on the indemnity bill (Dublin, 1799).

TIGHE, W., *Statistical observations relative to the county of Kilkenny* (Dublin, 1802).

TONE, W. T. W., *Life of Theobald Wolfe Tone, written by himself and continued by his son*, 2 vols. (Washington, 1826).

TRANT, D., *Considerations on the present disturbances in the province of Munster, their cause, extent, probable consequences, and remedies* (Dublin, 1787).

TYNER, G., *The traveller's guide through Ireland* (Dublin, 1794).

WAKEFIELD, E. G., *An account of Ireland statistical and political*, 2 vols. (London, 1812).

WALLACE, T., *An essay on the manufactures of Ireland* (Dublin, 1798).

WEEKS, J. E., *A new geography of Ireland* (Dublin, 1752, 1762).

WHYTE, M., *An inquiry into the causes of our want of tillage in Ireland* (Dublin, 1755).

WILSON, C. H., *A collection of the resolutions of the volunteers, grand juries etc. of Ireland which followed the celebrated resolves of the first Dungannon diet* (Dublin, 1782).

WILSON, W., *The post-chaise companion or traveller's directory through Ireland* (Dublin, 1786).

WOODWARD, R., *The present state of the Church of Ireland* (Dublin, 1787).

WYSE, T., *Historical sketch of the late Catholic Association of Ireland*, 2 vols. (London, 1829).

YOUNG, A., *A tour in Ireland with general observations on the present state of the kingdom made in the years 1776, 1777, and 1778 and brought down to the end of 1779*, 2 vols. (London, 1780; ed. A. W. Hutton, London, 1892; repr. Shannon, 1970).

Newspapers and Periodicals

Newspapers:
Clonmel Gazette (CG)
Clonmel Herald (CH)
Clonmel Journal
Cork Advertiser (CA)
Cork Evening Post (CEP)
Cork Hibernian Chronicle
Dublin Courant
Dublin Evening Post
Dublin Gazette (DG)
Dublin Newsletter

Dublin Weekly Advertiser
Ennis Chronicle (EC)
Faulkner's Dublin Journal (FDJ)
Finn's Leinster Journal (FLJ)
Freeman's Journal (FJ)
Limerick Chronicle (LC)
Limerick Journal (LJ)
Munster Journal
Pue's Occurrences
Southern Reporter (Cork)
Waterford Chronicle (WC)
Waterford Herald
Waterford Mirror (WM)

Periodicals:
Annual Register 1803 (London, 1805), *1816* (London, 1817)
Proceedings of the Dublin Society
Proceedings of the Incorporated Society
Transactions of the Dublin Society
Gentleman's and London Magazine
Walker's Hibernian Magazine
Wilson's Dublin Magazine

SECONDARY WORKS

A history of congregations in the Presbyterian church in Ireland 1610–1982 (Belfast, 1982).

AKENSON, D. H., *The Church of Ireland: Ecclesiastical reform and revolution 1800–1885* (New Haven and London, 1971).

ANON., *Genealogy of the earls of Llandaff of Thomastown Co. Tipperary, Ireland* (n.p., 1899).

BAGSHAWE, W. H. G., *The Bagshawes of Ford: A biographical pedigree* (London, 1886).

BALL, F. E., *The judges in Ireland 1221–1921*, 2 vols. (London, 1926).

BARKLEY, J. M., *A short history of the Presbyterian church in Ireland* (Belfast, 1959).

BARNARD, T. C., *Cromwellian Ireland* (Oxford, 1975).

BARTLETT, T., 'The Townshend viceroyalty', in Bartlett and Hayton (eds.), *Penal era*, 88–112.

—— 'The O'Haras of Annaghmore, *c.*1600–*c.*1800: Survival and revival', *IESH*, 9 (1982), 34–52.

—— 'An end to moral economy: The Irish militia disturbances of 1793', *Past & Present*, 99 (1983), 41–64.

—— 'The origins and progress of the Catholic question in Ireland, 1690–1800', in Power and Whelan (eds.), *Endurance and emergence*, 1–19.

—— and HAYTON, D. W. (eds.), *Penal era and golden age: Essays in Irish history, 1690–1800* (Belfast, 1979).

BARTON, B. F., *Some account of the family of Barton drawn from manuscript sources and records together with pedigrees of the various branches of the house* (Dublin, 1902).

BEAMES, M., 'Cottiers and conacre in pre-famine Ireland', *Jnl. of Peasant Studies*, 2 (1976), 352–4.

—— *Peasants and power: The Whiteboy movements and their control in pre-famine Ireland* (Hassocks, Sussex and New York, 1983).

BOLTON, G. C., *The passing of the Irish act of union* (Oxford, 1966).

BRENNAN, M., 'The changing composition of Kilkenny's landowners, 1641–1700', in Nolan and Whelan (eds.), *Kilkenny*, 161–95.

BRIC, M. J., 'The Whiteboy movement, 1760–1780', in Nolan (ed.), *Tipperary*, 148–84.

—— 'The tithe system in eighteenth-century Ireland', *PRIA*, 86 C (1986), 271–88.

BURKE, W. P., *History of Clonmel* (Waterford, 1907).

Burke's, *Irish family records* (London, 1976).

—— *Guide to Irish country houses* (London, 1976).

BURNS, A., *History of the British West Indies* (London, 1965).

BURNS, R. E., 'The Catholic relief act in Ireland, 1778', *Church History*, 32 (1963), 181–206.

BUTEL, P., *Les négociants Bordelais: l'Europe et les Iles au XVIIIe siècle* (Paris, 1974).

BYRNE, M., 'The distilling industry in Offaly, 1780–1954', in H. Murtagh (ed.), *Irish midland studies* (Athlone, 1980), 213–28.

CANNY, N. P., 'Migration and opportunity: Britain, Ireland, and the New World', *IESH*, 12 (1985), 7–32.

CARDEN, L. E. G., *Some particulars about the family and descendants of the first John Carden of Templemore Co. Tipperary and Priscilla his wife* (n.p., 1912).

CARTE, T., *History of the life of James, duke of Ormonde 1610–88*, 6 vols. (Oxford, 1851).

CLARK, S., and DONNELLY, J. S. (eds.), *Irish peasants, violence, and political unrest* (Madison, Wis. and Manchester, 1983).

CLARKSON, L. A., 'The demography of Carrick-on-Suir, 1799', *PRIA*, 87 C (1987), 13–36.

—— 'The Carrick-on-Suir woollen industry', *IESH*, 16 (1989), 23–41.

CONDON, J., 'Don Jorge Rian of Inch Co. Tipperary (1748–1805)', *Irish Ancestor*, 18 (1986), 5–10.

COOMBES, J. A., *A bishop of the penal times: The life and times of John O'Brien, bishop of Cloyne and Ross, 1701–1769* (Cork, 1981).

354   *Bibliography*

COOPER, R. A., 'Genealogical notes on the Cooper family in Ireland 1660–
1960', *Irish Genealogist*, 3 (1964), 351–5.

CORISH, P. (ed.), *Radicals, rebels, and establishments* (Belfast, 1985).

—— 'Two centuries of catholicism in county Wexford', in Whelan and
Nolan (eds.), *Wexford* (Dublin, 1987), 222–47.

✓ —— and BRADY, J., *The church under the penal code: A history of Irish
catholicism*, iv. fasc. 2 (Dublin, 1971).

COSTELLO, C., *In quest of an heir: The life and times of John Butler,
Catholic bishop of Cork, Protestant baron of Dunboyne* (Cork, 1978).

CRAIG, M., *The architecture of Ireland from the earliest times to 1800*
(London, 1982).

CRAWFORD, W. H., 'Change in Ulster in the late eighteenth century', in
Bartlett and Hayton (eds.), *Penal era*, 186–203.

—— 'Development of the county Mayo economy, 1700–1850', in
Gillespie and Moran (eds.), *'A various country'*, 67–90.

—— 'The evolution of the linen trade in Ulster before industrialization',
IESH, 15 (1988), 32–53.

CULLEN, L. M., 'The overseas trade of Waterford as seen from a ledger of
Courtenay and Ridgeway', *Jnl. Royal Society of Antiquaries of Ireland*,
88 (1958), 165–78.

—— *Anglo-Irish trade 1660–1800* (Manchester, 1968).

—— *Life in Ireland* (London, 1968).

—— (ed.), *The formation of the Irish economy* (Cork, 1969).

—— *Six generations: Life and work in Ireland since 1790* (Cork, 1970).

—— *Merchants, ships and trade 1660–1830* (Dublin, 1971).

—— *An economic history of Ireland since 1660* (London, 1976).

—— 'Eighteenth-century flour milling in Ireland', *IESH*, 4 (1977),
5–25.

—— *The emergence of modern Ireland 1600–1900* (London, 1981).

—— 'Landlords, bankers, and merchants: The early Irish banking world,
1700–1820', in A. E. Murphy, *Economists and the Irish from the
eighteenth century to the present day* (Dublin, 1984), 25–44.

—— 'Galway merchants and the outside world, 1650–1800', in D.
O'Cearbhaill (ed.), *Galway, Town and Gown, 1484–1984* (Dublin,
1984), 65–89.

—— 'The 1798 rebellion in its eighteenth-century context', in Corish
(ed.), *Radicals*, 91–113.

✓ —— 'Catholics under the penal laws', *Eighteenth-century Ireland*, 1
(1986), 23–36.

—— 'The social and economic evolution of Kilkenny in the seventeenth
and eighteenth century', in Nolan and Whelan (eds.), *Kilkenny*, 273–
88.

—— and BUTEL, P. (eds.), *Négoce et industrie en France et en Irlande aux
XVIIIᵉ et XIXᵉ siècles* (Paris, 1980).

—— and FURET, F. (eds.), *Ireland and France 17th–20th centuries: Towards a comparative study of rural history* (Paris, 1980).

—— and SMOUT, T. C. (eds.), *Comparative aspects of Scottish and Irish economic and social history, 1600–1900* (Edinburgh, 1977).

DE BRÚN, P., 'Scriptural instruction in Irish: A controversy of 1830–31', in P. De Brún, S. Ó'Coileáin, and P. Ó'Riain (eds.), *Folia Gadelica* (Cork, 1983), 134–59.

DEVINE, T. M., and DICKSON, D., *Ireland and Scotland 1600–1850: Parallels and contrasts in economic and social development* (Edinburgh, 1983).

DICKSON, C., *The Wexford rising in 1798, its causes and its course* (Tralee, 1955).

DICKSON, D., 'An economic history of the Cork region in the eighteenth century', Ph.D. thesis (University of Dublin, 1977).

—— 'Aspects of the rise and decline of the Irish cotton industry', in Cullen and Smout (eds.), *Comparative aspects*, 100–15.

—— 'Taxation and disaffection in late eighteenth-century Ireland', in Clark and Donnelly (eds.), *Irish peasants*, 37–63.

—— *New foundations: Ireland, 1660–1800* (Dublin, 1987).

—— 'Inland town: Reflections on eighteenth-century Kilkenny', in Nolan and Whelan (eds.), *Kilkenny*, 333–44.

—— 'Catholics and trade in eighteenth-century Ireland: An old debate revisited', in Power and Whelan (eds.), *Endurance and emergence*, 85–100.

DONNELLY, J. S., 'The Rightboy movement, 1785–8', *Studia Hibernica*, 17–18 (1977–8), 120–202.

—— 'The Whiteboy movement, 1761–5', *IHS*, 21 (1978), 20–54.

—— 'Propagating the cause of the United Irishmen', *Studies*, 69 (1980), 5–23.

—— 'Irish agrarian rebellion: The Whiteboys of 1769–76', *PRIA*, 83 C (1983), 293–331.

—— 'The social composition of agrarian rebellions in early nineteenth-century Ireland: The case of the Carders and Caravats, 1813–16', in Corish (ed.), *Radicals*, 151–69.

DUNBOYNE, LORD, *Butler family history*, 3rd. edn. (n.p., 1972).

ELLIOTT, B. S., *Irish migrants in the Canadas, a new approach* (Kingston, Montreal, and Belfast, 1988).

ELLIOTT, M., *Partners in revolution: The United Irishmen and France* (New Haven, Conn. and London, 1982).

Emmet, T. A., *The Emmet family* (New York, 1898).

EMPEY, C. A., 'The Norman period 1185–1500', in Nolan (ed.), *Tipperary*, 71–91.

EVANS, E. J., *The contentious tithe: The tithe problem and English agriculture, 1750–1850* (London, 1976). ✓

FITZPATRICK, W. J., *Ireland before the Union with revelations from the unpublished diary of Lord Clonmell* (Dublin, 1867).

FRASER, A. M., 'Joseph Damer a banker of old Dublin', *Dublin Historical Record*, 3 (1941), 51–3.

—— 'The Damer family in Co. Tipperary', *Clonmel Historical and Archaeological Journal*, 1 (1953–4), 52–4.

FROUDE, J. A., *The English in Ireland in the eighteenth century*, 3 vols. (London, 1872–3).

GAHAN, D., 'Religion and land tenure in eighteenth-century Ireland: Tenancy in the south-east', in R. V. Comerford, M. Cullen, J. R. Hill, and C. Lennon (eds.), *Religion, conflict, and coexistence in Ireland: Essays presented to Monsignor P. J. Corish* (Dublin, 1990), 99–117.

GARDINER, M. J., and RADFORD, T., *Soil associations of Ireland and their land-use potential* (Dublin, 1980).

Genealogy of the earls of Llandaff of Thomastown, Co. Tipperary, Ireland (London, 1899).

GILLESPIE, R., and MORAN, G. (eds.), *'A various country': Essays in Mayo history, 1500–1900* (Westport, 1987).

GLEESON, D. F., *The last lords of Ormond: A history of the 'Countrie of the three O'Kennedys' during the seventeenth century* (London, 1938).

√ GOUGH, H., and DICKSON, D. J. (eds.), *Ireland and the French Revolution* (Dublin, 1990).

GRATTAN, H., *Memoir of the life and times of the Rt. Hon. Henry Grattan*, 3 vols. (London, 1839–42).

GRUBB, G. W., *The Grubbs of Tipperary: Studies in heredity and character* (Cork, 1972).

GRUBB, I., *The Quakers in Ireland 1654–1900* (London, 1927).

HAYTON, D. W., 'The crisis in Ireland and the disintegration of Queen Anne's last ministry', *IHS*, 22 (1981), 193–215.

HEWETSON, J., *Memoirs of the house of Hewetson or Hewson of Ireland* (London, 1901).

√ HILL, J. R., 'The meaning and significance of "Protestant Ascendancy", 1787–1840', in *Ireland after the Union* (Oxford, 1989), 1–22.

HOFFMAN, R., ' "Marylando-Hibernus": Charles Carroll the settler, 1660–1720', *William & Mary Quarterly*, 45 (1988), 207–36.

JACOB, A. H., and GLASCOTT, J. H., *An historical and genealogical narrative of the families of Jacob* (n.p., 1875).

JOHNSTON, E. M., *Ireland in the eighteenth century* (Dublin, 1974).

—— 'Problems common to both Protestant and Catholic churches in eighteenth-century Ireland', in O. MacDonagh, W. F. Mandle, and P. Travers (eds.), *Irish nationalism 1750–1950* (London, 1983), 14–37.

JONES, H., *The Palatine families of Ireland* (Calif., 1965), typescript.

JONES, M. G., *The charity school movement* (London, 1938; new imp. 1964).

JUPP, P. J. 'Irish parliamentary elections and the influence of the Catholic vote', *Historical Journal*, 10 (1967), 183–96.

KEARNEY, H. F., 'The court of wards and liveries in Ireland, 1622–1641', *PRIA*, 57 C (1955), 29–68.

KELLY, P. H., 'The Irish woollen export prohibition act of 1699: Kearney revisited', *IESH*, 7 (1980), 22–44.

KEOGH, D., 'Thomas Hussey, Bishop of Waterford and Lismore, 1797–1803 and the rebellion of 1798', in W. Nolan and T. P. Power (eds.), *Waterford: History and society* (Dublin, 1992), 403–25.

KNOX, S. J., *Ireland's debt to the Huguenots* (Dublin, 1959).

LARGE, D., 'The wealth of the greater Irish landowners', IHS, 15 (1966), 21–47.

LECKY, W. E. H., *History of Ireland in the eighteenth century*, 5 vols. (London, 1892; 1913).

LEE, G. L., *The Huguenot settlements in Ireland* (London, 1936).

LEISTER, I., 'Orchards in Tipperary', *Irish Geography*, 4 (1962), 292–301.

—— *Peasant openfield farming and its territorial organisation in County Tipperary* (Marburg/Lahn, 1976).

LENIHAN, M., *Limerick: Its history and antiquities* (Limerick, 1866).

LENNON, P. [*recte* Connell], 'An economic geography of Co. Meath, *1770–1870*', *IESH*, 8 (1981), 103–5.

LEPPER, J. H., and CROSSLE, P., *History of the grand lodge of free and accepted masons of Ireland* (n.p., 1925).

LOGUE, K. J., *Popular disturbances in Scotland 1780–1815* (Edinburgh, 1979).

McCARTHY, S. T., *The McCarthys of Munster: The story of a great Irish sept* (Dundalk, 1922).

—— *The Trant family* (Folkestone [1924]).

McCRACKEN, E., *The Irish woods since Tudor times* (Newton Abbot, 1971).

McDOWELL, R. B., *Ireland in the age of imperialism and revolution, 1760–1801* (Oxford, 1979).

McLYNN, F. J., ' "Good behaviour": Irish Catholics and the Jacobite rising of 1745', *Éire-Ireland*, 16 (1981), 43–58.

MADDEN, R. R., *The literary life and correspondence of Marguerite Gardiner, Countess of Blessington*, 3 vols. (London, 1855).

MAGUIRE, W. A., *The Downshire estates in Ireland 1801–1845* (Oxford, 1972).

MAHER, J., *Romantic Slievenamon in history, folklore, and song: A Tipperary anthology* (Mullinahone, 1954).

MALCOMSON, A. P. W., *John Foster: The politics of the Anglo-Irish ascendancy* (Oxford, 1978).

—— 'The parliamentary traffic of this country', in T. Bartlett, and D. W. Hayton (eds.), *Penal era*, 137–61.

√ MALCOMSON, A. P. W., *The pursuit of the heiress: Aristocratic marriage in Ireland 1750–1820* (Belfast, 1982).

√ MANNION, J. J., 'Waterford merchants and the Irish–Newfoundland provisions trade, 1770–1820', in Cullen and Butel (eds.), *Négoce et industrie*, 27–43.

MARNANE, D. G., *Land and violence: A history of west Tipperary from 1660* ([Tipperary], 1985).

Memoir on the coalfields of Ireland, 2 vols. (Dublin, 1921).

MILNE, K., 'Irish charter schools', *Irish Journal of Education*, 8 (1974), 3–29.

MOODY, T. W., and VAUGHAN, W. E. (eds.), *A new history of Ireland*, iv. *Eighteenth century Ireland, 1691–1800* (Oxford, 1986).

—— MARTIN, F. X., and BYRNE, F. J. (eds.), *A new history of Ireland*, iii. *Early modern Ireland, 1534–1691* (Oxford, 1976).

—— —— —— —— *A new history of Ireland*, viii. *A chronology of Irish history to 1976* (Oxford, 1976).

NEELY, W. G., *Kilcooley: Land and people in Tipperary* ([Belfast], 1983).

√ NOLAN, W., *Fassadinin: Land, settlement, and society in south-east Ireland 1600–1850* (Dublin, 1979).

—— (ed.), *Tipperary: History and society* (Dublin, 1985).

—— 'Patterns of living in Tipperary, 1750–1850', in Nolan (ed.), *Tipperary*, 288–324.

—— and Whelan, K. (eds.), *Kilkenny: History and society* (Dublin, 1990).

—— and POWER, T. P. P. (eds.), *Waterford: History and society* (Dublin, 1992).

O'BRIEN, C. C., *The great melody: A thematic biography of Edmund Burke* (London, 1992).

O'BRIEN, G., *The economic history of Ireland in the eighteenth century* (Dublin and London, 1918; new edn. Philadelphia, 1977).

O'CONNELL, M. R., *Irish politics and social conflict in the age of the American revolution* (Philadelphia, 1965).

O'DONOVAN, D., 'The money bill dispute of 1753', in Bartlett and Hayton (eds.), *Penal era*, 55–87.

O'DONOVAN, J., *The economic history of livestock in Ireland* (Cork, 1940).

O'FEARGHAIL, F., 'The Catholic church in county Kilkenny, 1600–1800', in Nolan and Whelan (eds.), *Kilkenny*, 197–250.

√ O'FLAHERTY, E., 'The Catholic Convention and Anglo-Irish politics, 1791–3', *Arch. Hib.*, 40 (1985), 14–34.

√ —— 'Ecclesiastical politics and the dismantling of the penal laws in Ireland, 1774–82', *IHS*, 26 (1988), 33–50.

O'FLANAGAN, P., 'Markets and fairs in Ireland, 1600–1800: Index of economic development and regional growth', *Jnl. of Historical Geography*, 2 (1985), 364–78.

O'KELLY, E., *The old private banks and bankers of Munster* (Cork, 1959).

O'NEILL, T. P., 'Discoverers and discoveries: The penal laws and Dublin property', *Dublin Historical Record*, 37 (1983), 2–13.

O'SHEA, M. J., *The history of native Irish cattle* (Dublin, 1954).

PAKENHAM, T., *The year of liberty: the story of the great Irish rebellion of 1798* (London, 1978).

PORRITT, E., and PORRITT, A., *The unreformed House of Commons*, 2 vols. (London, 1903).

POWELL, T., 'An economic factor in the Wexford rebellion of 1798', *Studia Hibernica*, 16 (1976), 140–57.

POWER, P., *Waterford and Lismore: A compendious history of the united dioceses* (Cork & London, 1937).

POWER, T. P., 'Land, politics, and society in eighteenth-century Tipperary', Ph.D. thesis (University of Dublin, 1987).

—— 'Converts', in Power and Whelan, *Endurance and emergence*, 101–27.

—— 'Conversions among the legal profession in eighteenth-century Ireland', in D. Hogan, and W. N. Osborough (eds.), *Brehons, serjeants, and attorneys: Studies in the history of the Irish legal profession* (Dublin, 1990), 153–74.

—— and WHELAN, K. (eds.), *Endurance and emergence: Catholics in Ireland in the eighteenth century* (Dublin, 1990).

PRENDERGAST, J. P., *The Cromwellian settlement of Ireland* (London, 1922).

REID, J. S., *History of the Presbyterian church in Ireland*, ed. W. D. Killen, 3 vols. (Belfast, 1867).

RENNISON, W. H., *Succession list of the bishops, cathedral, and parochial clergy of Waterford and Lismore* (n.p. [c.1920]).

ROBERTS, P. E. W., 'Caravats and Shanavests: Whiteboyism and faction fighting in east Munster, 1802–1811', in Clark and Donnelly (eds.), *Irish peasants*, 64–101.

ROEBUCK, P. (ed.), *Plantation to partition* (Belfast, 1981).

—— 'Rent movement, proprietorial incomes and agricultural development, 1730–1830', in Roebuck (ed.), *Plantation*, 82–101.

ROHAN, P. K., *The climate of north Munster* (Dublin, 1968).

SAVORY, D. L.. 'The Huguenot–Palatine settlements in the counties of Limerick, Kerry, and Tipperary', *Proceedings of the Huguenot Society of London*, 18 (1949), 215–31.

SHEE, E., and WATSON, S. J., *Clonmel: An architectural guide* (Dublin, 1975).

SIMMS, J. G., *The Williamite confiscation in Ireland 1690–1703* (London, 1956).

—— 'Irish Catholics and the parliamentary franchise, 1692–1728', *IHS*, 12 (1960), 28–37.

SIMMS, J. G., 'The Irish parliament of 1713', *Historical Studies*, 4 (1963), 82–92.

SMYTH, P. D. H., 'The Volunteers and parliament 1779–84', in Bartlett and Hayton (eds.), *Penal era*, 113–36.

SMYTH, W. J., 'Estate records and the making of the Irish landscape: An example from Co. Tipperary', *Irish Geography*, 9 (1976), 29–49.

√ —— 'Land values, landownership and population patterns in county Tipperary for 1641–60 and 1841–50: Some comparisons', in Cullen and Furet (eds.), *Ireland and France*, 159–84.

—— 'Property, patronage and population: reconstructing the human geography of mid-seventeenth century Tipperary', in Nolan (ed.), *Tipperary*, 104–38.

STEPHENS, L., and LEE, S., *Dictionary of national biography*, 66 vols. (London, 1885–1901).

SULLIVAN, A. M., *New Ireland* (London, 1878).

VAUGHAN, W. E., and FITZPATRICK, A. J., *Irish historical statistics: Population, 1821–1971* (Dublin, 1978).

VAUGHAN-ARBUCKLE, C. L., 'A Tipperary farmer and Waterford tradesman of two centuries ago', *JWSEIAS*, 8 (1902), 80–9.

WALL, M., 'Catholic loyalty to king and pope in eighteenth-century Ireland', *Proc. Irish Catholic Hist. Comm.* (1961), 17–24.

—— 'The United Irish movement', *Historical Studies*, 5 (1965), 122–40.

—— 'The Whiteboys', in Williams (ed.), *Secret societies*, 13–25.

—— *The penal laws, 1691–1760* (Dundalk, 1976).

—— *Catholic Ireland in the eighteenth century: The collected essays of Maureen Wall*, ed. G. O'Brien (Dublin, 1989).

WALSH, J. R., *Frederick Augustus Hervey, 1730–1803, fourth earl of Bristol, bishop of Derry, 'Le bienfaiteur des Catholiques'* (Maynooth, 1972).

WARD, C. C., and WARD, R. E., The ordeal of O'Conor of Belangare', *Eire-Ireland*, 14 (1979), 6–14.

√ WHELAN, K., 'The Catholic Church in County Tipperary, 1700–1900', in Nolan, *Tipperary*, 215–55.

√ —— 'The religious factor in the 1798 rebellion in county Wexford', in P. O'Flanagan, P. Ferguson, and K. Whelan (eds.), *Rural Ireland, 1600–1900: Modernisation and change* (Cork, 1987), 62–85.

—— Review of E. Ó Néill, *Gleann an Óir*, in *Irish Review*, 7 (1989), 139–43.

√ —— 'Politicisation in county Wexford and the origin of the 1798 rebellion', in H. Gough, and D. Dickson (eds.), *Ireland and the French Revolution* (Dublin, 1990), 156–78.

—— and NOLAN, W. (eds.), *Wexford: History and society* (Dublin, 1987).

WHITE, J., *My Clonmel scrapbook* (Waterford, 1907).

WHITE, J. D., *Anthologia Tipperariensis* (Cashel, 1892).

WHITE, T. DE VERE, 'The Freemasons', in Williams (ed.), *Secret societies*, 46–57.

WILLIAMS, T. D. (ed.), *Secret societies in Ireland* (Dublin, 1973).

WOODWARD, D., 'The Anglo-Irish livestock trade of the seventeenth century', *IHS*, 18 (1973), 489–523.

—— 'A comparative study of the Irish and Scottish livestock trades in the seventeenth century', in Cullen and Smout (eds.), *Comparative aspects*, 147–64.

Index

Apart from well-known placenames and those indicated otherwise, all placenames are in Co. Tipperary